Praise for the second edition of
Writing Assessment and Instruction for Students with Learning Disabilities

"Too often, teachers view written language instruction as broad, vague, and overwhelming. This book is absolutely packed with information and strategies to make assessing and teaching all writers effective and easy."

—Wendy Randall Wall, educational consultant and owner,
Learning & Behaviour Specialists, LLC

"With the second edition of *Writing Assessment and Instruction for Students with Learning Disabilities*, the authors have set a new standard in creating an ultimate educational guide for written assessment. Well written and organized, and filled with practical strategies, this book should be required reading for every educator dedicated to teaching written language skills to all students, not just those with disabilities. It is an essential desk reference, one I will turn to again and again as a neuropsychologist and educator, and it will be on my short list of recommended volumes for all my future workshops."

—Sam Goldstein, Ph.D., editor-in-chief, *Journal of Attention Disorders,* and
co-editor-in-chief, *Encyclopedia of Child Behavior and Development*

"This book is brilliantly conceptualized and written. Without a doubt, it will become one of the most frequently used resources for educators who want to improve the written performance of their students."

—Donald D. Deshler, Williamson Family Distinguished Professor of Special Education, and
director, Center for Research on Learning, University of Kansas

"What every teacher needs to know about writing assessment and instruction . . . easy to read with practical research-based ideas for improving students' writing performance."

—Lynne Jaffe, Ph.D., learning disabilities consultant

"An excellent resource for teaching my high-school students who struggle with written expression. Teacher-friendly and effective, this text provides practical assessments with evidence-based interventions and strategies. A must for teachers of teachers of writers at all levels."

—Vesta Hamond Udall, M.Ed., secondary special education teacher
and college instructor

"The unique approach to assessing students' writing abilities through writing samples presented in this research-to-practice–based book is useful to teachers, psychologists, and diagnosticians. The comprehensive model of writing that structures the book enables teachers to use assessment results as the basis for designing effective instruction to overcome writing problems for students at all grade levels."

—Esther Minskoff, Ph.D., professor emerita of special education,
James Madison University, Harrisonburg, VA

"Nancy Mather's tests and books are the most useful resources that I have ever used. Her new book is an invaluable resource which shows educators how to use assessments to guide all aspects of writing instruction. It is based on years of research and experience with struggling learners."

—Rosalind Hill, consultant in the Boston Public Schools

Jossey-Bass Teacher

Jossey-Bass Teacher provides educators with practical knowledge and tools to create a positive and lifelong impact on student learning. We offer classroom-tested and research-based teaching resources for a variety of grade levels and subject areas. Whether you are an aspiring, new, or veteran teacher, we want to help you make every teaching day your best.

From ready-to-use classroom activities to the latest teaching framework, our value-packed books provide insightful, practical, and comprehensive materials on the topics that matter most to K–12 teachers. We hope to become your trusted source for the best ideas from the most experienced and respected experts in the field.

Writing Assessment and Instruction for Students with Learning Disabilities

SECOND EDITION

Nancy Mather, Barbara J. Wendling, and Rhia Roberts

Foreword by Noel Gregg

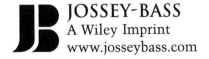

JOSSEY-BASS
A Wiley Imprint
www.josseybass.com

KH

Published by Jossey-Bass
A Wiley Imprint
989 Market Street, San Francisco, CA 94103-1741—www.josseybass.com

Library of Congress Cataloging-in-Publication Data

Mather, Nancy.
    Writing assessment and instruction for students with learning disabilities/Nancy Mather, Barbara J. Wendling, Rhia Roberts; foreword by Noel Gregg. — 2nd ed.
        p.   cm.
    Includes bibliographical reference and index.
        ISBN 978-0-470-23079-4
        1. Learning disabled children—Education—Language arts.   2. English language—Composition and exercises—Study and teaching (Elementary)   3. English language—Composition and exercises—Ability testing.   I. Wendling, Barbara J.   II. Roberts, Rhia.   III. Title.
    LC4704.85.M38   2009
    371.9'044623-—dc22

                                                                                                200902521

Printed in the United States of America
SECOND EDITION
PB Printing   10 9 8 7 6 5 4 3 2 1

8/17/11

About the Authors

Nancy Mather, Ph.D., is a professor at the University of Arizona in the Department of Special Education, Rehabilitation, and School Psychology. She is a coauthor on the Woodcock-Johnson III and has coauthored two books on interpretation and application of the WJ III: *Woodcock-Johnson III: Reports, Recommendations, and Strategies* (2002) and *Essentials of WJ III Tests of Achievement Assessment* (2001). In addition, she has recently coauthored the books *Learning Disabilities and Challenging Behaviors: A Guide to Intervention and Classroom Management* (2nd ed.) (2008); *Evidence-Based Interventions for Students with Learning and Behavioral Challenges* (2008); and *Essentials of Assessment Report Writing* (2004).

Barbara J. Wendling, M.A., has years of clinical experience as a general and special educator and diagnostician in public school settings. She has taught university courses, has worked in educational publishing, and is currently an educational consultant. In addition, she serves as the education director for the Woodcock-Muñoz Foundation. Barbara has coauthored a number of publications related to assessment and instruction. Recently, Wendling and Mather have also coauthored *Essentials of Evidence-Based Academic Interventions* (2009).

Rhia Roberts, Ph.D., specializes in assessment and learning disabilities. She worked as a professor of special education at Chapman University in San Diego for several years. She is now an educational consultant and currently trains teachers and school psychologists in districts around the country. She has coauthored the Illinois Test of Psycholinguistic Abilities, Third Edition (ITPA-3), the Test of Orthographic Competence (TOC), the Test of Silent Word Reading Fluency (TOSWRF), an intelligence test for a Canadian company, and the Phonic Reading Lessons program (PRL: Skills; PRL: Practice).

Dedication

To the many boys and girls in school and out whose lot is a hard one, and who must struggle against poverty and adverse circumstances and yet in whose souls is burning the unquenchable desire for knowledge and culture, this little book is respectfully dedicated.
—A. C. Butler, Copyright 1895, Persimmons: A Story for Boys and Girls and Men and Women Who Have Not Forgotten Their School Days

The qualities of good writing are complex and nuanced. But they can be named, and I'm convinced they can be taught. Of all the arts, writing should be among the most democratic: all one needs is paper and a pen—and, I would suggest, a teacher or two along the way who works to make the intangible tangible, so every student might know the joy of writing well.

—Nancie Atwell, 2002

To writers-in-development everywhere and those who seek to understand, support, and teach them.

Acknowledgments

We would like to thank Dr. Noel Gregg, a leading expert in the evaluation and treatment of writing disorders, for her thoughtful foreword to the second edition of this book. We also wish to thank Marjorie McAneny, senior editor for K–12 Education at Jossey-Bass, for her patience, support, and substantive suggestions for this text, as well as Nina Kreiden, our senior production editor, for her management and editorial assistance with this project, and David Horne for his careful review and editing suggestions. Warren Sammons was extremely helpful in scanning writing samples, and Susan Campbell provided several samples for CBM scoring practice. Vesta Udall and Wendy Wall contributed several samples from their students as well. Finally, we would like to acknowledge how grateful we are for the love and support of our wonderful families and friends.

Contents

List of Figures
and Exhibits

FIGURES

EXHIBITS

Foreword

Writing is the expression of ideas and feelings through the use of written symbols. Over the years, the rapid integration of technology into home and school environments has challenged traditional definitions of writing. Voice-activated software blurs the boundaries between oral and written language. Although the mediating tools for writing are changing, the process of coding experiences into symbols (words) to provide meaning continues to be central to written expression. The writer remains the essential catalyst. Critical to understanding a student's writing abilities is a professional's knowledge of how to analyze writing samples. Unfortunately, many teachers and psychologists lack experience in how to examine writing tasks. Often, standardized test scores become the sole criteria for determining writing performance. The primary purpose of this second edition of the Mather and Roberts textbook is to provide, through exposure to samples of student writing, effective strategies in using authentic text as a means of guiding writing instruction.

A growing number of students in our school systems experience difficulty with written expression. The causes of these problems usually are the result of a mixture of factors. The majority of students in our classrooms demonstrate no disabilities. However, some of these writers have developed inefficient writing strategies that result in below-average writing performance. For other writers, the source of underachievement in written expression rests with cognitive or oral language abilities. Learning to organize experiences or transform ideas to oral language is the key instructional goal for such individuals (for example, those with language or attention deficit/hyperactivity disorders). Other students are fluent in developing ideas and demonstrate adequate oral language abilities. However, the breakdown for these students might be in the coding of oral language into written symbols (such as dyslexia). Students demonstrating significant social cognition problems (for example, Autism or Asperger's Syndrome) encounter problems with sense of audience. Motivational or anxiety issues surrounding the process of writing will interfere with fluency and quality of text for any student. In addition, students coming from different cultures, as well as those for whom English is their second language, can struggle with aspects of writing.

For teachers faced with these different types of inefficient writers, *Writing Assessment and Instruction for Students with Learning Disabilities* provides systematic strategies to analyze classroom writing samples for the purpose of providing more valid writing instruction. A key to any assessment of writing is an understanding of the influence of the task demands (such as spelling, handwriting, written expression), the tools used for responding, and the topic. Before critical decisions related to a student's potential or ability are formed, this information should be put into proper perspective. Often, discrepant performance across measures purporting to evaluate a specific writing skill (such as spelling) is not the result of a student's motivation or the psychometrics of a measure. The task, the tool, or the topic demands may be very different across two measures of a single skill.

Three essential aspects of a writing task that teachers should consider are the modality demands, cognitive or language demands, and the degree of structure. Mather, Wendling, and Roberts provide teachers with many effective assessment and intervention strategies to address the influence of these factors on writing, particularly in regard to handwriting, spelling, and written expression (Chapters Five, Six, and Seven).

Consideration of the degree of structure that a task requires from a writer is very relevant to decision making. Evaluators often see the importance of this factor when they report that a student's performance was in the average range on a specific writing test. The general education teacher reports disbelief because in the classroom the student's writing performance is seriously impaired. Often this discrepancy can be traced to the difference in structure between the test and the classroom requirements. Mather, Wendling, and Roberts address many of these issues in Chapter Four ("Effective Accommodations for Struggling Writers"), Chapter Eight ("Informal Assessment and Curriculum-Based Measurement"), and Chapter Nine ("Analysis of Writing Samples").

Structure is best understood by considering two aspects, prompts and response types. Prompts are cues provided in the presentation of the task. For instance, a writer could be given a single picture, a series of pictures, a story starter, or a written topic. Writing from a series of pictures is the most structured while a written topic is the least structured writing task. The authors point out that during an evaluation of writing, one should collect information on the writing skill being assessed across varying levels of structure by collecting informal assessments and classroom products (Chapters Eight and Nine).

Mather, Wendling, and Roberts also discuss in great depth the importance of the meaningfulness of a task to a writer (Chapters One, Three, and Ten). They stress that the evaluator should give careful consideration to the background knowledge and motivation a student brings to the writing task. If a writer possesses information about a topic, the quality and fluency of his or her writing will often be positively influenced. Therefore, students should always be given a choice of writing topics during an evaluation of their performance. When using story starters or picture stimuli, there should be several to choose from that include age-appropriate themes and culturally appropriate experiences. Writers often produce more elaborate and better-organized text when they feel comfortable with the audience (for example, with the classroom teacher rather than the school psychologist). Unfortunately, many writing experiences provided in schools to students focus on the student writing to the evaluator, which shapes the writer's perspective on the function of writing.

Writing tasks provide opportunities for teachers to observe a student's ability to use writing for different functions (Chapters Four, Eight, and Nine). One function of writing is test-taking, such as fill in the blank, short answer, copying, dictation, and translation. The demand on planning and organization is far less with such tasks. Informational uses of writing such as note-taking, reports, and summaries are a second function of school writing. More emphasis of this function is on planning, organizing, and transcribing abilities. Often, fewer opportunities are provided to students to demonstrate their abilities with imaginative (stories, poems, plays) or personal (diary, journal, and notes to friends) writing. Each function of writing should be examined by an evaluator to determine if errors (such as in spelling) detected on one function are consistent across the others.

This book makes a compelling case for the unique and very significant needs of student writers demonstrating difficulties with the demands of writing. In addition, it does so in a way that other books do not. As discussed previously, written language underachievement is symptomatic of a large percentage of students. As the demands of literacy are increasing daily, skill with written language production becomes not only a theoretical interest but also a pragmatic necessity. In each classroom, teachers are faced with those students for whom writing is difficult—the inefficient writers. A key principle advocated by Mather, Wendling, and Roberts is that teachers and psychologists can learn best by analyzing authentic writing samples of inefficient writers as a means of developing effective writing interventions that lead toward successful outcomes. Writing interventions and strategies are provided throughout the text to help teachers pinpoint the critical learning needs of a wide range of writers' profiles.

The expertise surrounding the assessment and intervention for inefficient writers that Mather, Wendling, and Roberts bring cannot be matched by any other textbook. Mather, one of the leading experts in the field of learning disabilities, demonstrates throughout this entire text her remarkable breadth of knowledge about critical learner characteristics, interventions variables, and the interactions among these factors for struggling readers and writers. Wendling and Roberts also bring extensive clinical, research, and teaching expertise to enhance the ecological validity of the assessment and intervention suggestions presented throughout this textbook.

In light of the way that this book is structured, practitioners will find it to be one of the most valuable resources available to them for the following reasons:

- It is grounded in the literature.
- It is theory-based.
- It provides clear, step-by-step instructions for how to implement and interpret various informal and CBM writing assessments.
- It links assessment information to writing strategies and instruction.

I believe that this book will provide practitioners with the foundation that they need to promote optimal success for the heterogeneous group of inefficient writers they face. This very readable book is written with passion, provides poignant examples of writing samples, and suggests numerous practical assessment and teaching suggestions that can be readily implemented. It will add greatly to my abilities as an educator whose career has focused on inefficient readers and writers, and it will be a resource to which I will frequently turn.

Noel Gregg, Ph.D.
Distinguished Research Professor
University of Georgia
Department of Psychology
Department of Communication Sciences
and Special Education

chapter
1

Very Gently with No Red Marks

Writing is easy: All you do is sit staring at the blank sheet of paper, until the drops of blood form on your forehead.

—Gene Fowler

Writing is a key to successful school experiences and an essential means of communication that helps students learn how to structure and organize their thoughts. Some students with writing difficulties have language or learning disabilities, whereas others do not. Whatever the underlying reasons for the difficulties, for many students, writing is not easy. In fact, writing is the most complex of all the language tasks, and students of all ages can have difficulty becoming proficient writers. Many of you may remember feeling overwhelmed at some time in your school careers by the prospect of having to write a paper. As the due date rapidly approached, your anxiety about finishing the paper increased exponentially.

The numerous skills involved with writing are multifaceted, ranging from the production of legible handwriting to the production of organized discourse. Some students have difficulty with handwriting or with basic writing skills such as spelling, whereas others have difficulty expressing and organizing their ideas or taking notes quickly in a classroom. Think of the many skills that are involved in trying to take accurate notes quickly during a class lecture. You have to listen, identify and comprehend the important ideas, and then paraphrase the material to be written down. You then have to hold that information in memory,

while you quickly jot down the ideas and continue to listen. There is no time to think about letter formation or spelling, or about whether the ideas have been recorded in a meaningful sequence, but you know that the notes have to be written clearly enough that you will be able to read and study them at a later time.

The components of writing are interwoven, and difficulty in one aspect of writing, such as spelling, often contributes to difficulty in another aspect of writing, such as taking notes or expressing ideas. You will want to understand and consider the interplay of these components when you are planning appropriate instructional interventions for students who struggle with writing.

Too often students with writing difficulties develop counterproductive coping strategies, such as writing only words they know how to spell, avoiding expression of complex ideas, or writing as little as they can. For example, Spence, a fourth-grade student with strong verbal abilities, had difficulty with spelling. In answer to a question about how he chooses a topic to write about, Spence replied, "I look at the words on the board and on the walls, then I make up a story using those words and the extra ones I know how to spell, like *the*." He also noted that his stories usually involve the police because he finally knows how to spell that word. Figure 1.1 illustrates one of his stories involving the "police." Notice that he has spelled the word *again* four different ways on the last two lines. Clearly, difficulties with spelling affect Spence's word choice and writing facility.

The writing of Greg, another fourth-grade student, provides an example of the impact of limited spelling skill on writing. As part of a writing assessment, Greg was asked to write responses to several items on the Woodcock-Johnson III Writing Samples test (Woodcock, McGrew, & Mather, 2001). When shown a picture of a queen and king, Greg was given the following prompt: "This woman is a queen. Write a good sentence that tells what this man is."

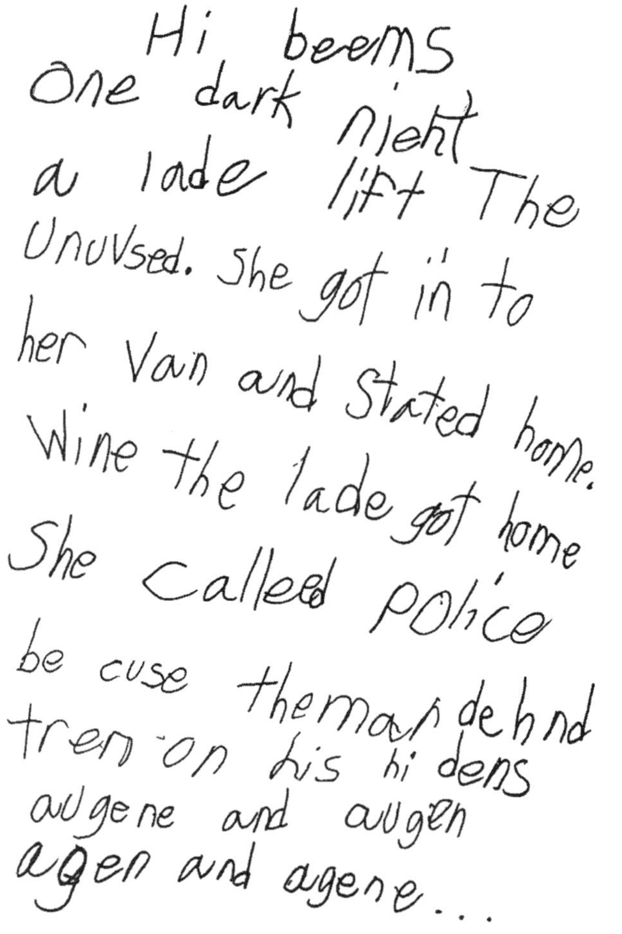

While contemplating the task, Greg mused aloud, "The man is a king. Oh boy! Hard words! I can't spell those words. The man is rich. Another hard word! What can I spell? I can spell mom and dad. Can I use mom in my sentence? The mom is rich. I don't know how to spell rich. What do I know how to spell? Thin! I can spell thin." Following this dialogue, Greg produced the sentence presented in Figure 1.2: *The mom is thin.* Presently, Greg's written expression is hampered severely by his limited spelling skill. Without knowledge of Greg's thought processes, one may surmise that his problem is with oral language and reasoning, rather than with spelling.

Unfortunately, students such as Spence and Greg have trouble constructing meaningful passages because so much of their attention is directed toward spelling. The important question then becomes, How can Greg's and Spence's teachers help them? Although many teachers recognize when a student is having trouble with writing, they may feel unsure of what to do about it.

Some teachers do not receive enough training on how to help students improve their writing. Other teachers received training, but did not have enough practical experience in analyzing written products, detecting the difficulties, and then implementing appropriate instruction. Without training in how to assist students with writing difficulties, teachers become frustrated. For example, during the second week of

Figure 1.1. Spence's Story with the Word *Police.*

Translation: High Beams One dark night a lady left the university. She got into her van and started home. When the lady got home she called police because the man behind turned on his high beams again and again and again and again . . .

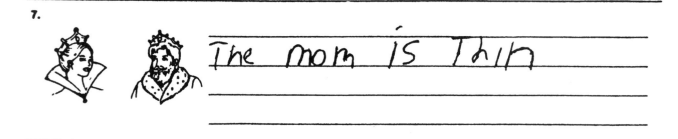

7.

The mom is Thin

Figure 1.2. Greg's Written Response on the WJ III Writing Samples Test.

school Ms. Wall, a third-grade teacher, entered the teacher's lounge with a story written by one of her students, Ann. Although Ann was trying to record her ideas, Ms. Wall was concerned about Ann's present level of development in writing skill. After showing her fellow teachers the paper, presented in Figure 1.3, Ms. Wall asked, "What should I do?"

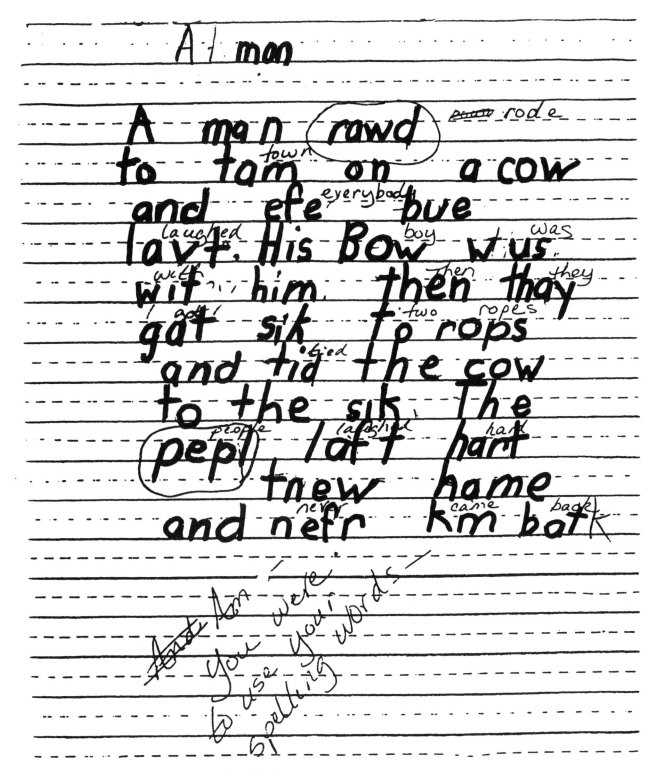

Figure 1.3. Ann's Story Using Her Spelling Words.

She had written a comment on Ann's paper noting the failure to comply with the assignment of writing a story incorporating the week's spelling words. Although failure to complete the assignment was the least of her concerns, Ms. Wall just did not know what else to say.

Older students also experience difficulty. For example, during the first week of eighth-grade English class, Ms. Downing asked the students to write something about themselves that they would like to share. She provided several examples: "Perhaps you have a special pet or you took an exciting trip this summer; or you could discuss your family or an activity that you really enjoy. The main requirement is to let me know something about you." At the end of the fifty-minute period, Carlos handed her the essay presented in Figure 1.4.

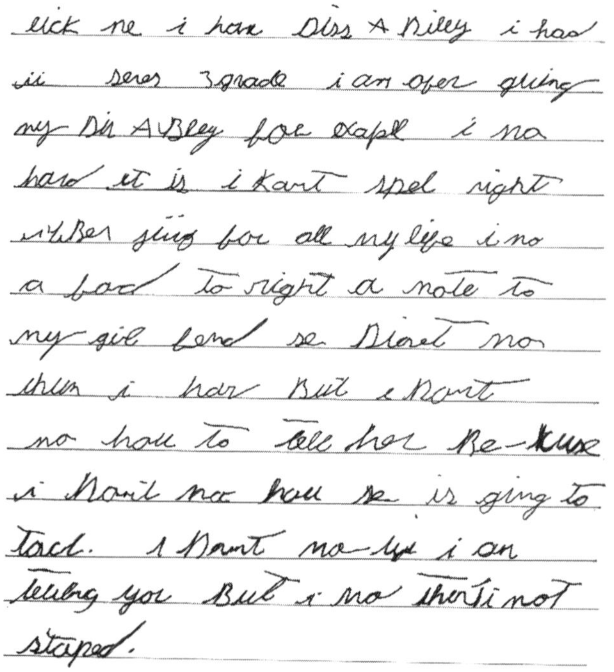

Carlos's difficulty with writing is readily apparent, as is his desire to communicate to the audience, his teacher. So how do we start the process of helping students improve their writing? The process begins *very gently with no red marks*. Ms. Downing appreciated and empathized with the message that Carlos was expressing. She responded to his writing with the following comment: "Thank you for telling me about your struggle with writing. I am looking forward to helping you this year. If you would like, I can help you write a note to your girlfriend." Clearly, students such as Carlos require a caring teacher and intensive, systematic instruction to improve their writing abilities.

Effective writing teachers are able to analyze a student's strengths and weaknesses in writing and then develop specific instructional plans. To select appropriate interventions, you must identify and prioritize the areas of concern, as well as identify the strengths on which to build. With careful analysis of a student's present performance level, instructional programs can be designed to increase writing competence. Recalling your own anxious moments related to writing may help you proceed gently with no red marks as you provide students with feedback on their writing.

Figure 1.4. Carlos's Essay to His Teacher.
Translation: Like me I have a disability. I've had it since third grade. I am often quitting because of my disability. For example I know how hard it is. I can't spell right. I've been trying for all my life. I know I am afraid to write a note to my girlfriend. She doesn't know that I have but I don't know how to tell her because I don't know how she is going to act. I don't know why I am telling you but I know I am not stupid.

The primary purpose of this book is to help educators become effective writing teachers. It is appropriate for both general and special education teachers who are working with students who struggle in various aspects of writing development. These students require teachers who understand the components of written language and are well versed in assessing difficulties, selecting appropriate interventions, and monitoring progress, all of which are addressed within. It is our hope that this book will increase your understanding of why students struggle with writing, enhance your sensitivity to the diverse needs of your students, and increase your proficiency in analyzing and teaching writing. This book will be useful in university courses that focus on writing assessment and instruction. It is also a reliable reference for practicing general education teachers at the elementary or middle-school level, as well as for special education teachers, speech-language therapists, and school psychologists who work with students across the grades.

In this second edition, we have maintained the focus on students with language and learning disabilities that affect aspects of written language development. Numerous intervention strategies have been developed for use with these students who often require differentiated instruction. The majority of accommodations and instructional strategies described in this text, however, are applicable to all students with writing difficulties, regardless of the cause.

The book is organized into ten chapters. Following this introductory chapter, the second chapter provides a review of the various components of written language and the types of difficulties students may have with handwriting, spelling, usage, vocabulary, and text structure. The third chapter provides an overview of theoretical perspectives, and the basic principles of an effective writing program. The fourth chapter reviews the various accommodations that can help students be successful. Chapters Five, Six, and Seven contain summaries of instructional strategies that can be used to enhance student performance in the areas of handwriting, basic skills, and written expression. Chapter Eight describes methods of informal assessment, as well as how to use measures of curriculum-based measurement (CBM) to monitor student progress. Chapter Nine presents analyses of student writing samples. Some of the analyses have been completed, whereas others have guided questions that could be used for independent study assignments or in-class discussions. Chapter Ten, the final chapter, discusses the concept of "voice" in writing, and reminds us that our first job is to listen to, respect, and respond to the messages that students share with us through their writing.

chapter

2

Components of Written Language

We need only try to imagine the enormous changes in the cultural development of children that occur as a result of mastery of written language and the ability to read—and of thus becoming aware of everything that human genius has created in the realm of the written word.

—L. S. Vygotsky (1978)

Many students have severe and persistent difficulties developing writing skill, particularly those who have language impairments or learning disabilities, or for whom English is not their primary language. Some students seem to make minimal progress in writing across the grades and each year get farther and farther behind their peers. The challenge for every teacher is how to address the diverse developmental levels of writing skill that exist in all classrooms. As an example of developmental differences, Figure 2.1 illustrates some of the results from a classroom of children

Figure 2.1. Written Names of Kindergarten Children.

writing their names in the second week of kindergarten. As can be seen, several children write their names clearly with ease, whereas others only produce wispy pencil strokes. In fact, Kenneth, Dominic, and Jaimi are already writing stories with complete sentences, whereas Ryan, Tony, and Sarah are just holding pencils for the first time. They do not know how to write any letters of the alphabet.

Throughout the grades, students' skill levels vary, as do the aspects of writing that cause them difficulty. When learning to write, students may have trouble generating content, creating organizing structures, formulating goals, executing the mechanical aspects of writing, and revising text and reformulating goals (Harris, Graham, Mason, & Friedlander, 2008). Some students struggle primarily with spelling, whereas others have trouble formulating their ideas into coherent messages. Thus you need a basic understanding of the major components of written language, including (a) handwriting, (b) spelling, (c) usage, (d) vocabulary, and (e) text structure. Figure 2.2 illustrates these components. A discussion of each component follows.

HANDWRITING

Handwriting is a fine-motor skill that enables students to record their thoughts. Rapid, legible, and comfortable handwriting facilitates writing production. Students who can write easily tend to write more, and their writing is

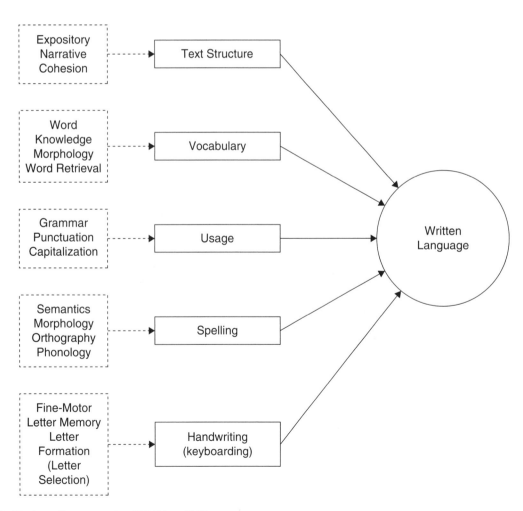

Figure 2.2. Various Components of Writing Skill.

evaluated more favorably by teachers. Even though a written text may be well composed, if the writing is illegible, the reader becomes annoyed and the meaning of the passage is lost. A student who cannot produce legible script or write quickly and easily is restricted in the ability to communicate ideas. In addition, legible handwriting supports the development and growth of other writing skills.

Some students have great difficulty developing legible handwriting. They have trouble coordinating the motor movements needed to form the letters, or visualizing a letter's or word's appearance. Figure 2.3 presents a report written by Taylor, a third-grade student. Although Taylor has several ideas that he wishes to express, he has difficulty forming the letters and spacing them evenly apart. On the average, he writes only two words per line. Writing requires so much effort for Taylor that he has trouble thinking about what he wants

to write. When speaking, however, Taylor has a lot to say.

The handwriting of students with severe visual-motor weaknesses can be nearly impossible to decipher. As an example, look at the story by Daniel presented in Figure 2.4. Daniel is a fourth-grade student who has written a story about his parents and his Game Boy. Unless Daniel reads the story to his teacher immediately after it is written, he cannot remember what it says, and she cannot read it.

Components of Handwriting

Handwriting requires numerous skills. To write legibly, students must recall the appearance of the letters and then coordinate the motor patterns needed to form the letters. They must also judge the amount of space that is needed between the letters and words and try to position the letters on the writing lines.

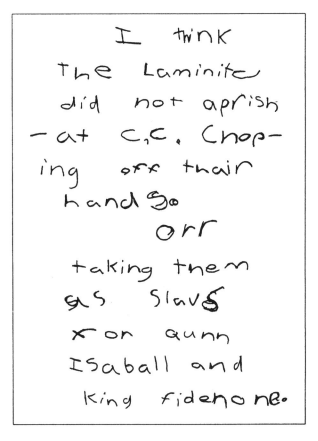

Figure 2.3. Taylor's Report.

Effective handwriting requires both legibility and fluency. Legibility refers to the clarity and accuracy of the letter forms, whereas fluency refers to the ease and quickness of formation.

Legible handwriting involves six interrelated characteristics: (a) letter formation, or the composition of the stroke; (b) size and proportion, or the size of the letters and the proportional size between uppercase and lowercase letters; (c) spacing, or the amount of spacing between letters and words; (d) slant, or the consistency in direction of the writing; (e) alignment, or uniformity of size and consistency on the writing line; and (f) line quality, or the steadiness and thickness of the line (Barbe, Wasylyk, Hackney, & Braun, 1984). You can evaluate these characteristics by analyzing a student's handwriting within a composition, on dictated sentences, and on tasks involving near- and far-point copying. In addition, you may ask students to copy sentences using their fastest writing, and then to copy the same sentences using their neatest writing.

Students who have the most severe problems with handwriting may be diagnosed as having dysgraphia, or what is referred to as a disturbance in visual-motor integration. The student may have trouble executing the motor movements needed to write or copy letters or have trouble recalling the letter forms or letter sequences. Memory for letter forms and letter sequences is commonly referred to as orthographic memory.

Faheem, an eighth-grade student with poor handwriting skill, discussed with Mr. Marcus, his science teacher, the difficulty he was having copying class notes from the chalkboard. Faheem explained that he did not have enough time to copy the lecture notes because he had to

Figure 2.4. Daniel's Story About His Game Boy.

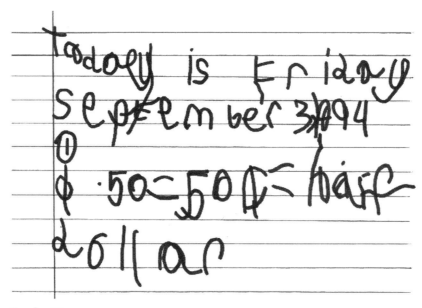

Figure 2.5. Frank's Handwriting.

look back and forth at every single letter. Each time he looked back up at the board, he had trouble finding his place again. In addition to having difficulty with copying, Faheem still has trouble remembering the orientation of the letters *b* and *d*.

For many students with poor handwriting, the quality of their handwriting decreases as they attempt to compose. Composing requires the writer to attend to all of the different simultaneous demands, such as paying attention to spelling, punctuation, and ideation, which results in an overwhelming task. For some writers, the actual task of writing is laborious, and their production speed is extremely slow. Figure 2.5 illustrates the writing of Frank, a third-grade student. Although the final product may be judged as legible, Frank spent over one hour writing this response.

In still other cases, handwriting is affected by a few specific illegible letters. Figure 2.6 illustrates a paragraph written by Jill, a ninth-grade student. Although she forms most letters correctly, her reversed formation of the letter *e* affects the overall legibility of her writing.

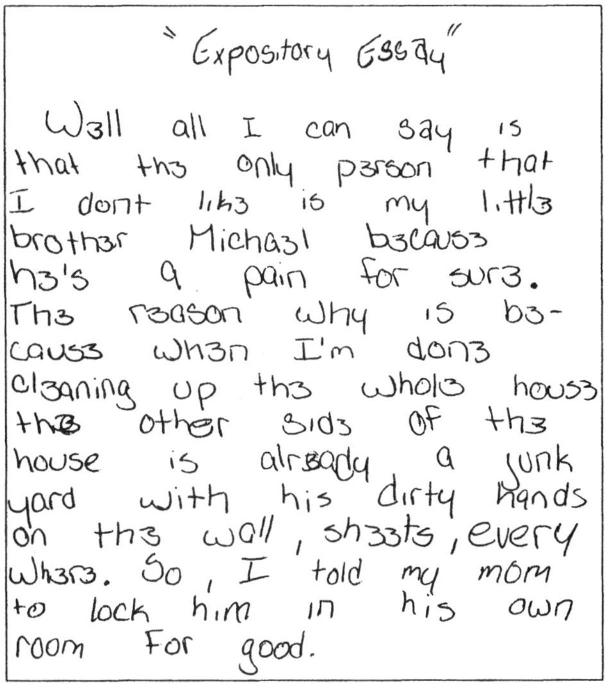

Figure 2.6. Jill's Handwriting.

Although handwriting skills usually improve as students progress through school, some secondary and postsecondary students still write slowly, and their writing is difficult to decipher. Figure 2.7 illustrates the class notes of Jeremy, a college senior, who was diagnosed as having dysgraphia in third grade. He was enrolled in an introductory course on learning disabilities. At the bottom of the notes, there is a definition of dysgraphia. Throughout his school career, Jeremy's instructors and teachers have complained about the limited legibility of his writing. Unfortunately, Jeremy has not yet learned how to use a word-processing program.

As a general rule, students with poor handwriting skill require a great deal of practice, but for some students, even additional practice does not result in legible writing. Jeremy reminisces that he had six years of intensive handwriting instruction in elementary school. When discussing his instructional history, he laughs and says, "A lot of good it did me."

Historically, individuals with poor handwriting received assistance from others with more talent, such as a writing master or scribe. Some students today would love the opportunity to hire a scribe who could recopy their writings. Fortunately, many students are able to take advantage of technology, such as using laptop computers to write their assignments.

SPELLING

Of all the basic skill areas, spelling is the most difficult for many students. When compared to their normally achieving peers, individuals with learning disabilities score significantly lower in most areas of written expression, but particularly on measures of spelling. Spelling is much more difficult than reading because the person has to recall and reproduce the entire word correctly, not just recognize it. As a general rule, even as their reading skill improves, their spelling difficulties persist.

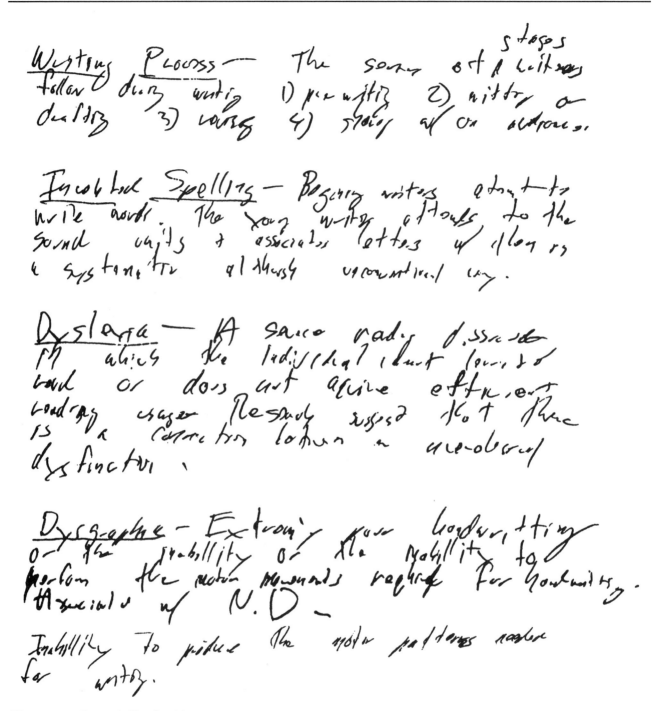

Figure 2.7. Jeremy's Handwriting.

Figure 2.8 presents a letter that Denny, a college senior, wrote to his professor to explain the tardiness of his assignment. Although his excuses are explained clearly, his difficulties with both spelling and handwriting are still apparent.

Even though the most critical aspect of written language is the ability to communicate ideas, both spelling and handwriting affect how writing is evaluated, the clarity of the thought, and the ease of deciphering the message. As Gearheart and Gearheart noted (1989): "There are students who can express themselves unusually well in writing despite inadequate spelling and handwriting, but these are the

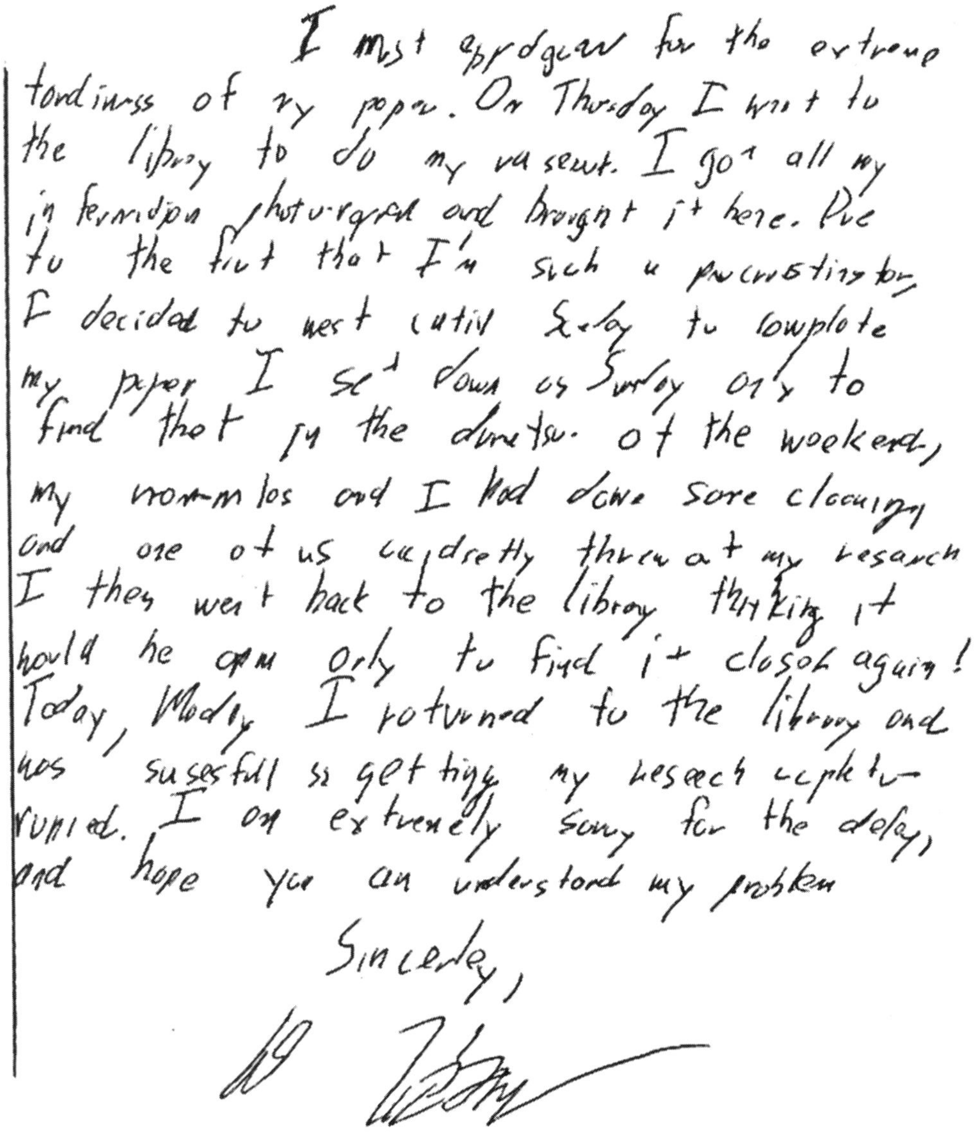

Figure 2.8. Denny's Letter to His Professor.

exceptions. Often their lack of ability in these other two areas 'masks' their potential ability in written expression" (p. 404). Unfortunately, poor spelling can even contribute to lowered grades in other, unrelated academic areas.

Figures 2.9 and 2.10 illustrate the thoughts of two fourth-grade students, Javier and Marge, writing about pollution. Javier writes, "Clean Air. Good to smell, good air. We can stop pollution now. Please keep our air clean." Marge writes, "Save the Earth. Keep the air clean here. Don't go in the car, just walk. We can pick up trash." Unfortunately, both of their compositions are compromised by poor spelling.

Students with spelling problems are often embarrassed by their limited spelling skill. For example, Dennis, a third-grade gifted student with a learning disability, commented that he would be very careful to make sure that no other students could ever see his writing assignments. When asked why, Dennis replied, "I know I'm smart, but my lousy spelling makes me look so dumb. Sometimes I can't think of how to spell even simple words like *house*."

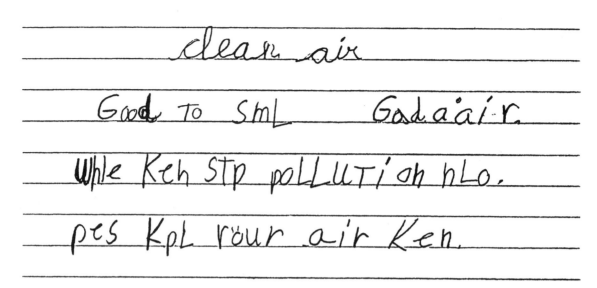

Figure 2.9. Javier's Descriptive Passage.

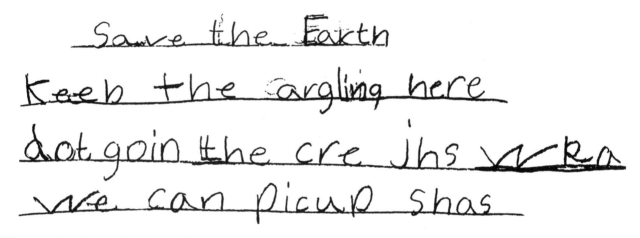

Figure 2.10. Marge's Descriptive Passage.

A characteristic of many students with learning disabilities is good written expression but poor spelling. Some students persist with writing despite their intense frustration with spelling. Amanda, a fourth-grade student, wrote a letter to her grandmother, presented in Figure 2.11. Although the letter contains many errors in spelling and punctuation, her ideas are carefully sequenced and her message is persuasive. She received help from a peer editor, but neither one of them knew how to spell *gorgeous* or *generous*, so they just crossed them out. They tried to correct the word *beautiful*.

Despite her poor spelling, Amanda was able to communicate her wishes clearly to her grandmother, and she did get the new bike before her birthday.

Sometimes spelling problems can affect a student's communicative attempts. For example, Figure 2.12 is an excerpt from a story written by Deval, a sixth-grade student. In this example, her poor spelling interferes with her ability to communicate.

Figure 2.13 shows Madison's first draft on an assignment to write how she would feel if she would encounter a dinosaur. Although you

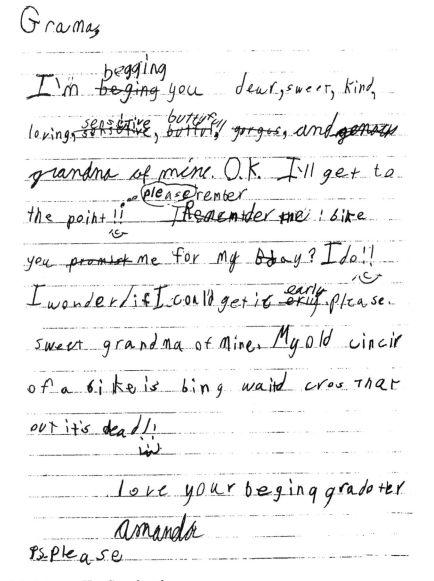

Figure 2.11. Amanda's Letter to Her Grandmother.

Translation: Dear Grandma,

I'm begging you dear, sweet, kind, loving, sensitive, beautiful, gorgeous, and generous grandma of mine. O.K. I'll get right to the point. Please remember the bike you promised me for my birthday? I do!! I wonder if I could get it early, please, sweet grandma of mine. My old clunker of a bike is dying. Wait cross that out. It's dead.

Love your begging granddaughter,

Amanda

P.S. Please.

can probably decipher what this third-grade student is writing, her spelling errors really detract from the content. Note that her teacher has stamped the paper with "Not Edited." Applying this type of notation is often a good idea for papers that may go home without any teacher feedback. When looking at the writings of Amanda, Deval, and Madison, we can clearly see that accurate spelling is very difficult for some students.

Components of Spelling

Accurate spelling requires knowledge of our English writing system. Four aspects of oral language have particular relevance to spelling:

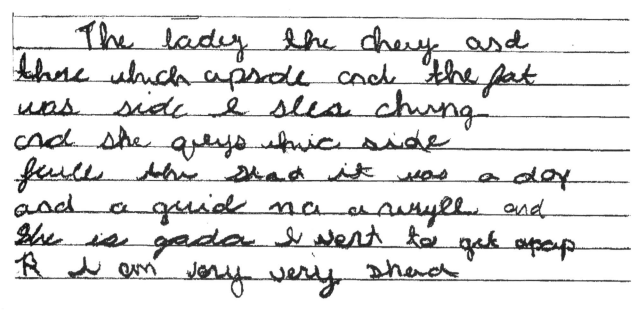

Figure 2.12. Deval's Paragraph.

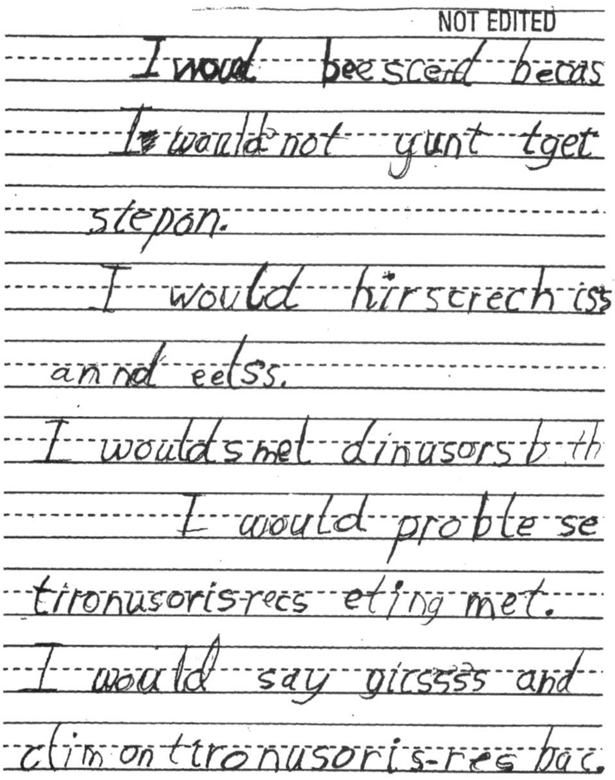

NOT EDITED

Figure 2.13. Madison's Thoughts About Dinosaurs.

phonology, orthography, morphology, and semantics.

Phonology

Phonology refers to the sounds of language. The individual units of speech sounds are called phonemes, and the sounds are usually represented with slashes (for example, /m/ for the *m* sound). English has an estimated forty to forty-four phonemes. The reason this number is inexact is that specific regional dialects can result in a different number of speech sounds. For example, in some parts of the country, it is hard to hear the difference between the short *i* sound and a short *e* sound so the words *pen* and *pin* sound very similar when spoken.

When first learning to spell, children must acquire knowledge of the sound-to-letter principles that govern English spellings, or what is known as the alphabetic principle, the knowledge that speech sounds are represented with letters. Although phonemes have no meaning in and of themselves, spelling requires the accurate sequencing of these phonemes to spell meaningful words.

Orthography

Orthography refers to the writing system of a language, including the spelling patterns, punctuation marks, and numbers. The writing system represents the phonemes through graphemes, or written letters and letter patterns. English has about 230 graphemes. The English language is complicated because the same phoneme /s/ can be spelled with different graphemes *c* and *s*, and the same grapheme *c* can represent different phonemes /k/ and /s/.

English is described as having a deep orthography because the correspondences between the sounds and letters are more complex than in some other languages, such as Spanish. Although many English words can be spelled by simply recording each of the individual phonemes (for example, *hat*), others have patterns that are not phonetic but are regular (for example, *ight*), and still others do not conform to common spelling rules (for example, *once*). These words with irregular elements are often referred to as "exception" words or "sight" words because the irregular element has to be memorized.

Morphology

In addition to learning the spelling of phonemes and specific letter combinations and patterns, children must also learn how to spell morphemes. Just as phonemes are the smallest unit of sound, morphemes, the components of basic word structure, are the smallest meaningful units of language. An understanding of morphology enables a student to form plurals, show possession, or change verbs to different tenses. Morphemes regulate word meaning and signal to us the difference between statements such as, "The dog smells bad" (he smells) and "The dog smells badly" (he has trouble smelling).

Morphemes include roots which are free morphemes that can stand alone, and affixes (prefixes and suffixes), bound morphemes that cannot stand alone. Affixes are attached to root words and alter their meanings. For example, if the prefix *pre-* is attached to the root word *view*, the new word *preview* has a different meaning. Morphology relates to the internal structure of words and is considered an element of grammar.

The word *girls* has two morphemes: one for the meaning of girl and the other for the plural marker. In some words, such as compound words, two root words are combined together to form a word, such as combining the words *rain* and *coat* to form the word *raincoat*. To spell words correctly, students must combine phonological knowledge with an understanding of both orthography and morphology.

Although the spellings of some English words do not adhere to regular phoneme-grapheme correspondence patterns, regularity is often more apparent at a deeper, morphological level. Knowledge of the morphological principles of English makes it possible to spell thousands of additional words. Figure 2.14 illustrates how the addition of morphemes to the root word *friend* alters the spellings, as well as the word meanings.

Many students with learning and language problems are not as proficient as their peers in using morphological knowledge to help with spelling. Students may have difficulty forming plurals, possessives, and verb tenses. They often omit word endings even though they say these endings when speaking. Other students have problems that involve many aspects of language. Figure 2.15 illustrates a descriptive paragraph written by Fiona, a tenth-grade student. Her difficulties with morphology and usage are readily apparent.

Semantics

Semantics or vocabulary knowledge aids a writer in word choice and in the spelling of homophones or words that differ in meaning but sound alike (such as *pair* and *pear*). Typically, the content of the sentence, especially the words preceding or following a given word, helps the writer determine the correct spelling. Students with learning disabilities often have difficulties producing the correct spellings of homophones and require a considerable amount of practice to master these words. A high school freshman may know that a "cent" is a penny, but not know that "scent" is an odor. Figure 2.16 illustrates a partial retelling of "The Night Before Christmas" written by Cathie, a fifth-grade student. Her confusion regarding the spelling of homophones is evident.

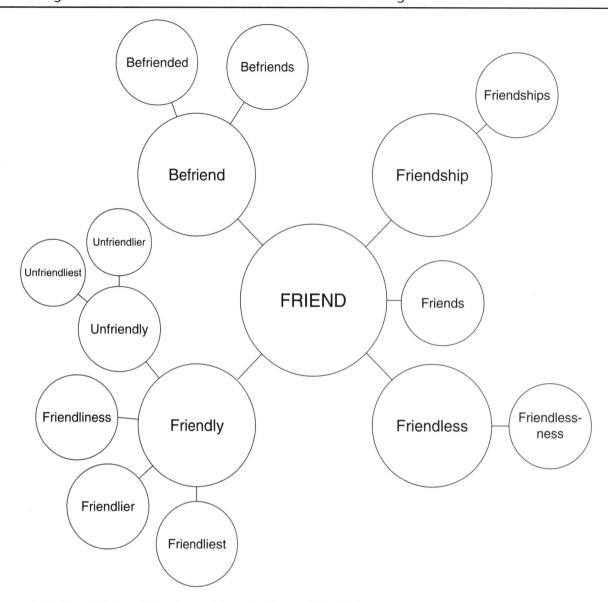

Figure 2.14. The Addition of Morphemes Alters Spelling and Word Meaning.

USAGE

The rules governing written language are more involved than those of spoken language. To communicate in writing with clarity, students must master rules involving capitalization, punctuation, and syntax. Both recollection and application of these English composition skills require knowledge of language structure and mastery of these written language conventions. Knowledge of these rules becomes particularly important when students attempt to edit their own assignments. Many of the written language conventions do not occur naturally in our oral language and therefore require conscious attention and instruction.

Correct use of punctuation and capitalization helps the reader understand the writer's intent. Figure 2.17 presents a paragraph written by Laurie, a fifth-grade student. Her run-on sentences detract from her message.

Syntax, frequently referred to as a component of grammar, represents the structure of a language and includes the rules for combining

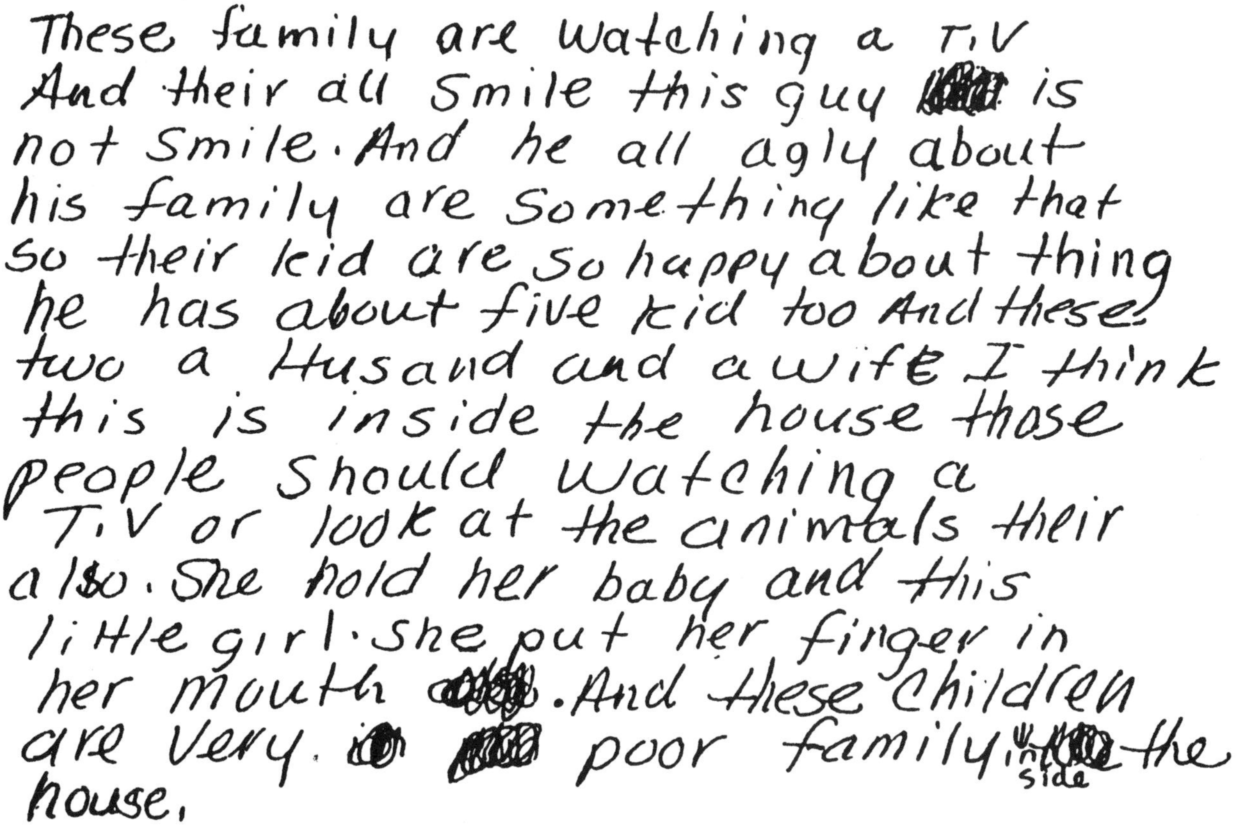

These family are watching a T.V
And their all smile this guy ~~⬛⬛~~ is
not smile. And he all agly about
his family are something like that
so their kid are so happy about thing
he has about five kid too And these
two a Husand and a wife I think
this is inside the house those
people should watching a
T.V or look at the animals their
also. She hold her baby and this
little girl. She put her finger in
her mouth ~~⬛⬛~~. And these children
are very. ~~⬛ ⬛⬛~~ poor family ~~⬛⬛~~ the
inside
house,

Figure 2.15. Fiona's Descriptive Paragraph.

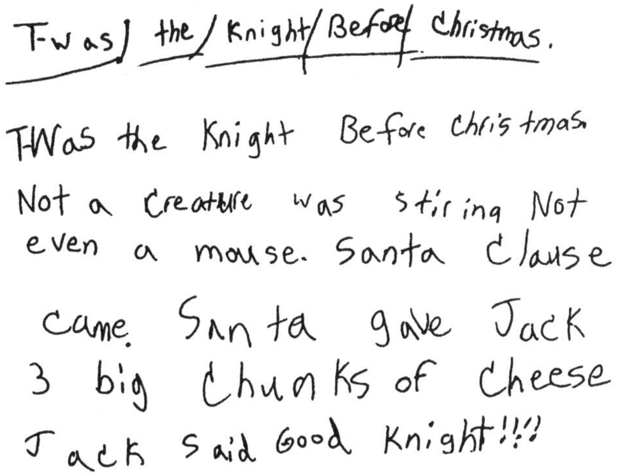

T-was) the/ Knight/ Before/ Christmas.

TWas the Knight Before Chris tmas.
Not a Creature was stiring Not
even a mouse. Santa Clause
came. Santa gave Jack
3 big Chunks of cheese
Jack said Good Knight!!!

Figure 2.16. Cathie's Retelling.

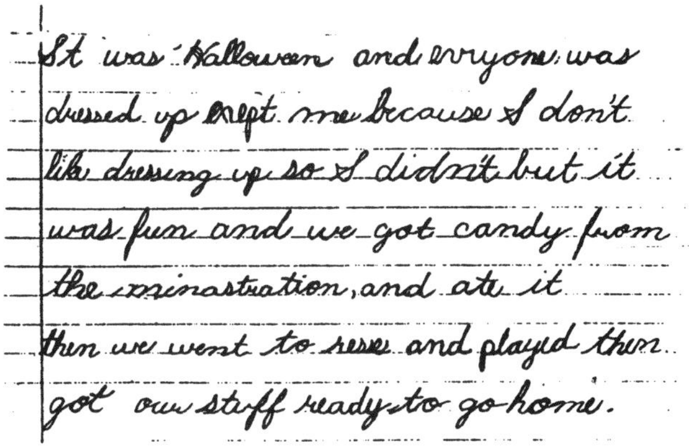

It was Halloween and evryone was
dressed up exept me because I don't
like dressing up so I didn't but it
was fun and we got candy from
the ministration, and ate it
then we went to reses and played then
got our stuff ready to go home.

Figure 2.17. Laurie's Paragraph.

words into sentences and identifying the relationships among the various words. Syntax includes knowledge of (a) clause structure, or noun phrases and verb phrases within clauses, and (b) the rules for forming negatives, questions, and complex sentences through embedding and conjoining (James, 1989). More simply put, syntax refers to the predictable patterns of language that are found in sentences. As Gould (1991) described, "Even in a nonsense sentence, 'The iggle oggled the uggle,' the actor, action, and recipient are known, as are the patterns for changing the form of the sentence to a negative or a question" (p. 134). "The iggle didn't oggle the uggle" and "Did the iggle oggle the uggle?" The selection and use of syntactic structures are essential for clarity. Understanding of sentence syntax enables one to construct a variety of sentence patterns that make one's writing more interesting. Knowledge of morphology is also important for understanding sentence structure. As morphological knowledge increases, a student's ability to produce more complex language structures evolves.

Figure 2.18 illustrates the writing of Joshua, an eighth-grade student who had an assignment to write a paragraph about his favorite sport. In this paragraph, Joshua overuses the conjunction *and* and he writes the phrase *I like* six times. Joshua's failure to expand and alter syntactic patterns results in uninteresting writing.

Struggling writers often have difficulty putting words in the correct order and applying punctuation and capitalization rules. Some common usage problems involve pronoun use, subject-verb agreement, and consistency of verb tense. Students who struggle with writing tend to write short sentences that lack complexity and variety. Also they tend to write

run-on sentences and sentences with too many clauses that are joined using words such as *and, but,* or *then.* They may have trouble identifying where the main sentence ends and a clause begins. Alexia, a third-grade student, wrote a description of what she liked about her trip to Disneyland, presented in Figure 2.19.

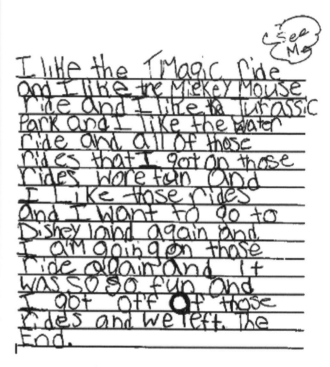

Figure 2.19. Alexia's Description of Her Trip to Disneyland.

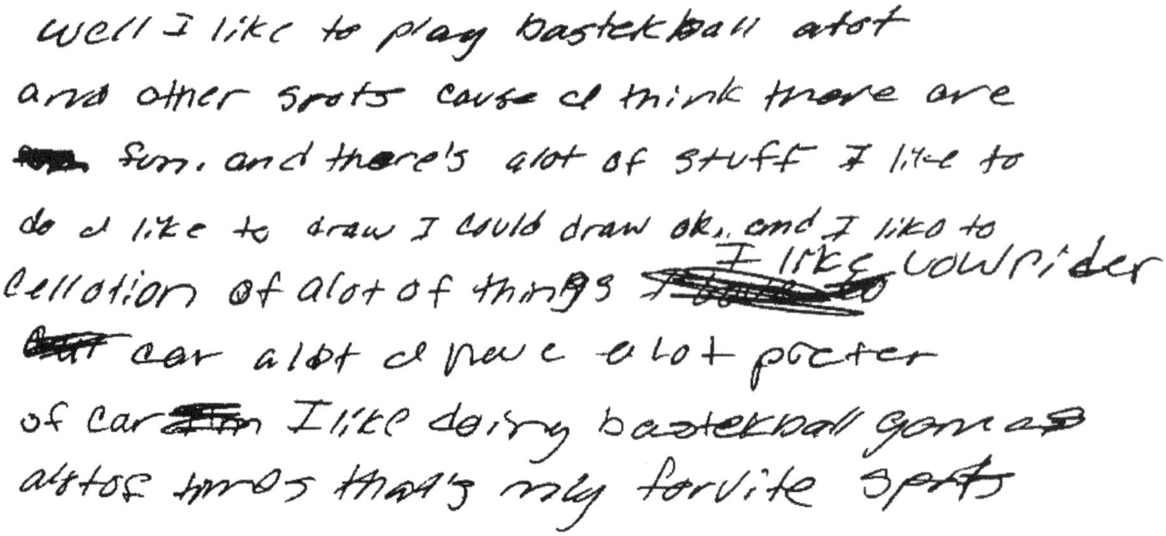

Figure 2.18. Joshua's Paragraph.

All of Alexia's thoughts are joined with the conjunction *and*. Alexia also tends to use fewer modifiers, such as adjectives, adverbs, and prepositional phrases, than her peers. One can sense her teacher's wish to provide direct feedback by her only comment of "See me."

Some students who experience delays in their ability to generate and use a variety of sentence patterns require intervention in oral language. Other students have adequate oral syntactic development, but have trouble formulating written sentences. In either case, intervention is necessary because the ability to vary syntactic structures in sentences by altering, expanding, and manipulating words and phrases adds variety and interest to writing.

VOCABULARY

Another critical aspect of effective writing is selecting descriptive words. For students with language impairments, their written language mirrors their spoken language. For students with learning disabilities, however, a discrepancy often exists between their oral and written vocabularies, with their oral vocabulary being far superior to the vocabulary words that they use when writing. When they are asked questions directly, they often have much more knowledge about a topic than is reflected in their written products.

As an example, Tom, a fifth-grade student, told his teacher about his favorite experience on his trip to Ohio:

> *Well, we went to see my grandma and my favorite part of all was that we spent two whole days at Cedar Point. It's like a big carnival. We rode the roller coaster, the Ferris wheel, and they had this rocket ship that really could spin you around. I even won a goldfish at one booth, but it took me three tries of tossing this little ball into a small bowl. My dad said that it probably would have been cheaper to buy one. It really was neat and even my grandma*

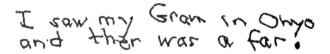

Figure 2.20. Tom's Summary of His Trip to Ohio.

> *went on the rides. Well, all of them except the rocket ship. She was kidding but she said that one would make her even more dizzy than she already is.*

Figure 2.20 presents Tom's written summary of this same experience. Tom has many ideas, but writing is so difficult that his written products are far inferior to his oral retellings.

The number of different words available to writers is determined by their breadth and depth of word knowledge and their ability to retrieve words as needed. In planning writing, skilled writers consciously select appropriate and descriptive words to convey their ideas. Students with more limited vocabularies may have difficulty with (a) word-retrieval ability, (b) knowledge of morphology, or (c) breadth and depth of word knowledge.

Word Retrieval

Word retrieval involves the ability to rapidly access the individual words that are stored in memory. When students have difficulty with word retrieval, the problem is not the lack of intact word knowledge, but rather quick and efficient access to these words. As he was turning in his essay, Jayden, a sixth-grade student, was trying to recall the word *staple*. He explained to his teacher, "It's the thing that holds the papers together, but not the one you take off easy. The one that is stuck." Although Jayden knows the word *staple*, he frequently has trouble retrieving words. He can often explain the function of the object but has trouble producing the object's specific name. On all word-retrieval tasks, Jayden makes more substitution errors than do his normally achieving peers. In addition, he is often slower to respond with answers in both conversation and writing than his peers.

Characteristics of students with word retrieval difficulties include (a) a delay in producing words, including common objects, letters, colors, or numbers; (b) omission and substitution of words; (c) circumlocutions (such as "the thingamajig you use after washing your hands so you can wipe your hands [towel]"); and (d) use of gesture, pantomime, or nonverbal vocalizations (Gerber, 1993). These problems may be apparent in both spoken and written language and can persist into adulthood. Figure 2.21 illustrates a paragraph written by Rebecca, a third-grade student. In both speaking and writing, Rebecca has difficulty using precise vocabulary.

Morphology

Students' knowledge of morphology helps them to gain meaning by recognizing how prefixes, suffixes, and roots contribute to and alter word meaning. Understanding both the meaning of root words and affixes can help increase vocabulary knowledge. Figure 2.14, presented in

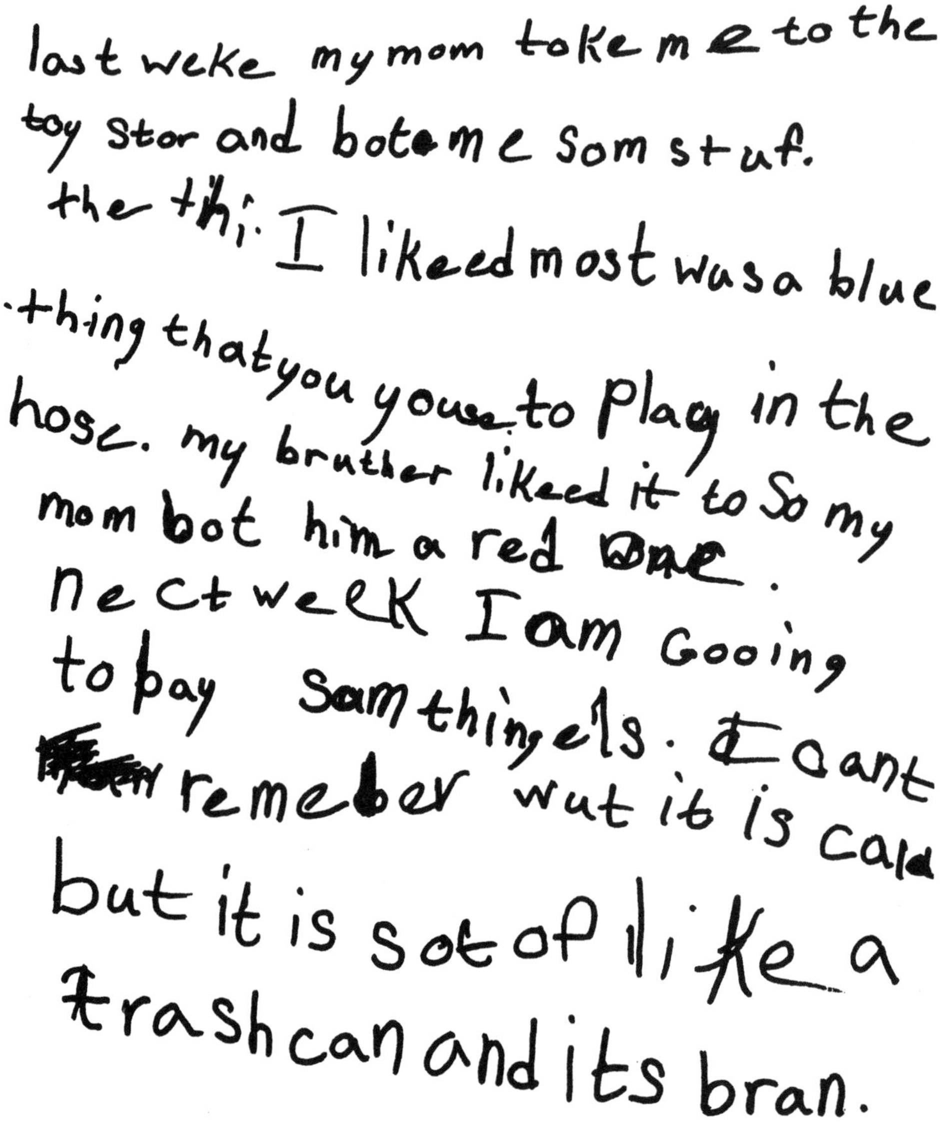
last weke my mom toke me to the toy stor and bote me som stuf. the thi. I likeed most was a blue thing that you youse to plag in the hose. my bruther likeed it to so my mom bot him a red one. nect week I am gooing to bay samthinels. I cant remeber wut it is cald but it is sot of like a trash can and its bran.

Figure 2.21. Rebecca's Paragraph.

the section on spelling, illustrates the addition of morphemes to the word *friend*, thus altering both spelling and word meaning. Morphology helps writers discriminate the parts of speech in sentences.

Affixes include both prefixes and suffixes. Prefixes are attached to the beginnings of root words. Each prefix has its own distinct meaning (or meanings), and when added to the root word, it alters the word's meaning. For example, the prefix *hyper-* means over, so when added to the root word *active*, the new word becomes hyperactive, meaning overly active.

Suffixes are attached to the ends of words and may be inflectional or derivational. When added to a word, an inflectional suffix creates a different form of the same word and alters the meaning. For example, the suffix *-ed* is added to the verb *walk* to demonstrate that that word is past tense. When added to a word, a derivational suffix generally makes a new word and changes the part of speech. For example, the suffix *-ness* is added to the adjective *happy* to form the noun *happiness*. For most students, knowledge of the meanings of common English suffixes undergoes significant development between fourth grade and high school. In general, derivational suffixes are the most abstract and difficult concept of morphology that students are asked to learn; this may be because derivational suffixes are used more frequently in the complex syntax of written language, rather than within common everyday speaking.

Breadth and Depth of Word Knowledge

Word knowledge, or semantics, includes both knowledge of word meanings and the various shades of meaning a word may have. Semantic knowledge helps one to differentiate between words that have shared yet different meanings, such as the difference between *dusk* and *night* or *sympathy* and *empathy*. Children with limited word knowledge often have difficulty expressing themselves because they have trouble selecting the right words to use. Some students overuse

general, nondescriptive words such as the word *nice*, and their writing lacks specificity and elaboration. Figure 2.22 presents a description by Emily, a third-grade student, regarding how she loves her nice teachers.

Weaknesses in vocabulary can persist into adulthood and hinder educational performance at all levels. Students may experience difficulties using homophones (words that sound the same but have different spellings), selecting vocabulary, generalizing word meanings across contexts, and forming associations among words. To enhance their writing performance, students with vocabulary difficulties need to receive instruction in a variety of strategies designed to increase their breadth and depth of word knowledge.

TEXT STRUCTURE

Written texts are designed and organized to convey and represent ideas for a particular purpose. The genres, or text structures, selected by writers enhance organization and the presentation of information in different ways. Organization of text requires the abilities to plan, translate, and review what has been written. In considering a writer's ability to organize and structure text, you must first examine the cohesiveness and coherence of a student's writing. Next, you must determine the student's knowledge of narrative and expository writing.

Cohesion and Coherence

It is the writer's job to present information in a connected, meaningful manner. A writer must attend to the transitions from one sentence to the next, as well as to logical sequencing of ideas. Text organization requires attention to both cohesion and coherence. Cohesion involves the specific ways sentences are integrated and linked together and the transitions within and between sentences. Coherence refers to the overall form and organization of the ideas in a text.

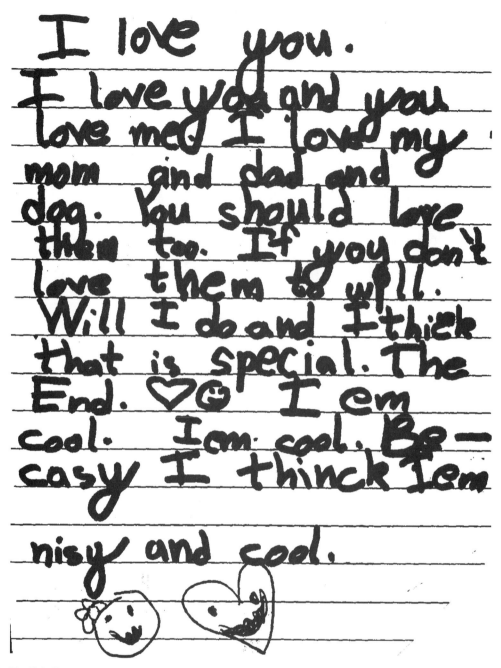

I love you.
I love you and you
love me. I love my
mom and dad and
dog. You should love
them too. If you don't
love them to will.
Will I do and I think
that is special. The
End. ♡☺ I em
cool. I em cool. Be—
casy I thinck I em
nisy and cool.

Figure 2.22. Emily's Description of Her Teachers.

Relationships between and among sentences are often established through the addition of cohesive ties. Cohesive ties help the reader recognize the relationships among thoughts. Two examples of types of cohesive ties are transitional and lexical ties. Transitional ties are words or phrases that illustrate the relationships between sentences, such as *for example* or *consequently*. Lexical ties are established through the selection of vocabulary, such as repeating a word more than once within a text or using a synonym. Good writers pay careful attention to these cohesive devices so that the content and structure of their writing interact to create meaning. Figure 2.23 illustrates the first draft of a descriptive paragraph about Christmas written by Myrna,

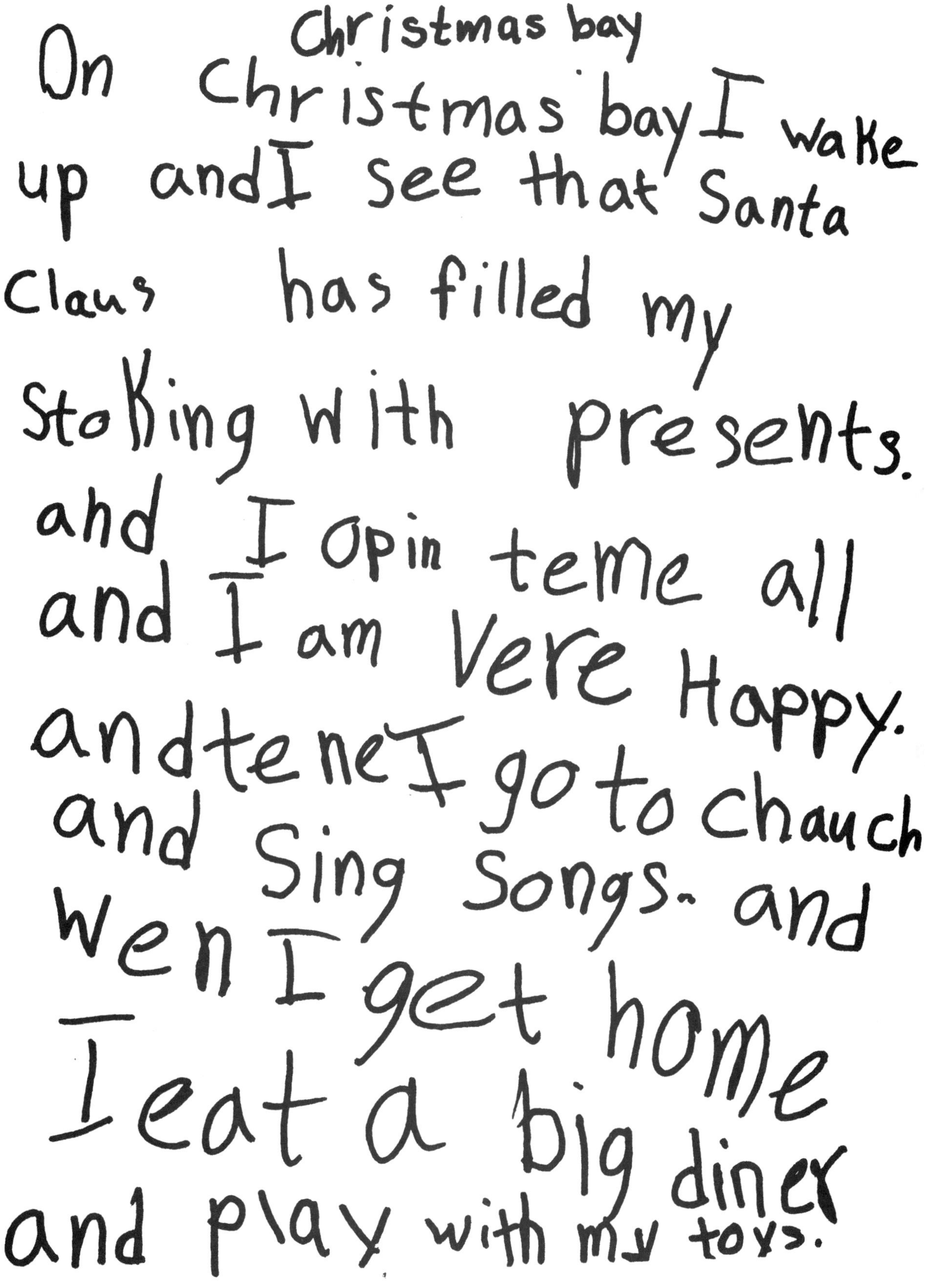

Christmas bay
On Christmas bay I wake up and I see that Santa Claus has filled my stoking with presents. and I opin teme all and I am vere Happy. and tene I go to chauch and sing songs. and wen I get home I eat a big diner and play with my toys.

Figure 2.23. Myrna's Descriptive Paragraph.

a third-grade student. She does not use cohesive ties and attempts to create unity to her ideas by using the conjunction *and*.

In contrast, Figure 2.24 illustrates a descriptive paragraph written by Olivia, a sixth-grade student, who was asked to describe a favorite place. Arrows were added to show Olivia's use of cohesive ties to sequence her text.

Text coherence then relies on both topic maintenance and the careful sequencing of ideas. Coherence and cohesion in writing also involve consideration of the reader's needs. Thus the text structure, the underlying organizational schema, allows the writer and the reader to communicate more easily because what has been written reflects an anticipated organization.

The two major types of text structure are narrative and expository writing. Narrative texts have syntactic patterns and cohesive characteristics that are different from expository text. For instance, the structure for a creative story differs from the structure of a chapter in a science textbook.

Narrative

Students often have to write stories, particularly in elementary school. Knowledge and understanding of the underlying framework or set of rules associated with narrative structure have been referred to as story schema and story grammar. *Story schema* refers to the mental representations an individual has of story parts and their relationships, whereas *story grammar* describes the organizational rules, relationships, and regularities found in text. Story grammar provides students with a framework that can help them produce narrative text.

The basic story grammar elements include (a) setting or place; (b) description of the main characters; (c) beginning, or what starts the story; (d) reaction, or how the main characters respond; (e) outcome, or the results of the attempt to reach the goal; and (f) ending, or the consequences and final responses of the main characters. A more simplified story grammar can include four major story parts: (a) setting (introduction of the characters, time, and place); (b) problem (the predicament that confronts the main characters); (c) action (the characters' attempts to solve the problem); and (d) ending (the characters' successes, or their failures to solve the problem).

Some students have good understanding of story grammar. The first drafts of their

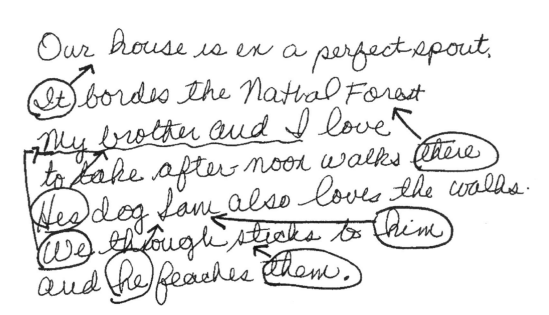

Figure 2.24. Olivia's Descriptive Paragraph.

narratives contain all of the story elements. For example, Luke, a fifth-grade student, wrote a horror story, presented in Figure 2.25. Although a teacher may have concerns in regard to his spelling and handwriting, Luke has created a setting, presented the main characters, designed a problem, and provided a resolution and ending.

Students differ in their abilities to use text structure. Analyses of students' writings indicate that some stories are limited in content and do not include explicit goals, starting events, or the characters' emotional reactions. In general, students who struggle to write stories include fewer story components. Figure 2.26 presents

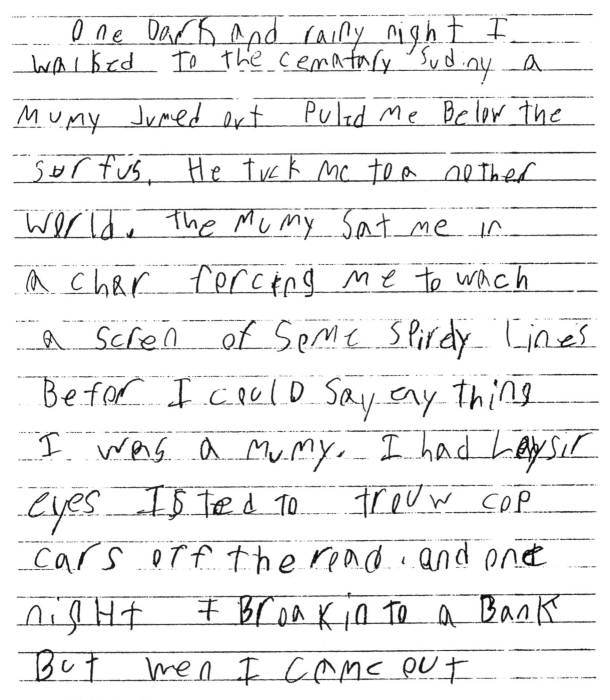

Figure 2.25. Luke's Horror Story.

I saw a man wiseling and snaping his fingers the cops came sudeny Iterned Back into a Boy againg. I went to Jajll for 20 years. Sence then I Never went Back To the semitry.

Figure 2.25. Luke's Horror Story. *(Continued)*

once apon a time their were some bears. They lived in the woods. They had some friends. they had a big house and they liked to go for walks in the woods with their friends. They were friendly Bears and liked to have partys. They would ask thir friends to come over one day. Thir friends came over to the party. They had food and then they saw the move. They liked the move because it was funny and everyone leaft. They all went home and thought it was a nice day.

Figure 2.26. Hefina's Beginning of a Story.

the initial draft of the beginning of a story by Hefina, a sixth-grade student. Although Hefina has described the setting, she has not determined the major problem or problems that the main characters will encounter. Consequently, the story line does not progress, and the presented ideas are disjointed. In addition to direct instruction in story grammar, Hefina would benefit from instruction designed to increase her ability to organize narrative text.

Expository

Expository text explains or provides information about a topic to the reader. Many children in elementary school have trouble relaying factual information in an appropriate written form. In general, expository writing is more complex than story writing because students must research the topic, determine ways to organize their findings, and consider the reader's prior knowledge. In addition, the importance of being able to create expository text structures increases as students progress through school.

A number of different expository text structures exist that can be applied to answer different text structure questions. Each structure is characterized by various semantic and syntactic techniques. Examples of text structure include descriptive, sequential, temporal, compare-contrast, explanation, problem-solution, and opinion. Some essays contain multiple text structures, rather than just one. For example, an author may develop a persuasive essay by comparing and contrasting various opinions (compare-contrast) and then discussing the reasons that support his or her own viewpoint.

Figures 2.27, 2.28, and 2.29 illustrate three student first drafts of different types of text structures. Casey, a tenth-grade student, wrote a descriptive paragraph about his cat, Max. Carl, a sixth-grade student, wrote a sequential paragraph about how to build a snowman. Marnie, a seventh-grade student, was instructed to write a compare-contrast paragraph reflecting traditional and modern views on family and marriage in Japan. Each of these writers has a sense of text structure.

Failure to attend to text structure can result in writing that has irrelevancies, redundancies, and poor organization. As an example of incorporating irrelevant details into an assignment, Figure 2.30 illustrates the writing of Sophia, a seventh-grade student. Sophia was asked to write an opinion paper expressing how she liked the assigned literature book,

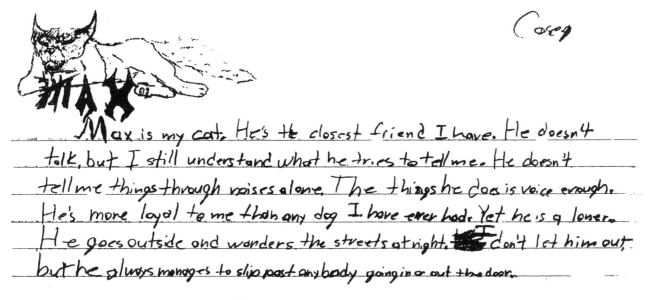

Figure 2.27. Casey's Descriptive Paragraph.

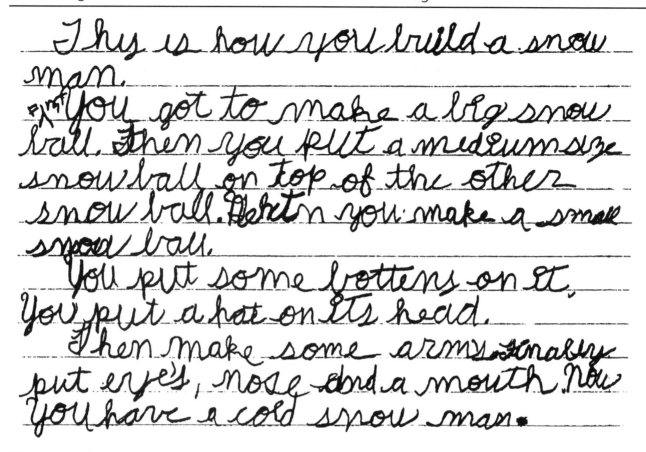

This is how you build a snow man.
You got to make a big snow ball. Then you put a medium size snowball on top of the other snow ball. Then you make a small snow ball.
You put some bottens on it. You put a hat on its head.
Then make some arms. Finally put eye's, nose and a mouth. Now you have a cold snow man.

Figure 2.28. Carl's Sequential Paragraph.

The Pigman. After commenting that she liked the book, Sophia writes a series of marginally related details (for example, there is a party; they did go to the zoo; the man dies; the kids were nice to him), but the combination of the loose connections integrated with her own personal experiences leaves the reader confused. Her writing is characterized by irrelevancies, mechanical errors, and poor organization. Rather than plan her composition, Sophia appears to have included any ideas that came to mind in order without regard to their relevance to her composition.

In contrast, Erik, a tenth-grade student, was asked to write an opinion paragraph on his feelings about guns. His first draft is presented in Figure 2.31. Erik attempts to introduce his topic by describing the function of guns. He then goes on to incorporate his personal experiences and reveal his concerns. Although

revisions and edits are needed, Erik includes several relevant details and supports his opinion with his prior knowledge and experience.

Clearly, students differ in their abilities to produce expository text. Some compositions contain unclear introductions, few details, and inadequate summaries or conclusions. In addition, some writers do not understand how to organize, monitor, and revise their texts on the basis of text structure. The sentences that are written may be unrelated rather than being combined into organized sections of related information in which main ideas are stated first followed by supporting facts and details.

CONCLUSION

Writers who struggle often require instructional techniques that differ from those provided to

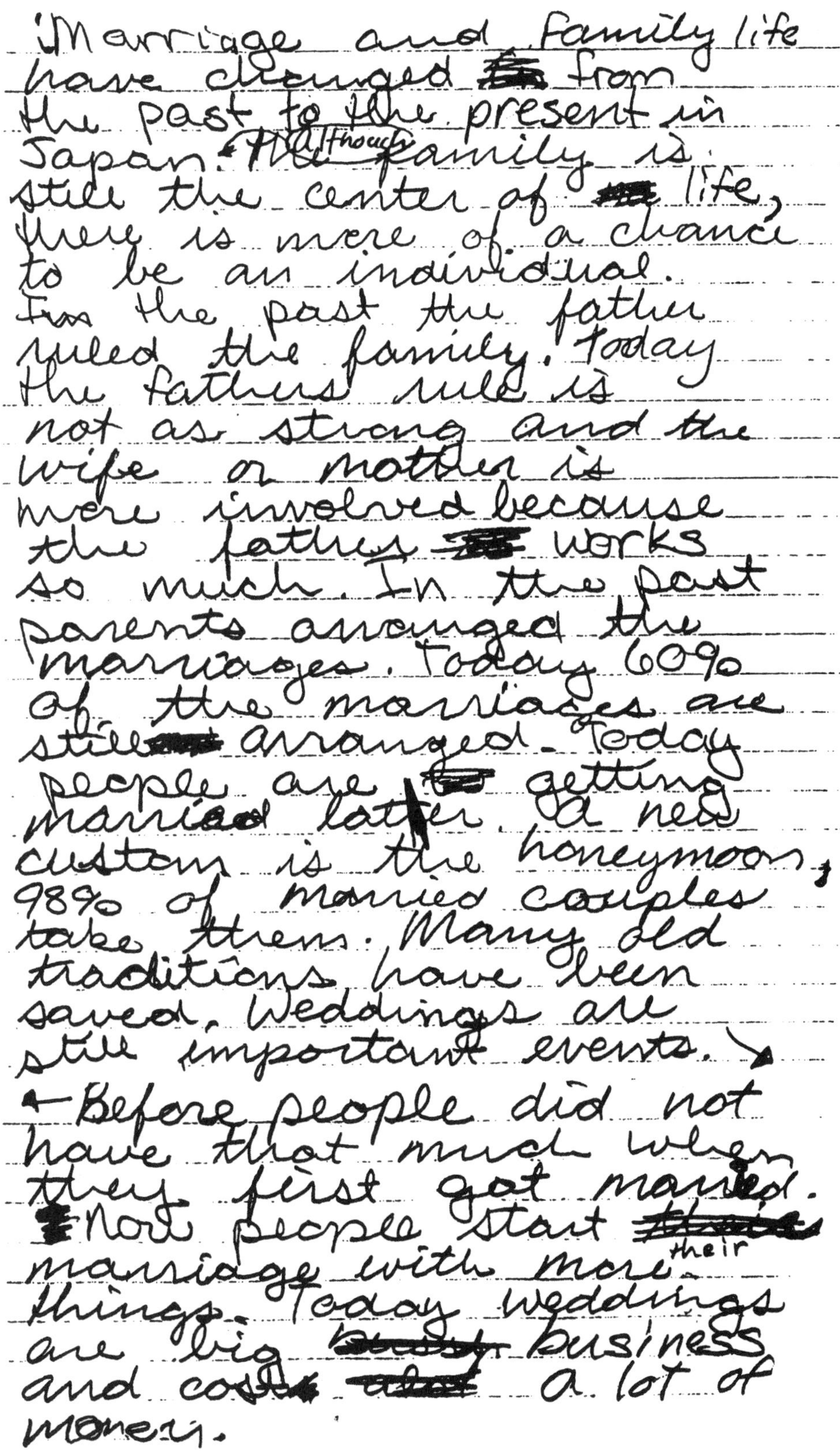

Marriage and family life have changed from the past to the present in Japan. Although family is still the center of life, there is more of a chance to be an individual. In the past the father ruled the family. Today the fathers rule is not as strong and the wife or mother is more involved because the father works so much. In the past parents arranged the marriages. Today 60% of the marriages are still arranged. Today people are getting married later. A new custom is the honeymoon, 98% of married couples take them. Many old traditions have been saved. Weddings are still important events. Before people did not have that much when they first got married. Now people start marriage with more their things. Today weddings are big business and cost a lot of money.

Figure 2.29. Marnie's Compare-Contrast Paragraph.

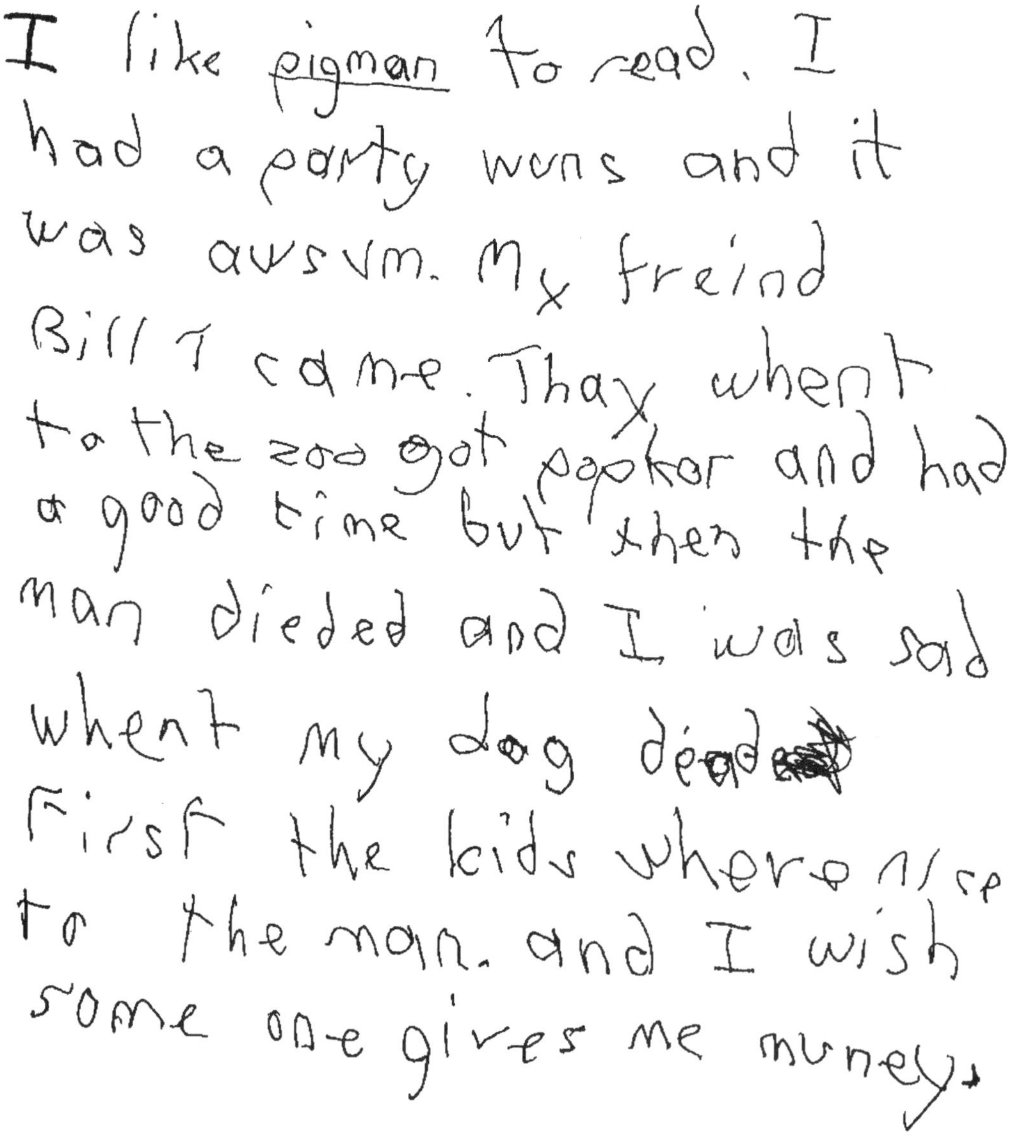

I like pigman to read. I had a party wans and it was awsvm. My freind Bill T came. Thay whent to the zoo got popkor and had a good time but then the man dieded and I was sad whent my dog dead First the kids where nice to the man. and I wish some one gives me money.

Figure 2.30. Sophia's Opinion Paper.

normally achieving peers. Learning to write involves the mastery of numerous skills, and students often show extreme variation in these skills. Assessment and treatment of written language difficulties therefore require an understanding of the different components of written language and the relationships and interactions among these different components. For example, Ms. Chen, a fifth-grade teacher, was well aware that Julio had a wonderful vocabulary, but his difficulty with spelling severely affected his word choice when writing. In contrast, Katie spelled with ease but her limited background knowledge and vocabulary made it difficult for her to formulate and express her ideas clearly. Writing involves both the author and secretary roles (Isaacson, 1989). The author works on effective communication of ideas, whereas the secretary concentrates on the more mechanical aspects, such as the correction of spelling and usage errors. Julio is well prepared for the author role, but not the secretary role. Katie is well equipped for the secretary role of locating spelling errors, but not the author role of organizing and expressing her ideas.

For students like Julio and Katie who struggle to acquire specific aspects of writing

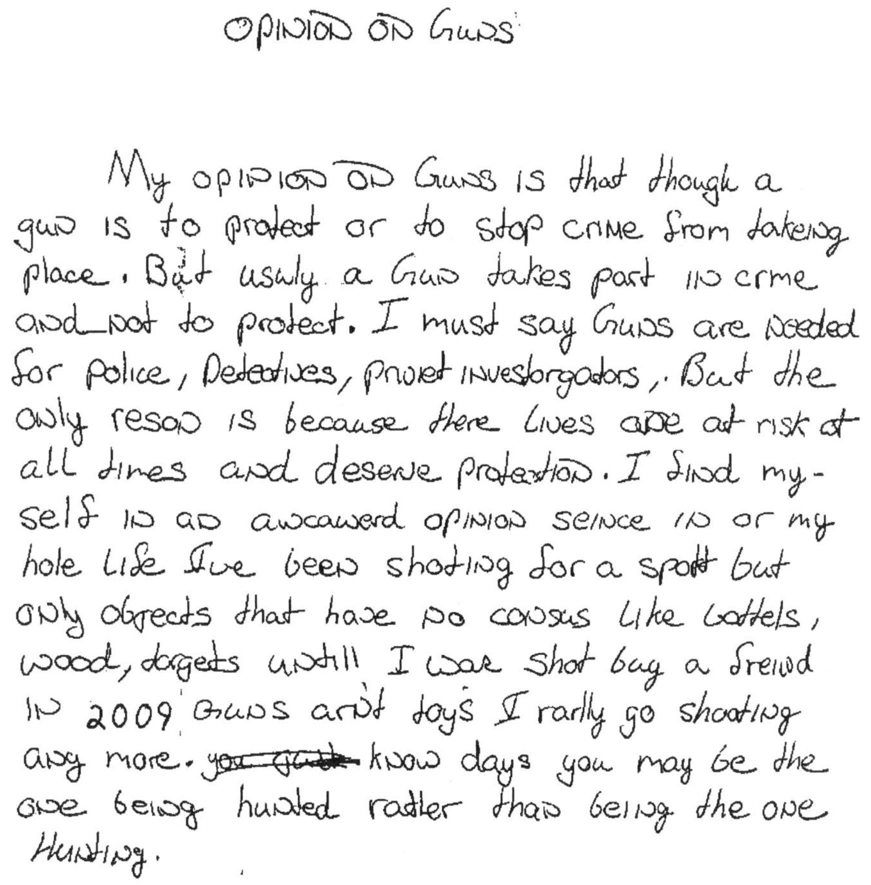

OPINION ON GUNS

My opinion on Guns is that though a gun is to protect or to stop crime from takeing place. But usuly a Gun takes part in crme and not to protect. I must say Guns are needed for police, Detectives, privet investorgators, . But the only reson is because there Lives are at risk of all times and desere protection. I find my-self in an awcawerd opinion seince in or my hole life I've been shoting for a sport but only objects that have no cousus like bottels, wood, targets untill I war shot buy a freind in 2009. Guns arnt toys I rarly go shooting any more. you ~~quit~~ know days you may be the one being hunted rather than being the one Hunting.

Figure 2.31. Erik's Opinion Paper.

competence, the obstacles they encounter can seem insurmountable. Even though these students attempt to produce coherent prose, the quality of their writing is often compromised by poor handwriting, spelling, usage, or ideation and organizational problems.

To become effective, independent writers, students who struggle with writing require intensive, systematic writing programs. Comprehensive writing programs include instruction to help students develop (a) procedural knowledge of the process of writing; (b) declarative knowledge about the purposes, text structures, and mechanical aspects of writing; and (c) conditional knowledge in regard to when to use the strategies (Isaacson, 1994). Sequenced, explicit instruction does work but you must select the instructional interventions by considering each student's present skill level and development. Chapters Five, Six, and Seven discuss instructional activities and present a variety of strategies for teaching handwriting, basic writing skills, and written expression. When skills are assessed and specific instruction is provided, students do become more competent writers.

chapter
3

Theoretical Perspectives and Effective Principles

Thought and language, which reflect reality in a way different from that of perception, are the key to the nature of human consciousness. Words play a central part not only in the development of thought but in the historical growth of consciousness as a whole. A word is a microcosm of human consciousness.

—L. S. Vygotsky (1962)

After making several changes and recopying his paper, Ravi, a third-grade student, asked his teacher, "How can I just write it perfectly the first time so I don't have to write it again?" Although everyone can empathize with his wish, Ravi hasn't yet realized that writing is a recursive process that requires extensive time for planning, composing, revising, re-revising, and editing. Even skilled, competent writers move back and forth through an interchange of self-expression and self-evaluation that can result in numerous revisions.

Many students struggle with writing because writers must direct their attention to a wide range of skills and processes simultaneously. The task of writing can be as daunting to a second-grader attempting to write a story as to an adult who is trying to write a book. The challenge is even greater for students who have difficulties in language and learning. Kerchner and Kistinger (1984) described a picture of a child with learning disabilities trying to write: "That

portrait depicts a child awkwardly grasping a pencil and much-used eraser, attempting to fulfill an assignment by writing words on paper. We might entitle this portrait 'Personification of Frustration'" (p. 329). This description captures the experience of students with learning disabilities, but it also portrays the many other students who struggle with writing as well.

Today's students appear to struggle even more with writing than did those of past generations. Some blame television and the lure of video games; some blame instant and text messaging on computers and cell phones; others blame the lack of time that teachers have to teach writing because of all the preparation time for mandated state testing. In spite of this seeming decline in writing performance, teachers are more aware than ever before of the importance of helping students become effective, competent writers. To provide quality writing instruction, you need to have a theoretical framework that encompasses the important role of language. This framework includes your theoretical perspective on teaching writing, as well as your adherence to basic principles of writing instruction.

THEORETICAL PERSPECTIVES

To understand written language, it is important to consider the differences between spoken and written language, the complexity of the writing task, and the influence of psycholinguistics.

Differences Between Spoken and Written Language

The skills required for conversation differ from the skills required for composing. Writing is not "talk written down." Writing is more complex than speaking. Oral communication occurs within a particular setting and is topic-oriented and spontaneous. To facilitate communication, a speaker uses many verbal cues (such as intonation) and nonverbal cues (such as eye contact or facial expressions) when conversing. A permanent record of the conversation does not exist. After the conversation has ended, both the speaker and the listener must rely on the memory of what was said, which may be colored by their personal emotional reactions to the event. Exhibit 3.1 summarizes several of the major differences between spoken and written language.

Writing requires more skills than speaking. The writer needs skill in motor control and dexterity with a pen or a keyboard, organization and clarification, knowledge of syntax and vocabulary, and the capacity to juggle these demands. The writer must also consider the response of the reader, or audience, and use reflective thinking when rereading and checking what has been written.

Teachers look at a student's writing and judge many factors. How neat is the handwriting? Are words spelled correctly? Is punctuation used correctly? Are ideas expressed in an organized way? Are various sentence structures used? Is the vocabulary appropriate for the topic? By the fourth grade, students' writings can reflect their ability to (a) organize their thinking, (b) set a goal and maintain focus on the goal, (c) draw upon background knowledge, (d) reflect on events and facts from another's perspective, and (e) review and revise what has been written for logic and coherence. Clearly, writing is not just "talk written down."

Complexity of Writing

Anyone who writes is aware of the multifaceted nature of the task, as well as the complexity of the act. When writing, the author must direct attention toward a wide range of skills. For students who struggle with writing, certain aspects of performance are not automatic.

Exhibit 3.1. Examples of Differences Between Spoken and Written Language.

Spoken Language	Written Language
Relies upon listening and memory	Provides a permanent record
Is less structured	Is more structured; requires exact word choice, and formal sentence and paragraph instruction
Relies upon immediate, personal, literal, inferential, and emotional interpretations	Provides opportunity for review and evaluation of interpretations
Requires dual monitoring (what is being said and what one plans to say)	Requires simultaneous monitoring of numerous abilities
Requires planning what will be said next, perhaps with a goal in mind	Requires planning large units of communication while keeping goals in mind
Involves communication with a known audience with immediate feedback	Involves an abstract, distant audience with delayed feedback
Provides visual cues to support meaning (such as gestures and expressions)	Provides punctuation marks to express a few meanings

The child may be thinking of how to form a cursive *j* or how to spell the word *dinosaur* while attempting to translate thoughts.

Writing involves at least three domains of knowledge that interact to shape what is written: (a) knowledge of the topic, (b) knowledge of language, and (c) knowledge of the audience. Knowledge of the topic allows a writer to incorporate background knowledge and experiences into his or her writing. Knowledge of language helps a writer to incorporate writing conventions governing the ordering of words into sentences. Knowledge of audience allows the writer to consider the reader or readers and their background knowledge. A writer may have difficulty with any, or all, of these three domains: retrieving and organizing information to be written, retrieving the words and formulating sentences for effective communication, or assessing the knowledge base of the readers. When Mark, an eighth-grade student, was asked to write an essay on his opinions regarding education, he eventually wrote the following sentence: *People need education, I guess. I just don't know how to explain why.* Evidently, Mark needed more background knowledge prior to writing.

The Influence of Psycholinguistics

Contributions from psycholinguistics are fundamental to the design of intervention strategies for struggling writers. Contemporary approaches in psycholinguistics are based on the work of Lev Vygotsky (1962; 1978). In Vygotsky's perspective, language plays an active role in the creation of thought. Thus the ability to put thoughts into writing helps children develop, clarify, and structure their ideas. Three aspects of Vygotskian theory are pertinent to the development of writing programs. The first involves the child's use of private speech and its regulatory function for the construction of content. The second incorporates concepts central to the zone of proximal development, a theoretical construct that underlies effective instruction. The third aspect deals with decentralization and the development of audience consideration and text cohesion.

Private Speech

Vygotsky believed that language is acquired as a result of collaboration with more competent speakers. The dialogues between adults and children facilitate use of words and the use of language. Between the ages of two and ten years, most children internalize language functions, developing and using what Vygotsky refers to as private speech. Private speech, defined as self-talk, accompanies the child's actions, assisting in cognitive development and metacognition.

The child takes a major step toward the ability to accomplish independent goal-directed behavior when he or she begins to use the strategies adults use to regulate behavior. The child may imitate verbal directions and formulate and carry out goal-directed actions. Language then comes to organize the child's thought. Initially private or inner speech plays an important role in the development of goal-directed activities. Later, it provides the foundation for written language development.

Vygotsky viewed writing as the elaboration of inner speech. As the writer establishes goals for writing, he or she transforms inner speech into written language through elaboration and extension. Thus thoughts and impressions are transformed and then expanded into written discourse. Some students have problems expressing their thoughts in writing. Due to their difficulties with language, these students have more limited private speech and cannot cope with the multiple dimensions of writing. In the Vygotskian view, writing is among the most intense of self-regulatory activities because of the need to coordinate the many aspects. The writer is expected not only to generate, organize, and control thought processes in light of the writing goals but also to manipulate the more mechanical aspects.

Zone of Proximal Development

In his book *Mind and Society*, Vygotsky introduced the concept of the zone of proximal development as a key construct for learning to occur (1978, p. 86). He defines the zone as the "distance between the actual developmental level as determined by independent problem solving and the level of potential development as determined through problem solving under adult guidance or in collaboration with more capable peers." The process of maturation makes possible specific learning processes that push forward maturation. Thus development is not seen as coinciding with learning but rather as evolving slightly behind it. Teaching is then directed at providing instruction that is slightly more advanced than development. Many educators use the more familiar terms *instructional range* or *instructional level*. Similar to the zone of proximal development, many informal reading inventories identify three levels of performance: the independent, instructional, and frustration levels. The independent level is below the zone; the person can perform the task with no assistance and with ease. The instructional level is within the zone and is the targeted area for instruction when help is provided by a more knowledgeable other. The frustration level is above the zone, and the concepts or tasks are too difficult for the student even with assistance.

The challenge to you as a teacher is fourfold: (a) to conduct task analysis and error analysis necessary to determine the point at which to intervene with instruction, (b) to determine the optimal distance between the child's independent level of functioning and his or her capabilities with assistance (the depth of the zone), (c) to prioritize intervention based on need, and (d) to motivate a reluctant learner to enter the zone. The first three challenges constitute a model for effective teaching. The final challenge recognizes the impact of writing difficulties on self-concept and motivation.

Some students are not yet capable of performing tasks without the support of others. As teachers, we can help students become more independent in thinking and problem solving by enhancing knowledge of the topic and knowledge of language. Reasoning and thinking are guided by language. Explicit instruction in language can provide students with opportunities to reach new insights and understandings. Language is the vehicle that pushes thinking toward higher levels, and writing is a permanent record of thinking processes. Writing then is a central means for helping children develop their thinking skills.

Awareness of Audience

As children continue to develop, they are able to take the perspective of the reader. They begin to conceptualize at more abstract levels and can decentralize, or meet the needs of an abstract and absent audience. The development of decentralization can be seen in children's play. For example, a child may refer to "this horse" when pointing to the broom, and "that horse" when pointing to an upside-down chair. These symbolic references provide the foundation for formal references in writing and are the predecessor to text coherence. When writing, the author must be sensitive to the reader's need for explicit and consistent reference to avoid ambiguity. For example, the writer avoids ambiguity through careful attention to pronoun referents and consistency in verb tense.

A writer's awareness of audience is intricately related to his or her ability to decentralize. A child at play takes the role of a significant other, fantasizing responses or reactions of a particular character. Similarly, the author takes the role of the reader when attempting to critique his or her own text. The more accurately the reader's knowledge is judged, the more cohesive the text will be.

These three aspects of Vygotskian theory, the development of inner speech, the zone of proximal development, and the process of decentralization, are directly related to writing instruction. Through modeling and questioning, you can help students transform their ideas into written text and consider the reader's perspective. You will also want to establish instructional goals that are slightly ahead of a student's developmental level. Essentially, your role is to enhance each student's ability to express their ideas effectively. This is the central goal of writing instruction.

EFFECTIVE INSTRUCTIONAL PRINCIPLES

In addition to a theoretical foundation, effective classroom writing instruction revolves around implementing and following several basic instructional principles. The list below provides an overview of general teaching tips. A more in-depth discussion of several of the key principles follows.

General Teaching Tips

- Provide students with rich experiences prior to assigning writing.
- Help students learn to plan and organize their thoughts prior to writing.
- Conduct a task analysis of students' writing skills and prioritize specific areas for instruction.
- Select only one or two skills to work on at a time.
- Help students recognize common errors in written language through class mini-lessons.
- Model and provide practice using various prewriting, drafting, revising, and editing strategies.
- Do not grade first drafts but provide ideas for revision.
- Provide students with meaningful writing assignments.
- Provide clear purposes for writing assignments.
- Instead of penalizing for errors, teach the student how to correct the mistakes.
- Read numerous examples of good writing to students and discuss the features that make the writing interesting.
- Encourage students to write their thoughts in journals or diaries and provide feedback to the students on their ideas.

- Ask students specific questions that will guide their revisions.
- Base final grades on the personal accomplishments of each student in the classroom, rather than on how they compare to others.

Determine the Student's Present Level of Writing Skills and Establish Realistic Goals

Before beginning writing instruction, you must first have an idea of how easily and well each student in your classroom can write. This can be accomplished by collecting several writing samples on different topics, as well as interviewing students about their understanding of writing. Figure 3.1 offers sample questions that you might ask to determine a student's knowledge of writing. By knowing a student's current level of writing skills, you are equipped to develop realistic goals and expectations for each student.

Once you have determined a student's level of skill, the next step is to establish instructional goals. When working with reluctant writers, you must first address the most important concerns. For example, if a student is having trouble forming complete sentences, you may not want to address her failure to use question marks. That can wait. Or, if a student is having trouble organizing his thoughts, you may want to wait before addressing his incorrect use of capital letters.

On occasion, a teacher may set unrealistic goals for a student and then assume that the student didn't try hard enough when the goal is not met. Figure 3.2 illustrates a paragraph written by Nick, a fourth-grade student. For an in-class assignment, he was asked to write a paragraph on the benefits of being healthy. Students worked independently on their paragraphs and were then to edit their own work. Nick's paper was returned the next day with the comment, "You must edit!" Nick's teacher was unaware that Nick had tried to edit his work, but he did not see any errors.

General

Does the student understand the purpose of the writing process approach?

What is the student's attitude toward the writing process approach?

Does the student take pride in his or her writing at the various stages?

Prewriting

Does the student understand the purpose of prewriting strategies?

What is the student's attitude toward prewriting?

What prewriting strategies does the student use?

Is information gathered from various sources?

Is the information adequate?

Does the student generate enough ideas?

Does the student define the topic and purpose?

Is there evidence of sufficient planning?

Does the student consider the intended audience?

What prewriting skills need attention?

First Draft

Does the student understand the purpose of writing a draft?

What is the student's attitude toward writing a draft?

Is the information from the prewriting activities used?

Is the focus on the main idea?

Does the student place more emphasis on content than on mechanics?

Does the student take time to think while composing?

What skills in composing a first draft need attention?

Revision

Does the student understand the purpose of revision?

What is the student's attitude toward revision?

Does the student respond positively to advice and feedback from others?

Does the student use a variety of sentence constructions, such as simple, compound, and complex?

Does the student attempt to select more precise vocabulary?

Is the student able to add, delete, and move sections?

Does the student read the draft to ensure clarity and logic?

Are new ideas and information added to the main and subtopics?

Does the student consider the audience while revising?

Are specific revision strategies used?

Does the student make changes to reflect the suggestions from both the teacher and peers?

Can the student explain how the revisions have improved his or her composition?

What revision skills need attention?

Editing

Does the student understand the purpose of editing?

What is the student's attitude toward editing?

Does the student identify many of his and her errors?

What types of errors does the student identify?

Does the student:

Write in complete sentences?

Use conjunctions correctly (such as *but, because, and*)?

Use correct subject-verb agreement?

Use correct verb tense?

Form plurals correctly?

Use possessives appropriately?

Use pronouns appropriately?

Use homonyms appropriately?

Figure 3.1. Questions for Evaluating Writing Knowledge.

Use comparatives and superlatives appropriately (such as *bigger, biggest*)?

Use word endings correctly (such as *ed, eg, ing, ly*)?

Apply correct punctuation rules?

Apply correct capitalization rules?

Use correct spelling?

Can the student correct identified errors?

What editing strategies does the student use?

Does the student use available resources (such as teacher or peer suggestions; a dictionary and a thesaurus)?

Can the student explain why the changes are necessary?

What editing skills need attention?

Final Draft

Does the student understand the purpose of writing a final draft?

What is the student's attitude toward writing a final draft?

Have all previous comments and feedback been taken into consideration?

Is the structure and sequence of the final draft appropriate?

Is the purpose of the writing clear?

Has the perspective of the reader been considered?

Were the majority of grammatical and spelling errors corrected?

What final draft skills need attention?

Sharing

Does the student understand the reason for sharing his or her work?

What is the student's attitude toward sharing his or her work with peers?

How does the student prefer to share his or her work (reading, displaying)?

Can the student suggest different ways in which she or he would like to share her or his work?

Dos the student participate when other students share their work?

Figure 3.1. Questions for Evaluating Writing Knowledge. (*Continued*)

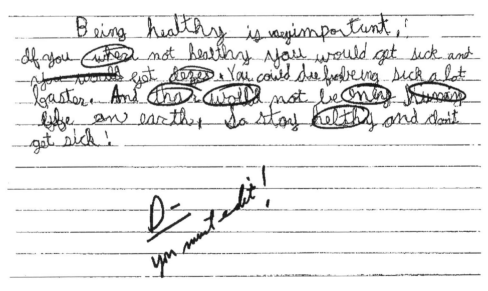

Figure 3.2. Nick's Paragraph.

We want to make sure that we do not lose sight of the most relevant instructional goals by focusing on issues of lesser significance. Figure 3.3 shows a fifth-grade student's spelling test with his teacher's comment, "Cody, the holes should be on the other side." Clearly, Cody's spelling difficulties are of far greater concern than the location of the holes on the notebook paper. We are reminded of the Gary Larsen cartoon where two people are flying in

Figure 3.3. Cody's Spelling Test.

an airplane that has a gaping hole in the top. The one passenger remarks to the other, "Oh great. Now, there goes my hat!" Don't focus your feedback on the little things. Focus on the most important instructional issues.

Sometimes you will want to give priority to what students perceive as their most troublesome aspect of writing, even if that difficulty is more perceived than real. Because of negative feedback from others, some students perceive their problems with writing as actually far greater than they really are. Figure 3.4 illustrates the first draft of Azumi, a seventh-grade student. Azumi is concerned about her poor spelling skill. Although her spelling is not perfect, she succeeds in communicating through writing. Somehow through her experiences, she has come to believe that her poor spelling is a major impediment to her writing. Although her teacher is more concerned about Azumi's limited use of descriptive adjectives, she knows she must first address Azumi's concerns about her spelling, so that Azumi can regain her confidence as a writer. Once Azumi understands that her misspellings can be easily corrected, her teacher will focus on the use of descriptive adjectives.

Ensure That Students Are Capable of Performing the Task

Sometimes students are unintentionally assigned writing tasks that are beyond their capabilities. Writing assignments should not be too difficult for a child or beyond his or her capabilities. Figure 3.5 shows one of Joey's spelling tests. Joey is in third grade and consistently gets only one or two of his spelling words correct each week even though he studies for hours. Although the lists may be appropriate for many of his peers, these words are too difficult for Joey. Lists containing high-frequency words such as *they*, *said*, and *people* would be far more meaningful and appropriate for Joey at his current skill level.

Although struggling writers are usually the ones who are given work that is beyond their skill levels, good writers may also be given assignments they do not want to do. Jacob, a kindergartener who entered school reading at a second-grade level, was identified by his teacher as someone who needed to be challenged in writing. Consequently, while other students were learning to write their letters, Jacob was asked to read a book and write a book report. Although he fulfilled the assignment for the

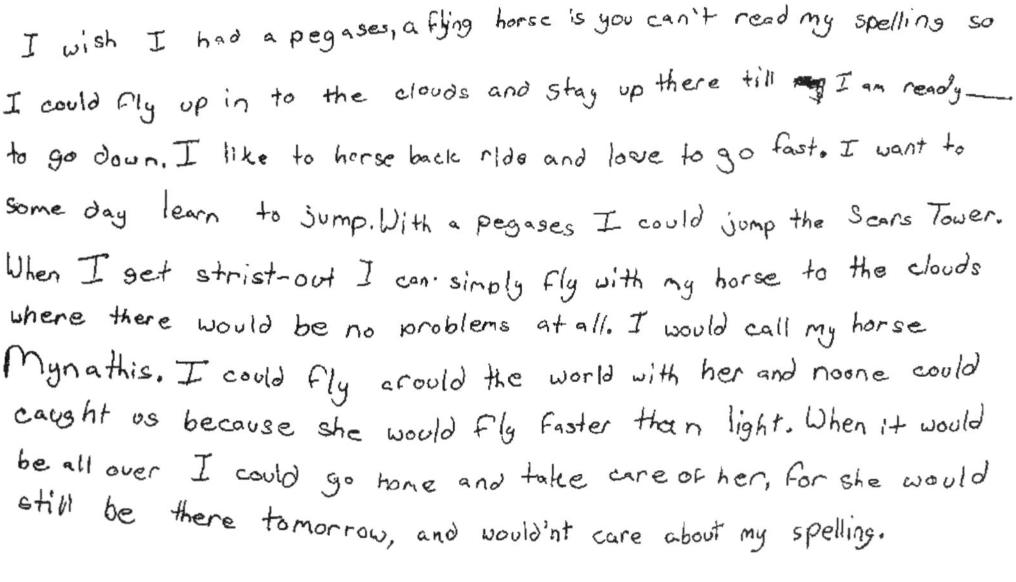
I wish I had a pegases, a flying horse is you can't read my spelling so
I could fly up in to the clouds and stay up there till I am ready
to go down. I like to horse back ride and love to go fast. I want to
some day learn to jump. With a pegases I could jump the Sears Tower.
When I get strist-out I can simply fly with my horse to the clouds
where there would be no problems at all. I would call my horse
Mynathis. I could fly arould the world with her and noone could
caught us because she would fly faster than light. When it would
be all over I could go home and take care of her, for she would
still be there tomorrow, and would'nt care about my spelling.

Figure 3.4. Azumi's First Draft of a Story.

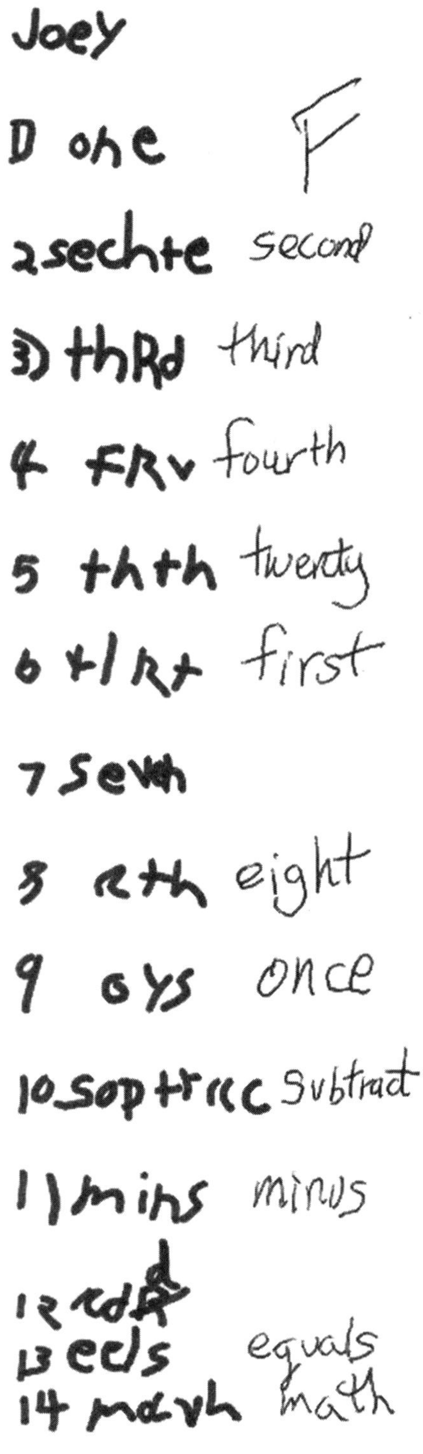

Joey

D one   F

2 sechte second

3) thRd third

4 FRv fourth

5 thth twenty

6 t/Rt first

7 Sevth

8 Rth eight

9 oys once

10 sop trcc subtract

11 mins minus

12 rdf

13 eels equals

14 mdvh math

Figure 3.5. Joey's Spelling Test.

first ten weeks, Jacob bemoaned his fate often, asking questions such as, "Why can't I just do the same as the other kids?" and "Why can't I just enjoy my book?" Although he was perfectly capable of writing book reports, Jacob was only five years old.

Sadly, the decision to have Jacob write book reports at the age of five seems to have had a long-lasting, negative effect. After ten weeks of writing book reports, he began to refuse to read. Thankfully, his teacher recognized the problem and changed Jacob's assignment to reading without having to write reports. These types of experiences, however, can have long-term impact. Three years later, Jacob continues to love to read but dislikes writing.

One common misperception among some teachers is that children can edit their own work independently. Even successful writers can only correct the errors they find, such as a lack of subject-verb agreement or the misuse of quotation marks. They may not, however, fix an error such as "the diamond weighs a caret" when they do not know that the word *carat* is misspelled. Even a computerized spell checker does not note this error because *caret* is a real word, spelled correctly. Thus a person's ability to detect errors can only be as accurate as his or her knowledge of those types of errors.

Ernie, a third-grader, was asked to fix any misspellings on his paper. Figure 3.6 presents the corrections Ernie made. Some of the spelling errors have been changed to different errors, whereas other words that were spelled correctly initially have been altered. Ernie cannot correct his spelling mistakes without receiving feedback and support from others.

Ensure That Writing Assignments Are Meaningful

Dynamic writing teachers always try to make each written assignment meaningful and appropriate. For example, Ms. McGrew, a fifth-grade teacher, had her students write letters to a newspaper in response to an article denouncing the "me" generation. Because the assignment was interesting, the students tried harder than usual and produced some thoughtful letters that they planned to send to the editor.

Although some worksheets can be meaningful, having children complete too many worksheets can have a negative effect on motivation. Also, because worksheets are mass produced,

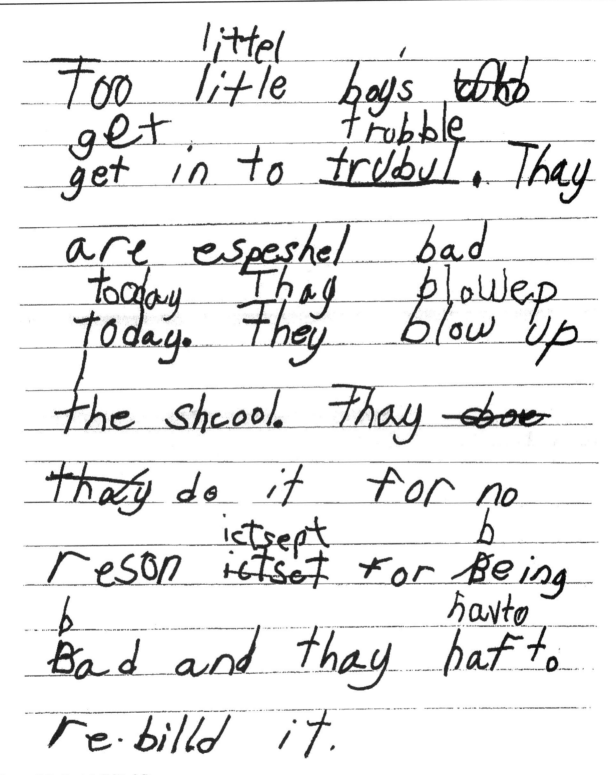

Figure 3.6. Ernie's Edited Story.

they are not tailored to each student's needs. In addition, some worksheets have some very strange questions. Figure 3.7 provides an illustration of the lack of clarity on some worksheets. Ben, a first-grade student, was asked to predict the weather by looking at some pictures. Although the meaning of most of the pictures was clear, he could not decide what the weather would be when a child dresses in shorts and a short-sleeved t-shirt and runs

Figure 3.7. Ben's Homework.

around carrying an unplugged fan. Ben had asked his mother for help, but she was not sure either. Ben's response of, "We don't have a clue" to the picture was humorous but he also remarked that the worksheet was really dumb and a waste of time. Having to complete too many worksheets that seem dumb can affect a student's attitude toward writing.

Spend Ample Time on Prewriting Activities

All students need to spend time on prewriting activities. In the past, written language instruction was far more product-oriented and prescriptive; students wrote on topics assigned by the teacher and then turned in their papers for grading. Thankfully, the days are gone when teachers would write a topic on the chalkboard and expect a finished product to be handed in at the end of the forty-five-minute period. Sometimes,

however, teachers do not spend enough time on prewriting activities and preparing students for their writing assignments.

Consider the topic of "Excitement at the Zoo." Even with little or insufficient prewriting activities, Rachael, a first-grader, has been to the zoo over a hundred times in her young life and has a lot to say. Zara, one of Rachael's classmates, however, has never been to the zoo so she has little to say. Unaware of their differences in background knowledge, the teacher may then compare Zara's writing to Rachael's. Although Zara had tried to think of something to write, she does not have the background knowledge she needed to complete the task. This type of assignment would be better after a class field trip to the zoo.

Students need to have something to say before they start writing. Elena, a sixth grader, was asked to write in her journal. Her response is presented in Figure 3.8. Elena cannot think of anything to write. She needs help generating ideas before sitting down to compose.

Students need to think about and develop their central ideas before writing the first draft. Common prewriting activities include brainstorming with peers, mentally rehearsing what one wants to write, creating various graphic organizers, or conducting research on a topic. Without enough time devoted to thinking about the topic, many students produce assignments that have limited content and are poorly organized. For example, when asked to write a story, Robbie, a fourth-grade student, wrote the draft illustrated in Figure 3.9. Although he begins the story naming several characters and students from his class, the remaining sentences seem unrelated. Two of the sentences were prompted by environmental stimuli: he looked at the "Say No to Drugs" poster on the classroom wall and observed another student writing about his Play Station.

Fortunately, when time and structure for planning are provided, students are more likely to produce a cohesive piece of writing. Figure 3.10 presents a sample from Doris, a fourth-grade student. Doris was provided with a story starter, and then she developed her central

I am haveing trouble thinking of some thing ~~it~~ to wright.

Figure 3.8. Elena's Comment.

Robbie   Writing May 4   Rough Draft

Once apon a time, there was a lady na me Wendy
Randall. she had six kids there names were Michael, Crystal,
Timothy, Lee, Gregory and Amanda. Robbie, Vy and David were
the farmers. wendy grew alot of flower's. Wendy's kids
played at the playground in the park. Wendy's husband
died of a plane crash. But michael had to say no to drugs.
Wendy took her kids to propark, timothy and the rest of
his brothers and sisters had a great time. Then
Wendy took her de rightful kids to Pizza Hut.
But Lee on the farm   had a sega Genisis.

Figure 3.9. Robbie's Initial Draft.

One day, while I was walking in the woods, I tripped over a
leg and found a little box in the grass. I open the
box caieles ly and I fond a little stuachow.
On ititseid posh butten and say vere you
wont to go. I posht the butten and said
"I wont to go to mars. and then evey
thing vent blank and I felt like I
was nuthing. then I fell a tigling in my
hand. I was on mars. I walkt arond and
stept in sumething I stared singking it
wasunt quiksant it was sumething like
lave coold bown. I prest the butten
and seid. "back to earth." When I got back
I put the sachuy back in its box and
berey it and that was that.

Figure 3.10. Doris's Story About Her Trip to Mars.

ideas on a story map prior to writing. She decided to write about taking an unexpected journey to Mars. Although you can see that spelling is difficult for Doris, she organizes her story in a logical sequence.

After a teacher reads books about the topic on hand, has guest presenters, shows video clips, takes the class to the library, or plans a trip to the museum or another pertinent place of interest, every child in the classroom has something to write about. With younger students, you should spend about 50 percent of total writing time on prewriting activities and helping children plan what to write. When students have a lot to say, they ask for more time to write, which is a nice request to hear.

Provide Instruction That Presents Multiple Opportunities for Idea Generation, Feedback, and Revision

Most teachers today view writing as an evolving process of thinking, formulating, drafting, rejecting, revising, and refining. Students are encouraged to develop their plans and review their texts as they put their words on the page. Thus writing involves stop, review, and start-again processes. This interactive process may be viewed as cyclical, involving prewriting, planning, writing, revising, and editing, with unfixed starting and ending points. For example, a student may realize when drafting an essay that she does not have enough information on the topic. Subsequently, she would return to a prewriting activity, such as going to the library to research specific facts, or interviewing a more knowledgeable other. After feedback from a peer or teacher, a student may revise sections of a paper that needed clarification. It is rarely appropriate to assign a grade to first drafts of papers. Instead, students should be provided with meaningful, constructive feedback on how to improve and revise their writings.

Instructional activities that provide students with ideas for writing and revision include brainstorming, focusing on students' ideas and interests, conducting small-group activities, holding conferences, providing specific feedback, and postponing editing skills until the final revision. Because of the ease of revision, the use of word-processing programs allows students to write their thoughts incrementally, recording and developing one idea before the others. If desired, a student can even write the ending of a story before creating the beginning.

Help Students Think About Their Audience Prior to and During Writing

When writing, students need to learn how to consider the audience. Sometimes students do not provide the reader with enough information to understand the meaning of their writing. The writers have difficulty predicting which parts of their writing may confuse their readers. Because the readers are often not present, writers must make frequent assessments and judgments to monitor the clarity of their messages.

Many students assume that the teacher is the audience, and therefore introductions to the topic are not needed. Caitlin, an eleventh-grade student, was asked to write an opinion paper, illustrated in Figure 3.11. She decided to write about someone stealing a car. Caitlin does not consider the needs of the reader because she fails to introduce her topic. She presents new information without explanation and makes erroneous assumptions in regard to the information the reader already possesses about the situation.

Similarly, Ian, an eighth-grade student, was asked to write a paragraph, illustrated in Figure 3.12, that presented the reasons why teenagers should not use alcohol or drugs. Although Ian has several ideas about the topic, he does not begin by explaining the topic. Consequently, his message becomes directed solely to his teacher. You can remind students to consider and remember their audience as they plan and revise their writing assignments.

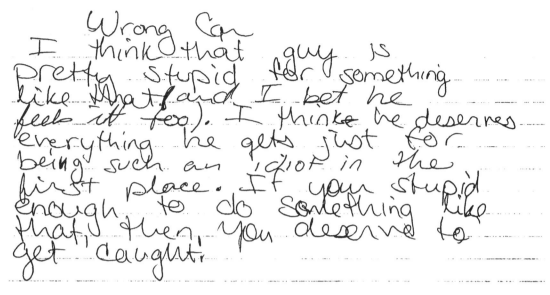

Wrong Can
I think that guy is
pretty stupid for something
like that (and I bet he
feels it too). I thinke he deserves
everything he gets just for
being such an idiot in the
first place. If you stupid
enough to do something like
that, then, you deserve to
get caught.

Figure 3.11. Caitlin's Opinion Paper.

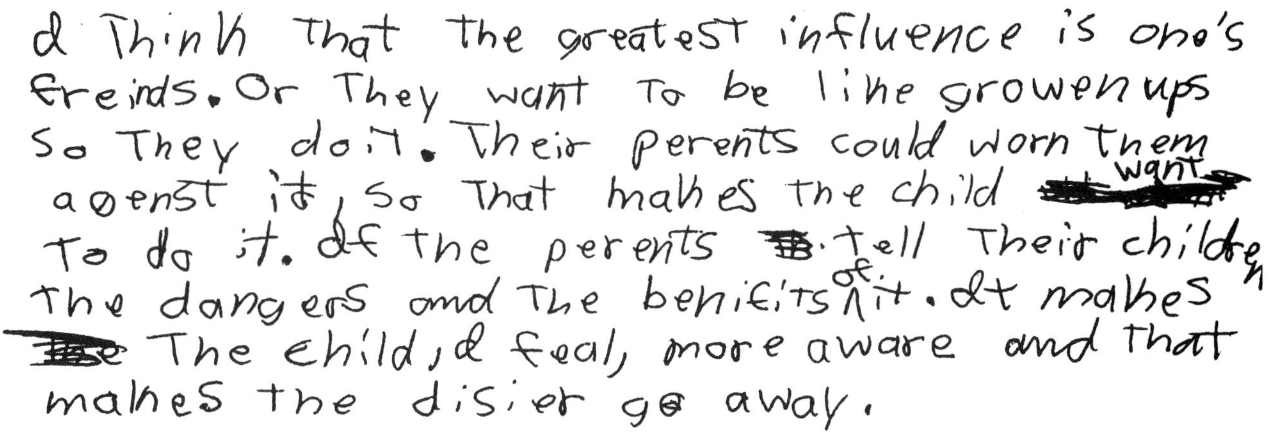

d Think That the greatest influence is one's
freinds. Or They want To be like growen ups
So They do it. Their perents could worn them
agenst it, so That mahes the child *want*
to do it. df the perents B. tell Their childre
The dangers and The benifits of it. dt mahes
The child, d feal, more aware and That
mahes the disier go away.

Figure 3.12. Ian's Paragraph.

Place Emphasis Initially on the Expression of Ideas and the Content of the Writing, Not on Basic Writing Skills or Handwriting

Students with learning disabilities place too much value on form and writing mechanics, rather than idea generation. As Graham and Harris reported: "When we asked a child with a learning disability to describe good writing, she responded, 'Spell every word right.' A second child recommended, 'Write as neat as you can.' A third child advised, 'Put your date and name on there . . . be sure to hold your pencil right'" (2005, p. 17).

Always remember to first respond to the content of what students write, rather than their spelling errors or the quality of the handwriting. First and foremost, writing is a method of communication that is shared between the

Figure 3.13. Dan's Letter to His Fourth-Grade Teacher.

Translation: Dear Ms. Caseman, Thank you for helping me with my writing this year. You listened to my ideas. Have a great summer. Dan

writer and the reader. The reader's first job is to acknowledge and respond to the message.

At the end of the school year, Dan, a fourth-grade student with very poor handwriting (see Figure 3.13), wrote a note to his teacher to thank her for her help with writing. He wanted her to know how much he appreciated the fact that she listened to his ideas.

Provide Meaningful, Positive Feedback to Students

To keep children motivated and willing to take chances in their writings, you should provide feedback with the ratio of four positive comments for each corrective comment. Even adults with good coping mechanisms and a history of success experience difficulty keeping motivated if they receive only corrective or negative feedback. Imagine, then, how difficult it must be for a child with poor coping mechanisms and a history of failure to continue to be motivated to write.

Diego, a third-grader, had been asked to write a paragraph about the desert. Although Diego had completed the assignment to the best of his ability, the only feedback he received was corrective. His teacher underlined

ten words, wrote seven *sp*'s to denote spelling errors, crossed off three *B*'s, added *e* to *snakes*, circled one word with two question marks underneath it, and put in one caret accompanied by a question mark. Diego's assignment consisted of twenty-two words; the teacher's feedback consisted of twenty-seven marks and culminated with the comment, "You must improve your spelling." Although the teacher marked all of the errors accurately, all of these corrections will just overwhelm Diego.

By following the four positive comments to one corrective comment rule, Diego's teacher can use positive remarks to make Diego receptive to corrective feedback. For example, she could circle any correctly spelled word and add happy faces to denote the correct spelling with a positive comment, such as "Good spellings." She could have also acknowledged the content by writing, "You know a lot of different types of desert animals." Such positive feedback would result in Diego being more receptive to correcting his errors and writing more about the desert.

One of the most effective ways of nurturing a child's self-esteem is for teachers to begin their feedback by praising the positive attributes of a student's paper and not marking all of the errors. Remember the principle from Chapter One: Proceed very gently with no red marks. Some students have difficulty with many aspects of writing skill. A paragraph written by Keisha, a fifth-grade student, is presented in Figure 3.14. Although Keisha has difficulties with ideation, usage, and spelling, her teacher's first comment was a compliment about her neat handwriting. This simple comment made Keisha feel good about her writing and want to continue to work on her assignments.

Feedback should be supportive rather than overwhelming. For example, Ana's teacher wanted to help Ana improve the story she was writing, but on Ana's first draft, her teacher made twelve corrective marks with one corrective comment. A better technique would have been to remember the four to one rule. She could offer comments, such as "Good use of a title," "You wrote more than you did last week—good," or "Your handwriting is neat." When critiquing writing, remember to tell students what they are doing correctly as well. In fact, telling students what they are doing right often improves writing more than only telling them what they are doing wrong.

Provide Concrete Suggestions for Ways to Improve Writing

When revising, writers evaluate what they have written and then make changes in meaning depending on their writing goals. Feedback is provided by a more knowledgeable other who makes suggestions with regard to how the writer can clarify organization and ideas. Peers and teachers can ask questions to help the writer clarify content and improve the sequencing of ideas with the emphasis placed on communication and content, rather than on form. Although the importance of revising writing on the basis of feedback is widely recognized, many writers dislike the process. Gage (1986) described how some students feel about revision:

Revision can be perceived by students as a perfunctory exercise in cosmetic editing

where they only correct the errors that the teacher has marked. When students revise in this way, they are responding to revision as a kind of punishment for their errors, rather than as a further opportunity to rethink what they have to say and their reasons for saying it. Revision cannot be a penalty for crimes against grammar; it must be an occasion for reassessing every aspect of the writing after having had the opportunity to see how others respond to it [p. 27].

Figure 3.15 presents the first draft of a fairy tale written by Andy, a fourth-grade student. In a revision conference, the teacher praised Andy for his creative first draft and made specific comments about his use of metaphors. She then noted specific areas in the story that required clarification. As Andy's story progresses, confusion exists regarding who is the prince and who is the princess. In one sentence, the princess is referred to with a masculine pronoun. With the guidance and questioning of his teacher, Andy identified ways to resolve the ambiguities and clarify his story. After Andy had revised his story, the teacher met with him again regarding how to correct his errors in punctuation and spelling.

Through active modeling and discussion of writing, you can help students become more adept at using revision strategies to improve their own writing. Students need to understand that revising is not a punishment, but rather a way to improve their abilities to communicate and express their ideas with clarity.

Provide Individualized Feedback

You can have frequent mini-conferences to provide students with individualized feedback on their writing. During these conferences, you can reinforce any concepts, rules, or strategies that have been taught and then discuss specific content. In addition, you can introduce more advanced composition skills such as how to write compound and complex sentences. When revising and editing, students need individualized

The mean Tiger

Keisha

That tiger was very very mean.
The maen tiger wit to sleppy he had
to give him some mediche to yoto
slepep we had some equipment on his
head he was dream about killing
pepole and eating tham and naving some
of the pepole of slaves tial wic his
dream but it well have naver some
of the ners was goin. I waa wer
thert cit that Tiger is os os os
mean. That Tiger is going to
get very very meaer and meare
he will not eat my for he
piffen or he lunch that tiger is os mere
The End
of the Tiger

Dow you No wut the
tiger did to the Mus he
Killing hern.
The End

Figure 3.14. Keisha's Paragraph.

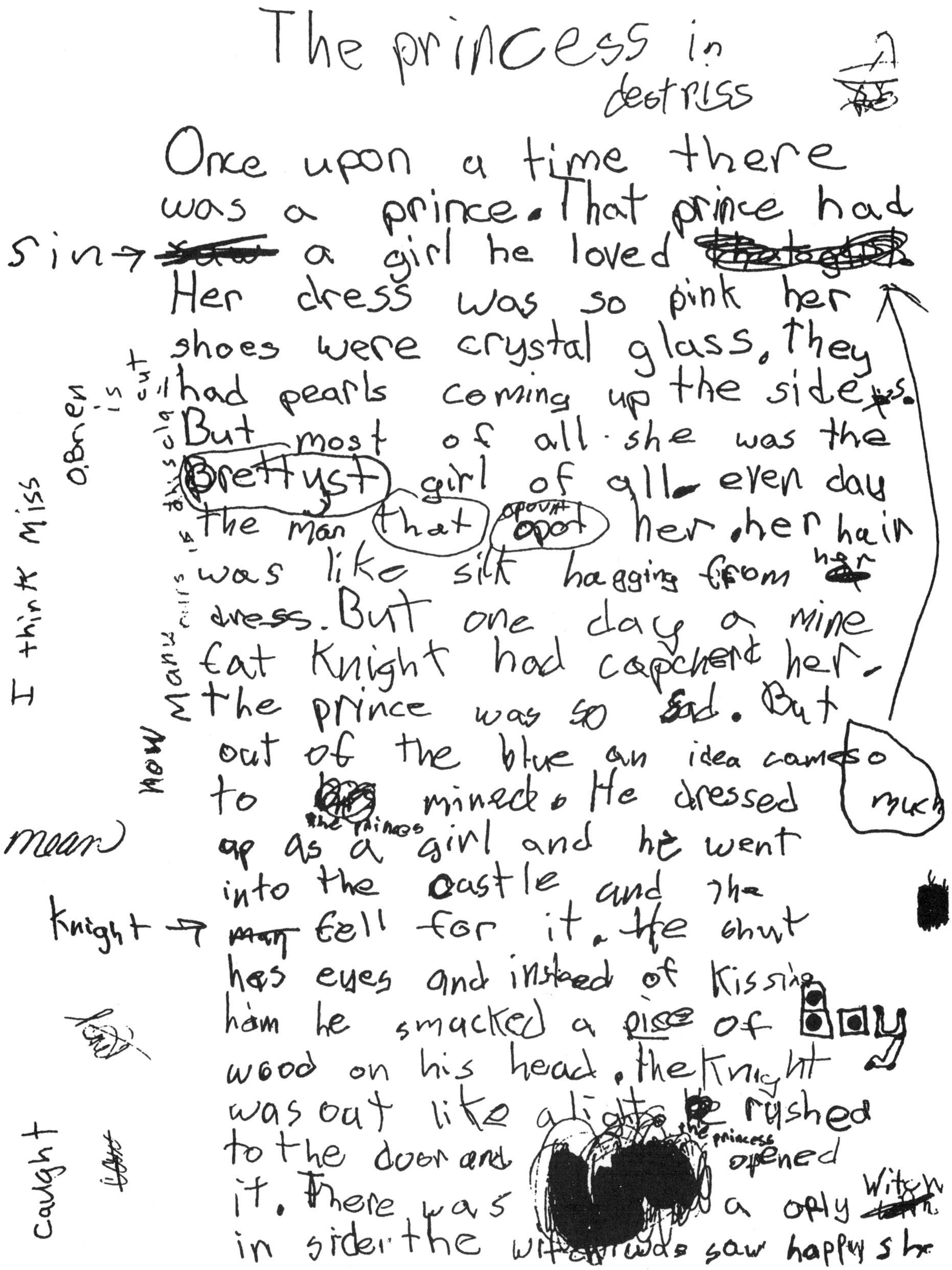

The princess in destriss
Once upon a time there
was a prince. That prince had
sin → a girl he loved
Her dress was so pink her
shoes were crystal glass, they
had pearls coming up the sides.
But most of all she was the
Brettyst girl of all even day
the man that opout her. her hair
was like silk hagging from her
dress. But one day a mine
fat Knight had capchert her.
the prince was so sad. But
out of the blue an idea came so much
to the prince's mined. He dressed
up as a girl and he went
into the castle and the
knight → fell for it. He shut
his eyes and instead of kissing
him he smacked a pice of
wood on his head. the knight
was out like a light. he rushed
to the door and the princess opened
it. There was a ugly witch
in sider the witch was saw happy she
I think Miss O'Brien is cut
mean
caught

Figure 3.15. Andy's First Draft of a Fairy Tale.

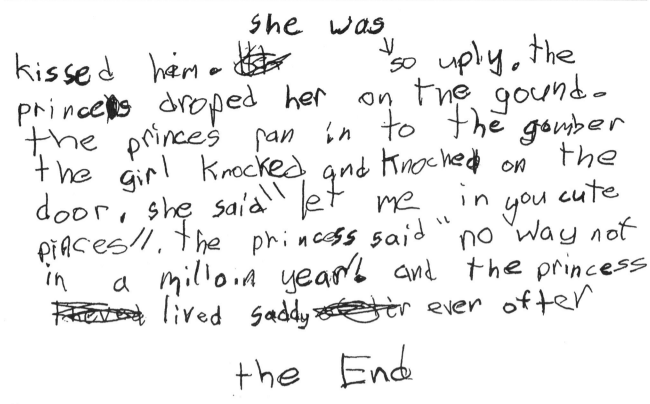

kissed him. ~~the~~ she was so ugly. the princess droped her on the gound. the princes ran in to the gomber the girl knocked and knocked on the door, she said "let me in you cute piAces". the princess said "no way not in a million yeart" and the princess ~~Ravert~~ lived saddy ~~after~~ ever offer

the End

Figure 3.15. Andy's First Draft of a Fairy Tale. (*Continued*)

feedback from the teacher, a small group of peers, or both. Without a conference when revising, students are unlikely to improve the content of their writing. Similarly, without feedback during editing, students are unlikely to be able to correct their errors.

Before providing peer conferences, students need specific instruction in how to conference. Students will benefit from a guide or checklist that indicates what they are to look for in the writing of others. For example, a checklist may remind the students to discuss whether the necessary elements of the writing assignment are included, or to comment on the parts that were well written, as well as the parts that were unnecessary, or needed clarification. You might also provide input to the peer conference by demonstrating how to ask questions and make comments. It is always good to start the conference by telling the student what you liked about his or her writing. You could then ask questions to clarify parts of the writing or to help the student revise and clarify parts of the paper. Ask questions that are open-ended, guiding the student, and provide comments that are specific rather than general. Although the majority of students appear to profit from peer feedback, some students prefer to meet individually with their teachers as they do not want other students to see their poor handwriting or spelling errors. Be sensitive to these individual differences. Figure 3.16 provides an example of a checklist that students may use when conferencing with peers.

Comment on Improvement

As a learner, it is satisfying to have even small improvements recognized. There is a lot of ground between a correct and an incorrect response. Take, for example, Tara trying to spell the word *because*. Improvement can be seen if, one week, Tara writes "btrs" and the next week she writes "bcs." Tremendous improvement is noted when she writes the word as "bekus." Although each of the three attempts is

Name: _____   Date: _____

Conferenced with: _____

Title of Paper: _____

Please discuss some of the following questions in each section as appropriate.

Check the questions discussed.

Beginning

☐ I like your beginning because . . .

☐ Your beginning is unclear because . . .

Middle

☐ I would like to know more about . . .

☐ I like the way you describe . . .

☐ What else do you want the reader to know?

☐ This part is a little confusing; can you tell me more?

☐ Have you stayed on topic?

☐ Do you like what you have written?

☐ Are your ideas in a good order?

Ending

☐ Your ending is clear because . . .

☐ Your ending is unclear because . . .

Editing

☐ Did you check your punctuation?

☐ Did you check your spelling?

☐ Did you check your capital letters?

☐ Are all of your sentences complete thoughts?

Figure 3.16. Peer Conference Checklist.

incorrect, if we were to wait until Tara spelled the word correctly, she would have to go a long time without positive feedback about her effort and improvement. Commenting on improvement provides positive feedback immediately. The first week you could say or write: "You've got the first and last sounds down—good." The next week, you could say, "Last week, you had the first and last sounds down; this week, you have the first and last sounds AND one of the middle sounds—well done."

As another example, Charlie, a third-grade student, was given the same standardized spelling test in January and April. Although his score did not improve much (he had four out of twenty correct in January and six out of twenty correct in April), an analysis of his spelling attempts highlights the progress he made in those three months. For example, *kitchen* improved from "kitten" to "kitchon," *purchase* improved from "puras" to "purchus," *imaginary* improved from "imanaro" to "imnmagenary," and *society* improved from "sosite" to "sosioty."

You can find evidence of improvement in all aspects of written language. For a child who forgets to capitalize the first word of a sentence, remembering to capitalize two out of six sentences shows improvement. Instead of pointing out the four errors, you could comment on the improvement by highlighting the two capitalized words and writing, "You remembered to start these two sentences with capital letters—great!" For a child who usually writes only two sentences, writing three sentences is an improvement. For a child who uses the word *good* over and over, writing *warm* or *smart* is an improvement. Recognizing improvement motivates children to want to become better writers.

Usually when some aspect of writing is noted as a weakness, you and the student need to work together to address the problem. Spence, a fourth-grade student, over-relied on the word *nice* because he knew how to spell it. Before writing a paragraph about paradise, his teacher worked with him to think of some alternative words for *nice*. Spence, a student with a good vocabulary but poor spelling, generated the following list of words: *fantastic, amazing, colossal, energy-efficient, impervious, healthy,* and *glorious.* He then wrote the paragraph and underlined the words from his list. Not only was the result, shown in Figure 3.17, a paragraph that showed great improvement, but also his teacher was able to write positive and encouraging comments.

Few students create a perfect piece of writing on the first draft, but all students can improve their first drafts with guidance and feedback. Instead of comparing the progress of Spence, Charlie, and Tara to each other, compare the progress of Spence to Spence, Charlie to Charlie, and Tara to Tara. You want to evaluate whether or not Spence's current paragraph is better than the ones he wrote in previous weeks.

Focus on Editing Papers After Revisions Have Been Completed

In most instances, you will want to focus on spelling and punctuation errors after the revisions to content have been completed. In the editing stage, the writer proofreads a piece to detect and correct errors in spelling, punctuation, capitalization, and usage. The majority of students require specific assistance to recognize and correct their errors. Students with poor spelling skill or poor grammar cannot edit without the assistance of a more knowledgeable person. Typically, you will want to focus on one or two skills during editing, rather than reviewing all of the errors. Concentrating on only a few skills can help the student learn to use those skills effectively and not become overwhelmed.

Do Not Penalize Students for Incorrect Spellings or Poor Handwriting

Some students have trouble with spelling, whereas others have trouble producing legible handwriting. These difficulties should not influence the grades on their papers. Consider, for example, Steven, an eighth-grade student with

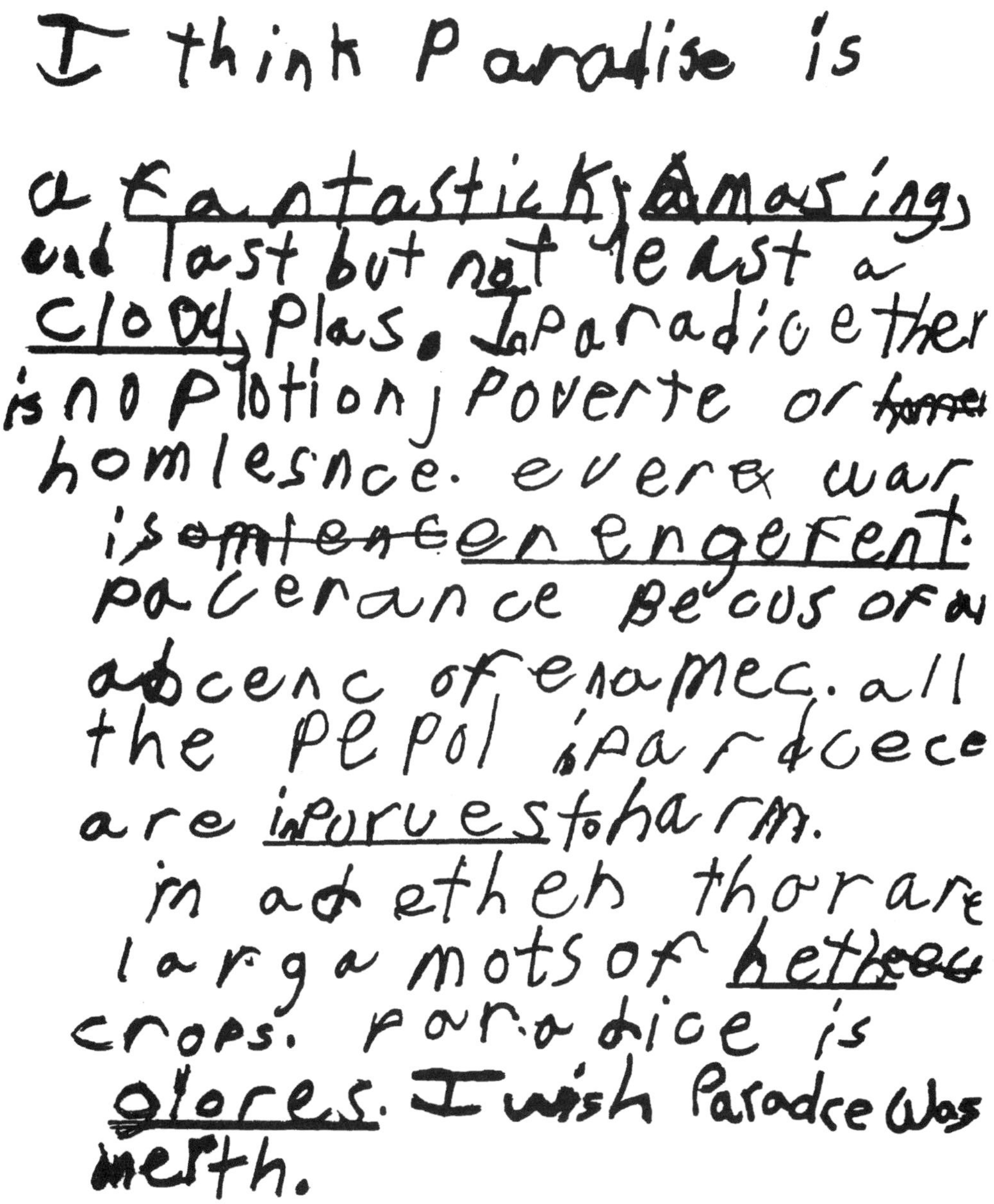

I think Paradise is a fantastick, Amasing, and last but not least a cloody plas. In Paradice ether is no plotion, Poverte or homlesnce. evere war is ener engerent. pacerance Becous of a abcenc of enamec. all the pepol iparicece are inpuruestoharm. in ad etheh thorare larga mots of hethea crops. paradice is glores. I wish Paradce was merth.

Figure 3.17. Spence's Paragraph.

Translation: I think Paradise is a fantastic, amazing, and last but not least, a colossal place. In Paradise, there is no pollution, poverty, or homelessness. Everywhere is energy-efficient. Peace reigns because of an absence of enemies. All the people in Paradise are impervious to harm. In addition, there are large amounts of healthy crops. Paradise is glorious. I wish Paradise was on earth.

expertise in history but poor spelling. Steven was failing in history, and when an explanation was sought, the teacher commented that she marked all answers that were not spelled correctly as incorrect. Steven's failing grade, therefore, was the result of his poor spelling, rather than a lack of content knowledge.

Similarly, Maricel, a sixth-grade student, was graded on her spelling errors rather than on her knowledge of verb use. Maricel completed the assignment presented in Figure 3.18 from her grammar book, where she was asked to select whether the verb in the sentence should be *do* or *does*. Although only one

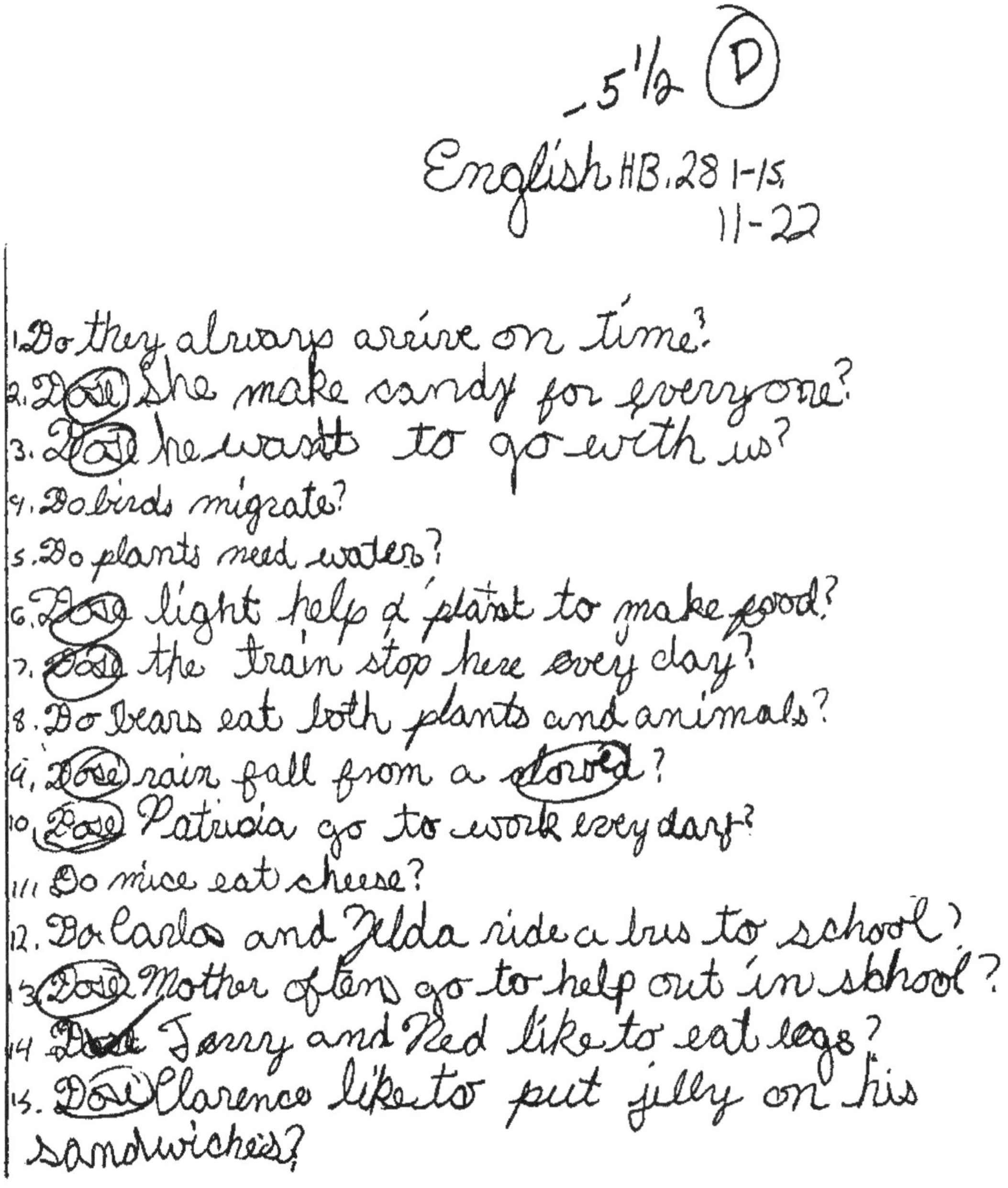

_-5½ Ⓓ_

English HB. 28 1-15,
_11-22_

1. Do they always arrive on time?
2. Do/Does she make candy for everyone?
3. Do/Does he wants to go with us?
4. Do birds migrate?
5. Do plants need water?
6. Does light help a plant to make food?
7. Does the train stop here every day?
8. Do bears eat both plants and animals?
9. Does rain fall from a cloud?
10. Does Patricia go to work every day?
11. Do mice eat cheese?
12. Do Carlos and Zelda ride a bus to school?
13. Does Mother often go to help out in school?
14. Does Jerry and Ted like to eat eggs?
15. Does Clarence like to put jelly on his sandwiches?

Figure 3.18. Maricel's Grammar Assignment.

response was actually incorrect, she received a D on the assignment because of her incorrect spelling of the word *does*. It is important for Maricel to learn to spell the word *does* correctly, but the assignment was not a spelling test.

Students can also be penalized for poor handwriting. Vanna, a sixth-grader, had been asked to write an imaginary story on a topic of her choice. After jotting down some notes, she fulfilled the assignment. Sadly, she was given a low grade because her handwriting was judged to be not neat enough. It is important to assign grades based on how well the student fulfilled the requirements of the assignment, not just on the aesthetics.

Avoid Writing Negative Marks and Comments

For many children, putting words on paper seems to require a tremendous leap of faith, faith that their writing will be valued. Question

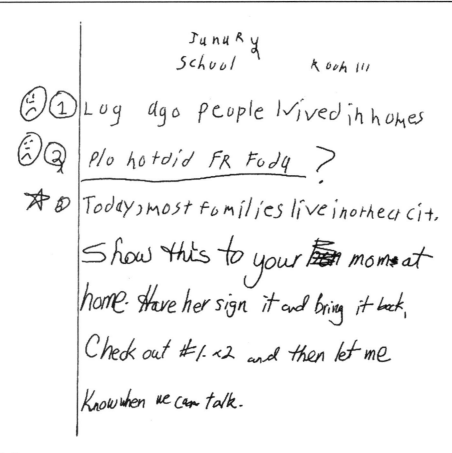

Figure 3.19. Jed's Paper.

Translation: Long ago people lived in homes. People hunted for food. Today, most families live in or near cities.

marks and sad faces just discourage children. A question mark seems to denote, "I haven't a clue what you are trying to say," and the sad face seems to suggest, "This is not your best work and it makes me feel sad and disappointed." Although very few teachers place sad faces on children's papers in response to their writings, we have come across a few. One wonders how Jed, a third-grade student, felt when his response to questions on a "Digging for Dinosaurs" chapter was returned. Figure 3.19 shows that he not only received two sad faces, but also a note of concern to his mother.

Jed, having tried his best on the assignment, is now faced with a choice. He can continue to risk getting negative responses to his written work or he can stop writing. Either way he gets a poor grade, so he wonders why he should bother to write.

Although it is understandable that as teachers, we too can feel frustrated and overwhelmed, it is important not to forget to be gentle when responding to children's writings. Figure 3.20 shows an entry from Melinda's journal. In response to her statement of "I got nothing to rite," her third-grade teacher wrote, "Did you get up this morning? How did you feel about coming to school today?" The comments, although clearly coming from a place of frustration, are rhetorical and serve no real purpose. They are certainly not gentle, nor encouraging. Perhaps Melinda was being candid by writing that she had nothing to write. Better then to write a comment such as, "I understand. Some days I don't feel like writing either. The next time you don't have anything to write, let's try to think of some ideas together."

In contrast, look at Ms. Gerner's feedback to a third-grade student on two assignments presented in Figure 3.21. Ms. Gerner knows that her student, Ben, struggles with writing. In the first sample, she thanks him for

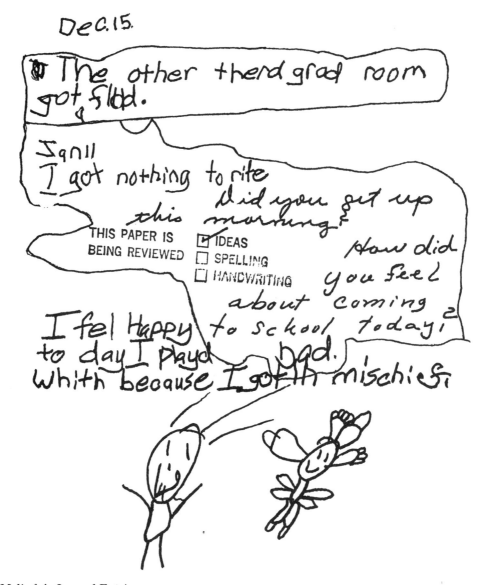

Figure 3.20. Melinda's Journal Entries.

writing about his fishing trip, and asks him if he saw any sharks. She also comments that his picture looks scary. In this second sample, she notes that the game was close and that she knows that he likes pizza. She then asks him some questions about his weekend. Notice that after receiving his paper back, Ben wrote in answers to her questions. These types of positive comments that address the content of the writing will encourage Ben to keep sharing his ideas and experiences and improving his writing skills.

Write Meaningful Comments on Papers

If the comments you write on papers are not meaningful to students, they will learn very quickly to ignore them and look only at the grade. Mike, a fourth-grade student, was very confused with a comment written by his teacher. He had been asked to write five sentences that would be considered to be a "fact" and five sentences that would be considered to be an "opinion." Figure 3.22 presents his paper and his teacher's

Ben
Thanks for writing about your fishing trip!
Did you see sharks? Your picture looks scary!

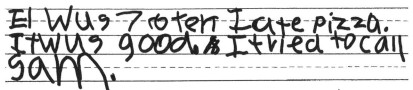

The game was pretty close.
Was the pizza good? yes Was
Sam at home when you called?
I can read every bit of your
weekend update, Ben. Good job!

Figure 3.21. Ben's Stories About Fishing and Pizza.

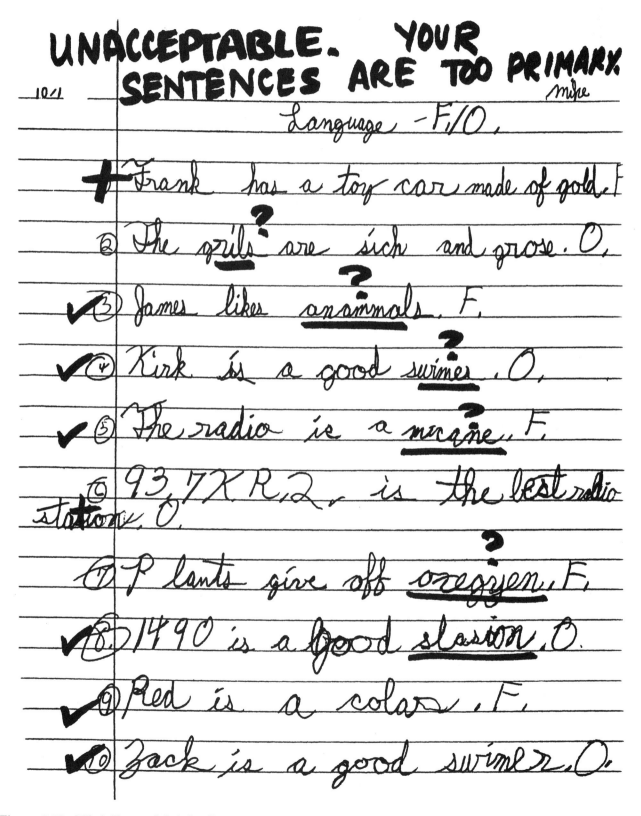

Figure 3.22. Mike's Fact and Opinion Sentences.

feedback, which was written in bright red ink. Mike thought he had followed the assignment and was confused both by his grade, "Unacceptable," and the teacher's comment, "Your sentences are too primary." Mike did not know what the word "primary" meant, so he just threw the paper in the wastebasket. The teacher did not acknowledge Mike's performance on the actual assignment: writing five fact sentences and five opinion sentences. Clearly, Mike understands the difference between fact and opinion, and this should have been acknowledged. Unfortunately, the teacher focused feedback on Mike's spelling and the lack of complexity of his sentences, rather than on the requirements of the actual task.

Although the meaning was readily apparent, the comment in Figure 3.23 written on Suri's spelling test "Study to take over" made her feel very discouraged. Suri, an eighth-grade student, understood that the teacher was telling her to study harder but she had studied the list for five hours throughout the week. The words that she was trying to learn to spell were not ones that she could easily read, and she never used them in her writing. In an effort to protect her self-esteem, Suri reacted to the comment by giving herself a couple of stars for her effort. The importance of giving meaningful and appropriate feedback cannot be overemphasized. Not all students are as resilient as Suri. They will not be able to protect their self-esteem from too much negative feedback. As a teacher, make it your goal to follow the four to one rule: four positive comments to one corrective comment.

Do Not Associate Writing with Punishment

When teachers or parents use writing as a punishment, children are likely to want to avoid writing as much as possible. Writing is often inadvertently paired with punishment when children are asked to write letters of apology for misbehavior or when they have to stay in the classroom during recess to write some statement regarding their behavior numerous times

Figure 3.23. Suri's Spelling Test.

(for example, "I will raise my hand before talking."). If children are to learn to become good writers, parents and teachers need to pair writing assignments with positive ideas and events. It is appropriate, however, to provide writing as a choice of a way to express one's thoughts and feelings. You might ask the student: "Would you rather talk about or write about what happened this afternoon on the playground?"

Help Students Develop and Maintain Positive Attitudes Toward Writing

One important goal of writing instruction is to help students develop and maintain positive attitudes toward writing. Within a supportive classroom environment, teachers are both instructors and coaches. They are collaborators, not evaluators or judges, and they help students toward becoming the best writers they can be by furnishing guidance while simultaneously fostering self-direction. Children feel free to experiment and take risks.

Nearly all classrooms have some unmotivated writers. Some may have learning disabilities. Others may have had negative experiences with writing and are discouraged about their lack of success in writing. Still others may feel they cannot think of things to write. Whatever the reasons for poor motivation toward writing, a lack of effort contributes to the students' writing difficulties. Some students dread the task of writing and comment when faced with a writing assignment: "Do I have to?" "How long does it have to be?" In one instance, a student may refuse to complete an assignment. In another, a student will do the least amount of writing that is needed to fulfill an assignment. In other words, the primary motivating force for the student is avoiding failure by complying with the task, rather than a desire to communicate through writing and do the task.

Furthermore, students with motivational or writing difficulties often stifle their own creative ideas because of difficulties with basic writing skills. As a nine-year-old, Anton was extremely bright and motivated, but his teacher complained about his lack of creativity and poor organization of details when writing. Anton had severe difficulties with spelling. His spelling challenges would not have affected his creativity if there were no penalty for misspellings on initial drafts, but his classroom teacher expected students to hand in a spelling-error-free product at the end of the lesson. An observation and a quiet conversation with Anton made it clear that he had no trouble expressing his ideas in writing, but that his creativity was being affected by the expectation for correct spelling. Anton would look to see what words the students sitting next to him were using, and he would supplement those words with others he could find in his personal spelling dictionary. He then created his assignment around this group of words that he knew were correctly spelled. Even expert writers would have difficulty with creativity if they were confined to a given set of words.

Anton confided that he was feeling frustrated because he was trying his best but it didn't seem to be good enough, and he didn't know why he should bother with such silly assignments anyway. Anton's attitude is somewhat reminiscent of the words of Graves (1985): "If I arrive at the blank page with a writing history filled with problems, I am already predisposed to run from what I see. I try to hide my paper, throw it away, or mumble to myself, 'This is stupid'" (p. 38).

Motivating reluctant writers need not be time-consuming for you, but it does require careful thought and planning and a gentle touch. You can help guide all students toward becoming the best writers they can be by remembering that once children are motivated to write, the process can begin. The most important factors are that you provide positive comments and ensure that all students experience success.

Consider the Roles of Both Extrinsic and Intrinsic Motivators on Performance

To understand the effect of motivation on performance, you must consider both intrinsic and extrinsic motivators. Intrinsic motivation comes from within the individual and is based on a person's experiences, perceptions, and emotions. One facet of intrinsic motivation is self-efficacy, or one's beliefs about one's own abilities; the greater one's self-efficacy, the greater one's motivation. For example, Matthew, an efficient and effective writer, may complete his writing assignments because he enjoys writing and has a history of past successes on similar assignments. Students with writing difficulties, however, are unlikely, at least initially, to seek out writing activities. Consequently, they often require extrinsic incentives and motivators to facilitate their engagement in writing tasks.

Extrinsic motivation originates from sources outside the individual and is fostered by external rewards or the threat of punishment. For example, Liam, a tenth-grade student, was asked to write an essay describing a person whom he admired. The teacher informed Liam that if he had not started his essay, he would have to stay in and miss his morning break. Although he was not intrinsically motivated to complete the assignment, Liam did not want to miss his morning break. In response he wrote, "I admire my mom because she owns her house and car. Everything is paid for. I didn't know what to write about but I did it anyway so I can go on break." The goal is for teachers to guide students from being motivated by extrinsic to intrinsic factors. The best way to accomplish this goal is by helping students succeed, which increases both self-efficacy and independence.

Ensure That Students Are Successful

Because success breeds success, it is extremely important to ensure that children are successful on their writing assignments. Sometimes students feel humiliated by the responses of their peers. Figure 3.24 shows a math writing assignment by Marcos, a fourth-grader. Marcos was asked to write several math word problems for a peer to solve. Although he completed the assignment, his peer informed him that he was unable to read any of the problems, and, consequently, could not solve them. In response,

Marcos grabbed his paper back and commented that it was a "dumb assignment" anyway. One can only surmise that Marcos's frustration will negatively affect his motivation for future writing assignments. A simple accommodation would have saved Marcos from this embarrassing situation. His teacher could have helped Marcos rewrite his problems with correct spelling before handing the problems to his peer. Find ways to help each student succeed.

Similarly, Padma, a third-grade student, was not able to finish an assignment in the allotted time. Unfortunately, instead of giving Padma more time to finish, her teacher assigned her a D. A positive response would have encouraged Padma to finish her paper, but the low grade made her feel frustrated and mad that she did not have enough time. Padma, an already reluctant writer, will probably remain so until she succeeds on writing tasks. If Padma's teacher had provided her with more support, such as the use of a paragraph frame, Padma could have filled in the blanks, completed the assignment, and received a passing grade, and would then be more motivated to do her best on the next assignment.

Setting a child up for success takes a bit of thought and planning, but the rewards are significant. For example, Tyler's teacher knew that he had trouble writing so she sat with the third-grader during journal writing time for a question-and-answer session. Tyler commented years later that it was because of this teacher that he persevered and knew he would become a competent writer.

Respect a Student's Opinions

Sometimes it is difficult to accept opinions that differ drastically from our own. When a writer shares an opinion, however, it is important that we respect it and do not assign a grade based on that opinion. After all, people will typically only share their thoughts when they feel that it is safe to do so.

Unfortunately for Ivan, his eighth-grade English teacher did not like his choice of topic.

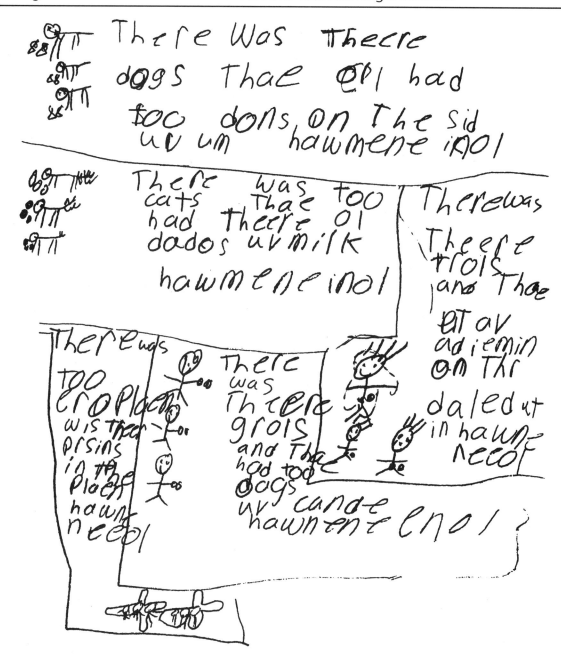

Figure 3.24. Marcos's Word Problems.

Ivan was asked to write a paragraph that provided support for his opinion on a topic. After being given several sample paragraphs to read, he selected the topic, "Mondays Are Boring." His first draft is presented in Figure 3.25. Although one can empathize with the teacher's concerns, the comment and assigned grade will not motivate Ivan to revise his paragraph.

Sometimes it can be challenging to respect an opinion if that opinion is perceived to be the result of lack of effort or care or a failure to follow the instructions of the assignment. Carl, a fourth-grader, is the type of student whom many teachers would find taxing. For a book report, he decided instead to write a sentence about the author's picture in a calendar. The teacher knew he should make comments that respected Carl's opinions so as to nurture a working relationship. He responded to Carl's paper with, "It seems you are quite the critic

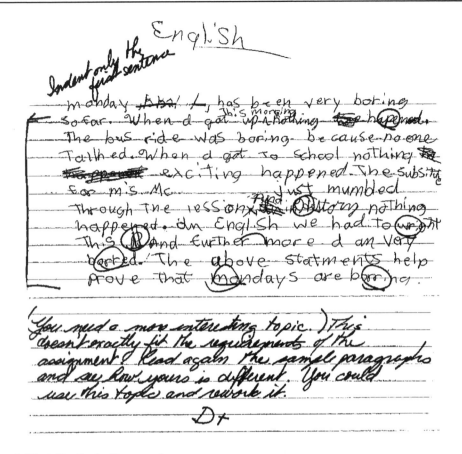

Figure 3.25. Ivan's First Draft of a Paragraph.

Figure 3.26. Carl's Book Report.

of pictures! I agree that picture in the calendar isn't the greatest. Even though you did not like his picture, can you write about the part in the book that you liked the best?"

Acknowledge a Student's Voice

Students who can express themselves in writing are able to share their major concerns in regard to their experiences and emotions. Writing thus becomes a vehicle for expanding and clarifying one's own thoughts and feelings. We want to encourage all students to share their thoughts, particularly those for whom writing is the most difficult. Jermaine, a sixth-grade student, wrote a paragraph, presented in Figure 3.27, in regard to how he wished people would view him. Although the writing is difficult to read because of his poor spelling, Jermaine's ideas and feelings about his situation are clear. Fortunately,

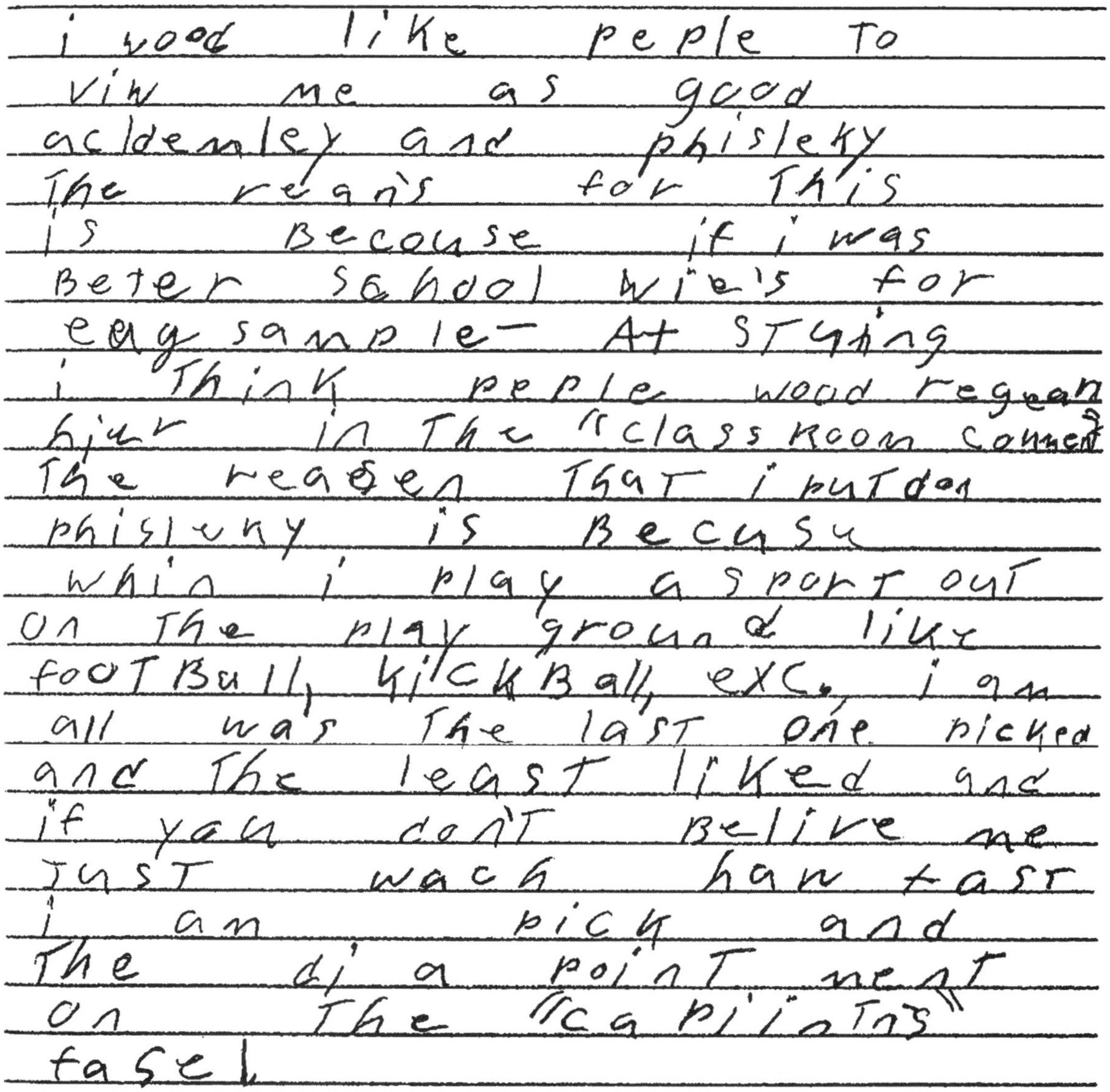

i vood like peple To
viw me as good
acldemley and phisleky
The reans for This
is Becouse if i was
Beter school wie's for
eay sample— At STuying
i Think peple wood regean
hiur in The "class koom connet
The reaßen That i putdon
phislukny is Becusu
whin i play a sport out
on The play ground liky
footBull, kickBall, exc. i am
all was The last one picked
and The least liked and
if you donT Belive me
JusT wach han tasr
i am pick and
The di a point next
on The "capiinTns"
fasel.

Figure 3.27. Jermaine's Paragraph.

Translation: I would like people to view me as good academically and physically. The reason for this is because if I was better school wise for example, at studying. I think people would regret their in the classroom comment. The reason that I am put down physically is because when I play a sport out on the playground like football, kickball, etc. I am always the last one picked and the least liked and if you don't believe me just watch how fast I am picked and the disappointment on the "captain's" face.

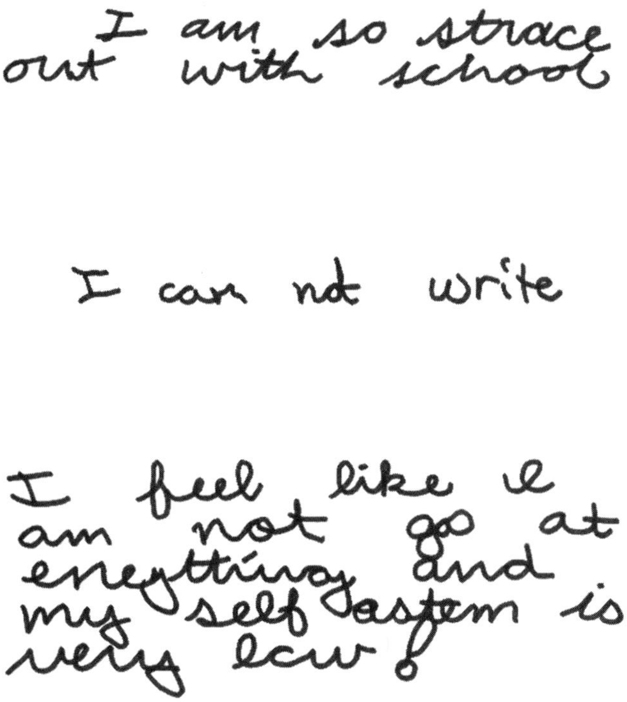

I am so strace out with school

I can not write

I feel like I am not go at eneytting and my self astem is very low

Figure 3.28. Notes from Maria's Journal.

Jermaine's teacher provided him with positive feedback on his first draft and commented that she knew exactly how he felt being the last one picked on the playground.

CONCLUSION

Effective writers know that writing is a recursive process. Although the goal is for children to be intrinsically motivated to write, you can guide and encourage reluctant writers so that they keep on writing. Figure 3.28 presents an excerpt from Maria's journal. Because of her difficulties with writing, this eighth-grade girl feels that she is not good at anything at all. By following the effective principles for writing instruction, you can provide a safe environment in which students like Maria can take risks and not be fearful of failure.

chapter
4

Effective Accommodations for Struggling Writers

The essence of our effort to see that every child has a chance must be to assure each an equal opportunity not to become equal, but to become different to realize whatever unique potential of body, mind and spirit he or she possesses.

—John Fischer

School places heavy demands on writing, and many students fail courses, particularly at secondary levels, because of poor writing abilities. These students are at tremendous disadvantages if curricular adjustments and accommodations are not made regarding writing requirements throughout their school careers. Although classroom accommodations are unnecessary for most students, special accommodations, such as extra time to complete exams and written assignments or permission to take reduced class loads, are essential for students with writing difficulties.

The purposes of this chapter are to consider (a) the definitions of accommodations and compensatory strategies, (b) the determination of the amount of support, (c) the selection of appropriate accommodations, (d) specific legal requirements related to provision of accommodations, and (e) examples of the specific accommodations that you might implement.

ACCOMMODATIONS AND COMPENSATORY STRATEGIES

Accommodations do not replace the need for interventions, but rather are adjustments in curricular demands that allow students to succeed. The purpose is to provide equal opportunity and equal access to all students, so that all may benefit from instruction. Accommodations may be procedural or attitudinal, may involve environmental accessibility, or may include the use of assistive equipment or technology.

Compensatory strategies are not the same as accommodations. Instead, compensatory strategies are the techniques that students use to help themselves perform tasks. These strategies may be developed instinctively by the student or taught by a teacher familiar with the student's learning style and the task demands. The ultimate goal of teaching students compensatory strategies is to help them develop the skills needed to complete challenging tasks independently. For some students, the use of compensatory strategies allows them to meet the general education classroom expectations.

Ryan, a seventh-grade student, required both compensatory strategies and accommodations to succeed in his general education classes. Ryan's vocabulary and ability to generate ideas in writing were age appropriate. In contrast, he had very poor visual-motor skills. When he tried to write down his ideas, his handwriting speed was so slow he forgot what he was saying. For Ryan, compensatory strategies included the development of both keyboarding and word-processing skills. In addition to compensatory strategies, Ryan required procedural accommodations. Procedural accommodations have an impact on the policies and practices teachers use in managing their classrooms. For Ryan the procedural accommodation was permission to use a computer for all of his written assignments in all of his classes.

DETERMINATION OF THE AMOUNT OF SUPPORT

Unfortunately, a standard, universal accommodation plan does not exist. Little guidance is available to assist you in judging whether an accommodation for a particular student is both appropriate and reasonable. The types of writing difficulties experienced by individuals are varied, and so the accommodations must be varied as well. You must consider both a student's strengths and educational needs to determine the appropriate educational adjustments and supports. When determining the amount of support a student needs, consider two student-related factors, the zone of proximal development and the need for instructional scaffolding.

Zone of Proximal Development

As discussed in Chapter Three, Vygotsky (1978) distinguished between two developmental levels: the actual level of development and the level of potential development. He called this distance between a student's present level of performance and the level of potential performance "the zone of proximal development." Potential performance is defined as that which can be obtained when instruction is provided by more knowledgeable others, such as adults or more knowledgeable peers. Vygotsky recognized that good instruction is one step beyond a student's present performance level or just slightly in advance of development. In other words, good instruction cannot be too easy or too hard. Like Goldilocks's quest for the perfect porridge, instruction must be "just right," not too hard and not too easy.

Two implications are inherent in the implementation of this concept. When making curricular adjustments, you should (a) ascertain that students are working within their instructional levels and (b) attempt to create situations that involve purposeful pairing of students with more knowledgeable others. Most students are able to perform at higher levels when paired with partners who have more extensive knowledge and can discuss, demonstrate, and model ways to complete the task.

Instructional Scaffolding

With the correct supports or "scaffolding," all students can experience success. Scaffolding can be used with individual students or groups. Building on the work of Vygotsky, Applebee and Langer (1983) developed the concept of instructional scaffolding, in which learning is seen as a process of gradual internalization of procedures within the context of a collaborative role between the student and teacher.

Instructional scaffolding, therefore, allows for collaboration in tasks that would be too difficult for students to undertake alone, but which can be accomplished with adult support and interaction. Learners are supported while they obtain the skills necessary to succeed on tasks. To provide scaffolding, you must reduce the number of components that a student must manage by following three steps: (a) determine the difficulties that may be encountered in a new task, (b) select specific strategies to help the student overcome the anticipated problems, and (c) structure the activity so that the strategies are explicit and appropriate.

The particular writing tasks that will require instructional scaffolding will vary from grade to grade and will vary with regard to the intensity of a student's needs. Scaffolding may be needed in the instructional materials (textbooks and assignments) as well as within teacher-student interactions (Applebee, 1986). Effective instructional scaffolding incorporates (a) student involvement, (b) assurance of task appropriateness, (c) provision of a structured learning environment, (d) shared responsibility, (e) use of a variety of strategies to address difficulties, and (f) gradual transfer of control. When using instructional approaches incorporating these principles, you encourage students to select their own topics and then write their own opinions and solutions. In addition, your role shifts from teacher to evaluator of quality or the judge of success to that of an interested reader and skilled editor.

You need to evaluate the appropriateness of supports or scaffolds periodically to determine their effectiveness in meeting students' needs. As students assume more responsibility for their own learning, you gradually withdraw the supports. When scaffolding instruction, you model or demonstrate the activity, provide guided practice with frequent corrective feedback, and then provide opportunities for students to perform the task independently.

In the dictionary, the word *scaffold* has two distinct meanings:

- A temporary supporting structure, usually made of wood or metal, put up for workers when they are building.
- A high platform used for execution, usually by hanging.

Unfortunately, for many students with writing difficulties, the educational system has afforded them academic experiences reminiscent of the second definition. By setting standards and competencies that are out of their reach, the students cannot achieve success even when they try their hardest. How long would you continue trying if you knew you could not succeed?

SELECTION OF APPROPRIATE ACCOMMODATIONS

As a teacher, you assume the responsibility of judging when certain accommodations are and are not appropriate. In some cases, accommodations are critical; in other cases, accommodations are not needed because the student is capable of managing the task without assistance. How do you determine what accommodations are necessary? To make this judgment, you need information regarding the student's current level of writing proficiency, as well as information about the amount of time and effort the student expends completing the assigned tasks.

Bashir, an eighth-grade student, failed his first spelling test. When he met with the special education teacher, he informed her that he had studied for the test for over four hours. She then determined that Bashir could not read any of the spelling words. Clearly, the selected spelling words were too difficult for him. Without a shorter or an easier list of spelling words, Bashir would be unable to succeed.

Five years later, when Bashir enrolled in college, his English professor informed him that he would not pass the course with "spelling like that." When Bashir told his instructor that he had dyslexia, which made it difficult for him to spell, she was unsympathetic. After failing several in-class essays, Bashir dropped his English course and, subsequently, left college. In this instance, Bashir did not receive appropriate accommodations (such as no penalty for in-class spelling or permission to complete in-class assignments out of class), nor did he take responsibility for the use of appropriate compensatory strategies (for example, the use of a spell checker or editor).

Accommodations can be the key to success for students with written language difficulties. Mohammed, a sixth-grade student, was receiving failing grades due to his incomplete work. During the first grading period, his behavior and attitude toward school deteriorated. On one occasion, the class was given an assignment to conduct library research for a report. Mohammed used the library computer and located the books. He then read everything about Henry VIII that he needed for his report. When asked, Mohammed could describe all of Henry's wives and how they died. Mohammed refused, however, to write note cards and would not begin a first draft. The teacher, annoyed with Mohammed, sent him to the office. Instead of going to the office, Mohammed hid in the boys' bathroom. When he was discovered, the principal called his parents to inform them of Mohammed's actions.

After multiple meetings at school, Mohammed's parents sought psychological counseling. The psychologist suggested an evaluation for learning disabilities. Results of the evaluation indicated that Mohammed had an extensive vocabulary but had difficulty formulating written sentences because of very poor visual-motor ability. With diagnostic information in hand, the parents returned to the school seeking not special education services, but appropriate accommodations. Mohammed was soon allowed to use a computer for all of his written assignments. Instead of illegible printing, Mohammed was able to produce neat word-processed text. In addition, the printed copy allowed his teacher to provide direct feedback on his writing. Within four months, Mohammed was turning in quality work on time, and his grades and self-concept improved dramatically.

On occasion, unnecessary accommodations are made that actually inhibit student progress. Chayanne, a fifth-grade student with a mild hearing impairment, had made limited progress in writing. In an initial interview, Chayanne's mother commented that the hardest accomplishment for a child with a hearing impairment was learning to write. The results of an educational evaluation indicated that although Chayanne had reading skills at grade level, her writing performance was significantly below average and she had difficulty with speed of production and letter formation. The examiner noted further that Chayanne could hear speech sounds easily and had minimal difficulty pronouncing phonically regular nonsense words.

Because Chayanne had no difficulty hearing English language sounds, one would predict that she would be able to learn to translate sounds into words and learn to spell.

When asked about her school writing program, Chayanne noted that for the past two years she had had a peer transcriber who did all of her writing. She further explained that the hardest thing for a child with a hearing impairment to do was to learn how to write. In this situation, expectations communicated from others, as well as the specific accommodations that were made for Chayanne, adversely affected her writing skill development. As Johnson (1991) commented, "All too often, poor readers and writers are permitted to listen to tapes or give oral responses in class. While these temporary accommodations may be necessary for students to obtain and convey knowledge, we should not deprive them of a valuable form of communication for themselves and others" (p. ix). As a general rule, the selected accommodations should not interfere with instruction, be seen as a substitute for intervention, or inhibit student writing progress.

The Negotiation Process

Often the process of determining appropriate accommodations involves negotiations between teacher and student or at other times between teacher and teacher. Students should take part in determining appropriate accommodations or they may feel that the adjustments are unjustified. Figure 4.1 illustrates a note written by a fourth-grade student, Jay, after the teacher had tried to help him position his paper by placing a piece of tape diagonally across his desk (Maniet, 1986). One can see from the student's written response that he found this adjustment to be unnecessary, as well as a little insulting.

Initially, resistance to curricular adjustments by the student or teacher may prove problematic. For example, some students may reject the idea of altering assignments or requirements. At the beginning of the school year, Ms. Turnbull, Matthew's fifth-grade

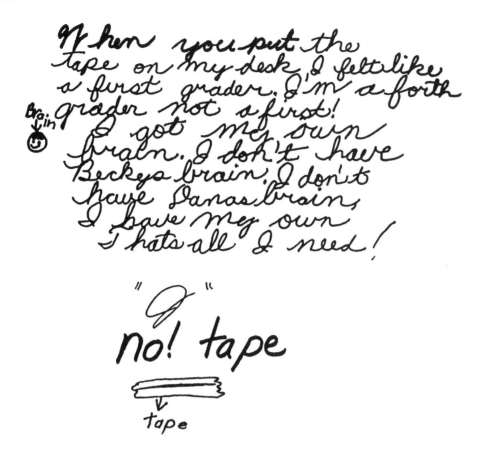

Figure 4.1. Jay's Note.

teacher, noticed that he was struggling with mastery of the twenty words on the weekly spelling test. After two weeks of poor grades, Ms. Turnbull met with Matthew to discuss possible adjustments in the spelling program. She began by commenting about Matthew's neat handwriting and then noted Matthew's difficulty on the two final tests. Ms. Turnbull asked Matthew his opinion in regard to his performance. Matthew informed her that he had studied for the tests but the words were too hard and he just could not remember them. In response, Ms. Turnbull suggested that Matthew's weekly list be reduced to five words. At this suggestion, Matthew responded that he wanted his list to have twenty words, just like all the other kids. Ms. Turnbull then suggested that Matthew take the twenty-word spelling test, but that she would grade only the five words that they had preselected. Matthew commented that this adjustment would be

"just great." Matthew does the same thing as the other students, but has a private agreement with this teacher.

Although many general education teachers are receptive and quite accustomed to making adjustments, a few may initially resist changing standards for just certain individual students. They may feel that the request to modify instruction for one or two students is not fair to the others. When asked to reduce the number of spelling words for Matthew, Ms. Turnbull could have responded, "If I alter the expectations on the spelling test for Matthew, it would not be fair to the other children."

In the classic video *How Difficult Can This Be?* Rick Lavoie presents two important points with regard to this type of argument: (a) Matthew's needs have nothing to do with the other children, and (b) the word *fair* has been misinterpreted (Lavoie, 1990). *Fair* does not mean equal, but instead that every student gets what he or she needs to succeed. Matthew needs five spelling words to be successful, whereas Jonathan, his classmate, can handle all twenty words. If you, or a colleague, are struggling with this concept of different work not being fair, ask the following questions. What is fair about asking students of differing abilities to do exactly the same work? You know that you would not refuse to allow a student to take his medicine because everyone else in the class doesn't need it or not allow a child to use assistive technology because everyone else does not need it.

On rare occasions, a teacher may be unwilling to make specific accommodations for a student. Xavier, an eighth-grade student with a learning disability, requested oral examinations as specified in his Individual Educational Program (IEP) from his science teacher, Mr. Janus. Mr. Russell, the special education teacher, also spoke to Mr. Janus regarding the need for alternative methods of assessment for Xavier. Mr. Janus responded to both that he was unwilling to make this adjustment. Fortunately for Xavier, Mr. Janus is obligated legally to make classroom accommodations for Xavier; individuals who have been diagnosed as having language impairments or learning disabilities and have qualified under the Individuals with Disabilities Education Improvement Act (IDEA, 2004) or Section 504 (1973) have certain legal protections relative to appropriate school accommodations.

LEGAL REQUIREMENTS FOR INDIVIDUALS WITH LEARNING DISABILITIES

Provision of services in school settings for individuals with specific learning disabilities has been problematic. A major source of confusion involves the interpretation of legal requirements and protections. The following sections provide brief reviews of the general legal requirements pertaining to learning disabilities. The first section discusses requirements under the IDEA 2004. The next section discusses requirements for accommodations under Section 504 of the 1973 Rehabilitation Act (PL 93-112) and the Americans with Disabilities Act of 1990 (ADA, PL 101-336).

Eligibility Under IDEA 2004

Among the various disability areas, the most controversy exists with regard to the eligibility criteria for learning disabilities (LD) services. That definition in the law (20 U.S.C. §1401 [30]) reads as follows: "The term 'specific learning disability' means a disorder in one or more of the basic psychological processes involved in understanding or in using language, spoken or written, which disorder may manifest itself in the imperfect ability to listen, think, speak, read, write, spell, or do mathematical calculations. Such term includes such conditions as perceptual disabilities, brain injury, minimal brain dysfunction, dyslexia, and developmental aphasia. Such term does not include a learning problem that is primarily the result of visual, hearing, or motor disabilities, of mental retardation, of emotional disturbance, or of environmental, cultural, or economic disadvantage."

To be diagnosed as having a specific learning disability (SLD) under IDEA 2004, an individual must (a) exhibit underachievement (not achieve adequately for the individual's age or meet state-approved grade-level standards in one or more of the specified eight areas when provided with learning experiences and instruction appropriate for the individual's age or state-approved grade-level standards); and (b) make insufficient progress OR exhibit a pattern of strengths and weaknesses in performance, achievement, or both relative to age, grade-level standards, or intellectual development, that is determined by a multidisciplinary evaluation team to be relevant to the identification of SLD. The eight areas are oral expression, listening comprehension, written expression, basic reading skill, reading fluency, reading comprehension, mathematics calculation, and mathematics reasoning. The multidisciplinary evaluation team may not identify an individual as having a specific learning disability if the difficulty is *primarily* the result of a visual, hearing, or motor impairment; mental retardation; emotional disturbance; lack of appropriate instruction; limited English proficiency; or environmental, cultural, or economic disadvantages.

The most significant change in IDEA 2004 is the elimination of the requirement that a student had to have a severe discrepancy between intellectual ability and achievement. Although school districts can still use a discrepancy approach, they cannot be required to use this for determining SLD. IDEA included an additional provision allowing school districts to use a process designed to determine if the student responds to research-based interventions. This process is often referred to as Response to Intervention (RTI). For written language, depending on the student's specific needs, school personnel could monitor progress when explicit and systematic instruction is provided in handwriting, word processing, phonemic awareness, spelling, vocabulary, or written expression.

As part of the eligibility determination process, general and special education teachers and school psychologists are to provide systematic monitoring of the effectiveness of the instruction, as well as the student's progress. This is often accomplished through the use of curriculum-based measurements (CBMs), which can be administered frequently. Procedures for using CBMs to monitor growth in written language are presented in Chapter Eight. You can also collect dated samples of writing from a portfolio to demonstrate a student's progress. Figure 4.2 shows a paragraph written by Jesse in January, prior to receiving special education services. In April, his special education teacher dictated the same paragraph to him orally to transcribe, which is presented in Figure 4.3. Although Jesse still needs further assistance, it is easy to see how much his spelling has improved in just a few months.

These types of work samples and evaluation provide useful information to help the multidisciplinary team decide if a student is in need of more intensive interventions than can be provided by a general education teacher. More comprehensive evaluations are often then conducted to determine specifically why the student is having such difficulty. In cases of writing problems, the more comprehensive evaluations would include standardized measures or norm-referenced measures of both oral and written language abilities.

One major problem regarding IDEA eligibility for a learning disability in written language is that the category for writing is simply

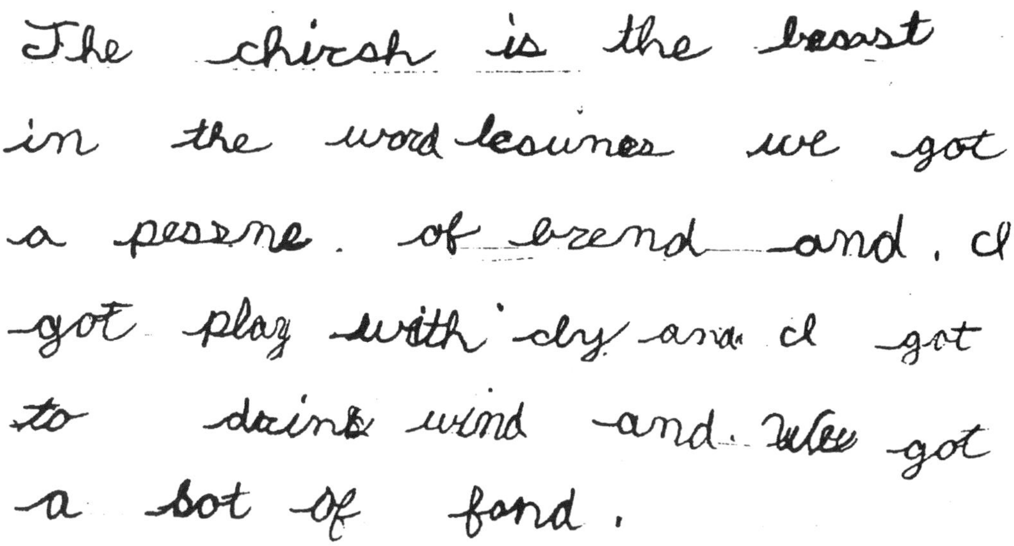
The chirsh is the beasst
in the word leaunes we got
a pessne. of brend and. I
got play with dy and I got
to daink wind and. Wee got
a bot of fond.

Figure 4.2. Jesse's Paragraph in January.

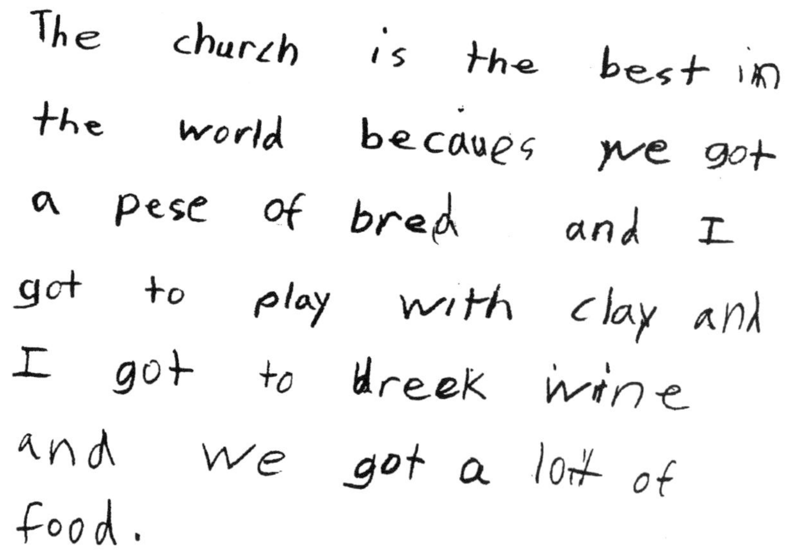

The church is the best in the world becaues we got a pese of bred and I got to play with clay and I got to dreek wine and we got a lott of food.

Figure 4.3. Jesse's Paragraph in April.

called "written expression." Unlike reading, which is broken into three major components, all aspects of writing are grouped together. Writing, like reading, also has major components and students struggle with different aspects. Some students have trouble spelling but can express their ideas clearly; some students spell with ease but have trouble organizing and expressing their ideas; still others have trouble with the motor aspects of writing and produce illegible handwriting. If the problem is just spelling or just handwriting, some multidisciplinary teams may determine that the student does not qualify for SLD services. This is in spite of the fact that poor spelling is one of the major characteristics of a specific writing disability.

Figure 4.4 presents a writing sample from Krista, a third-grade student who is able to express her ideas with clarity but struggles with mastery of grapheme-phoneme connections, as well as the recall of common spelling patterns. She was asked to write a make-believe story about why a student was late for lunch. Krista is a student with a spelling disability, and she should receive appropriate help. Spelling and handwriting are integral to written expression, and problems in these areas should not be disregarded, as they will affect the overall quality of written expression.

Eligibility Under Section 504 and the Americans with Disabilities Act

Eligibility for services under Section 504 differs from the IDEA 2004 qualification criteria. As the law mandates equal access and equal opportunity, a lack of responsiveness to treatment or the existence of a severe discrepancy are not required for accommodations. Eligibility procedures are not clearly addressed in Section 504, but have been clarified to some extent by court rulings and legal experts.

The regulations governing implementation of Section 504 provide a broader definition of a disability than is found in the IDEA 2004 regulations. In Section 504, a disability is defined as any physical or mental impairment that substantially limits a major life activity [34 CFR Section 104.3(j)]. Because learning is a major life activity, educators are mandated to make reasonable accommodations for students with learning disabilities. For a student to receive accommodations, however, the disability must be currently affecting learning.

The law states

No otherwise qualified individual with a disability in the United States . . . shall, solely by reason of his disability, be excluded from the participation in, be denied the

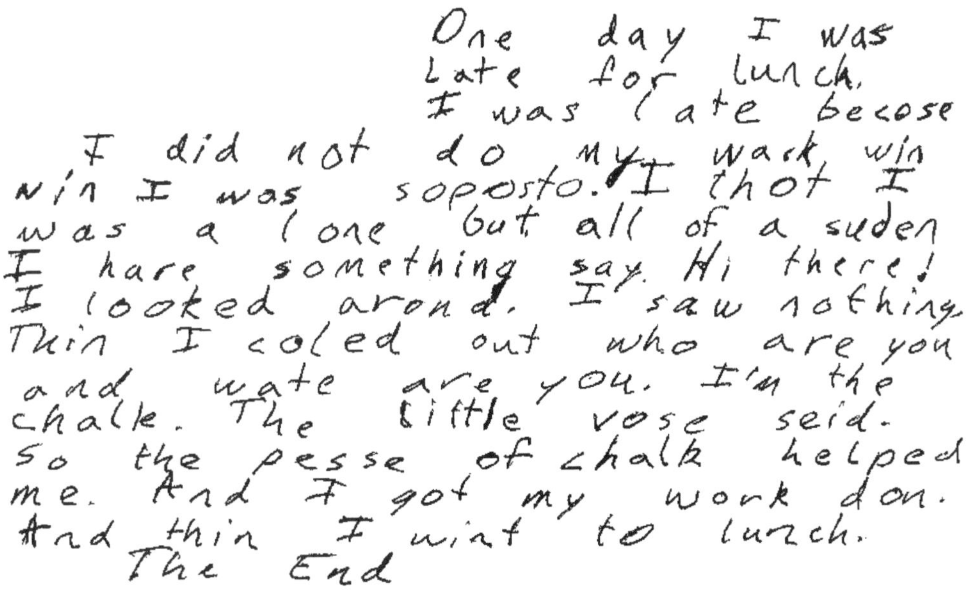
One day I was
Late for lunch.
I was late becose
I did not do my wark win
win I was soposto. I thot I
was a lone but all of a suden
I hare something say. Hi there!
I looked arond. I saw nothing.
Thin I coled out who are you
and wate are you. I'm the
chalk. The little vose seid.
So the pesse of chalk helped
me. And I got my work don.
And thin I wint to lunch.
The End

Figure 4.4. Krista's Story About Being Late for Lunch.

benefits of, or be subjected to discrimination under any program or activity receiving Federal financial assistance [34 CFR Section 104.4(a)].

The wording is the same in the Americans with Disabilities Act (ADA, 1990) and the Americans with Disabilities Act (ADA) Amendments Act of 2008 as in Section 504, and the three acts are identical in regard to the accommodations mandated for individuals with disabilities. The ADA, however, extends the mandates to private institutions with fifteen or more employees. The schools specifically mentioned in the ADA are nursery, elementary, secondary, undergraduate or postgraduate private school, or other places of education.

As a result of the ADA, individuals with learning disabilities in most private schools are now afforded the same legal protections that their counterparts in public schools have been provided for over three decades. Individuals in some private institutions, however, continue to be protected by Section 504 rather than the ADA. For example, a private school that receives any federal funding (such as funding to provide federal loans to students) is responsible for providing accommodations whenever necessary under Section 504. Only private institutions that are independent and self-supporting are regulated solely by the ADA.

One exception exists to the extension of the legal mandates to private schools. An exemption was granted to schools directly affiliated with religious organizations. If a student in a parochial school is not being provided with appropriate accommodations, the parents may not have the recourse mandated by Section 504 and the ADA.

Although both laws mandate that reasonable accommodations be made, much latitude exists in the interpretation of "reasonable." Reasonable accommodations must be determined for the student on an individual basis. Under Section 504 mandates, services are provided primarily in the general education classroom. Unfortunately, although accommodations place minimal demands on teacher time or school funds, some classroom teachers perceive these adjustments as being inherently problematic. Teachers must provide accommodations that are listed on either a student's IEP or 504 Accommodation Plan. Individuals with writing disabilities often require adjustments or accommodations such as access to a spell checker, or provision of a scribe on certain types of tests. Often they are no more complex than providing computer access in a central location, not penalizing for spelling on in-class assignments, or arranging for extended time on tests. Modifications on examinations should not, however, alter the measurement of skills or knowledge that the exam is supposed to test. The purpose of the law is to accommodate a disability by providing equal opportunity, not to favor an individual. All written and approved accommodations are legally binding. Although no funding is available for services to students who qualify under Section 504 or the ADA, both laws provide for enforcement of mandates by authorizing the removal of federal financing of schools found to be out of compliance.

Interpretation and implementation of Section 504 have proven troublesome to many school districts due to a lack of information or clarifications. One major misconception is that compliance with the IDEA is equivalent to compliance with Section 504. This is not so: every student covered by the IDEA is also covered by Section 504, but the reverse is not true. A student could fail to qualify for services under the IDEA, yet still qualify for accommodations and procedural safeguards under Section 504.

The mandates of Section 504 do not cease with high school graduation. Section 504 requires that postsecondary institutions (from technical training schools to private four-year universities) make reasonable accommodations for the physical and mental limitations of individuals. Individuals with written language disabilities, therefore, are entitled to accommodations not only as children but also as adults pursuing advanced degrees.

Responsibility for accommodation is shared equally by the individual student and the school. Unlike students in elementary and secondary education, postsecondary students are obligated to notify their institution of their disability and the necessary academic accommodations. Each individual needs to inform the appropriate personnel and provide documentation as to the nature and severity of their writing disability, as well as the recommended accommodations. For students of all ages, it must be determined that (a) the student has a disability, (b) the documentation is adequate, (c) the student is qualified, and (d) the accommodation is reasonable.

Specific Accommodations for Writers with Disabilities

How do you choose the appropriate accommodations for a student? The answer is whichever and however many are necessary to give the individual an equal opportunity to achieve in the specific setting. Depending on the type and severity of the writing problem, students will vary in the type and number of accommodations needed. Some individuals may need to present assignments orally or on tape; others may need extended time on tests. As with teaching strategies, curricular adjustments are tailored to unique individual needs.

Once the need for specific accommodations has been determined, the question then becomes what accommodations are available and viable to the ecology of the classroom. In many school districts, a team meets to identify appropriate student accommodations.

Although Section 504 mandates that reasonable accommodations be made, an official list of acceptable accommodations does not exist. The following academic adjustments, however, are noted specifically in the law: (a) modifications to the method of instruction, (b) extended exam time, (c) alternative testing formats, and (d) increased time in which to complete a course [34 CFR Sections 104.44(a)(b)(c)]. In general, the three major accommodations for students with moderate to severe writing difficulties are to provide more time for writing; access to technology, such as the use of a laptop; and ways to express themselves that require limited or no writing.

Some school personnel have questioned whether or not educational institutions must purchase computers for students who require these aids. The ADA codifies that institutions may not charge individuals with disabilities for the provision of necessary auxiliary aids and services [28CFR Sections 35.130(f),

Assignments
Adjust the difficulty level of in-class and homework writing assignments.
Reduce the number of written assignments.
Reduce the length of assignments both in the classroom and at home.
Provide extended time on writing assignments.
Accept tape-recorded assignments as an alternative to written assignments.
Teach the student how to use a tape recorder to complete specific assignments. For example, provide practice preparing and orally dictating an essay for an English class.
Permit oral dictation of written assignments to a teacher, parent, or peer.

Examinations
Provide more time on in-class exams.
Administer exams orally. Give exams individually or have the student dictate responses into a tape recorder for grading at a later time.
Allow alternative methods for displaying content mastery, such as allowing oral presentations or special projects.
Provide alternative exam formats that do not require extensive writing, such as multiple-choice, short answer, or fill-in-the-blank.
Divide written exams into several sections that can be administered over several days.
Allow the student to write all exam responses on a computer.

Taking Notes
Provide the student with copies of class notes from the instructor or a peer.
Provide tape recordings of the class lectures rather than require the student to take notes.
Limit or eliminate copying requirements from both the blackboard and textbooks.

Grading
Grade on individualized, preestablished criteria. You might grade a particular writing assignment on content only, whereas on another you might focus on form, such as the use of capitalization.
Provide many ungraded opportunities for writing skill development.
Modify the grading system for writing assignments. Assign grades to reflect effort or on the basis of individualized progress.
Modify the grading system for the student by placing greater emphasis on special projects, rather than on performance on written assignments.
Grade the student on improvement in writing skill, rather than comparing his or her writing performance to peers.
Provide the student with structured assistance with editing prior to grading a paper.
When grading assignments, do not penalize for errors in basic skills, such as punctuation errors, misspellings, or poor handwriting.

Peer Support
Provide opportunities for the student to work on writing assignments in small groups.
Provide the student with a cross-age tutor to help with writing tasks.

Technology
Encourage the student to use a spell checker when editing papers.
Encourage the use of technology, such as a word-processing program.
Encourage the student to use spelling and grammar correction programs before turning in assignments.
Teach the student how to use voice recognition software.

Figure 4.5. Examples of Accommodations and Adjustments.

36.301(c)]. The regulations in Section 504 and the ADA clarify, however, that institutions are not mandated to provide services of a personal nature, such as individualized tutoring [34 CFR Section 104.44(d)(2); 28 CFR Sections 35.135, 36.306]. Figure 4.5 provides examples of adjustments and reasonable accommodations that may be needed by an individual with writing difficulties.

CONCLUSION

Many individuals with writing difficulties can succeed in general education classrooms provided that specific accommodations and curricular adjustments are made. The type and amount of support needed will vary from individual to individual, task to task, and course to course. You can decrease the amount of scaffolding provided as students become more proficient on tasks. Most accommodations and modifications are not expensive or time-consuming.

The provision of support for individuals with writing disabilities is mandated by federal laws. Personnel in both public and private schools are required to adhere to these legal protections. Legal policies protect the needs of individuals with writing disabilities, but educators must ensure that these policies are turned into practice.

chapter
5

Helping Students with Handwriting

One thing only is certain—that the written language of children develops in this fashion, shifting from drawings of things to drawing of words.

—L. S. Vygotsky (1978)

As Vygotsky described, most children first attempt to draw things and gradually progress to writing letters and words. Figure 5.1 shows the drawings of Winnona, a three-year-old. The picture illustrates all of her extended family and then her family entering their house. Children like Winnona who begin drawing at early ages usually develop the motor control they need for letter formation.

Some children, however, spend little time drawing and coloring prior to entering school, and for them, letter formation and handwriting are difficult. In addition, little instruction regarding handwriting is provided in preschool and kindergarten classrooms. Thus many students invent ways of forming letters, such as drawing the letter *p* from the bottom around the top. Although this approach results in legible writing in early education, it makes the transition to cursive writing in second or third grade very difficult.

Even though many students of all ages have poor handwriting, handwriting has been considered to be neglected because few teacher education programs train teachers how to evaluate and teach handwriting. Handwriting is often thought to be an unimportant subject. Although students should not be required to demonstrate neat handwriting every time they

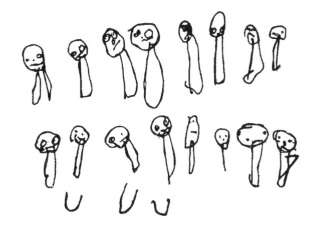

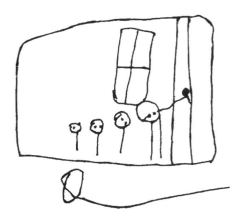

Figure 5.1. Winnona's Drawings of Her Family.

write, even in this age of technology, students need to develop a legible writing style. Even into upper grades, a few children still struggle with handwriting. Figure 5.2 shows a request from Dan, a fourth-grade student, for school supplies. Although several of the words are legible, several are not.

In some instances, nearly all of the writing is illegible. Figure 5.3 depicts the writing of

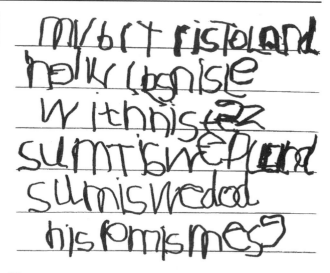

Figure 5.3. Inessa's Handwriting.

Translation: My brother is tall and he works nicely with his friends. Sometimes we play and sometimes we don't. His room is messy.

of informal assessment techniques, commercially available products, and a brief discussion of the role of technology.

GENERAL PRINCIPLES

When teaching children how to write letters, remember that tracing letter forms is much easier than copying letters onto a blank page. The most difficult skill is to reproduce the letter without visual or verbal cues. An effective program for teaching letter formation is based on the following four principles: (a) forming letters with verbal cues and tracing until the patterns become automatic; (b) copying letters and practicing letters in isolation and then within words; (c) encouraging students to critique their own handwriting; and (d) providing students with help maintaining a clear, legible writing style. Important elements of instruction include modeling and describing proper letter formation with practice, feedback, and reinforcement. Many students require explicit, direct instruction to establish legible, fluent writing. As skill progresses, students can improve their handwriting as they write meaningful text.

Figure 5.2. Dan's Handwriting.

Translation: I am Dan. Dear whomever would be concerned. We at Canyon View think we need help and supplies so if you could help that would be great. Thank you

Inessa, a fourth-grade student. Inessa is writing about her brother. The only sentence that is easy to decipher is the last one: "His room is messy." Inessa's ability to communicate through writing is very limited because of her poor handwriting.

This chapter begins with a review of handwriting principles. Next, various writing styles, the instructional needs of left-handed writers, and the use of word processing are discussed. Specific instructional strategies are then provided for the areas of: (a) readiness, (b) letter formation, (c) reversals, (d) fluency, (e) self-evaluation, and (f) appearance. The chapter concludes with a review

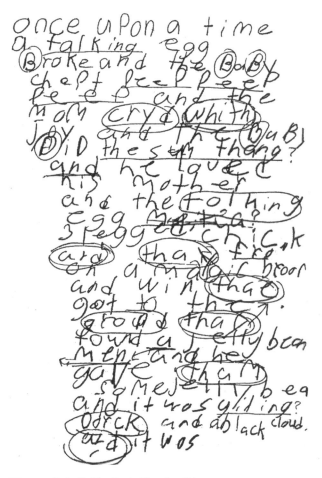

Figure 5.4. Tabbatha's Handwriting.

On rare occasions, handwriting improves without direct intervention. Figures 5.4 and 5.5 illustrate two writing samples from Tabbatha, a third-grade student. The second sample was written two weeks after the first sample. When the second sample was written, Tabbatha had started receiving medication for Attention Deficit Hyperactivity Disorder (ADHD). Clearly, her difficulties with handwriting were related to ADHD, as the appearance of her writing improved substantially with this treatment. Medication alone, however, does not usually cure the handwriting problem. It may facilitate the process for a few students, but most will also need explicit instruction.

The numerous instructional programs for handwriting have the following common elements:

1. Opportunities to practice handwriting skill; with older students, functional opportunities to practice handwriting (for example, filling out job applications, bank forms, and so on)
2. Teacher modeling of correct handwriting with direct instruction in letter formation

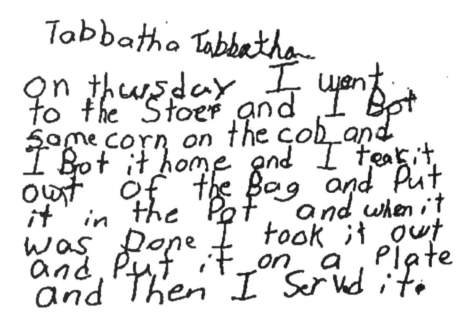

Figure 5.5. Tabbatha's Handwriting Two Weeks Later.

3. Opportunities to practice handwriting by tracing over models, with gradual fading of the models

4. Provision of primary paper with a middle line in order to foster the correct size of letters; as skill develops, provision of standard paper

WRITING STYLES

In many school districts, handwriting instruction begins with manuscript writing and then progresses to cursive writing at the end of the second or beginning of the third grade. A general consensus does not exist regarding whether children with handwriting difficulties should be taught manuscript or cursive writing first. Some children find printing to be easier, whereas others find cursive to be easier.

Manuscript or Cursive

Some students appear to profit from early instruction in cursive writing. Several advantages exist regarding teaching students cursive writing rather than manuscript in kindergarten or the first grade. First, the students only have to learn one handwriting system. Second, because all cursive letters are made from left to right, a student may have fewer letter reversals. Third, the continuous writing motion can help with spacing, speed, and alignment.

Other young children seem to find that manuscript is an easier style to learn. Because the letter forms are composed of simple sticks and circles, the shapes may be more familiar and thus easier to form than cursive letters. In addition, the print style matches what children see in books. Cursive writing can be difficult for some young children, as they do not have the fine-motor skills necessary to sustain the movement required for continuous strokes.

This problem is not always limited to young children. In some instances, an older student has such difficulty learning cursive writing that learning the new style becomes counterproductive. For example, Frank, a third-grade student, had extreme difficulty developing a legible manuscript style. Fortunately, his teacher realized that it was more important to spend time on authentic writing activities than to insist that Frank spend time mastering cursive writing. We want to introduce students such as Frank to keyboarding and word processing as soon as possible.

Learning a new writing style appears to be particularly problematic for students with poor memory for letter forms or poor visual-motor skill. When new writing styles are introduced, other aspects of writing performance often deteriorate. For example, when a student changes from manuscript to cursive, he or she may make more errors in spelling and punctuation. Shawn, a fourth-grade student, enjoys writing in cursive and is proud of the neat and legible work that he produces, but he makes twice as many spelling and punctuation errors.

Shawn explained to his teacher, "It's like my brain's a battery that has enough energy to make nice handwriting or to spell right, but not enough to do both." Shawn and his teacher agreed that every first draft would be printed so he could direct his attention to expressing his ideas. During the editing stage, they would correct his errors in basic skills. Shawn would copy the final draft in cursive so that he could continue to be proud of his work.

Manu-Cursive

One way to avoid having to teach a new writing style is to begin instruction with a manu-cursive style. Manu-cursive is a writing style that combines elements of both manuscript and cursive letter formation. The most well-known example of a manu-cursive writing style is D'Nealian (Thurber, 1983). In this method, the majority of letters are formed with a continuous motion, thus providing a natural progression from manuscript to cursive letter formation. Letters are connected by adding joining strokes. Manu-cursive approaches are effective for students with handwriting difficulties for several reasons. First, in using this writing style, students make fewer reversals and transpositions. Second, they do not need to learn two different methods for writing, and third, letters are formed in a single, continuous motion. In addition, D'Nealian offers visual, auditory, and tactile-kinesthetic clues to aid in memory of the letter forms. As students form the letters they say the verbal directions. To make a cursive *a,* the writer would say, "middle start, around down, close up, down, and a monkey tail." To make an *e,* the writer would say, "start between the middle and the bottom, curve up, around, touch down, up, and stop." Having students verbalize the motions helps remind them how to make the letter forms.

Depending on a student's age, ability, and interest, instructional training in a particular writing style may be recommended. As a general principle, permit variation in handwriting styles and allow students to use the style that they prefer. If a student is producing legible work at an adequate speed, ignore small irregularities in style that do not detract from communication. Some students will always prefer to use manuscript writing, whereas others will prefer a manu-cursive or cursive writing style. The important point to remember is that in designing an instructional program for handwriting, your goal is to help students develop a fluent, legible handwriting that other people can read with ease.

Figure 5.6 illustrates a retelling of an event by Jorge, a third-grade student. Although Jorge has average oral language abilities, his problem with visual-motor skill makes writing extremely difficult. His mother spends time each evening trying to teach Jorge how to form letters, but his writing does not seem to improve. Although most individuals will master a legible handwriting style, a few will not even with years of practice. As we described in Chapter Two, Jeremy, a senior in college, still had illegible handwriting after six years of instruction, and had still not acquired keyboarding skills. Students such as Jorge and

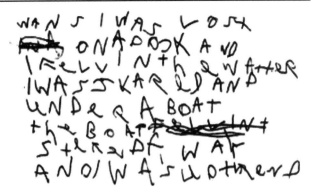

Figure 5.6. Jorge's Retelling of an Event.

Translation: Once I was lost on a dock and I fell in the water. I was scared and under a boat. The boat (steered off away?) and I was up. The End.

Jeremy will need to write the majority of their assignments on computers.

Word Processing

Computers can help students bypass handwriting difficulties, allowing all students to produce neat, clean copies of their written work. Because of severe difficulties with handwriting or difficulties focusing on handwriting, spelling, syntax, and ideation simultaneously, some students need to begin word-processing instruction as early as second or third grade. To become efficient at word processing, students require instruction in both keyboarding skills and the operation of the word-processing program. Students should learn how to enter, save, edit, and print text.

In today's technology-driven world, children should be taught keyboarding skills early in their school years, perhaps as early as first grade for those struggling with handwriting. A number of software programs designed to develop keyboarding skills are available. Two such programs are "Mavis Beacon Teaches Typing" (www.broderbund.com) and "Read, Write, and Type" (www.talkingfingers.com).

Many inexpensive computers for simple word processing are available. One commonly used word processor is the AlphaSmart, which provides several styles of portable, easy-to-use, inexpensive laptops available for school and home use. Teachers and students can use the NEO 1 or 2 and the Dana or Dana Wireless, which has WiFi capabilities. Dana is also compatible with Palm OS educational applications. Students can easily share and send files, as well as do peer editing.

Many students could benefit from instruction in both handwriting and word processing. Consider the journal entry of Philip, a third-grade student (Figure 5.7). His rate of production is extremely slow. He spent twenty minutes on this journal entry, which says something about things or people. He writes at the end that he likes them all.

Given the severity of Philip's fine-motor difficulties, his teacher developed a program that included a structured, multisensory method for handwriting as well as instruction in keyboarding skills. In addition, the teacher implemented some specific accommodations because of Philip's extreme difficulties in handwriting. For example, on occasion the teacher substituted oral book reports for written ones and encouraged Philip to work on assignments with a peer who did the majority of the writing. Although computers can be vital for the success of students such as Philip, they still can benefit from handwriting instruction.

Left-Handed Writers

Students who write with their left hand often require some special adjustments. First, have students who write with their left hand hold the pencil about an inch farther back than right-handed writers do. Encourage children not to hook their wrists when writing, but if they do and can write with ease, do not try to change the positioning. Second, have students slant their papers slightly to the right when writing with cursive. The bottom right hand corner of the paper should be pointed at child's navel, so if you drew a line from the navel to the right hand corner and continued in a straight line, it would end at the upper left-hand corner. Essentially, the paper lies parallel to the writing arm. Finally, permit these writers to write letters vertically or with a slight backward rather than forward slant.

Readiness Activities

Some young children may not have developed the prerequisite motor skills needed for handwriting. For these students, provide activities that focus on the development of necessary fine-motor and visual-motor skills. You can help children develop readiness skills by providing

Figure 5.7. Philip's Journal Entry.

activities such as cutting, tracing, coloring, and copying. Prior to formal handwriting instruction a student should be able to (a) trace and copy simple shapes and lines; (b) connect dots on paper; (c) draw horizontal, vertical, curved, and slanted lines; (d) draw backward and forward circles; and (e) note likenesses and differences in letter forms. Many of these prerequisite skills can actually be developed within drawing and writing activities.

Simply encouraging children to color and draw can help them develop the motor skills necessary for handwriting. Errol, a first-grade student, was resistant to writing, although he liked to draw. Initially, his teacher allowed him to work on his drawings during writing time. After one month, Errol began to want to place a title on his pictures, and soon thereafter he began to put his thoughts on paper. Figure 5.8 illustrates Errol's portrayal of his superheroes. For this illustration, he wanted to label each character.

Common examples of readiness exercises include:

1. *Scribbling.* Encourage the child to scribble using different mediums, such as finger-paints, pencils, and crayons.
2. *Tracing.* Have the student trace over letters and words with different color markers.
3. *Copying.* Have the student copy letters and words.
4. *Writing.* Have the student write letters or words on lined paper.

Several factors may interfere with handwriting, including (a) hand preference, (b) pencil grasp, (c) posture, (d) paper positioning, (e) copying, and (f) spatial organization.

Hand Preference

Prior to formal handwriting instruction, a few students need help establishing hand preference. If a preferred hand has not been identified by first grade, you should determine the hand that is better coordinated or used more often for eating, throwing a ball, and so on. If the more skilled hand is not readily identified, you might consult with an occupational therapist. Initially, the child could wear some type of jewelry or a sticker on that hand as a reminder of which hand to use when writing. Because many children with delayed hand dominance have trouble crossing the midlines of their bodies, encourage children to place papers on the same side of the desk as their preferred hands.

Pencil Grasp

Some students with low muscle tone often persist in using ineffective pencil grips. They use their shoulders and elbows to control the pencil, rather than their fingers. In general, these children can benefit from a variety of sensorimotor activities and exercises. Examples of activities include: (a) tracing around stencils or templates, (b) drawing in clay with a stylus, (c) drawing on sand or sandpaper, or (d) writing while standing at a chalkboard.

Two pencil grasps have been found effective. In the first, the pencil is held lightly between the thumb and first two fingers with the index finger placed on top of the pencil. The pencil rests upon the first knuckle of the middle finger. As an alternative, a student may prefer the D'Nealian pencil grasp. For this grasp, the pencil is held between the index and middle fingers with about a 25-degree slant. The two fingers and thumb grip the pencil about one half inch above the point. In addition, a student's pencil grasp might benefit from a molded finger grip on the pencil.

Posture

Poor posture can also contribute to handwriting difficulties. Ensure that children are provided with the proper size chairs and desks. Children should have chairs that have flat backs and seats so that they may maintain symmetrical body positions. Their feet should rest flat on the floor and the desk height should be slightly

Figure 5.8. Errol's Drawings of His Superheroes.

above the elbows so that both forearms can rest comfortably. As a rule, children should be able to move their writing arms smoothly and easily across the paper.

Paper Positioning

Paper position can also affect legibility. Some students have difficulty positioning their papers on their desks and may benefit from taping the paper in the correct position or using a clipboard until they learn to position the paper at the correct angle automatically. If the student has trouble keep the paper in place, you could tape a large sheet of construction paper on the desk to keep the paper from slipping. Students who avoid crossing the midline may be helped by slanting the paper toward the dominant hand or placing the paper to the side of their midline. When writing in cursive, right-handed students typically slant papers to the left, whereas left-handed students slant papers to the right.

Copying

In general, do not require students who have difficulty copying to copy large amounts of material from the chalkboard or their textbooks. When copying is necessary, seat these students as close to the material as possible. For some students, you can: (a) reduce the amount of material to be copied, (b) use colored chalk to highlight certain words or phrases, (c) provide a printed copy of the assignment, or (d) have a peer provide a copy of the notes.

Students who have a tendency to reverse letters often have trouble copying work from the board or from their books. You can use several strategies to help students improve their copying skills. Have the student put his or her finger under the first letter of the word, say the letter aloud, and then copy it. Have the student move to the next letter and follow the same procedure. After the word has been copied, ask the student to say "space" before copying the next word. Repeat the procedure until the sentence has been copied. If needed, the student can cross out each letter once it has been copied. When sufficient fluency and speed have been achieved copying individual letters, have the student repeat the procedure copying words, phrases, and then sentences.

Spatial Organization

Students with problems in spatial organization may have difficulty writing letters on the appropriate lines or observing the margins on the paper. They often have trouble organizing their writing neatly on the paper. These students may benefit from highlighting the lines on the paper with colored markers or, in some instances, using paper with raised lines. Students with severe difficulties may benefit from the use of a cardboard frame that forces the pencil to stop when it hits the top or bottom of the line. For students who fail to observe margins, place a piece of clear tape along the sides of the paper as a reminder to stop writing.

LETTER FORMATION

This writing business. Pencils and what-not. Over-rated, if you ask me. Silly stuff. Nothing in it.
　　　　　　　　—Eeyore (A. A. Milne)

Although many commercial workbooks are available to provide students with practice in letter formation, these exercises do not provide sufficient instruction to achieve the result of fluent, legible handwriting. For teaching letter formation, you need to use a combination of instructional methods that includes modeling, practice, self-evaluation, and provision of feedback. Students need guidance to improve in handwriting. Zoya, a second-grade student, was given a worksheet with a sentence to copy, presented in Figure 5.9. As feedback, her teacher instructed her to "work carefully." This kind of feedback will not improve handwriting skill. Zoya is working carefully, but because of

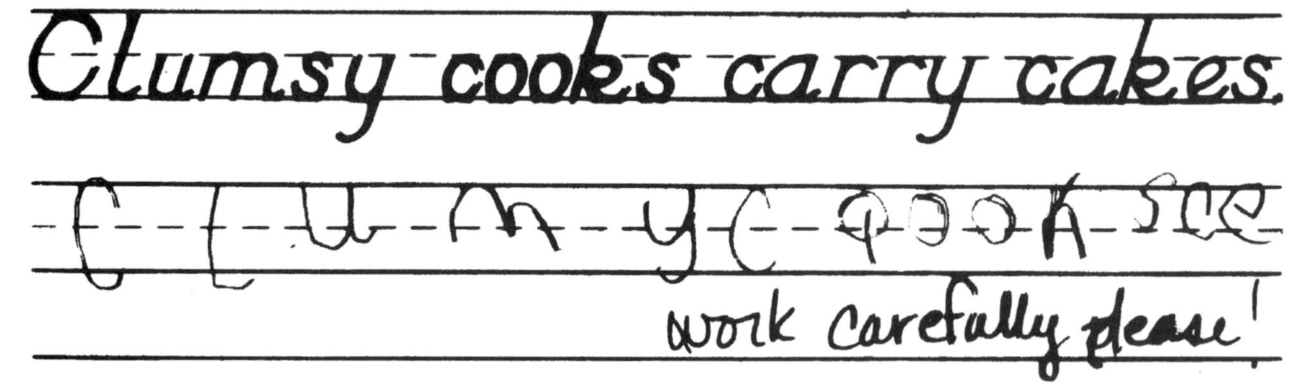

Figure 5.9. Teacher's Comment on Zoya's Paper.

poor visual-motor skills, this is the best that she can do.

Instructional methods typically begin with letter forms, then progress to words and short phrases, and finally to sentences. Many methods contain a number of systematic steps that are multisensory. Multisensory (visual-auditory-kinesthetic-tactile, or VAKT) strategies help children learn to form letters easily and automatically.

Standard Procedure for Letter Formation

When teaching beginning writers how to form letters, you can use the following steps:

1. Model correct letter formation with verbal instructions.
2. Discuss how to form the letter and review any unique features of the letter.
3. Have the student name and then trace the letter with a finger and then with a pencil or marker.
4. If needed, provide more tracing practice with raised letter cards. These may be made by writing colored letters on cards and then outlining them with Elmer's glue. When the glue dries, the raised letters can be traced.
5. Have the student write the letter while looking at the model. Have the student compare the letter to the model.
6. Have the student write the letter from memory three times and then compare the letters to the model.
7. Provide feedback on correctly and incorrectly formed letters and then more practice with incorrectly formed ones.

Even when a student has mastered the majority of letter formations, some letters may continue to be problematic. When an error is made on a letter, you can mark over the error with a highlighter, and then have the student erase the incorrect part, correct it, trace over the correctly formed letter, and then write the letter correctly.

Self-Guided Symbol Formation Strategy

This self-guided strategy was developed to help students master the formation of particular letters (Graham & Madan, 1981). The procedure is practiced on lined paper, and students can use either cursive or manuscript writing. The strategy consists of the following five steps:

1. Identify the letter that the student typically forms incorrectly. Ask the student to write a sample sentence that contains all of the letters, such as *The quick brown fox jumps over the lazy dog.*

2. Select one letter that the student has trouble forming. Model the correct letter formation with a crayon, marker, or chalk. Write the letter again while verbally describing the process. Continue until the student can repeat the verbal description with the teacher.

3. Have the student trace the letter until he or she can verbalize the steps alone. If needed, guide the student's tracing through the use of arrows or colored dots. Encourage the student to act as his or her own instructor, by defining the task, correcting errors, and praising accurate letter formation. Continue with step 3 until the student can copy the letter five times correctly.

4. Describe the formation of the target letter while the student attempts to visualize and write the letter. Provide corrective feedback. Continue until the student can write the letter five times from memory.

5. Have the student practice the target letter in meaningful contexts. Begin with practice of single words, phrases, and then sentences.

Fernald Multisensory Method

Many decades ago, Fernald (1943) described an approach that has formed the basis of many instructional procedures for handwriting. This multisensory method for teaching letter formation reinforces learning through tracing. To use the method, follow these steps:

1. Ask the student to watch you as you write the letter in crayon on an index card.

2. Have the student trace the letter numerous times, while saying the letter name.

3. When the student feels ready, ask him or her to turn over the card and form the letter properly from memory.

Gillingham and Stillman Multisensory Method

Some students enjoy writing on a chalkboard, and the kinesthetic feedback from the chalk's movement on the board may help with memory. Gillingham and Stillman (1973) incorporated a chalkboard into their multisensory approach that involves tracing, writing, and saying the letter name. You can use the following steps:

1. Write a letter on the chalkboard. Model correct letter formation while you say the letter name.

2. Have the student trace the letter while saying the letter name. Have the student continue to trace until he or she is comfortable with formation and knows the letter name.

3. Have the student copy the letter while saying the letter name.

4. Have the student write the letter from memory while saying the name.

VAKT Multisensory Approach

Students need varying amounts of repetition when learning letter forms. Choosing a method must, therefore, be dictated by individual needs. The best method will be the one that provides sufficient practice for learning to occur but not so much that the student becomes bored. For individuals in need of more support, another multisensory approach, similar to the Fernald method, involves systematic repetition and practice (Graham & Miller, 1980). The procedure consists of the following steps:

1. Write the letter with a crayon while the student observes.

2. Say the name of the letter with the student.

3. Have the student say the name of the letter while tracing it with his or her index finger.

4. Repeat step 3 until the student is successful on five consecutive trials.

5. Have the student write the letter while looking at the model.

6. Repeat step 5 until the student copies the letter successfully three times.

7. Have the student say the name of the letter while writing it from memory.

8. Repeat step 7 until the student has written the letter successfully three times.

Dotted Representations

Many of the methods and programs for teaching letter formation have children practice tracing letters with dotted representations. Prior to practice, you prepare a dotted representation of the letter to be learned or use a computer software program that can generate worksheets of dotted letters. Follow these steps:

1. Give the student a dotted representation of the target letter.
2. Have the student trace over the dotted letter.
3. Repeat steps 1 and 2 several times until the student can form the letter with ease.
4. Have the student copy the letter several times.
5. Repeat step 4 as many times as needed until the student can form the letter correctly with ease.

D'Nealian

You can also use a six-step procedure for teaching letter formation using manu-cursive or D'Nealian letters (Thurber, 1983). This method introduces letters in groups of similar formation and incorporates visual, auditory, tactile, and kinesthetic modalities. The following steps are used:

Step 1: Tell the student what letter will be formed ("Now, we will make the letter ___.").

Step 2:
  a. Make eye contact with the student.
  b. Orally state the directions ("up," "around," "down," and so on) for writing the letter while simultaneously writing the letter in the air. If facing the student, write the letter backwards, so that the child can see the correct formation of the letter.

Step 3: Have the student repeat the directions while you trace the letter in the air.

Step 4:
  a. When letter formation is mastered, have the student practice writing the letters on paper with a marker or pencil.
  b. Have the student write the letter with a few other letters in groups of three; two or three different groups may be needed for learning the correct formation.
  c. Have the student repeat the directions for the letter when writing.
    At this point, ask the student to simply cross out errors and practice again so that progress can be seen. Students should know that when they are practicing something, new mistakes are expected as part of the learning process.

Step 5: Trace the letter on the student's arm, hand, or back with a finger while saying the directions. Repeat this step if necessary.

Step 6:
  a. Have the student trace the letter on your hand and say the directions.
  b. When the student succeeds, check to see if he or she has memorized the letter's formation. Do this by saying the directions and tracing the letter inaccurately on the child's hand. Encourage the student to indicate the error.

Self-Instructional Procedures

Some students learn easier and faster when a visual method of teaching is used. Other students benefit with more tracing practice. Still others prefer to rely upon their memorization of the oral directions of letter formation. One procedure emphasizes oral directions using the following steps (Graham, 1983):

1. On the basis of the student's needs, select a letter.
2. Write the letter as the student watches closely.
3. Describe the movements that are made when the letter is formed.

4. Have the student repeat the verbalization of the steps of letter formation.
5. Repeat steps 1 through 3 two more times.
6. Form the letter while describing the mechanics of the process.
7. Repeat step 5 until the student can verbalize the movements of the process in unison with the teacher.
8. Have the student trace the letter with his or her index finger while verbalizing the process with the teacher.
9. Repeat step 8 until the student can trace the letter and verbalize the steps simultaneously.
10. Trace the letter with a pencil while
    - Defining the task ("I have to write the letter *a*.")
    - Verbally directing the process ("I have to start on the midline.")
    - Correcting errors as they occur ("No, that's not on the midline.")
    - Self-reinforcing ("That's a good curve.")
11. Model step 10 both with and without errors.
12. Continue until the student can imitate the steps of the strategy successfully.
13. Have the student continue to use the procedure until the process is repeated successfully three times.
14. Describe the steps of the letter formation while the student writes it.
15. Repeat step 14 until the student can write the letter from memory successfully three times.

Instructional Sequence for Manuscript and Cursive Letters

Even though no rule exists about the order for introducing letters, some type of consistent sequence is likely to benefit students with learning disabilities. You do not want to introduce letters following the sequence of the alphabet as this does not factor in how the letters are formed. Instead you should use sequential groupings for introducing both lowercase and uppercase manuscript and cursive forms

(Polloway & Patton, 1993). You can group the letters by common features:

Manuscript Lowercase

1. o a d g q
2. b p
3. c e
4. t l i k
5. r n m h
6. v w
7. x y
8. f j
9. u
10. z
11. s

Manuscript Uppercase

1. L H T E F I
2. J U
3. P R B D K
4. A M N V W X Y Z
5. S
6. O Q C G

Cursive Lowercase

1. i u w t j
2. a d g q
3. n m x y v
4. r s p
5. c e
6. o z
7. b f h k l

Cursive Uppercase

1. N M H K U V Y W X Q Z
2. P B R
3. T F
4. C E
5. A
6. D
7. G
8. I
9. L
10. O
11. S
12. J

Whatever sequence you use to teach letter formation, it is important that you use the terms uppercase and lowercase consistently.

Hanover Cursive Writing Method

Cursive letters are also learned easier and faster when similarly formed letters are presented and practiced in groups. You can present and have students practice the letters in the following order (Hanover, 1983):

1. The *e* family: *e, l, h, f, b, k*
2. The *c* family: *c, a, d, o, q, g*
3. The hump family: *n, m, v, y, x*
4. Letters with tails in the back: *f, q*
5. Letters with tails in the front: *g, p, y, z*
6. *r* and *s*
7. Letters with a handle: *b, o, v, w*

Some letters are included in more than one letter family to emphasize the important characteristics. Once one group has been mastered, instruction progresses to the next. Once the lowercase letters are learned, uppercase letters are introduced in groups.

Reversals

Although reversals are common before the age of six or seven, a few older students continue to reverse letters. When second- and third-grade students still reverse letters and numbers in writing, it is important to address this confusion. If the problem is persistent or interrupts the student's train of thought, you can use a variety of instructional strategies to help the student reduce or eliminate reversals. To reduce anxiety regarding letter orientation errors, treat reversals as minor errors that will be corrected when the paper is edited. The following general principles and activities can help children eliminate reversals:

1. Do not emphasize timed writing activities, as reversals are more frequent in this type of activity.
2. Help the student create a list of the more common words containing the reversal(s) and review these words that contain the problematic letters through a multisensory approach. Have the student say the individual letter sounds as he or she traces over the whole word.
3. Draw directional arrows under letters or words that tend to be reversed.
4. For a younger student, print the letters frequently reversed in a different color: all letters that aren't reversed in green, and the letters that are reversed at times in red. Remind the student to observe the traffic sign colors and to stop and think before writing the red letters.
5. Write the commonly reversed letters (or transposed words, such as *was* for *saw*) on a transparency. Put a green dot where the student is to begin forming the letter or word, directional arrows throughout, and a red dot at where to stop. Project the image onto a chalkboard or whiteboard and have the student trace over it. On a daily basis, have the student trace over the letter or word several times.
6. Use a multisensory method to teach a simple, common word beginning with one of the problematic letters. For example, if a student reverses *b* and *d*, teach *dad* and point out that all three letters are formed in the same way. Encourage the student to think of the word (for example, *dad*) when uncertain about the direction of a *b* or *d*.
7. Use visual clues for teaching the student the forms of frequently confused letters. For example, show the student that the letter *b* can be formed with the fingers of the left hand and *d* with the right. Tell the student that because the alphabet is written from left to right and *b* comes first in the alphabet, *b* is the letter made with the left hand. Because the letter *d* comes after *b*, it is made with the right hand.
8. Have the student trace problematic letters or words on different surfaces (for example, on sandpaper or by finger-painting).
9. Encourage the student to use cursive writing rather than manuscript, as reversals appear less frequently in cursive.
10. Do not penalize the student for reversals, but reinforce the correct letter formations.

11. During the editing stage, give the student an index card with the problematic letter or word written on it. Have the student check the spelling.

12. Help the student recall the orientation of letters by using language clues. For example, remind the student that a lowercase *b* is just an uppercase *B* that lost its top.

13. Have the student name the letter and state aloud the movement pattern made when writing a frequently reversed letter. For example, when forming the letter *b*, the student may say, "start high, line down, back up and around."

14. Place a manuscript alphabet at the student's desk so that the child may self-check letters when editing. Highlight reversed letters on the strip.

15. Separate instruction for frequently reversed letters. Practice *b* and *d* on different occasions.

16. Show the student how to trace confusing letters by writing the cursive form of the letter over the manuscript form. A cursive *b* will fit nicely over a printed *b* but not a printed *d*.

17. Teach the student that the letter *b* has a hump on its right side, the letter *d* has a hump on its left side, and the letter *p* has a tail that goes down.

18. Use a mnemonic device to distinguish between difficult-to-remember letters or numbers (for example, teach that the upward strokes in *b* and *d* form the headboards in the word *bed*).

19. Write a cue word and provide an illustration for any commonly reversed letters, such as the letter *b* with a picture of a boy, and the letter *d* with a picture of a dog. Have the student keep the words on the corner of the desk or in a spelling dictionary.

You can use the following steps to practice frequently reversed letters or numbers:

1. Write a large letter or number on a piece of paper or on the chalkboard.

2. Have the student trace over the letter or number several times while saying the letter or number name.

3. Have the student write the symbol while looking at a model.

4. Have the student write the symbol from memory and compare it to the model.

In addition to reversing letters, some students transpose letters in words. Common examples include writing *saw* for *was* or *on* for *no*. Similarly to working with letters, you might use the following steps to help students eliminate transpositions:

1. Have the student write the confusing word on a card.

2. Have the student say the word while tracing it with his or her finger.

3. When the student feels comfortable, remove the card and ask the student to write the word from memory.

4. If the word is spelled incorrectly, repeat steps 1 through 3 until the word is spelled correctly.

WRITING SPEED

As increased writing demands are placed on students, handwriting speed increases in importance. One central instructional goal of handwriting instruction is to help students develop a fluid, rapid style. Practice contributes to automaticity as the motor patterns needed for legible writing become more firmly established.

Timed Writings

One technique that can be used to improve writing rate and fluency and to encourage reluctant writers to increase their productivity is daily timed writings. Several variations have been suggested (Alvarez, 1983). You can use the following steps:

1. Choose a topic or have students choose a topic for writing.

2. Have students write about the topic for a set amount of minutes.
3. Encourage students to try to write more words than they did on the previous day.
4. At the end of the time period, have students count the number of words, and record the word count on the top of the paper. You might also have students count the numbers of letters written or the numbers of sentences.
5. Check the scores and record the word count on a chart or graph. Do not count words from repetitious or incomplete sentences.
6. If desired, provide points for the number of written words that may be exchanged for certain privileges.

SELF-EVALUATION

Self-evaluation can help students during the handwriting process. Because self-appraisal is important to all learning, you will want to encourage students to evaluate their own skill development.

Self-Evaluation Strategy

One easy-to-follow self-evaluation strategy uses the following steps (Blandford & Lloyd, 1987):

1. Am I sitting properly for handwriting?
2. Do I have my paper positioned properly?
3. Do I have a correct pencil grip?
4. Do all my letters seem to be on the line?
5. Do all my tall letters seem to touch or come close to touching the top line?
6. Do my short letters take up only half the space between lines?
7. Do I have the right amount of space between words?

Where necessary, you can expand this strategy as follows:

1. Have the student use a card to guide handwriting. Add two reminders to the bottom of the card:
   a. Consult the letter chart on the desk when you forget how to form a letter.
   b. Strive for neat handwriting.
2. Read the statements and questions on the task card to the student.
3. Model how to perform each of the activities referred to in the questions.
4. In a grid to the right of the questions, model the recording of student performance:
   a. Place a check by each question followed.
   b. Place an X by those not followed.
5. Provide the student with practice using the task card with teacher guidance and feedback.
6. Have the student read the task card before attempting any written assignment.
7. During all written assignments, have the student follow the self-instructional questions and record performance on the grid.

Self-Evaluation Checklist

You might also have students complete checklists to evaluate how they feel about their handwriting. Students read the questions and check "yes" or "no" next to each question. Figure 5.10 presents a sample handwriting evaluation scale.

Appearance

A school boy brought home his card with a teacher's notation to his parents: "Your son's handwriting is so bad that we don't know if he can spell."

—Earl Wilson

Because the appearance of assignments may influence a teacher's grading, all students can benefit from knowing what factors help to make a paper more attractive. You can help students acquire this knowledge by discussing why papers should have a neat appearance, providing

Name: _____

Handwriting Evaluation Scale

		Yes	No
1.	I would rather print than write in cursive.		
2.	I combine print and cursive when I write.		
3.	I would like my writing to look better.		
4.	It takes a lot of energy for me to write.		
5.	Writing is hard for me.		
6.	Teachers think my writing looks neat.		
7.	I have to think about how to make the letters when I write.		
8.	I write lowercase letters correctly.		
9.	I write uppercase letters correctly.		
10.	I hold my pencil too tightly.		
11.	My hand gets tired when I write.		
12.	My letters all have the same slant or go in the same direction.		
13.	My letters are the right size.		
14.	I like the way my papers look.		
15.	I have trouble writing on paper without lines.		
16.	I would rather write with a pen than a pencil.		
17.	I pay attention to the margins on the paper.		
18.	My writing is easy for others to read.		
19.	I can write quickly and easily.		
20.	I would rather write on the computer than with a pencil or pen.		

Figure 5.10. Handwriting Evaluation Scale.

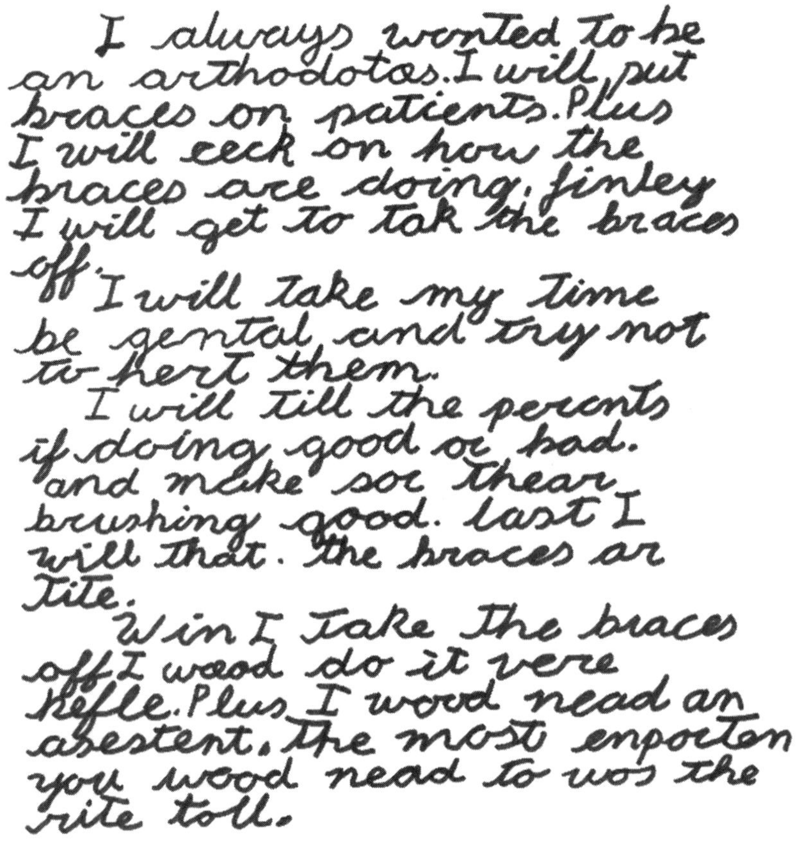

I always wonted to be an arthodotas. I will put braces on patients. Plus I will eeck on how the braces are doing. finley I will get to tak the braces off. I will take my time be gental, and try not to hert them. I will till the perents if doing good or bad. and make soc thear brushing good. last I will that. the braces ar tite. Win I Take the braces off I wood do it vere tefle. Plus I wood nead an abestent. the most enporten you wood nead to wos the rite toll.

Figure 5.11. Yuji's Paper.

examples of good papers, and encouraging students to evaluate the appearance of their own papers. Figure 5.11 illustrates the writing of Yuji, an eighth-grade student. He was asked to write about what kind of job he would like to have as an adult. Although his severe difficulties with spelling are readily apparent, it is clear that he is trying to present a neat paper. (His name, date, and class were deleted from the top of the paper for confidentiality.) You can see that Yuji has observed margins and indented his paragraphs.

Neat handwriting and efficient keyboarding are particularly important for students who struggle with spelling. In general, people tend to be far more forgiving of spelling errors when the handwriting is neat and the paper has an attractive appearance. Michael, a fifth-grade student, struggles with spelling, but has developed nice handwriting. In Figure 5.12 he retells one of his favorite jokes. Notice how his neat handwriting reduces attention to his spelling errors.

How Strategy

One strategy for evaluating the appearance of finished products is the HOW strategy (Archer, 1988). The mnemonic HOW helps students determine HOW your paper should look. To use this strategy, students review the following elements:

H = Heading provided

1. Write your name on the paper.
2. Write the date.
3. Name the subject.
4. Write a page number if necessary.

O = Organized

1. Use only the front side of the paper.

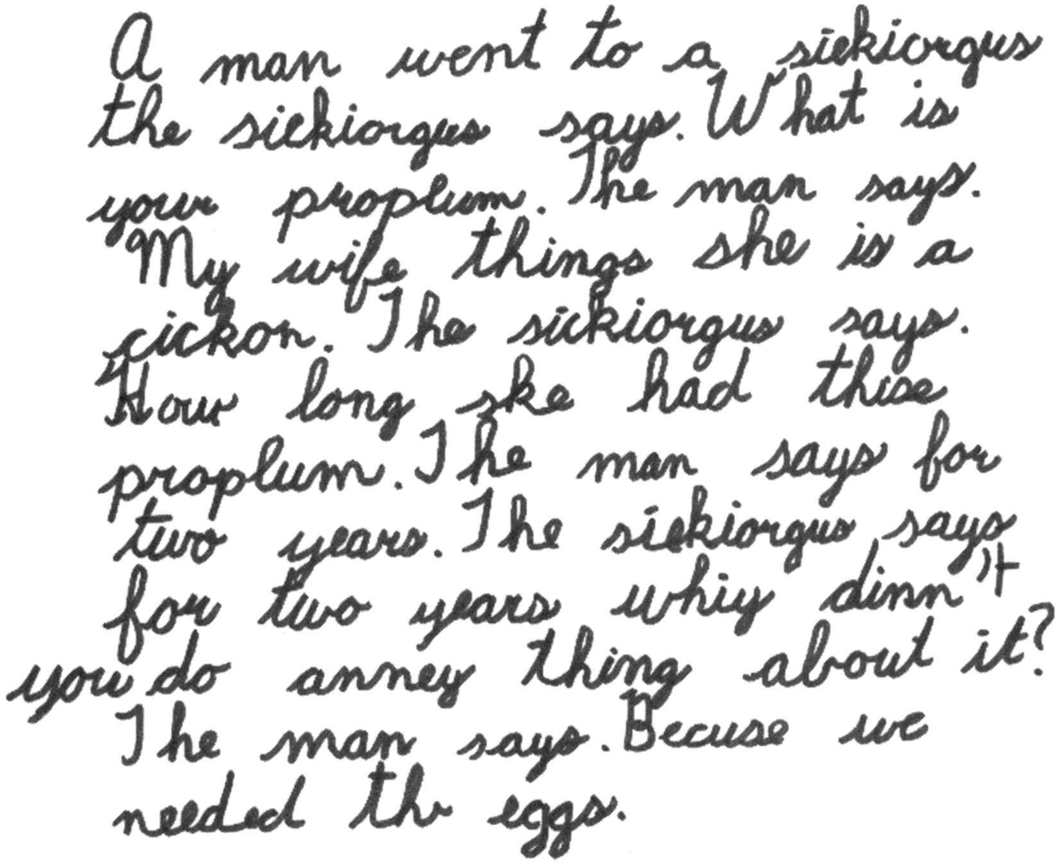

A man went to a sickiorgus the sickiorgus says. What is your proplem. The man says. My wife things she is a cickon. The sickiorgus says. How long zke had this proplum. The man says for two years. The sickiorgus says for two years whiy dinn't you do anney thing about it? The man says. Becuse we needed th eggs.

Figure 5.12. Michael's Joke.

2. Write within the left margin.
3. Write within the right margin.
4. Leave at least one blank line at the top.
5. Leave at least one blank line at the bottom.
6. Check for spacing.

W = Written neatly

1. Check that words and numbers are written on the lines.
2. Write words and numbers neatly.
3. Check that erasures and crossed-out words or numbers are neat.

Visual Illustration

Some students may benefit from an example that illustrates how a paper should look, such as the one presented in Figure 5.13.

Students can actually write drafts into this type of frame.

INFORMAL ASSESSMENT

Handwriting is a foundational skill that underlies and influences the quality of a student's written expression. It is an important skill needed for academic success throughout the school years and is a critical life skill in adulthood. Therefore, as a teacher you need to monitor your students' performance and progress in handwriting so that you can provide appropriate instruction. The simplest means of evaluating a student's handwriting is to use your powers of observation. Examine a student's writing and writing behaviors closely and make note of any errors or problem areas. You can

Figure 5.13. Visual Illustration.

observe each area reviewed in this chapter, such as the student's pencil grasp, pressure, orientation, spacing, posture, or letter formation.

Maintaining a portfolio of the student's writing samples is another way to monitor progress and identify instructional needs. Comparing a student's writing to rubrics, or grade-level exemplars, is still another means of evaluating handwriting. Any writing assignment, such as a spelling task or composition, is an opportunity to observe the quality of the student's handwriting.

Many teachers are using curriculum-based measures (CBMs) to monitor progress and inform instructional planning. These measures are short, standardized, and easy to score. They directly measure the skill and are sensitive to changes across time, making them ideal for monitoring growth. You can even develop your own curriculum-based measures. More information about CBMs is provided in Chapter Eight of this text.

One area of focus for informal assessment of handwriting is to count the number of letters or words written correctly within a given time period, such as one minute. Timed writings, discussed in this chapter, are an informal means to assess a student's skill level, to monitor progress, and to make adjustments to instruction. For example, you might use the "mad minute printing" or the "mad minute cursive" activity to encourage speed and fluency of writing. You could ask students to write the alphabet, or a sentence containing all the letters of the alphabet, as quickly as they can for a one- to three-minute period of time. The students can record and graph their letters-per-minute progress, which motivates them and encourages them to be responsible for their own learning. Your state standards, or your handwriting curriculum, may provide specific benchmarks for each grade. On average, you may expect third-grade students to print about forty letters per minute (lpm), fourth-grade students fifty lpm, and fifth-grade students sixty lpm.

EXAMPLES OF COMMERCIAL PROGRAMS

Several commercial programs are available to assist students with the development of handwriting skill. One example is *Handwriting without Tears* (www.hwtears.com). The program is comprehensive and relatively inexpensive, and it provides instruction in readiness, printing, and cursive. Readiness activities are presented using wood pieces that represent big and little curves and big and little lines. The program is developmentally based and can assist students who have difficulty with legibility, spacing, or reversals. The materials for printing and cursive instruction include both teacher guides and student workbooks. The *Getty-Dubay Italic Handwriting Series* published by Portland State University provides a comprehensive handwriting curriculum for grades K–6 (http://www.cep.pdx.edu/titles/italic_series/index.shtml). It provides easy-to-follow directions, tips, and practice materials. In addition, it uses a unique "Look-Plan-Practice" approach to self-assessment that increases students' abilities to monitor their own performance.

Startwrite Handwriting Software (www.startwrite.com) allows parents or teachers to create customized handwriting worksheets in manuscript, manu-cursive, or cursive. Letters can be printed in dotted or solid line formats up to a maximum size of two inches. You can incorporate shading, stroke arrows, guidelines, and letter starting dots. *Fonts4Teachers* provides similar software for making customized handwriting sheets in a variety of fonts (http://fonts4teachers.com). *Pencil Pete's Educational Software and Worksheets* is another software program that provides a handwriting curriculum and worksheets for practice (http://www.jjmdesigns.com). An animated Pencil Pete illustrates letter formation so that students can see how to form the letters before practicing on their own.

CONCLUSION

With the use of computers, legible writing is accomplished with ease. Many students find that it is easier to write on computers than with pencils and pens, particularly because word processors make it so easy to revise and edit. Teachers also find papers easier to read and can respond more readily to content. The question may then arise: "Why should we care about handwriting skill in the age of computers?" Conceivably, the time may come when handwriting skill decreases in value because word-processing programs are available in all classrooms. But even though the information-processing age is here, the resources are still not. Computers for every student are not standard equipment in the majority of classrooms.

Furthermore, even if a time comes when each elementary child has a laptop computer, handwriting will still be a necessary skill. Situations will always exist in and out of school in which handwriting is needed. Handwriting difficulties still will interfere with note-taking and performance on essay exams and even affect the judgment of an employer when reading a job application. In addition, people will always find themselves in places where computers are impractical, unavailable, or unnecessary. Many people will still, at times, prefer to use handwriting for (a) writing letters to friends and relatives, (b) writing short notes to others, (c) filling out forms, (d) taking notes in classes, or (e) recording messages and ideas when away from school or the workplace. Although technological advances have had an impact on the daily use of handwriting for some people, handwriting skill is still important.

Development of legible, fluent handwriting is an important goal for all students. Students who have trouble writing legibly often require specific instructional strategies that provide enough practice to make the actions automatic. Many handwriting difficulties are related to inadequate classroom instruction, as students do not spend enough time in regular, systematic practice with feedback. In general, effective handwriting programs provide students with modeling, practice, review, reinforcement, and feedback. Fortunately, with sufficient practice and guidance, most children do develop legible writing styles.

chapter
6

Building Basic Writing Skills

"You ought to write 'A Happy Birthday' on it. That was what I wanted to ask you," said Pooh. "Because my spelling is Wobbly. It's good spelling but it Wobbles, and the letters get in the wrong places. Would you write 'A Happy Birthday' on it for me?"

—A. A. Milne

As noted by Winnie the Pooh as he attempts to write a birthday card, poor basic skills, particularly spelling, can affect one's ability to communicate clearly in writing. Unfortunately, many students have difficulties mastering basic writing skills and, consequently, require systematic interventions. In some classrooms, however, teachers focus mainly on providing instruction in written expression, and even question the importance of or need for direct instruction in basic skills. They believe that instruction in basic skills can be accomplished within natural writing tasks. Other teachers believe that skill instruction is accomplished more easily out of context. In reality, both approaches can be effective and are appropriate depending on the needs of the writer. As a general rule, however, writing instruction is most meaningful when it is provided within a student's own written communications, but struggling writers often need more explicit, targeted instruction in basic skills.

This chapter discusses educational interventions, as well as a few commercial programs, for the areas of spelling, usage (punctuation, capitalization, and syntax), and editing for errors in basic skills. Each section provides descriptions of specific instructional strategies. Although the majority of the strategies are not presented within the context of writing activities, they can be easily incorporated into the editing of papers or used as supplementary instructional techniques.

SPELLING

It is a damn poor mind indeed which can think of only one way to spell a word.

—Andrew Jackson, 1833

Correct spelling is one important component of written expression. Because of the pervasiveness of spelling problems among students with learning disabilities, quality spelling instruction is essential. Although knowledge of linguistic principles related to spelling increases developmentally, many students with learning disabilities develop more slowly in spelling skill than their peers without disabilities. They also have more difficulty detecting and correcting their spelling errors. Bradley, a fourth-grade student, completed the worksheet presented in Figure 6.1. He was asked to answer questions about the story in complete sentences. Although he received credit for most of his responses, the teacher wrote the comment, "Please spell words correctly."

NAME _Bradley_   DATE _2-20_

90%

ANSWER THESE QUESTIONS ABOUT THE STORY IN COMPLETE SENTENCES.

SOCKS   _Please spell words correctly_

1. How did Socks feel about the diet the Brickers put him on? Why did he feel this way?

    He did not like it becas they were st starving him. _because_ _starving_

2. How did Tiffy feel when Socks left her house? Why did she feel this way?

    Whid Hmo the eat ne food, _any_

3. What did Mrs. Risley do that made Socks liker her immediately?

    She scratr his back and camd hin

4. What was Socks really hungry for and who gave it to him?

    Mrs. Risley gave him Love and attention.

5. If you were Socks, how would you let the Brickers know that you needed love and attention?

    I Wood talk them _would_

Figure 6.1. Bradley's Worksheet.

Although one can empathize with the teacher's frustration regarding Bradley's spelling performance, merely asking him to spell words correctly will not improve his spelling. The important consideration is that students spell the best they can using their present level of knowledge. Bradley is spelling words as accurately as he can at this point in his development.

Invented Spelling

As children develop as writers, they demonstrate increasing knowledge of the letters and sounds of the English language. When first learning to write, they articulate the individual phonemes of spoken language to guide their spelling attempts. In many classrooms, beginning writers are encouraged to write words

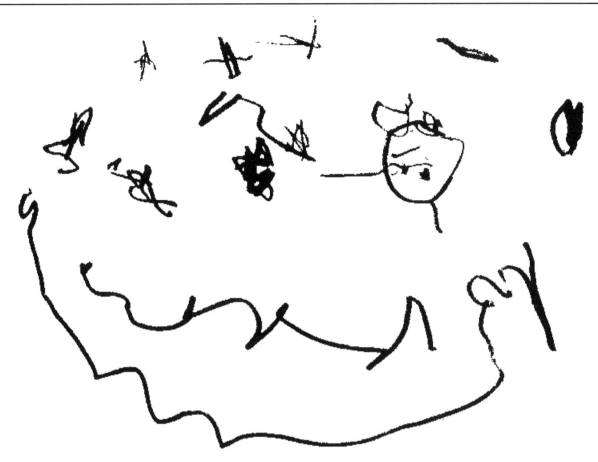

Figure 6.2. Graham's Story.

the way they sound or to "invent" their spellings. These invented spellings reveal a child's developing understanding and knowledge of sound-symbol relationships and the rules that govern our writing system. Encouraging kindergarten and first-grade students to engage in invented spelling during writing can increase both their reading and spelling skills. A more accurate description than invented spelling (which sounds like the spellings are being made up again each time they are written) is "temporary" spelling. Students are learning to put sounds in order, which is an initial (temporary) phase of learning to spell.

Beginning writers often draw and scribble, attempting to create forms that resemble symbols. Graham, a two-year old, tells his parents that he is going to do his homework. He grabs a piece of paper and a marker pen and prepares his story in Figure 6.2. When finished he says that he will write his name. At the top he attempts to make an *H* and then an *A*,

the first two letters of his sister's name, Haley. Graham has watched Haley write her name many times, and he assumes this is how you write your name.

As knowledge of the English spelling system develops and students become more familiar with print, they exhibit increasing sensitivity to English spelling patterns, and their attempted spellings evolve systematically toward more standard forms. This evolving knowledge of our spelling system appears to be reflected in several developmental stages or phases.

Spelling Phases

Research regarding spelling errors indicates that children appear to progress through several developmental phases when learning to spell. Although theorists vary somewhat in the number and description of these phases, the basic developmental progressions are similar.

Figure 6.3. Alexis's Story.

Figure 6.4. Toby's Story.

For the last two lines she proudly announced, "I'm just going to write the rest in cursive."

Gradually, a student's written products start to look more like real stories. Figure 6.4 illustrates a story written by Toby, a first-grade student. Toby understands that written symbols convey meaning, but he does not understand that letters represent sounds.

A few older students also have not grasped what is known as the alphabetic principle, or the knowledge that the letters of our language represent the sounds of our language. Edgar, a sixth-grade student, was asked to write several responses to questions by his teacher, Mr. Steen. Figure 6.5 presents Mr. Steen's questions, Edgar's responses, and Edgar's oral explanation of his responses.

Major Sounds

At the next phase of development, children understand that letters are used to represent sounds, but they only represent the sounds that are easiest to hear. In some instances,

No or Limited Sound-Symbol Correspondence

In the initial stages of learning to spell, a child will combine a string of unrelated letters to communicate a message. Figure 6.3 presents a story by Alexis, a kindergarten student. Notice that her story contains both letters and numbers.

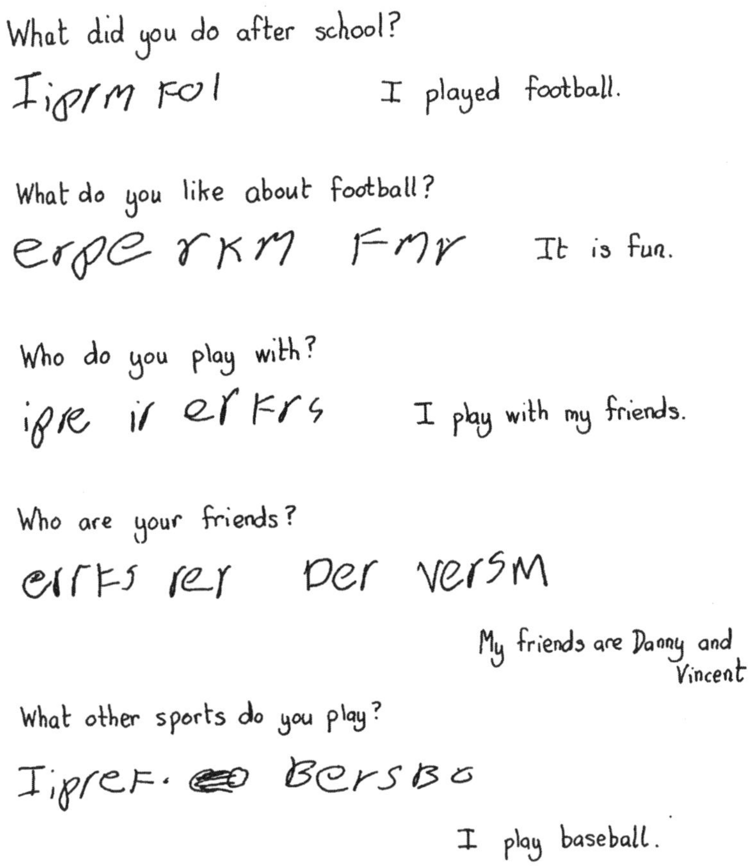

What did you do after school?

Iiprm Fol   I played football.

What do you like about football?

erpe rKm Fmr   It is fun.

Who do you play with?

ipe ir erFrs   I play with my friends.

Who are your friends?

erFs rer   Der versM

My friends are Danny and
Vincent

What other sports do you play?

Iipref. eo BersBo

I play baseball.

Figure 6.5. Edgar's Responses to Questions.

Figure 6.6. Luca's Picture of an Alien.

I got bt bi a r.c.pn.
and wnt to the sbl
nrsi. She gav. me ier.
Andy

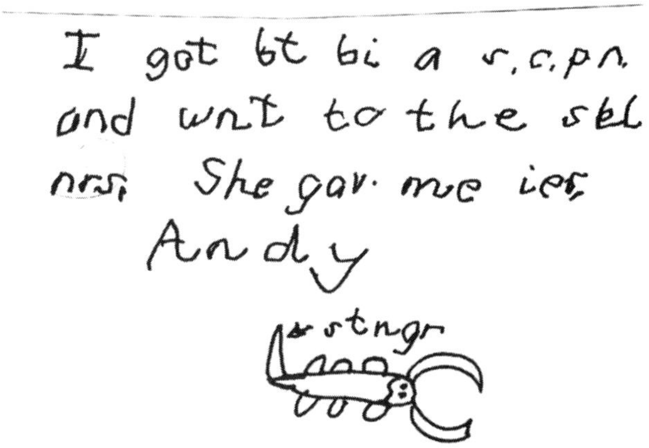

Figure 6.7. Andy's Writing.

students will write the names of letters that are close to the letter sounds, such as spelling the word *while* as "yl." During this stage, although spellings may follow logical linguistic patterns,

very few correct spellings are known. Figure 6.6 show's Luca's picture of an alien. Notice that he writes the letters from right to left, but does include the three easiest-to-hear sounds.

Toward the end of this phase, a student may know consonant sounds, long vowel sounds, and an occasional sight word. Figure 6.7 illustrates the writing of Andy, a third-grade student.

Figure 6.8. Emily's Note to Her Sister.

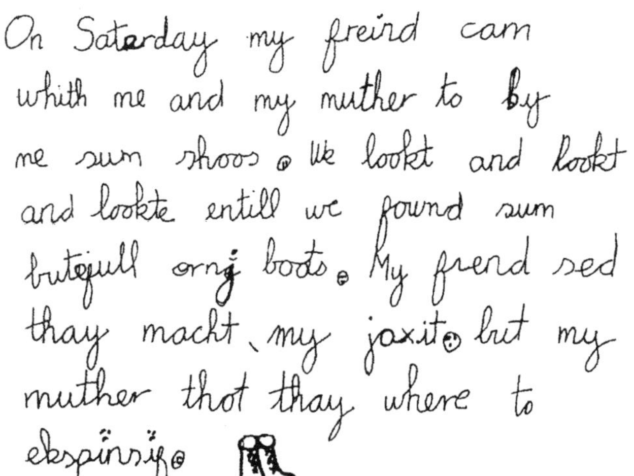

On Saterday my freird cam
whith me and my muther to by
me sum shoos. We lookt and lookt
and lookte entill we found sum
butejull ornj boots. My frend sed
thay macht my jaxit but my
muther thot thay where to
ekspinsiv.

Figure 6.9. June's Writing.

Most Sounds

During the next phase, writers produce spellings that demonstrate good sound-symbol correspondence. They attempt to record all of the sounds within a word and order them in the correct sound sequence. Vast levels of developmental differences exist among children. Figure 6.8 shows a note that Emily, a kindergarten student, put on her door for her sister Joanna. The word *quiet* is spelled exactly as it sounds, and she even has spelled the word *knock* with a *-ck* at the end. Clearly, Emily will have little difficulty learning how to spell.

By the end of third grade, most students are able to use both sounds and visual features when spelling words. A few students, however, seem to get stuck within a phase. Figure 6.9 illustrates the writing of June. Although she is in sixth grade, June still tries to spell words as they sound, not as how they look.

Visual Patterns

During the next phase, the writer demonstrates awareness of many of the conventions of English spelling or orthography. For example, the student spells the past tense of a verb as *-ed* even when the ending sounds like a /t/, such as in the word *trapped*. During this phase, the writer shows increasing understanding of English morphology and orthography and can spell words, both the way they look and the way they sound.

Correct Spelling

Correct spelling requires the use of multiple strategies. The writer must be able to sequence sounds correctly and recall the word-specific features and orthographic patterns of English spelling. The writer is also able to use knowledge of morphology and vocabulary as aids to accurate spelling. This final phase does not mean that the writer spells all words correctly, but rather that he or she is able to use all facets of language when spelling: phonology, orthography, morphology, and semantics. In addition, spelling errors that are made are usually minor in nature and reflect possible English spellings (for example, spelling *receive* as *recieve*).

Some children progress through these phases very rapidly, whereas others progress more slowly. For some students learning to spell is easy, whereas others find it extremely difficult. Poor spellers would like to become good spellers, but many times they do not. Their spellings do not improve simply by being exposed to correct spellings while reading. Instead, each word has to be practiced and learned systematically. Although many students with learning disabilities go through the same phases as their peers, their rates of development are slower and they seem to get stuck in certain phases unless targeted intervention is provided.

Latif, an eighth-grade student, is a good reader but a poor speller. When writing his book report on *Tom Sawyer*, he spelled the name *Becky* as "Beacy," "Beckey," "Becky," "Becy," "Beecy," and "Beacey." Despite numerous exposures to her name when reading the book, Latif did not retain the correct spelling. This is partially because reading is so much easier than spelling. All you have to do is recognize the word, whereas with spelling you have to reproduce the word in its entirety. Spelling skill is not, however, highly related to general verbal competence. Some students who speak well and may even have advanced vocabularies have trouble learning to spell.

In contrast to students such as Latif, good spellers learn to spell easily. They note spellings when reading and quickly acquire a substantial spelling vocabulary. For them, progress in spelling is rapid, and they retain the correct spellings of words once they have been mastered.

Factors Affecting Performance

Several cognitive and linguistic factors affect spelling development. Some students may have trouble learning how to put the sounds of the words in order because of poor phonological awareness. Others can order the sounds, but have trouble memorizing the orthographic patterns, particularly in words that contain irregular spelling patterns. Knowledge of phonology (the speech sounds), orthography (the visual spelling patterns), morphology (the meaning units), and semantics (vocabulary) are all necessary for spelling words correctly. A writer may have difficulty with one or all of these linguistic abilities.

Phonology

Phonology encompasses the sound system of a language. Phonological awareness then refers to knowledge of speech sounds in spoken words. This awareness is often measured by tasks involving rhyming words, matching initial or ending consonants, isolating single sounds from words, deleting phonemes, or counting the number of phonemes in spoken words. Phonological awareness is a prerequisite skill for learning how to spell. In order to spell, one has to listen to the sounds and then assign specific letters to represent these sounds. Some students with spelling difficulties do not understand that spoken words can be segmented or broken into syllables and syllables can be segmented into distinct phonemes. Thus they have limited knowledge of sound-symbol relationships.

Figure 6.10 presents the writing of Kirsten, a second-grade girl. The title of the assignment, taken from a popular children's book, was written on the board. Although Kirsten has specific ideas with regard to her horrible day, deciphering the meaning of her passage is difficult because she does not represent many of the phonemes (speech sounds) with possible graphemes (letter or letters).

Phonological processes are most critical for early spelling development. Knowledge of phonology precedes knowledge of orthography and morphology. When students have poor phonological awareness, they have difficulty segmenting, analyzing, and synthesizing speech sounds. Even young adults with spelling difficulties can still struggle with the associations between sounds and spellings. In some cases, the problem is severe. Figure 6.11 illustrates

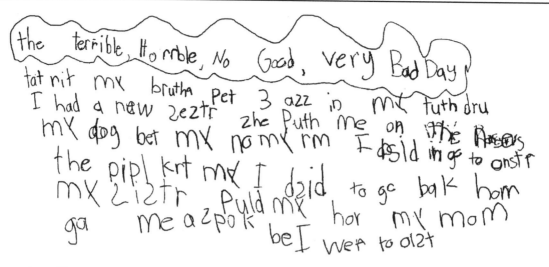

Figure 6.10. Kirsten's Passage.

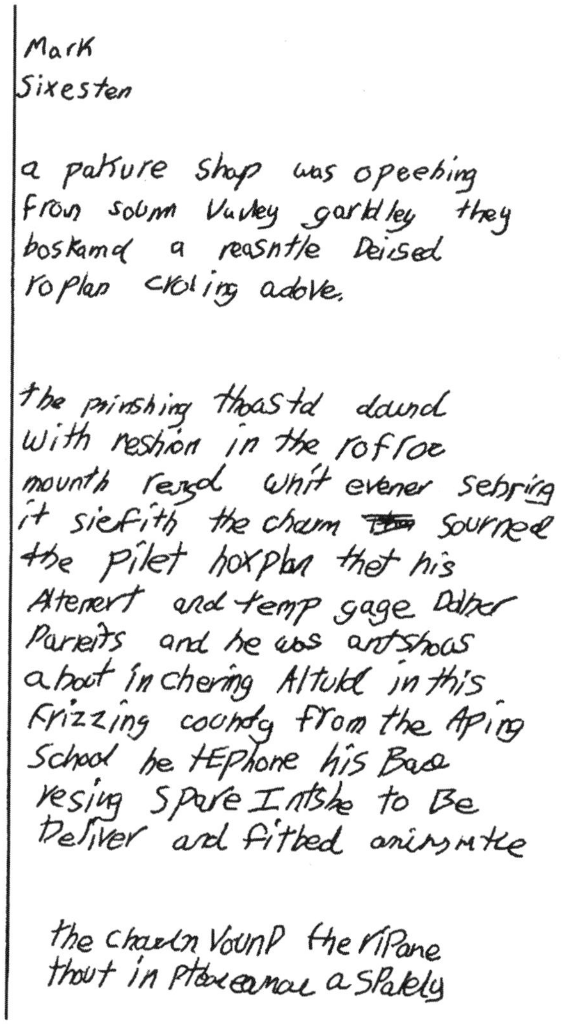

Mark
Sixesten

a paKture shop was opeehing
from sobm Vuvley garldley they
boskamd a reasntle Deised
roplan croling adove.

the pinshing thoastd daund
with reshion in the rofroe
mounth reagd whit evener sehrig
it siefith the chuwm ~~t~~ sourned
the pilet hoxplan thet his
Atenert and temp gage Dther
Pareits and he wos antshous
about inchering Altuld in this
frizzing countg from the Aping
school he tEPhone his Bad
resing spore Intshe to Be
Deliver and fitbed aniysmtte

the charln vounP the riPane
thout in ptoxeanac a sPakely

Figure 6.11. Mark's Paragraph.

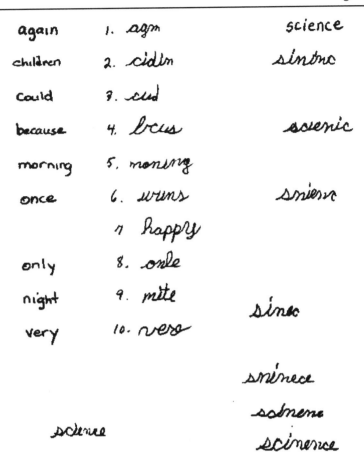

Figure 6.12. Nalan's Spellings.

a paragraph written by Mark, a sixteen-year-old with extreme difficulty translating English phonemes into graphemes. Although Mark knew what he was trying to write, his thoughts are very difficult to decipher.

Orthography

Orthography is the writing system of a language. Spellings are represented by graphemes, which are the letters and letter strings that are used to represent the phonemes. Knowledge of letter patterns is critical for words that contain irregular spelling elements. To spell some words correctly, one must be able to get a mental picture of the word or the specific orthographic patterns. Some students have great difficulty retaining visual images of words.

Figure 6.12 shows the attempted spellings of Nalan, a fifth-grade student. Nalan is shown the correct spelling of a word from her adapted spelling list, such as *because* or *once*. Notice that Nalan has just viewed the word, but she still writes "bcus" and "wuns," spellings that show knowledge of phonology but not orthography. Her teacher next showed Nalan the word *science*, then covered the word, and had Nalan attempt to write it. Because the word was incorrect, she showed Nalan the word seven more times. Finally, Nalan was getting frustrated so her teacher asked her to just copy the word, which appeared in the bottom left corner. Nalan looked up at the word *science* five times as she was attempting to reproduce it correctly.

Similarly, take a look at Ethan's attempts to spell the word *game* (Figure 6.13). His teacher wrote the word *game* on the top of the page, and then asked Ethan to study it until he thought he could write it from memory. It took Ethan several attempts to be able to do this. Imagine how hard it would be to learn to spell if you could not retain mental images of the words.

game

gm

gem

gem

gemr

gamr

game

Figure 6.13. Ethan's Attempts to Spell the Word *Game*.

Difficulty recalling orthographic patterns can result in spellings that often violate basic spelling rules. The spellings may reveal good knowledge of sound-symbol relationships but poor memory for letter sequences. The writer tends to write words the way they sound,

rather than the way they look. In contrast, writers who are good spellers use orthographic knowledge well.

Figure 6.14 presents the writing of Felicia, a seventh-grade student with a severe spelling disability. Analysis of Felicia's spelling reveals her insensitivity to and difficulty with the recall of English orthographic patterns. Because she has trouble remembering letter sequences, she spells words primarily the way they sound. Felicia even has trouble remembering how to spell simple words such as *when*.

Joseph, a fifth-grade student, has similar difficulties. Several of his journal entries are presented in Figure 6.15. Within the same page of his journal, he has spelled the word *yesterday* three different ways. He also reversed the letters *b* and *d* several times.

As can be seen from the writings of Felicia and Joseph, spelling can be a significant, persistent problem if you have trouble recalling the visual images of words. Unfortunately, markedly impaired spelling skill can affect the development of other aspects of writing as well.

Morphology

Morphology represents the meaning units in language. Difficulties with morphology can affect both spelling and vocabulary development. Essentially, morphology forms a bridge between spelling and vocabulary. Orthographic development and morphological knowledge often develop in tandem. Just as a phoneme refers to the smallest unit of sound, a morpheme refers to the smallest unit of meaning. For example, the word *girls* is composed of two morphemes, the meaning unit *girl* and the plural marker *s*. Understanding that past tense is typically spelled with the letters -*ed* can guide a student to spell the words jumped and walked correctly, even though they sound like they end with the letter *t*.

Semantics

The main way that knowledge of word meanings affects spelling is in understanding and

sevent grade is werd. Your alwase moving and enstad of a dechs you have a lock. It werd the first day of tonur hiashool aspeshole at Safford which the rotating sistane. Evabody is midst ye and youwoe wandring ware yougo nexcot. The best part about the rotating sistem is evie three days it in nomte I like it but wen it is moml is maast of the time wene it is 1-2-3 I get to lunch ner the frunt df I'm not the frist wn one.

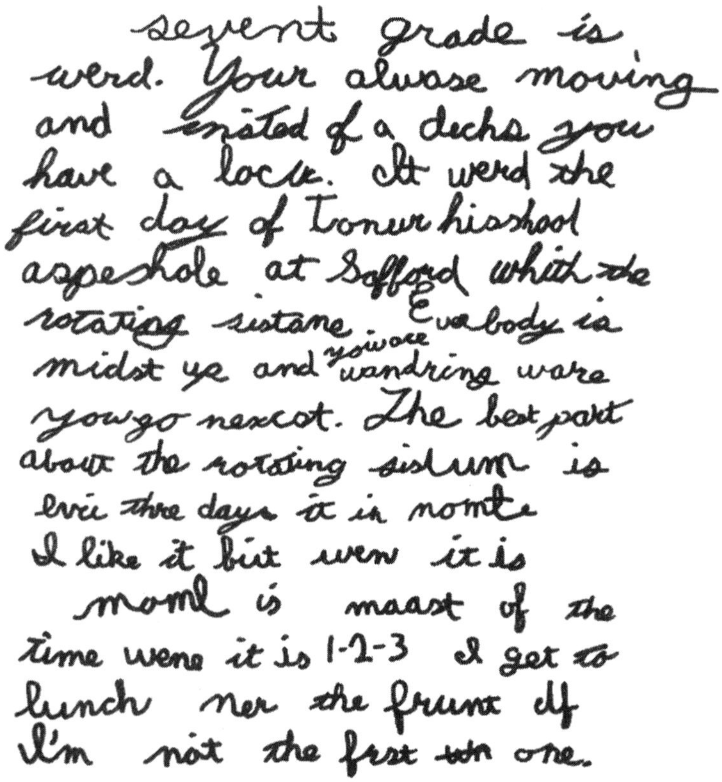

Figure 6.14. Felicia's Writing.

I got noting to rite Adout Begse I Didnt Do a tin Ersday

EstDay me and my Boutreing wat to the river Jongrs I sasd Brid

esat beay I went suming at rive r

satre Day I uin tot the indan rens and I went hunting

yserday done Baivndr

Bure a windoe with my BeBe gun

Figure 6.15. Joseph's Journal Entries.

choosing the correct homophones when writing. Homophones are words that are pronounced the same way, but differ in meaning and often in spelling (for example, *pear* and *pair* or *air* and *heir*). Many of the most commonly used homophones can be quite confusing to students who struggle with spelling (such as *to, too*, and *two* and *there, their*, and *they're*), and explicit instruction with practice is required to master these spellings. As noted before, poor spelling can also limit word choice and affect vocabulary development if students do not feel safe experimenting with and writing words that they are uncertain of how to spell.

Information about word origins can also help students understand why words are spelled in certain ways. For example, many scientific terms are of Greek origin, so a /f/ sound is spelled with a *ph*, such as in photosynthesis. Words of Greek origin with a /k/ sound are often spelled with a *ch*, such as in chromosome. You will find that the more you understand about spelling and English speech sounds, the better equipped you will be to understand children's misspellings and to guide them effectively in their development.

Children's ability to spell gradually increases as their linguistic knowledge expands. Once children can segment sounds and have some knowledge of sound-letter connections, they spell the sounds that they hear. They have knowledge of some aspects of the English sound system, and their misspellings reflect their developing knowledge.

Spelling and Speech Sounds

This information was adapted from four sources (Mather & Goldstein, 2008; Moats, 2000; Read, 1971; Wilde, 1997). Although this information is somewhat technical, you will find that if you understand the English sound system, it will help you to understand why students spell words the way they do, as well as what you can do to help them.

Phonemes are the smallest sound units that are represented by graphemes (various letter units). Although the English language has approximately 42 to 44 phonemes, there are approximately 250 graphemes. For example, consider the phoneme /f/. This sound can be spelled with several different graphemes: *f, ff, ph, gh*, and even *lf*, as in *half*. As a result of several alternative spelling possibilities, spelling is much more difficult than reading words. Certain rules, however, regarding the allowable position of letters within words underlie the spelling system. For example, an English word cannot begin with the letters *ff* or end with the letter *v*. Although sometimes a beginning writer may start a word with the letters *ck*, they soon realize that this spelling does not occur at the beginning of words.

English is composed of two types of sounds: consonants and vowels. If someone were to ask you what a vowel is, you would probably say: *a, e, i, o*, and *u*. Although these letters do represent vowel sounds, they do not define a vowel. The definition of vowels and

consonants has to do with the flow of air as the sound is produced. For vowel sounds, the air flows through the mouth unobstructed, whereas for consonant sounds, the airflow is cut off partially or completely.

Consonants

Consonants can be single letters or they can also be combined into blends, digraphs, and trigraphs. Blends are two or more consonant sounds that occur in sequence but retain their identity (for example, *bl* and *fr*). Digraphs and trigraphs refer to two or three adjacent letters that represent only one phoneme that is not represented by the pronunciation of either letter alone (such as *sh, gh*, or *tch*). Digraphs are particularly hard for children to spell because they cannot hear the letter sounds or names. Therefore, children may leave out one letter in a digraph, spelling /ch/ with the letter *c* or *h*.

Linguists classify consonants by both the place of articulation and the manner of articulation. What we will see is that children's spelling errors are often reasonable and involve confusions either about voicing (such as /b/ for /p/) or the place or manner of articulation (such as a fricative for a stop).

Place of Articulation

We pronounce various sounds using different parts of our mouths. Sounds can be made in the following places:

1. Labial: lips
2. Dental: teeth
3. Alveolar: ridge behind the teeth
4. Palatal: roof of the mouth
5. Velar: soft palate at the back of the mouth cavity
6. Glottal: vocal folds

Manner of Articulation

Some consonants are voiced (the vocal cords vibrate), whereas others are unvoiced (the vocal cords do not vibrate). Put your hand on your throat and say the words *pig* and *big*. Can you feel which beginning consonant uses the vocal cords?

English has the following eight pairs of unvoiced and voiced consonants:

Unvoiced	Voiced
/p/	/b/
/t/	/d/
/k/	/g/
/f/	/v/
/th/	/th/ (such as *thin* (unvoiced) and *th*umb (voiced)
/s/	/z/
/sh/	/zh/ (ship-genre)
/ch/	/j/

When letters are closed within slashes, they represent the letter sound and not the letter name. Because these pairs of sounds are so similar in production, children often confuse them when spelling. Look at Annmarie's list of her lunch at the picnic (Figure 6.16). Notice how she spells the word *potato*.

Consonants are further divided into the following five groups on the basis of how the air stream is affected as it travels through the mouth: (a) stops, (b) fricatives and affricates, (c) nasals, (d) liquids, and (e) glides.

Stops are formed by closing the stream of breath (/b/, /p/, /d/, /t/, /g/, /k/). When the /t/ and /d/ phonemes are in the middle of a word, they are often reduced to a tongue flap and are hard to distinguish (for example, *ladder* and *latter*), so a child may spell "lidl" for *little* or "spitr" for *spider*.

Fricatives are formed with friction in the mouth and a slight hissing sound (/v/, /f/, /th/, /z/, /s/, /zh/ /sh/). When writing /s/ or /z/, children often do not make a distinction between the voiced and unvoiced variants. In most instances, they choose to represent both sounds with the letter *s*.

Affricates are a stop followed by a fricative. There are only two affricates: /j/ and /ch/. Examples include *chill, chip*, and *gypsy* (has the /j/ sound). In certain contexts, /t/ and /d/ are articulated much like affricates (for example, *dress* or *trash*). Before the letter *r*, the sounds /t/ and /d/ are affricated (that is, released slowly with a resulting /sh/ sound). The affrication of stops before an /r/ is common for young children. Often, children notice this and thus produce the following types of spellings: "chran" for *train* or "jragn" or "jragin" for *dragon*. Children are likely to spell the /t/ sound as /ch/ and the /d/ sound as /j/, particularly before the letter *r*. The affrication of stops before an *r* in English continues until children learn that this pronunciation is predictable.

Nasals are formed by air going through the nose (/m/, /n/, /ng/). Say the words *went* and *wet* while holding your nose. You can tell by the sound which one travels through the nose. These consonant sounds are acquired later in development than other consonant sounds. When a nasal or liquid occurs before a voiceless stop consonant (such as /t/, /p/, or /k/), children often omit the letter for the nasal sound because it is not pronounced as strongly (for example, "jup" for *jump*). Figure 6.17 depicts a note written by Natasha, a second-grade student. Notice how she omits the nasal sound from the word *stranger*. Also, refer back to Annmarie's note in Figure 6.16. You will see

Sadwig btatow chips ice strobery

Figure 6.16. Annmarie's Picnic Lunch.

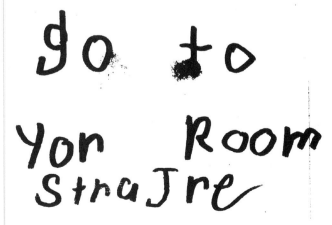

Figure 6.17. Natasha's Note.

that she is missing the letter *n* in the word *sandwich*.

The tongue does not move between a nasal with a following consonant, so the sound is much more difficult to hear. Children can learn how to detect words with nasals by holding their noses and pronouncing the words. Children may also overgeneralize the spelling of the /ng/ sound (for example, "thingk" for *think*). Or they may use the letter *g* to represent the /ng/ sound, such as in spelling the word *finger* as "fegr." They also tend to spell *-ing* endings as "eg" or "ig." You will find that errors with nasals are very common in the spellings of young children, as well as in older students who struggle with spelling.

Liquids are formed when the air stream is interrupted but with no real friction (/r/, /l/). Both liquids and nasals have an apparent vocalic quality, or vowel-like nature. When the letters *r, l, m,* or *n* come between two consonants or at the end of a word after a consonant, children perceive and write them as a separate syllable. Children thus often omit vowels with liquids and nasals. Although the vowel is usually an *e*, children rarely represent such a vowel in early writing, writing "tigr" for *tiger* or "tabl" for *table*. This omission of vowels with

liquids and nasals applies to medial consonants as well (for example, "hrd" for *heard*, "grl" for *girl*). Omissions of liquids and nasals from consonant blends account for a large proportion of spelling errors through sixth grade. When liquids and nasals are not involved, children are more likely to include a vowel in the syllable.

Glides are considered semivowels (/w/, /y/). Sometimes diphthongs or glided vowels sound like /w/ or /y/, so children spell them that way. Because they both have a vocalic quality, sometimes children confuse the /w/ sound with the /l/ sound and spell the word *saw* as "sal" or "soll."

Figure 6.18 shows a story about a giraffe by Haley, a beginning second-grade student. Notice how she spells the word *saw*, as well as her omission of the nasal sound in *went*" and her substitution of a *d* for a *t* in the word *eating*. These kinds of spellings are very typical of beginning writers.

Vowels

Children spell vowel sounds according to where they occur in the mouth. They don't know this, but that is what ends up happening. Vowels are described in terms of the position of the tongue during articulation: front or back, and

Figure 6.18. Haley's Giraffe Story.

high, mid, or low. English has about sixteen vowel sounds, thirteen simple sounds, and two or three diphthongs (sounds that are made by gliding one vowel sound to another within the same syllable, such as the *oi* in coin). Pronunciation of vowel sounds varies in different parts of the country.

Long and Short Vowel Sounds

Long (or tense) vowel sounds are often used to represent their own names in words. So a child may write "da" for *day* or "lade" for *lady*. Children often substitute long vowel sounds for the short (or lax) vowel sounds that are most similar in sound. So a child might spell *igloo* as "egloo." Vowel sounds are often distorted when they are followed by an /r/ sound, making them harder to spell than other vowels.

Diphthongs

A diphthong is a vowel that has two distinct parts that glide from one location in the mouth to another (for example, oi, ow). In certain positions, vowels are elongated. For example, the long /i/ vowel sound in the word *ride* is held out longer than in the word *write*. Children may represent this with a diphthong, especially in words in which the vowel is followed by a voiced consonant such as /d/ (for example, spelling "raed" or "riyd" for *ride* or *fly* as "fliy" and *try* as "triy").

Digraph

A digraph is one sound represented by two vowels. Children often omit one vowel from a digraph, representing the most salient sound (for example, "fet" for *feet* or "bot" for *boat*). Vowels with back glides as in *boat* or *boot* are often spelled by children with *ow*.

Schwa

A schwa sound is a weak mid-central vowel sound in an unaccented syllable (such as the first syllable in *about* and *upon*). In phonetics, this sound is represented by an upside-down lowercase *e*. The schwa sound is the most likely vowel sound to be misspelled because one cannot hear a distinct letter sound. The spelling of the unstressed schwa sound becomes particularly problematic in third grade and beyond.

Vowels are further classified by whether the tongue is high or low in the mouth and according to which part of the tongue is used—the front or back. Pronounce the following sequence of words while exaggerating the vowel sound: *beet, bit, bait, bet, bat, butt, body, bore, boat, book, boot*. Notice how your mouth moves from a closed, smiley position to a rounded, closed position (Moats, 2000). Children tend to substitute vowel sounds that are adjacent in articulation, particularly the short /e/ and /i/ sounds. Most children do not master vowel spellings until fourth grade.

As children practice applying their increasing knowledge of sound-symbol relationships to their temporary spellings, their proficiency with these connections increases. Through repeated exposures to phonological, orthographic, and morphological patterns, most children gradually come to master conventional spellings. Children with weaknesses in phonology, however, often continue to make these types of errors even into adulthood unless they are provided with intensive, systematic instruction.

Approaches

Classroom teachers provide different types of approaches to spelling instruction. As noted previously, the current instructional focus in some classrooms is on holistic writing activities and the natural development of spelling skills. Within these settings, spelling is viewed as a language-based activity that is best achieved in an environment that emphasizes the functional use of language, as well as practice of words in meaningful contexts. Errors are viewed as a natural part of learning. In these types of classrooms, students with spelling difficulties are given opportunities to experiment with our writing system in supportive environments.

This type of approach has numerous benefits for many students. A few students, however, require more intensive interventions because they do not acquire basic spelling principles just through exposure to words and word patterns.

Traditionally, many teachers have taught spelling through the use of weekly tests. Ms. Gowan, a second-grade teacher, follows this procedure. On Monday, she gives the entire class a pretest on a list of ten words presented in the reading series. On Tuesday, each student receives a copy of the list. On Wednesday, students write the words five times each. On Thursday, students are asked to study the words at home. On Friday, she gives a posttest. Although this procedure is effective for some of the students, several students have still not mastered many of the words by Friday. Ms. Gowan decides that these students require a more individualized approach.

Ms. Rollins, a third-grade teacher, decides to incorporate spelling instruction into her classroom writing activities. She abandons the weekly spelling tests and instead assists students with spelling as they edit their writing. She believes that as students write, they will naturally improve their spelling skills. Although her approach is effective for the majority of students, a few of her students do not appear to be improving in their spelling at all. Bashir, Janis, and Myeesha are not retaining any of the spelling words reviewed even when she provides mini skill lessons. As Ms. Rollins has discovered, students with limited spelling skill often require considerable practice to master the spelling of words that they use in their writing. Similar to Ms. Gowan, Ms. Rollins decides to create individualized spelling programs for these students.

Traditional approaches to spelling, such as having students study for and take weekly spelling tests, as well as more holistic approaches, such as assuming children will learn to spell by writing, are ineffective for students who struggle. For spelling tests, many of the words are too difficult or unfamiliar, or too many words are presented for students to master. By only addressing spelling errors through writing experiences, not enough time is devoted to practice and mastery of individual words and spelling patterns. Students who struggle with spelling require direct, systematic instruction regarding the English spelling system combined with meaningful classroom writing experiences. Knowledge of a few basic principles will help you provide effective spelling instruction.

Principles

For individuals who struggle with spelling, your instruction will be most effective if you follow these general principles:

1. Do not limit spelling instruction to weekly spelling tests. Discuss spellings and explain spelling patterns when editing papers.
2. Encourage children to write. Provide many opportunities to use spelling in writing.
3. In the initial phases of their learning to spell, encourage children to break apart and record each sound (phonemic segmentation).
4. So that children do not get discouraged, place emphasis on expression and content versus their spelling errors.
5. Provide daily opportunities for students to observe, verify, and correct spelling mistakes.
6. Teach children a systematic way for studying unknown words. Use a variety of word study approaches and determine which one is most effective for each child.
7. Provide at least an hour of formal spelling instruction per week.
8. Provide positive comments about spellings that are good attempts or nearly correct.
9. Teach and reinforce common patterns (for example, when teaching the word *other*, practice the words *mother, brother,* and *smother*).
10. Provide students with instruction in a few basic spelling rules.

One more important instructional principle is that students should not be penalized for poor spelling on the first drafts of assignments. In fact, you want to encourage students to focus on using descriptive vocabulary, rather than on selecting only the words they know how to spell. All in-class written products are then considered to be rough drafts, and correct spelling is not part of the grading criterion. Unfortunately, as discussed in Chapter Two, some students receive low grades on content area assignments because of poor spelling.

One final caution regarding teaching spelling is that you need to know how to pronounce the phonemes of English correctly. You want to say the sounds clearly and accurately. One common mistake that some teachers make is adding a schwa sound (unstressed vowel sound) to consonants. They will describe the /b/ as "buh" and the /m/ sound as "muh." Although this makes it easier to project the sound, it really makes the consonant have two phonemes, rather than just one. Look at Aaron's spelling test in Figure 6.19. When dictating his spelling words, his fourth-grade teacher was elongating the phonemes to help him hear the sounds. Notice the extra schwa sound Aaron is placing at the end of the words *dream* and *called*. Also, imagine how slowly his teacher must be saying the word *hole*. Although her intentions were good, you can see the importance of pronouncing speech sounds clearly and accurately.

Spelling Rules

Although you do not want to teach too many spelling rules, instruction in a few basic spelling rules can help students avoid certain types of spelling errors. As you introduce each rule, provide practice in using the rule. Here are several of the most important spelling rules:

1. The most common way to form the plural of nouns is to add the letter *s* to the singular (example, *cat, cats*).

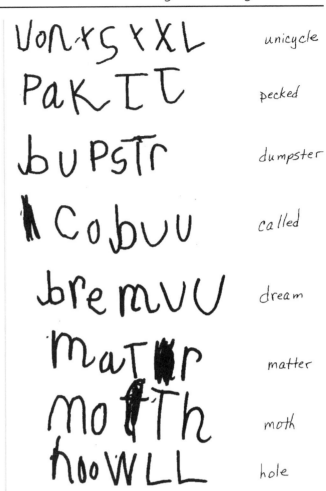

Figure 6.19. Aaron's Spelling List.

2. The plural of words ending in *s, x, z, ch,* and *sh* is formed by adding *-es* to the singular (example, *bench, benches*).
3. The plural of words ending in *y* after a vowel are formed by adding an *-s* (example, *toy, toys*) but for words ending in *y* after a consonant, change the *y* to an *i* and add *-es* (example, *baby, babies*).
4. The Doubling Rule (1-1-1 Rule): When a one syllable word ends in one vowel followed by a consonant, double the final consonant of the word when adding a vowel suffix (such as *-ing*). Do not double the ending consonant if the suffix starts with a consonant (such as *-ness*).

    sad + er = sadder

    sad + ness = sadness

    Note: the following letters rarely ever double in English words: *w, x, y, h, k, j, v*.

5. The Silent -*e* Rule: When a word ends in a silent *e*, drop the final *e* before adding a suffix that begins with a vowel. If a consonant suffix is being added, keep the *e*.

    like + ing = liking

    like + ness = likeness

Spelling Books

You should also not limit your spelling instruction to what is provided by a spelling book or basal spelling series. Usually these books provide a spelling list for the week that all class members are supposed to master. These lists are too difficult for struggling spellers, and too easy for the more accomplished spellers. Figure 6.20 presents two journal entries by Kevin, a fifth-grade student who struggles with spelling. Clearly, he is not fond of the spelling book. Students who struggle with spelling will require individualized approaches.

Spelling Lists

Students who struggle with spelling will usually require individualized spelling lists. Depending on a student's needs, you can provide different types of spelling lists that differ in the number and types of words that you select for study or in the format of presentation. For example, if you are trying to teach a student to sequence the sounds in words correctly, you would only assign spelling words that conform completely to English spelling rules. Each sound of the word can be easily heard and is spelled with the most common grapheme for that spelling. Initially, this list might involve simple consonant-vowel-consonant (CVC) words, such as *cat*, and then gradually progress to words involving consonant blends (such as *stop*). For other students who have mastered sound sequencing, you can focus on high-frequency words and common spelling patterns. You can also color-code spelling words using the concept of a traffic light: green (go) for phonically regular words, yellow (slow down) for words with irregular but frequent patterns (such as *ight, ould*), and red (stop) for words with an irregular element that must be memorized (for example, *once*). You will want to assign green words to students who still struggle with the sequencing of sounds in words until they learn how to put the sounds in order.

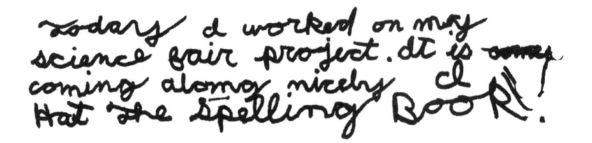

Figure 6.20. Kevin's Comments in His Journal.

When selecting the words for a student to spell, keep the following points in mind.

1. Make sure that the student knows the meanings of the words and uses the words in writing.
2. Make sure that the student can read the word with ease. Remember reading is much easier than spelling, and if the student struggles with reading the word, it is too difficult as a spelling word.
3. Focus on important, commonly used words for spelling instruction. Do not give spelling tests on content area words, such as words from a chapter in the science book.
4. Reward good spelling attempts, even when they are incorrect.
5. Have students grade their own tests.
6. Encourage students to use words from their spelling tests in their writings.

High-Frequency Lists

Many students with writing difficulties need specific assistance in learning how to spell high-frequency words, the most commonly used words in writing. The "Spelling for Writing List" presented in Figure 6.21 includes the 335 words that primary-grade children use most frequently in their writing (Graham, Harris, & Loynachan, 1994). The list was generated from the most commonly occurring words on four different vocabulary lists. Each word was assigned a grade placement based on difficulty level. This list of high-frequency writing words can be used with students of any grade level who have not mastered the spellings of basic words. Although the words are ordered by grade level, they can be reordered to illustrate specific phonics principles.

Another helpful list is the "300 Instant Words" list presented in Figure 6.22 (Fry, 1977). This list contains 60 percent of the words that make up all of written language. You can use this list to teach students high-frequency spelling words. Begin by identifying which words the student knows and does not

know how to spell. Then establish a program to help the student master the spellings of the unknown words. Mastery of high-frequency words may be accomplished more effectively using a flow list versus a fixed list.

Flow List

One way you can orchestrate an individualized spelling program is to use a flow list, or a list that evolves with mastery, as opposed to a fixed list in which new words are presented each week. The purpose of using a spelling flow list is to provide systematic instruction and review in order to promote mastery and retention of spelling words. Essentially, the spelling list evolves as the student learns to spell each word. Figure 6.23 presents an example of a flow list for Matthew, a fifth-grade student, and Figure 6.24 presents a blank form. The following steps were adapted from McCoy and Prehm (1987):

1. Help the student identify three to six words that he or she uses in writing but spells incorrectly. Words for the flow list may be taken from a student's writing or from a high-frequency word list, such as those presented in the previous section.
2. List the words in the first column on the spelling flow list form.
3. Have the student study the words with a strategy and then test the student on the words.
4. Mark each correctly spelled word with a *C* and each incorrectly spelled word with a check.
5. Provide daily practice and testing with the words.
6. If a word is spelled correctly three days in a row, cross it off the list and add a new word.
7. Have students file mastered words alphabetically into a word bank. Provide periodic review of the words to ensure retention, such as testing the word one week later.

Grade 1 Word List		Grade 2 Word List				Grade 3 Word List	
a	no*	about*	going*	over	well*	again*	lunch
all	not	after	happy	park	went*	air	maybe*
am	of	an*	hard	playing	were*	almost	might*
and*	oh	any	has*	put	what	also	money*
at	old	are*	have*	read	when*	always*	morning*
ball	on*	as	help	room	while*	another*	Mr.*
be	one*	ask	here*	said*	white*	anything*	Mrs.*
bed	out*	away	hit	same	who	around*	Ms.
big	play*	baby*	hope*	saw*	why	because*	never
book	ran	back	horse*	say	wish	better	nothing
box	red	bad	house*	school*	with*	can't*	once*
boy*	ride	been*	how*	sea	work	catch	own
but	run	before*	just*	ship	your	children*	party*
came*	see	being	keep	show*		class	people*
can*	she	best	kid	sleep		didn't	person
car	so	black	know*	small		dinner	place
cat	stop	boat	land	snow		does	ready
come*	the*	both	last	some*		don't*	real
dad	this	brother*	left	soon*		earth	right*
day*	to	buy*	little*	start		even	running*
did	two*	by	live	stay		ever	says
do	up	call	long	still		every*	should
dog*	us	candy	looking	store*		everyone*	sister
for*	was*	city	lot	story		everything*	someone*
fun*	we*	coming*	love	take		eye	something*
get*	will*	could	mad	talk		face	sometime*
go	yes	doing	made*	tell		family*	stopped*
good*	you*	door	make*	than*		few	summer*
got*		down*	many*	that		found*	talking
had*		each	men	them*		friend*	teacher*
he*		eat	more	then*		front	team
her*		end	most	there*		getting*	that's*
him*		fast	mother*	they*		great	their*
his*		father*	much	thing		hair	these*
home*		feet	must	think*		half	thought*
I*		fell*	myself*	three		having*	trip
if		find	name*	time*		head	trying
in*		fire	new*	today*		heard*	turn
into*		first*	next	told		hour	walking
is		fish	nice*	too*		hurt*	wasn't
it*		five	night	took		I'll*	watch
its*		food	now*	tree		I'm*	water
let		four	off*	try		it's*	where*
like*		from*	only	used		kind	which
look		funny	open	very*		knew*	won
man		game	or*	walk		lady	world*
may		gave	other	want*		later	would*
me*		girl	our*	way		let's*	year
my*		give	outside*	week		life	you're

Figure 6.21. Spelling for Writing List.

*Spelling demons or commonly misspelled words. This list may be photocopied for noncommercial use only. Copyright © 1994 by PRO-ED, Inc.
Source: From "The Spelling for Writing List" by S. Graham, K. R. Harris, and C. Loynachan, 1994, *Journal of Learning Disabilities*, 27, 210–214. Copyright © 1994 by PRO-ED, Inc. Reprinted by permission.

First Hundred		Second Hundred		Third Hundred	
1. the	51. will	101. new	151. put	201. every	251. until
2. of	52. up	102. sound	152. end	202. near	252. children
3. and	53. other	103. take	153. does	203. add	253. side
4. a	54. about	104. only	154. another	204. food	254. feet
5. to	55. out	105. little	155. well	205. between	255. car
6. in	56. many	106. work	156. large	206. own	256. mile
7. is	57. then	107. know	157. must	207. below	257. night
8. you	58. them	108. place	158. big	208. country	258. walk
9. that	59. these	109. year	159. even	209. plant	259. white
10. it	60. so	110. live	160. such	210. last	260. sea
11. he	61. some	111. me	161. because	211. school	261. began
12. was	62. her	112. back	162. turned	212. father	262. grow
13. for	63. would	113. give	163. here	213. keep	263. took
14. on	64. make	114. most	164. why	214. tree	264. river
15. are	65. like	115. very	165. ask	215. never	265. four
16. as	66. him	116. after	166. went	216. start	266. carry
17. with	67. into	117. thing	167. men	217. city	267. state
18. his	68. time	118. our	168. read	218. earth	268. once
19. they	69. has	119. just	169. need	219. eye	269. book
20. I	70. look	120. name	170. land	220. light	270. hear
21. at	71. two	121. good	171. different	221. thought	271. stop
22. be	72. more	122. sentence	172. home	222. head	272. without
23. this	73. write	123. man	173. us	223. under	273. second
24. have	74. go	124. think	174. move	224. story	274. late
25. from	75. see	125. say	175. try	225. saw	275. miss
26. or	76. number	126. great	176. kind	226. left	276. idea
27. one	77. no	127. where	177. hand	227. don't	277. enough
28. had	78. way	128. help	178. picture	228. few	278. eat
29. by	79. could	129. through	179. again	229. while	279. face
30. word	80. people	130. much	180. change	230. along	280. watch
31. but	81. my	131. before	181. off	231. might	281. far
32. not	82. than	132. line	182. play	232. close	282. Indian
33. what	83. first	133. right	183. spell	233. something	283. real
34. all	84. water	134. too	184. air	234. seem	284. almost
35. were	85. been	135. mean	185. away	235. next	285. let
36. we	86. call	136. old	186. animal	236. hard	286. above
37. when	87. who	137. any	187. house	237. open	287. girl
38. your	88. oil	138. same	188. point	238. example	288. sometimes
39. can	89. now	139. tell	189. page	239. beginning	289. mountain
40. said	90. find	140. boy	190. letter	240. life	290. cut
41. there	91. long	141. follow	191. mother	241. always	291. young
42. use	92. down	142. came	192. answer	242. those	292. talk
43. an	93. day	143. want	193. found	243. both	293. soon
44. each	94. did	144. show	194. study	244. paper	294. list
45. which	95. get	145. also	195. still	245. together	295. song
46. she	96. come	146. around	196. learn	246. got	296. leave
47. do	97. made	147. form	197. should	247. group	297. family
48. how	98. may	148. three	198. America	248. often	298. body
49. their	99. part	149. small	199. world	249. run	299. music
50. if	100. over	150. set	200. high	250. important	300. color

common suffixes: -s, -ing, -ed   common suffixes: -s, -ing, -ed, -er, -ly, -est

Figure 6.22. Fry's 300 Instant Words.

Source: Copyright by Edward B. Fry. Reprinted by permission of author.

Spelling Flow List

Name: Matthew   Starting Date: 11/12

Word	M	T	W	TH	F	M	T	W	TH	F	M	T	W	TH	F
they	C	C	C					C					C		
said	C	√	√	C	C	C					√				
people	√	C	C	C					√						
would	√	C	√	C	C	C					√				
could	√	C	C	C					C					C	
should	√	C	C	C					C					C	
were			√	C	√	C	C	C					C		
any				√	C	C	C							√	
people					C	√	√	C	C	C					C
said										√	C	C	√	√	C
would											C	√	C	C	
every											C	C	C		
busy										C	C	C			
because											C	C	√	C	
any													C	C	
friend													C	√	

C = Correct
√ = Incorrect

Figure 6.23. Matthew's Flow List.

Spelling Flow List

Name: _____   Starting Date:_____

Word	M	T	W	TH	F	M	T	W	TH	F	M	T	W	TH	F

C = Correct

√ = Incorrect

Figure 6.24. Sample Flow List Form.

8. If the word is missed on review, add it back to the flow list.
9. Once mastery is ensured (the word is correct on several retention checks), remove the known spelling word from the word bank.

This type of procedure seems to be more effective for students who struggle with spelling than the use of traditional weekly spelling tests.

Personalized Spelling Dictionaries

Many students with spelling difficulties can benefit from keeping an individualized spelling dictionary that contains their own frequently misspelled words from a flow list, as well as daily writings. You can write each letter of the alphabet in order on a separate page and then have the students write the words causing them spelling difficulty in their dictionaries.

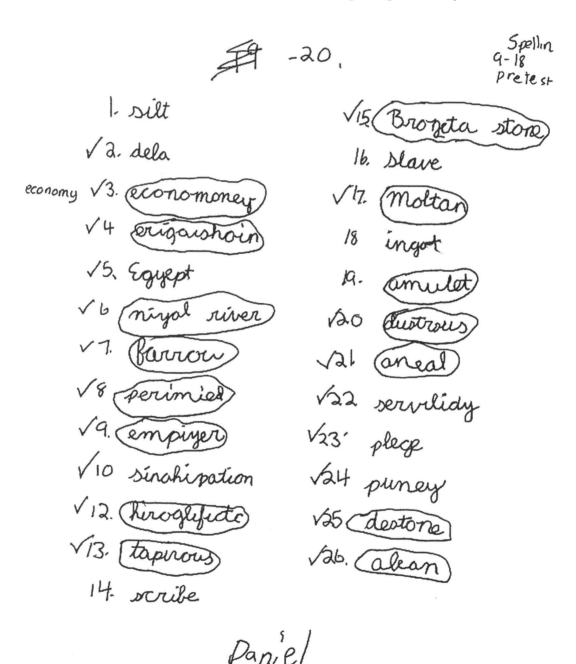

Figure 6.25. Daniel's Spelling Test.

They would then consult these dictionaries when writing or editing their work. In addition, high-frequency word lists in alphabetic order can be placed up on the wall so that students have access to these spellings and are expected to use these correct spellings at all times.

Grading Spelling Tests

For students who struggle with spelling, adapting the grading criteria may be beneficial. Instead of marking words correct or incorrect, you would assign a point value based on how close to correct the spelling is. Depending on the grade and skill level of a student, you can establish different criteria. For example, with beginning spellers you assign the following points to each word (adapted from Tangel & Blachman, 1992).

4—The word is spelled correctly.
3—All sounds are represented.
2—Some sounds are represented.
1—One sound is represented.
0—No sounds are represented.

For older students, you can assign more points and include other criteria, such as correct, the spelling is a possible English spelling, the word contains a vowel in each syllable, all phonemes are represented, and so on. Providing a continuum of scoring responses rewards students with points for good spelling attempts and allows you to monitor their progress and development.

Also when you are grading spelling tests, you will want to put the number of words spelled correctly on the top of the paper (or the number of points earned) rather than the number of incorrect words. Look at Daniel's spelling test in Figure 6.25. Notice that he has a –20 on the top of the paper. Clearly, the words are too difficult for him. One must also question the value of assigning these types of words as a spelling test. Although it is of historic significance, you do not need to know how to spell *Rosetta Stone*. His teacher could have also drawn a smiley face by his spelling of the word *economy* as "economoney."

Figures 6.26 and 6.27 illustrate two spelling tests by Adriana, a third-grade student who struggles with spelling. Her teacher has placed her score on each of the tests. You can easily see which one is more supportive of Adriana's attempts. Positive comments are helpful.

Word Study Methods

Students can study words in a variety of different ways. Some students benefit from tracing words, whereas others do not. Some students learn more effectively by saying the letter names aloud, rather than the letter sounds. Some students can picture a word in their minds, whereas others find it much easier to write the word. Regardless of what approach is selected, the following general research-based principles result in the most effective spelling instruction:

1. Present words for spelling tests in lists, rather than in sentences.
2. Encourage students to pronounce the words slowly as they spell the words.
3. Provide students with systematic review.

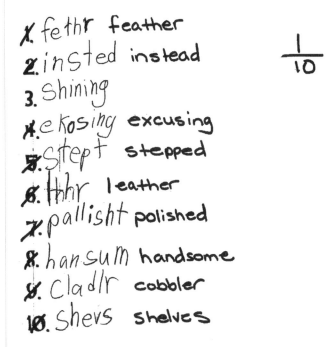

Figure 6.26. Adriana's First Spelling Test.

1. Serve ✔
2. Stagre
3. manner ✔
4. unyoushol
5. trafler
6. tresher
7. begele
8. seine
9. fostit
10. ?

(+2) Good!

On Wednesday, let's work on this together. 😊

Figure 6.27. Adriana's Second Spelling Test.

4. Determine words that are developmentally appropriate for the student.
5. Do not have students copy or write words several times as a study technique. Instead, have them write the word from memory without looking at the word.

Often when students are copying a word, they are not paying adequate attention to the word's spelling, and they end up writing the word numerous times incorrectly. Look at the papers presented in Figures 6.28 and 6.29. Brandon, a third-grade student, was asked to write his spelling words five times each. You can see that the words are not copied correctly. Similarly, Robert's eighth-grade English teacher asked him to recopy his spelling words, even asking him to rewrite one of the words fifty times! Spelling strategies that require more active participation are far more effective than simply writing words.

Many of the study strategies also involve a multisensory component in which the student looks at the word, traces the word while

April 13.   Room 111

1 dont doht dont dont doht
2 hasnt hasnl hashi hasni
3 we ye wevewevewe wv
4 yoy lf yoyll yoyll yoyll yoyll
5 yoyre yoyre youre yoyre
6 canht canht canht canht canht
7 I'll I'll I'll I'll I'll I'll I'll
8 well well well well wall
9 ishi ishi ishi ishi ish
10 Ive Ive Ive Ive Ive
11 ido hoit
12 coh hoi-
13 hasht hot
14 I well hot
15 youll ho t
16 you're not

Figure 6.28. Brandon's Spelling Words.

Figure 6.29. Robert's Spelling Words.

saying it, covers the word, and writes the word from memory. In addition, practice, review, and feedback are critical. In general, students who struggle with orthography tend to benefit from a method with a visual emphasis, whereas students who struggle with phonology tend to need a method with the emphasis on sounds.

Word Study Methods with a Visual Emphasis

Students who have trouble recalling letter sequences often will benefit from a method that emphasizes the visual features of a word.

The majority of these techniques involve three components: (a) multisensory word study, (b) emphasis on visual imagery, and (c) writing the word from memory.

Fernald Method

Use of the Fernald Method can help a student develop a visual image of the word and, subsequently, spell the word accurately (Fernald, 1943). For spelling, the method involves tracing and simultaneously pronouncing a word. This is an effective study technique for students who have trouble recalling the visual appearance of word spellings. The technique ensures that the student is paying attention to the word and making the link between the phonemes and graphemes. You can use the following steps:

1. Have the student select the word to be studied.
2. Write the selected word on a chalkboard or a piece of paper.
3. Pronounce the word clearly and distinctly. Have the student repeat the correct pronunciation while looking at the word.
4. Provide the student with time to study the word. You might encourage a student to picture the word, to say the word, and to trace the word with his or her finger.
5. When the student says that he or she knows the word, erase the word or remove it and have the student write the word from memory.
6. If the word is written incorrectly, return to step 3. If the word is written correctly, have the student turn the paper over and write the word another time from memory.
7. Create opportunities for the student to use words in writing.

For some students, visual imagery, or "seeing" words in their minds, can help with retention of spelling patterns.

1. Have the student look at the word carefully and say the word aloud.
2. Ask the student to close his or her eyes and try to picture the word.
3. Ask the student to write the word without looking at the spelling and then check the spelling against the correct spelling.
4. If the spelling is incorrect, have the student repeat steps 1 through 3.

Cover-Write Method

For students who have trouble recalling word images, a cover-write method may be useful. Several adaptations exist. You can use the following steps:

1. Select a word for the student to learn, write the word on a card, and pronounce it.
2. Have the student look at and say the word.
3. Have the student look at the word and say the letter names or the letter sounds while tracing each letter.
4. Have the student continue to trace and say the letters or letter sounds until the spelling is known.
5. Have the student cover the word and then say the word while writing it on paper. If the word is spelled incorrectly, repeat steps 2 to 4.
6. Review the spelling of the words periodically.

You can modify the cover-write method in many different ways to address a student's needs. Another example would be to use the following steps:

1. Write three to five words on a word card.
2. Have the student look at and say the first word.
3. Cover the word and have the student pronounce the sounds of the word while writing the letters.
4. Have the student compare the written word letter by letter with the model.
5. When the word is written correctly, cover the word again and ask the student to write the word while pronouncing it.
6. Repeat steps 2 to 5 with the new words.

To further draw attention to a word's visual details, you might show a student a group of words that are similar in appearance (for example, *thought, though, thorough*) and then ask the student to select the correct spelling. You could use colored markers to highlight the unique visual features. Some children also can be helped by providing a verbal mnemonic (memory aid) for words with confusing letter strings, such as *ould* or *ight*. Ms. Patel, a fifth-grade teacher, taught Ben to say "oh you little dog" when writing the words *would, could,* and *should* and "I go home tonight" when writing words with the *ight* spelling pattern.

Oral Spelling

Saying the word aloud while looking at the word can also help some students recall the word's spelling. Some students retain words better when they say each letter name, rather than each letter sound. You can use the following steps:

1. Ask the student to look at the word and say it aloud.
2. Have the student spell the word orally using the letter names and then say the word again.
3. Cover the word and have the student spell the word aloud.
4. If the spelling is correct, have the student write the word several times. If incorrect, repeat steps 1 and 2 until the word is spelled correctly.

Alternative Pronunciation

One strategy that can help with the recall of a few words with unusual spellings is to have students pronounce the word the way it is spelled, rather than the way it is spoken. For example, to remember how to spell the word *Wednesday*, you may deliberately articulate three distinct syllables "Wed-nes-day" when spelling the word. Or when writing the word *February*, you can place an extra emphasis on the first /r/ sound.

Computer Software

You can use computers to aid in the effective study of spelling in elementary and secondary schools, both in general and special education classes. Software programs using a "look and write from memory" approach have been developed by a number of companies. The word is flashed on the screen for a preselected length of time, and then the student types the word from memory. Whenever an error is made, the computer flashes the word again. This process continues until mastery is achieved. In some programs, the model can be programmed to disappear after the second letter is typed. Some students may prefer use of the computer for practicing spelling because of the immediate feedback and correction of errors.

Word Study Methods with an Auditory Emphasis

When a student has difficulty sequencing sounds (seen when misspellings contain many of the correct letters but in the incorrect order), a spelling method that emphasizes listening to the sounds of the word will be beneficial. For these students, effective spelling programs begin with a study of the sounds we hear in words and then a study of the letters we use to represent those sounds.

Phonological Awareness

The most effective way for improving the spelling performance of beginning writers is to provide training procedures that involve manipulating letters in conjunction with the letter sounds. By providing training in phonological awareness, you can help students improve their spelling skill. You can present activities that involve rhyming words, clapping out and counting the number of syllables in words, and pronouncing words by syllables. You can use a variety of manipulatives, such as alphabet blocks, poker chips, Scrabble tiles, or magnetic letters to help students begin to make the connections between the speech sounds and the letters that represent them. Colored chips can represent the consonant and vowel sounds (for example, make consonant sounds blue and vowel sounds red).

Segmentation is the most important phonological awareness skill for spelling. You can think of this ability as a necessary prerequisite for learning how to spell. If students cannot segment sounds, they will have trouble placing the sounds of a word in the correct order. Using tiles, letters, or both you can demonstrate how to pull the sounds of a word apart and then push the sounds back together again to spell a word. You can begin instruction using compound words (for example, *baseball*).

Say: "When I say the word *baseball*, how many words do you hear?" If needed, you can use pictures or hand gestures to reinforce how to break the two words apart. Once students can separate compound words, progress to syllable units (for example, *car-pen-ter*). An easy way to help children learn how to count the number of syllables is to have them place their hands under their chins and then say the word aloud. The number of syllables is equal to the number of times that the chin drops. One rule of English spelling is that each syllable must have a vowel, and the vowel sound forces the mouth to open. You might next want to provide practice with onsets and rimes (for example, *c-at*). The onset is the consonant or consonants that start an English syllable, and the rimes are the ending units that begin with a vowel. The rime is the part that rhymes. Finally, help children learn how to break words apart into their individual phonemes (for example, /b/ /a/ /t/). Have them pronounce each sound and then blend the sounds back into whole words. As skill improves, you can move from instruction in segmentation and sound-letter relationships to spelling approaches with an auditory emphasis. These approaches are designed to improve phonological awareness and teach students how to sequence sounds correctly.

Adapted Elkonin Procedure

D. B. Elkonin, a Russian psychologist, developed several simple procedures for helping students increase their understanding of the relationships between speech sounds and printed letters (Elkonin, 1973). Using the following procedure, adapted from Elkonin, you first teach the student how to count speech sounds and then how to translate these sounds into letters using the following steps:

1. Select a simple picture of a familiar object.
2. Place a rectangle for a word under the drawing and then divide the rectangle into the number of squares equal to number of phonemes. Begin with words in which the number of phonemes matches the number of graphemes (letters).
3. Ask the student to say the word slowly while pushing a chip forward for each sound. You can use blue and red poker chips or colored tiles. Practice with different words. Once a student can perform this step confidently, progress to Step 4.
4. Repeat the procedure in Step 3, but color-code vowels and consonants. Once a student can identify and differentiate vowel and consonant sounds, proceed to Step 5.
5. For this step, use letter tiles, magnetic letters, or letter cards to push into the boxes. At first, use words in which single phonemes are represented by the single most common graphemes. Once a student is able to spell words with predictable spelling patterns, introduce additional graphemes. For example, demonstrate how the word *sight* has three speech sounds but five letters and the word *came* has three speech sounds but four letters. In these examples, the number of boxes does not match the number of speech sounds, so make larger squares for the speech sounds that can be heard and smaller boxes for the speech sounds that are silent. Write consonant and vowel digraphs (one speech sound spelled with two letters) in one box. For example, when writing the word *boat*, make three boxes, placing the *oa* into the middle box. Discuss with the student the difference between how a word is spelled and how it sounds. Figure 6.30 illustrates three Elkonin boxes. The first represents the simplest type of word, when the number of letters matches the number of sounds. The second one illustrates a word that has a silent letter, and the third illustrates a word that contains a vowel digraph.

Sound-Letter Sequencing

Other methods begin with using both letters and sounds. They are designed to ensure that students attend to the sequence of sounds

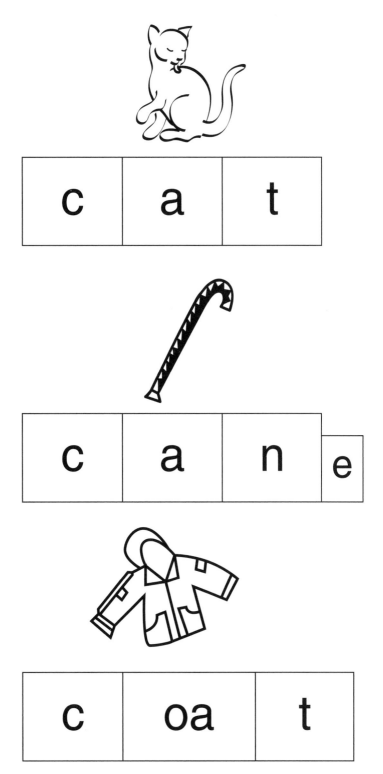

Figure 6.30. Examples of Elkonin Boxes.

when they are spelling. You can use the following steps:

1. Get some letter tiles, such as Scrabble tiles or magnetic letters.
2. Sound out a word slowly phoneme by phoneme. Have the student say each sound of the word and place the letter tiles in correct sequence from left to right. (Use sound-letter combinations that the student knows.) If necessary, demonstrate how to say the sounds and arrange the tiles before the child attempts to build the word.
3. After building the word, have the student point to each letter, say the sound, and then say the whole word.
4. Have the student write the word while saying each of the sounds.
5. As skill increases, you can use individual letter tiles to demonstrate how to spell letter combinations and syllables.

Making Words

Making Words is a guided invented spelling task (Cunningham & Cunningham, 1992). The purpose of this procedure is to help students develop phonemic awareness and discover how our alphabetic system works by increasing their understanding of sound-letter relationships. Making Words activities begin with short, easy words and then end with a big word that uses all of the letters. Children manipulate the letters to produce a variety of words. For the first lessons, provide students with several consonant letters but only one vowel, which is presented in a different color. As skills improve, you can give students two or more colored vowels. This activity helps children see how words change when letters are moved and different letters are added. Two samples of vowels and consonants for Making Words lessons are presented below:

Letters for a lesson with one vowel: *u k n r s t*
Examples of words to make: *us nut rut run sun sunk runs ruts rust tusk stun stunk trunk trunks*

Letters for a lesson with two vowels: *a e h n p r t*
Examples of words to make: *an at hat pat pan pen pet net ate eat heat meat path parent panther*

You can use this strategy, which takes about fifteen minutes, along with regular writing activities. Before starting, begin by choosing the longest word that will be the final word that uses all of the letters. Write the words on index cards and then put them in order from the shortest words to the longest words. Prepare sets of letters for each student, making vowels a different color from consonants. Use the following steps:

1. Give each student six to eight letters that will be used to make about twelve to fifteen words.
2. Say the shortest word and ask each student to form the word.
3. Ask each student to make other three-letter and four-letter words using the letters.
4. You may continue a pattern, increasing a word length by one letter during each step. The final word includes all of the letters the student has for that day. For example, ask the students to spell *it*, then add letters to spell *sit, slit, split*, and *splint*. As words evolve, discuss the spelling patterns.

You will want to work with students with the lowest skills in a small group, or ideally one-to-one. Begin with consonant-vowel-consonant (CVC) words and one short vowel sound. First teach the student how to change the first letter to make new words (for example, *hat, bat, rat, sat*) and then the last letter (for example, *sat, sad, Sam*) and then the vowel sound (for example, *hat, hit, hot, hut*). On following days, add in only one or two more sounds to replace the ones that have been mastered. Provide review of sounds on subsequent days. As skill improves, more letters may be added and longer words formed.

Multisyllabic Words

Once students can sequence phonemes and have mastered basic phonic elements, you can have them practice words with more than one syllable. Begin by selecting words with regular spelling patterns. By focusing on syllables, you can help students see that most words are composed of a series of manageable shorter units.

You can use these steps:

1. Write the words on word cards.
2. Say the word and have the student repeat the word, syllable by syllable, looking at and pointing to each syllable as it is pronounced.
3. Have the student pronounce the letter sounds in each syllable, pausing between the syllables.
4. Have the student write the word without looking at the spelling, slowly pronouncing each syllable.

As another example, if a student wanted to learn how to spell a longer word, such as *consideration*, you could use the following steps:

1. Identify and discuss the parts, common letter clusters, and syllables in the word.
2. Ask the student to write the letter(s) that make the "con" sound, then the "sid" sound, then the "er" sound, then the "a" sound, and finally the "tion" sound.
3. Have the student write the word *consideration* while pronouncing each syllable slowly: "con-sid-er-a-tion."
4. Have the student turn the paper over and write *consideration* from memory while saying each part of the word as it is written.
5. Have the student write the word from memory two more times.

You could also use a Making Words type of activity with syllables. Write syllables on index cards. Have the student pronounce the syllables and then move various syllables together to form both real and nonsense words

(for example, *protention*). Then ask the student to write the words while pronouncing each syllable.

Spelling Chart

Some students can improve their spellings of multisyllabic words through the use of a spelling chart (see Figure 6.31). The purpose of the chart is to increase the student's ability to break words into syllables. You can use the following steps:

1. Write the spelling word in column one and then pronounce the word and discuss its meaning. Have the student read the word.
2. In column two, have the student count and write the number of syllables in the word.
3. In the next columns, have the student divide the word into syllables and write one syllable in each column.
4. In the last column, have the student write the whole word.
5. As a final step, have the student turn over the paper and write the word from memory while pronouncing each syllable.

Word Study Strategies

You can also help students increase their knowledge of word patterns and the linguistic structure of words by teaching specific strategies. Students can then be encouraged to use the patterns to spell new words. Teaching students self-questioning strategies and providing guided practice with dictation exercises can help students improve their spelling skills. In addition, specific instruction in morphological rules will benefit students with spelling difficulties.

Rhyming Strategy

Helping students notice similarities among words that share orthographic patterns may

Name: _____   Date: _____

Multisyllabic Word Spelling Chart

Instructions
1. Write the word.
2. Say the word. (Put a check.)
3. Count and write the number (#) of syllables.
4. Write each syllable.
5. Write the whole word.
6. Turn the paper over and say and write the word.
7. Check the word.
8. If incorrect, repeat steps 1 to 7.

Word	Say	#	1	2	3	4	5	Word

Figure 6.31. Spelling Chart for Multisyllabic Words.

help them apply those patterns to new words. You can use the following procedure:

1. Identify the words that a student has misspelled on a spelling pretest or within written papers.
2. Develop a spelling bank of ten to fifteen words that rhyme with one of the misspelled words. For example, you may choose the word *other* if the student misspelled the word *mother*.
3. Explain that the rhyming parts of words are often spelled the same.
4. Present a list of words. Say one word and ask the students to identify the word in the spelling bank that rhymes with the stimulus word. Have students identify which letters of the printed and orally presented words would be spelled the same, based on the rhyming rule.
5. Have students spell the words orally several times and then write the words three times correctly from memory.
6. Test the students on the words and then review the words again a week later.

Five-Step Study Strategy

The five-step study strategy has been used effectively with elementary school students (Graham & Freeman, 1985). After memorizing the steps and practicing them with a teacher, students use the procedure independently. Due to the simplicity of the procedure, upper-elementary and secondary students could use the method when studying unknown words, as well. Students can eliminate tracing if it doesn't help with word retention. You can use the following steps:

1. Have the student say the word.
2. Have the student write, while saying the word.
3. Have the student check the correctness of the word.
4. Have the student trace and say the word.
5. Have the student write the word from memory and check it.

Repeat all the steps as necessary.

Self-Questioning Strategy

Some students may benefit from use of a self-questioning strategy to help improve their spelling skill. Self-questioning is a primary means of developing self-monitoring skills. Getting your students to think about their performance is an effective way to improve their accuracy. When using this strategy, encourage the student to read what has actually been written as opposed to what he or she thought they wrote. To implement self-questioning, Wong (1986) described the following strategy:

1. Read the words aloud.
2. Teach students how to break words into syllables.
3. Show students how to identify root words and suffixes.
4. Point out the changes occurring in the root words when suffixes are added.
5. For self-evaluation, have students ask the following questions:
   a. Is this a word I know?
   b. How many syllables do I hear in this word? (Have each student write the number.)
   Alternatively, write the following prompts for self-questioning on an index card:
   a. Do I know this word?
   b. Do I have the correct number of syllables?
   c. Is there a part of the word I am not sure how to spell?
6. Each student attempts to spell the word.
7. Students check to see that all syllables are written.
8. Students ask themselves if the word looks correct. If not, they underline the part that seems incorrect and try to spell the word again.
9. If the word does not have the correct number of syllables, the word is pronounced again while trying to identify the missing syllable.
10. Have students redo steps 6 through 9 until the word is correct.

11. Students provide self-reinforcement by acknowledging their attempts to improve spelling.

Dictation Spelling Methods

You can supplement spelling instruction by dictating sentences for students to write that contain the words they are learning or that target specific spelling patterns (for example, "the fat cat is on my hat") or contain previously learned words and new words. Students may give themselves one point for accurately spelled words, as well as for correct capitalization and punctuation, such as each sentence beginning with a capital letter and ending with the correct punctuation mark. Have them circle correct capital letters and end punctuation marks and underline each correctly spelled word. Students may record the number of points by each sentence and place a total on the top of their papers. Remember that when you engage your students in monitoring their own performance, you are helping them become more independent.

Morphology

Students who have difficulty with word endings often benefit from direct instruction in morphological rules. When incorporating morphology into spelling instruction, you will want to follow a specific sequence, such as teaching noun plurals, noun possessives (such as *boy's*), past tense, comparative and superlative forms of adjectives (for example, *funnier, funniest*), and common prefixes and suffixes.

Technology

The challenge of spelling can be partly reduced through the use of electronic aids. As is true for students with handwriting difficulties, students with spelling difficulties can benefit from the use of word processors and spell checkers. Although these programs differ in size and content, most have high-frequency lists to which students can add other words. If the spell checker has a speech synthesizer,

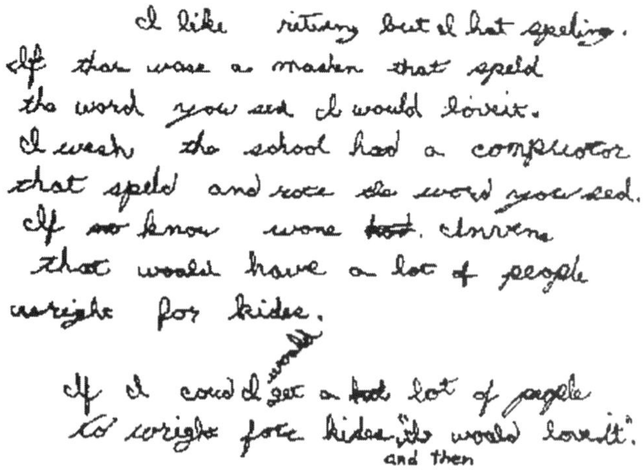

Figure 6.32. Melissa's Paragraph About Spelling.

the student can have the words read aloud to assist in selecting the correct option.

Sometimes people assume, however, that poor spellers can resolve their difficulties by simply using a computer or spell checker. Many students with severe spelling problems have not developed sufficient skill to use these tools independently. In order to use a spell checker, an individual must be able to spell phonetically; otherwise, the computer will not recognize the entry. The computer may mark the questionable pattern, but be unable to generate the correct spelling. Also, in many instances, the student must select the correct spelling from a list of words, and some students have difficulty choosing the correct option. The spell checker also overlooks certain errors. Because the computer operates at the letter pattern level, it cannot detect errors in meaning such as between common homonyms. Consequently, words that are misspelled within the context in which they are used are not detected as errors. The important point to realize is that a student must be a fairly proficient speller to operate a spell checker independently.

Figure 6.32 illustrates a paragraph written by Melissa, a seventh-grader with poor spelling skill. She comments that she loves writing but hates spelling. She hopes that someday she will have a computer to help her spell or, if not, she will hire people to write for kids. Unfortunately, Melissa's spelling skill is not yet accurate enough for her to use a spell checker.

USAGE

Basic writing skills also include the correct use of capital letters and punctuation. Some students can learn common punctuation and capitalization rules within the context of their writings, whereas others need to learn the rules out of context, be shown how to apply the rules, and then practice using the rules. You might begin with structured lessons and then help students to apply the rules to their own work. Start with the most common rules and provide practice and reinforcement until the student has mastered the rule.

Even though direct instruction with supervised practice in context appears effective for teaching both capitalization and punctuation rules, some students may not always apply the rules in their own writing. Consequently, you must help students learn and then apply these skills. To master both capitalization and punctuation rules, a student should be able to recognize when an element should be used and then how to apply it in new situations. Students must first learn the rule (for example, sentences begin with a capital letter), practice the rule, and then apply the rule in their written work. In regard to basic capitalization and punctuation rules, by the end of elementary school, students should be able to consistently start sentences with capital letters, end sentences with appropriate marks, use commas in lists, use apostrophes in contractions, and use quotation marks for dialogue.

Usage also includes the socially preferred way of using language or the dialects that are used within different cultures. Special considerations are often required when you are teaching standard English to speakers with differing dialects. As a caution, do not view variations in cultural syntax (for example, black dialect) as incorrect. Explain to students that standard English is usually used in formal types of written communications, whereas dialects are appropriate for more informal and oral communications. Both forms are appropriate, therefore, in different situations and for different audiences. For example, the language a student uses in a business letter will differ from the language used in writing a letter to a friend. Or, the use of a dialect may be appropriate in a narrative, but not in an expository essay. By encouraging students to write for different purposes, you provide them with the breadth of experiences necessary to communicate effectively to a variety of audiences.

In addition, the English language is constantly changing. Some traditionally objectionable constructions are now viewed as acceptable. For example, in the past the accepted plural of *curriculum* was *curricula*, and the accepted plural of *cactus* was *cacti*. Presently, both *curricula* and *curriculums* and *cacti* and *cactuses* are considered acceptable.

Punctuation

When to use certain punctuation marks, such as commas, requires some judgment. Although the rules regarding punctuation can vary, your job is to ensure that students know how to use basic punctuation marks correctly within writing. You can teach and reinforce many punctuation rules within the context of a student's writing. The key to successful instruction appears to be mastery of the rule, followed by application in authentic writing activities.

Sequence of Instruction

As a general rule, you want to introduce the most commonly used punctuation marks first, as well as the context in which they are used. A possible sequence would be:

Period
Question mark
Comma
Exclamation point
Apostrophe
Quotation marks
Colon
Semi-colon
Hyphen
Parentheses

A more expanded list sequenced according to the order of presentation in a writing curriculum follows (Cohen & Plaskon, 1980):

1. Period
   a. At the end of a sentence
   b. Following a command
   c. After an abbreviation
   d. After numbers in a list
   e. Following an initial
   f. After letters and numbers in an outline
2. Comma
   a. In dates (between the day of the month and the year)
   b. In addresses (between the name of the city and the state)
   c. After the greeting of a friendly letter
   d. After the closing of a friendly letter
   e. Between the words given in a series
   f. To set off appositives
   g. After *yes* and *no* when they are used as parenthetical expressions
   h. After the name of a person being addressed
   i. To separate a quotation from the explanatory part of a sentence
   j. After a person's last name when it is written before the first name
3. Question mark following a question
4. Quotation marks
   a. Before and after the direct words of a speaker
   b. Around the title of a story, poem, or an article
5. Apostrophe
   a. To establish a possessive noun
   b. In a contraction
6. Exclamation point
   a. At the end of an exclamatory sentence
   b. After a word or group of words showing surprise or strong feeling
7. Hyphen
   a. In compound words
   b. In compound numbers (for example, telephone numbers)
   c. Separating syllables of a word that is divided at the end of the line
8. Colon
   a. Between the hour and minutes in the time of day (for example, 3:25)
   b. After the salutation in a business letter

You will want to introduce only one punctuation mark at a time. You can use the following steps to teach any type of punctuation mark, from periods to quotation marks:

1. Explain when and how the punctuation mark is used.
2. Initially, have the student practice the use of the punctuation mark in sentences.
3. Encourage the student to try to use the punctuation mark correctly in written assignments.
4. If errors are made, review the use of the mark, and have the student proofread written work for the punctuation mark.

Capitalization

You can use a variety of techniques, such as letter-writing activities, to teach capitalization skills. You will want to begin instruction by identifying what rules a student has mastered and what ones need still to be learned.

Sequence of Instruction

As with punctuation, you would teach capitalization rules in the order of most frequent use. One possible instructional sequence to teach these rules would be as follows:

1. First and last names
2. First word in a sentence
3. The word *I*
4. Days, months, and holidays
5. Proper nouns: people (Frank, Mother), schools, parks, rivers
6. Addresses: streets, roads, cities, states, countries

7. Personal titles: Mr., Mrs., Ms., Dr.
8. Commercial product names and organizations (such as Cheerios, YMCA)
9. Abbreviations and initials
10. First words in the salutation and closing of a letter
11. Time
12. School subjects
13. First word of a quotation
14. Books, compositions, and songs
15. Degrees
16. Race and nationality

Cloze Procedure

You can also use the cloze procedure to help students practice and review capitalization rules. You can delete a variety of letters, some that require capitalization and others that do not, from a short passage. Have students read the passage and then reconstruct it by selecting either lowercase or uppercase letters to appear in the blanks. You could adapt this activity for students with limited skill by placing both forms of the letter that has been deleted underneath the blank.

Syntax

Students who struggle with writing often benefit from modeling, reinforcement, and explicit instruction in syntax. This does not mean formal grammar instruction, as research has demonstrated that traditional grammar instruction is ineffective for improving writing. You can teach most syntactic rules within the context of a student's writing. In addition, a variety of sentence-building strategies exist that help students become more aware of and more proficient with varying sentence structures. These strategies often begin with simple sentence patterns and then encourage students to expand the basic sentences through elaboration.

CATS Strategy

One simple strategy is known by the acronym CATS (Giordano, 1982). The acronym is a reminder to: copy, alter, transform, and supply. Prior to beginning the strategy, you would write three sentences with a space in between and then use the following steps:

C   Have the student *copy* a favorite sentence. If unable to copy, have the student trace the sentence with a yellow marker pen.

A   Help the student *alter* one word in the copied sentence.

T   Have the student *transform* the sentence into a different form, such as turning a statement into a question.

S   Have the student *supply* a response to the transformation, such as answering the question.

Sentence Guides

Use sentence guides to help students learn how to construct basic sentence patterns. For example, you might write a series of questions across the top of a paper, such as "Who?" "Did what?" "To whom?" Or, you may use more complex patterns, such as "Who?" "What doing?" "When?" "Where?" "Why?" The questions may be open-ended or refer to a picture or a story. The student would answer the questions and then write a sentence. As skill develops, you can reverse the order of questions. For example, instead of starting the sentence with the word *who*, you could make the first question be *when*. Once a student has mastered sentence writing, you can use pictures that tell a story in sequence to develop beginning skill in paragraph writing.

You also can have students write a basic sentence that contains a subject and a verb. They can then respond to additional questions to expand the sentence, such as Where? Why? How? When? For example, a student may write

Basic sentence: *Dan swam.*
Where? *in Lake Michigan*
Why? *he wanted some exercise*

How? *rapidly*

When? *Saturday morning*

Expanded sentence: *Dan swam rapidly in Lake Michigan on Saturday morning to get some exercise.*

Sentence Expansion Charts

As an alternative, some students may benefit from practice with sentence expansion charts. These charts may be developed to illustrate a variety of sentence types. Two samples are presented in Figures 6.33 and 6.34. As a final step, students then write the expanded sentence.

Sentence Construction

Have students practice syntactic rules as they learn the specific terminology associated with parts of speech. You can use the following steps:

1. Write several headings on a chalkboard, such as Article, Noun, Verb (easy) or Possessive Pronoun, Adjective, Noun, Verb, Adverb, Preposition, Article, Adjective, Noun (more difficult).

2. Ensure that all students understand what type of word is represented by each of the headings.

3. Have students brainstorm for words under each heading. For example,

   Possessive pronoun—*my, our, their, his, her, its, your*

   Adjective—*beautiful, mean, cowardly, enormous*

   Noun—*skyscraper, monster, acrobat, toothbrush*

   Verb—*crawled, bounced, sang, laughed*

   Adverb—*energetically, noisily, shyly, laughingly*

   Preposition—*under, in, beside, after, above, by*

   Article—*the, a,* an

   Adjective—*gigantic, stocky, intelligent, athletic*

   Noun—*candlestick, dictionary, dog, bottle, grass*

Article	Noun	Verb			
Article	Adjective	Noun	Verb		
Article	Adjective	Noun	Verb	Adverb	
Article	Adjective	Noun	Verb	Adverb	Prepositional Phrase

Final Sentence: _____

Figure 6.33. Simple Sentence Expansion Chart.

Article	Noun	Verb	Conjunction	Article	Noun	Verb
Article	Adjective	Noun	Verb	Conjunction	Article	Adjective	Noun	Verb
Article	Adjective	Noun	Verb	Adverb	Conjunction	Article	Adjective	Noun	Verb	Adverb

Final Sentence: _____

Figure 6.34. Compound Sentence Expansion Chart.

4. Have students create sentences by choosing one word from each list. The sentences may be nonsensical.

When a sentence pattern has been mastered, teach students how to write compound sentences by using conjunctions such as *but, and, although*, and *because*. Then have your students rewrite nonsensical sentences so they make sense.

Sentence Combining

Sentence-combining strategies help writers develop their skill in writing more complex sentence structures. For these activities, a writer is asked to combine several short sentences into one longer sentence.

To begin, write two or three simple sentences on the chalkboard, and ask students to combine the sentences to form one longer, more elaborate sentence. Discuss all suggestions and write all acceptable sentences produced by students on the board. Provide oral practice with the sentences before asking the students to combine them in writing. Next, take sentences directly from a student's written work. If desired, you might use exercises that focus on a specific aspect of syntax. For example, you may want to help students learn how to join sentences using a variety of conjunctions such as *because, but*, and *or*. You may also construct simple sentences from a student's spelling words or break apart longer sentences from the student's textbooks.

Sentence Writing Strategy

The Sentence Writing Strategy is one of six strategies included in the Expression and Demonstration of Competence Strand of the Learning Strategies Curriculum from the University of Kansas (Schumaker & Sheldon, 1985). Through this institution, you can receive specific training in the use and application of these strategies. This comprehensive strategy is designed to help students learn to write four kinds of sentences: simple, compound, complex, and compound-complex.

A simple sentence consists of one independent clause or a group of words that makes a complete statement and can stand alone. Four formula types of simple sentences are (a) single subject and verb, (b) compound subjects and single verb, (c) single subject with compound verbs, and (d) compound subjects and compound verbs.

Examples:
a. Martha jumped.
b. Martha and Bill jumped over the gate.
c. Martha jumped over the gate and ran.
d. Martha and Bill jumped over the gate and ran.

A compound sentence consists of two or more independent clauses that can each stand alone. Seven coordinating conjunctions are presented that may be used to connect the two independent clauses: *for, and, nor, but, or, yet, so*. Two formula types of compound sentences are (a) independent clauses joined by a coordinating conjunction and (b) independent clauses joined by a semicolon.

Examples:
a. Martha skipped and she jumped rope.
b. Martha was late; she missed the show.

A complex sentence consists of one independent clause and one or more dependent clauses. A dependent clause contains a subject and verb but cannot stand alone. The dependent clause starts with a word that shows the relationship between the two clauses. The related words are called subordinating conjunctions. Two formula types of complex sentences are (a) independent clause placed before the dependent clause and (b) the dependent clause preceding the independent clause.

Examples:
a. Martha had dinner before she went to the show.

b. Because she was late, Martha missed the show.

A compound-complex sentence combines compound and complex sentences and consists of two or more independent clauses and at least one dependent clause (for example, Martha had dinner and finished her homework before she went to the show). Compound-complex sentences with two independent clauses and one dependent clause can be formed in three ways: the dependent clause may be followed by, between, or after the two independent clauses. Formula types of compound-complex sentences are (a) two where the dependent clause is first, (b) two where the dependent clause is second, and (c) two where the dependent clause comes third.

Examples:
a. Before she went to the show, Martha ate dinner and exercised.
Before she went to show, Martha ate dinner; it was delicious.
b. Martha exercised before she ate, and later she went to the show.
Martha had dinner; because she exercised, she was late for the show.
c. Martha had dinner and exercised, before she went to the show.
Martha had dinner and exercised; however, she missed the show.

Use of this strategy will help students learn to recognize and write different types of sentences.

Cloze

You can also use the cloze procedure to help students learn how to expand sentences. You might delete words or phrases from sentences and place blanks for the student to complete. You may also write the type of grammatical structure under the blank, such as adjective or prepositional phrase.

EDITING

Editing usually refers to detecting and correcting errors in basic skills. Revision, on the other hand, is designed to improve, clarify, and expand content. Procedures that are more skill-based and used for editing are presented in the following section. Procedures that focus on the revision of content are presented in Chapter Seven.

Strategies

When helping students improve their editing skills, it is often best to limit your instruction to one or two types of error patterns at a time. When you focus on only one or two types of errors, such as starting sentences with capital letters or using quotation marks, students can focus their attention on mastery of just that skill.

COPS Strategy

The COPS strategy helps students identify four basic error types (Schumaker, Deshler, Nolan, Clark, Alley, & Warner, 1981). The mnemonic represents the following steps:

C Capitalization—check capitalization of first words in sentences and proper nouns
O Overall appearance of work—check for neatness, legibility, margins, indentation of paragraphs, and complete sentences
P Punctuation—check commas and end punctuation
S Spelling—check to see if the words are spelled correctly

Using this strategy, students can check their writing independently before submitting their work. They may write the acronym at the top of their papers and then place a check after they review their papers for each type of error.

SCOPE

A similar strategy, with the acronym of SCOPE, may be used to help students develop proofreading skills (Vaughn & Bos, 2009). The mnemonic represents the following series of questions:

S Is the *spelling* correct?

C Are the first words of sentences and proper names and nouns *capitalized*?

O Is the syntax or word *order* correct?

P Are there *punctuation* marks where needed?

E Does the sentence *express* a complete thought? Does the sentence contain a noun and a verb?

After you teach students the mnemonic SCOPE, model the strategy, and then have students apply the strategy to their own writing.

Spelling Proofreading Exercises

You can use a variety of proofreading activities that will help students. For example, underline your students' misspelled words and errors in punctuation and then have them attempt to correct the mistakes using a spell checker or by consulting with a peer. Place the number of misspelled words at the top of the paper or by each line or sentence. You might also list the different types of errors that were made, with the number of errors for each type. Provide supports as needed to help the student identify and correct the errors. As skill improves, encourage students to find and correct the misspellings independently. Another way to practice proofreading is to provide students with uncorrected writing samples from previous classes. Make sure all names are removed. Encourage them to read the samples aloud twice, once for content and then once for spelling and usage errors.

Some students make numerous errors in spelling on papers, so take extra care in providing feedback. Review the essay written by Marco, a seventh-grade student, who has decided to write about how he overcame Science class (see Figure 6.35). Clearly, the content is appropriate, as is his choice of words. Notice his teacher's question at the end: *Did you try using the dictionary?* Students who struggle with orthography have a very difficult time learning to spell basic common words, and a dictionary will not address this problem.

Corrective Strategy

As with all teaching, good instruction involves modeling, demonstration, practice, and application of a skill. Use the following steps to help students correct specific errors:

1. Select one error in a student's writing.
2. Discuss the error and explain the importance of the skill.
3. Demonstrate how to correct the error in the context of the student's paper.
4. Write another example of the error and ask the student to correct it.
5. Use a colored marker and highlight other examples of the error in the student's paper.
6. Have the student obtain help from a peer, if needed.
7. Have the student write "Proofread for [insert type of error]" on the top of the paper.

Editing Errors in Syntax

For errors in syntax, you can use a variety of activities to help students rewrite sentences. For example, use sentence-building activities to help students replace overused and nondescript words or to replace short, simple sentences with more complex ones.

Proofreading Checklist

Provide students with a proofreading checklist to help them remember what to check in their work. You can develop individualized lists for specific students or use a more generic form with an entire class. Figure 6.36 illustrates a sample proofreading checklist.

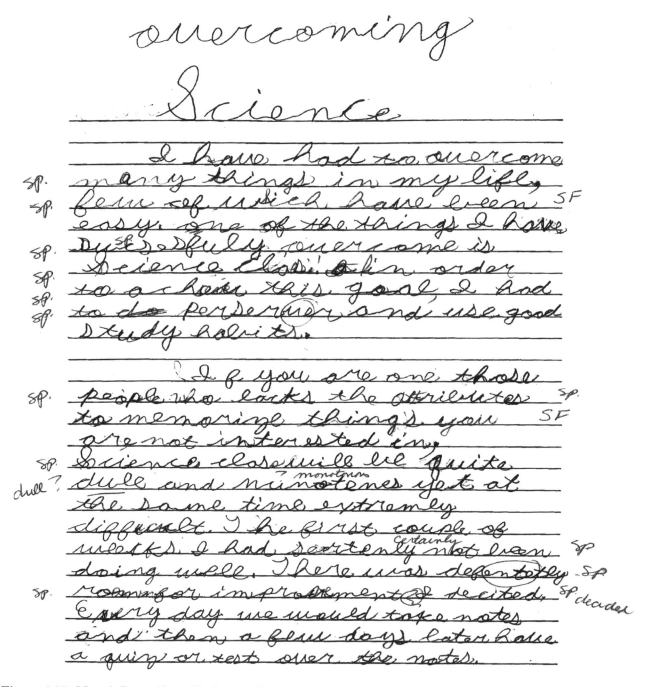

Figure 6.35. Marco's Paper About His Science Class.

Sentence Errors

You may also draw attention to specific sentences that are incorrectly or poorly constructed. Ask the students questions, such as:

1. Are the words in the sentence in the correct order?

2. Does the sentence say what you want to say?

3. Does the sentence sound right?

4. How can you make the sentence clearer?

Technology

Several grammar programs exist that are designed to help students correct usage errors.

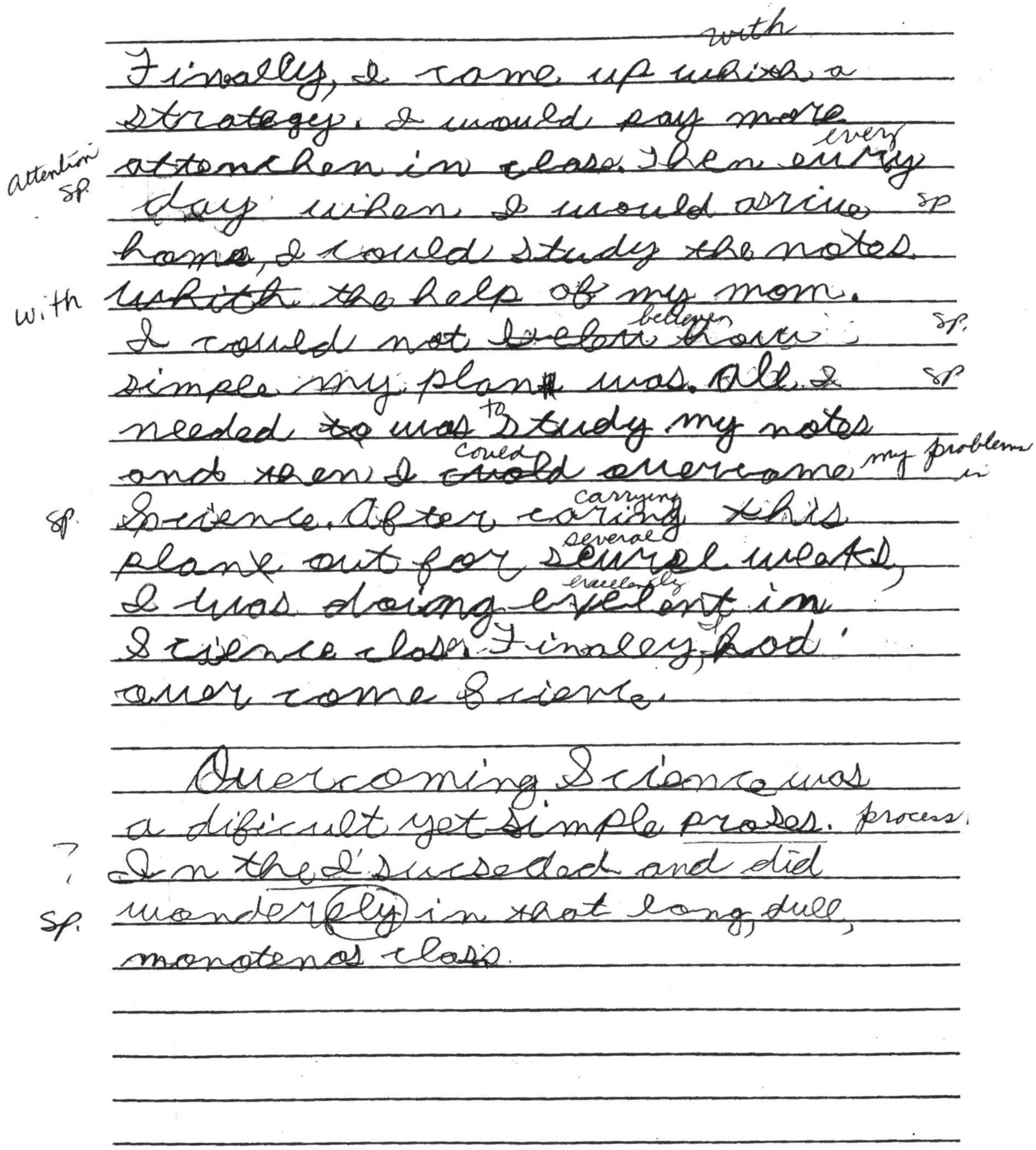

> with

Finally, I came up with a
strategy. I would say more
attention in class. Then every
day when I would arrive
home, I could study the notes.
with the help of my mom.
I could not believe how
simple my plan was. All I
needed to was study my notes
and then I could overcome my problem in
Science. After carrying this
plan out for several weeks,
I was doing excellent in
Science class. Finally, I had
overcome Science.

Overcoming Science was
a dificult yet simple proses. process
In the I sucseded and did
wonderfuly in that long, dull,
monotenas class.

Figure 6.35. *(Continued)*

In word-processing programs, these are usually integrated with the spell checker. After students enter text, they can check their work for grammatical errors, such as subject-verb agreement and incomplete or run-on sentences, as well as capitalization and punctuation errors.

In addition, students can vary syntactic structure by rewriting and expanding sentences. Students can either proofread a document as it is being written or wait until they have written the first draft. Although grammar-check programs are not as widely used as spell checkers, applications such as grammatically based word cueing can help students increase their syntactic competence. This type of program applies the syntactic rules of

Figure 6.35. Marco's Paper About His Science Class. (*Continued*)

English and then offers words to a student from which to choose. For example, if the student types in a noun, a list of verbs will appear. If the student types in a word such as *tomorrow*, a list of future tense verbs will appear. Other word prediction programs provide the student with choices of words as they enter in the first few letters.

EXAMPLES OF COMMERCIAL PROGRAMS

Many materials and programs are available to help you teach students basic writing skills. A simple Internet search of each specific skill area will yield numerous resources. If you

Name: _____

Date: _____

1.	I reread my paper looking for errors.
2.	I started all sentences with a capital letter.
3.	I ended all sentences with a period or question mark.
4.	I capitalized the word "I".
5.	I have tried to find and correct any misspelled words.
6.	I have used commas where they are needed.
7.	I have indented paragraphs.
8.	I have provided margins on both sides of the paper.
9.	I have checked for complete sentences.
10.	All of my sentences make sense.

Figure 6.36. Proofreading Checklist.

would like to implement a more comprehensive approach, consider using a multisensory, structured-language program. These programs require direct teaching of all skills and concepts. Nothing is left to chance, and the teacher continuously interacts with the students. Another common characteristic of these structured programs is that they present instruction in a logical sequence, beginning with the most basic elements such as phonemes and graphemes, and progressing to more difficult elements, such as expressing ideas. Both decoding and encoding skills are developed when using these multisensory structured-language programs, as reading and spelling are taught together. As examples, explore any Orton-Gillingham approach, the *Slingerland Multisensory Approach* (www.slingerland.org), *Project Read* (www.projectread.com), the *Herman Method* (www.cambiumlearning.com), *Wilson Reading* (www.wilsonlanguage.com), or *Language!* Designed for students in grades 3–12, *Language! A Comprehensive Literacy Curriculum* is available from Sopris West (www.sopriswest.com). It uses cumulative and sequential multisensory activities to engage students while establishing skills in phonemic awareness and phonics, word recognition and spelling, vocabulary and morphology, and grammar and usage.

If you are primarily concerned about developing a student's spelling skills, many additional materials exist. For example, *SpellWell*, from Educators Publishing Service (EPS) (www.epsbooks.com), is designed for grades 2–5. The skills taught throughout the program are cumulative. Each book is consistently organized to include grade-appropriate words that follow a particular spelling rule or pattern. Sight words frequently used in writing are also included. *Spellography* by Sopris West (www.sopriswest.com) is a classroom-tested spelling program for teaching word roots and multisyllabic spelling skills through a variety of games and activities. For older students, grades 7 and higher, *Spell of Words* from

EPS (www.epsbooks.com) covers phonograms, syllabication, word building with prefixes, word patterns, suffixes, plurals, and possessives. Chapters contain explanations of spelling rules, exercises, and suggestions for short compositions. *Spelling Through Morphographs* from SRA McGraw (www.sraonline.com) uses direct instruction to help develop spelling, reading, and vocabulary skills, especially for older students. Content focuses on learning the meaningful units of words, morphemes, which include affixes and base words. This knowledge fosters spelling, builds word knowledge, and increases the student's ability to decode multisyllabic words.

For teaching grammar, consider *Getting It Right: Fresh Approaches to Teaching Grammar, Usage, and Correctness* for grades 4 and higher or *Noun Hounds and Other Great Grammar Games* for grades 3–6, both from Scholastic (www.scholastic.com). *G.U.M. Grammar, Usage, & Mechanics That Really Stick* for grades 3–8 offers fifty flexible lessons in each book and is available from Zaner-Bloser (www.zaner-bloser.com). *Grammar Rock*, a software program, is part of the *Schoolhouse Rock!* series (www.schoolhouse-rock.com) and provides a multimedia approach to teaching grammar. Again, a simple Internet search will produce many alternative materials.

CONCLUSION

Students who struggle with writing often have extreme difficulty mastering basic writing skills. When provided with precise feedback and practice, however, students can learn specific skills that are necessary for writing. Provision of instruction in basic skills requires you to perform a balancing act between process and product. You may wonder how you can help students develop their basic writing skills and reinforce the accurate use of skills without discouraging their willingness and desire to write. If you provide students with meaningful and interesting writing activities, they will see the purposes and the benefits of writing. As a result, their commitment to correcting errors in spelling and usage will increase, as will their skills. The key ingredient for ensuring that students improve their basic writing skills is not a particular program but an effective teacher.

chapter 7

Improving Written Expression

Beneath the rule of men entirely great,
The pen is mightier than the sword.
  —Baron Bulwer-Lytton in *Richelieu*,
        Act II, sc. ii

Recent conceptualizations of writing have focused on how writers generate and organize ideas and how they can use strategies to facilitate this process. As noted by Strickland (1972, p. 498): "The quality of what is expressed in writing depends upon the quality of thinking that undergirds it." This reminds us of the important connection between oral language and written expression. Without an adequate language base, the quality of our thinking and thus the quality of our writing will be limited. In fact, it is often necessary to first teach oral language skills as a bridge to written language or to work on oral and written language simultaneously through the combination of speech and print. Many of the methods used to enhance skill in written expression involve the application of strategies and require thinking with language. These strategies are designed to assist students in thinking (cognition), in thinking about their own thinking (metacognition), and in thinking about their language (metalinguistics).

This chapter begins with a brief discussion of the relationship among metacognition, metalinguistics, and strategy instruction. Next, a variety of prewriting activities are presented. Instructional programs for the areas of vocabulary, text structure, and revision are then discussed. Each section discusses general instructional principles and then provides descriptions of specific instructional strategies.

METACOGNITION, METALINGUISTICS, AND STRATEGY INSTRUCTION

Metacognition involves awareness of our own thinking processes—in other words thinking about our thinking. For example, when approaching a new task, we may think, "What do I know about this topic? How will I accomplish this task?" When we are aware of our thinking, we can step back and look at what we are doing and evaluate our performance. "Am I on task?" "I don't know how to do this. What should I do?" Self-questioning is an important metacognitive activity and a powerful and necessary learning strategy. This is the primary way we monitor our own writing performance. As you can see, language plays an important role in metacognition.

Metalinguistics refers to our awareness of language and involves our ability to think about language. For example, phonological awareness and word awareness illustrate aspects of metalinguistic awareness—being aware of the nature and components of our language. Blending and segmenting phonemes and recognizing words as a unit of language are just two examples of metalinguistic tasks that are necessary for developing literacy skills.

Strategy instruction fosters both metacognitive and metalinguistic awareness. Through explicit instruction, students are taught strategies that help develop their awareness of their thinking and their language. They learn how to monitor and regulate their own performance through self-questioning and self-talk strategies. Examples of the types of self-questioning we use during writing would include

Am I considering my reader?

Do I need more specific wording?

Did I change subjects without realizing it?

Am I connecting my new ideas with the old ideas?

Are there better words to make my writing clearer?

Have I used cohesive ties to strengthen the connections within and between sentences?

Because written expression is so complex, it is essential that students be taught how to use metacognitive strategies. Your role is to teach your students to be self-aware learners so they can successfully translate their thoughts and ideas into writing.

Figure 7.1 illustrates an example of poor self-monitoring, a metacognitive process. Hope, a sixth-grade student, was asked to write a compare-contrast essay on the major differences between humans and apes. Although she introduced the topic appropriately, she failed to maintain her focus. Because Hope did not monitor her thinking or her performance, her essay got off track. Fortunately, you can teach students many strategies to help them with self-monitoring.

Principles of Strategy Instruction

Several principles apply to strategy instruction. The majority of metacognitive intervention strategies share the following features:

1. Explicit instruction in regard to the goal and purpose of the strategy.

2. Explicit instruction in regard to how to apply the strategy.

3. Provision of feedback in regard to how use of the strategy improves task performance.

4. Monitoring the effectiveness of the strategy in improving writing.

Exhibit 7.1 provides an overview of the process used to teach various strategies. As with all strategy instruction principles, the process moves from helping students know the what, how, when, where, and why of the strategy followed by teacher demonstration of the strategy using a think-aloud procedure. Then the process moves to student practice with corrective feedback and ultimately to using the strategy independently.

As a general principle, guided discussions can help students become aware of what strategies they use when writing. Through individual teacher-student conferences, you can help students understand how they approach writing tasks and discuss alternative strategies that would be more effective. Following is a transcription of a brief dialogue between Irene, who struggles with spelling, and her fourth-grade teacher. This example illustrates the relationship between oral language and writing. Good oral language is necessary but not sufficient for good written expression. In this case, when writing, Irene limits her word choices on the basis of her ability to spell the words.

Teacher: Your story writing skill has improved tremendously in the last few months, Irene. How do you decide what to write about?

Irene: I sit and think of something that I like or something good that I saw on TV or read in a book. Then I look around the room and in my spelling dictionary to see the words that I can use because I know how to spell them.

Teacher: And then what do you do?

Irene: Then I think out my story but I have to change it sometimes because I can't think of how to spell the words. But I can spell words like "and" and "there" and I couldn't even do that last year.

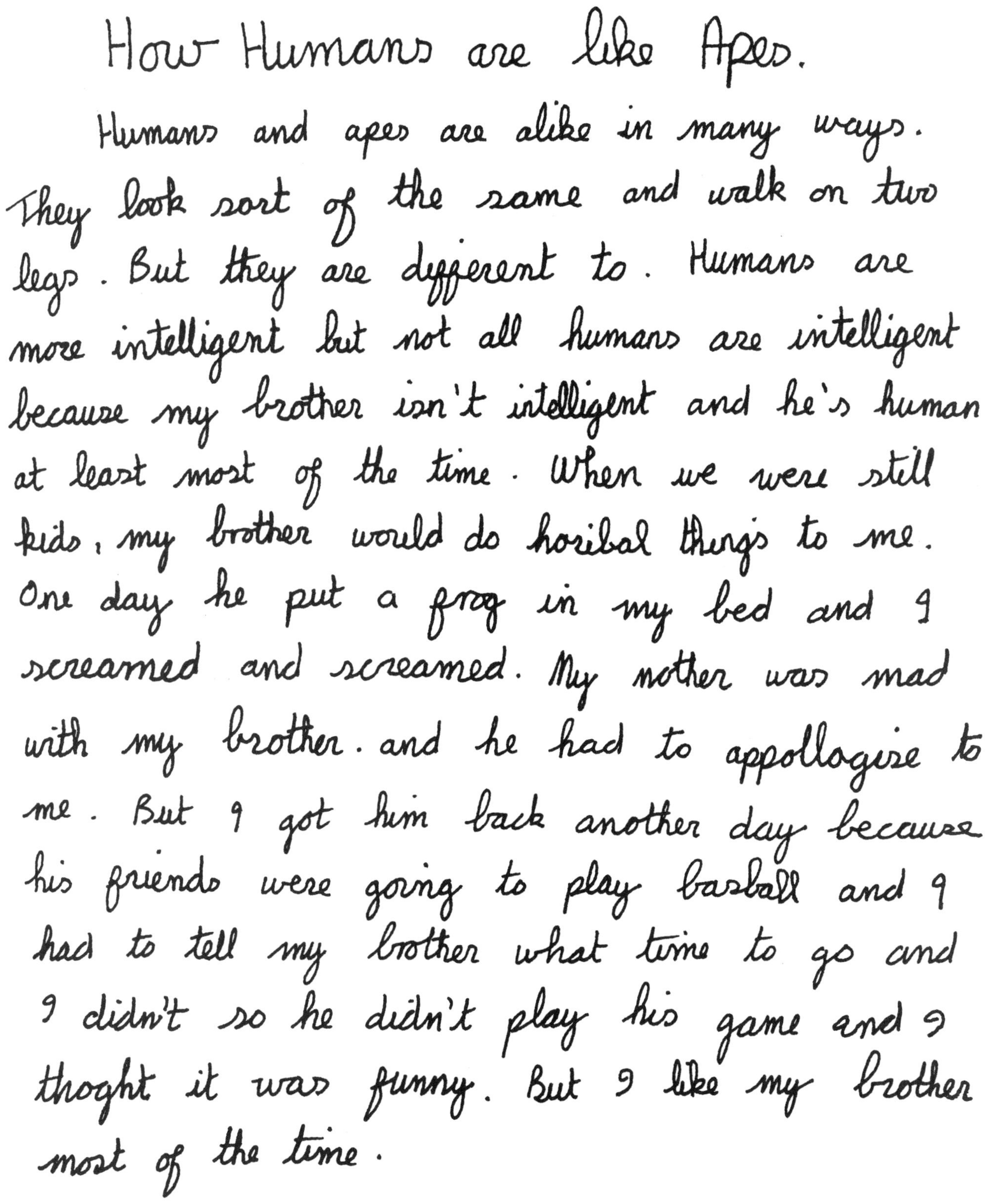

How Humans are like Apes.

Humans and apes are alike in many ways. They look sort of the same and walk on two legs. But they are different to. Humans are more intelligent but not all humans are intelligent because my brother isn't intelligent and he's human at least most of the time. When we were still kids, my brother would do horibal things to me. One day he put a frog in my bed and I screamed and screamed. My mother was mad with my brother. and he had to appollogise to me. But I got him back another day because his friends were going to play basball and I had to tell my brother what time to go and I didn't so he didn't play his game and I thoght it was funny. But I like my brother most of the time.

Figure 7.1. Hope's Compare-Contrast Essay.

Teacher: You have so many good ideas but I would rather you were not so concerned about your spelling. Try to get down part of the word you want to write, or just make a blank line and then later when we are editing your story we can put in the correct spelling. You could even draw a little picture of the word if you want.

Exhibit 7.1. Stages of Strategy Instruction.

Discuss the strategy: The teacher and students are active collaborators who discuss the purpose and benefits of the strategy. The students commit to learning and using the strategy. The teacher explains how they can measure the impact of the strategy on writing performance through progress monitoring.

Model it: The teacher models how to use the strategy, employing self-talk and self-instructions. Students may set performance goals for improving their writing.

Memorize it: Students memorize the mnemonic, the steps of the strategy, and their personal performance goals. They may use strategy reminder charts until the steps have been learned.

Support it: Students practice using the strategy until they can use it independently, receiving help from the teacher and peers. Each student receives as much individualized instruction as needed.

Independent use: Students use the strategy independently, trying to find new situations to apply the strategy.

Feedback: The teacher and students reflect upon how use of the strategy has helped improve writing.

Source: Adapted from Graham, S., & Harris, K. R. (2005). *Writing better: Effective strategies for teaching students with learning difficulties.* Baltimore: Paul H. Brookes.

Irene: That sounds okay because I remember the words that I want to write, I'm just not sure how to spell them. You know I can tell better stories than I can write.

Teacher: You are a good storyteller, but tell me, how else do you get ideas?

Irene: Well, sometimes I get ideas from talking with the other kids in class, and other times I look at Brian's paper and see what he's writing about. Sometimes he asks me what I am writing about because he can't think of anything either. Sometimes when I ask him, he helps me with spelling.

Teacher: Maybe next time, before we write, you and Brian could work together and see if you can come up with some ideas that you both would like to write about.

Irene: That would be fun because he can help with spelling and most days I can tell a good story.

Steps in Strategy Instruction

The first step in teaching strategies is to develop students' interest in writing as a form of communication and their understanding of the purpose of the strategy. When you make assignments, make sure that the activities are meaningful. Once students are fully involved in a writing activity, you can select specific strategies that will help increase their skill.

Most learning strategies involve the following steps:

1. Students learn and practice the skills necessary for using the specific strategy.
2. The teacher and students determine the present level of performance in the selected skill.
3. The teacher discusses the rationale for the use of the strategy.
4. The teacher describes the steps and models the strategy.
5. Students memorize the steps of the strategy.
6. Students practice the strategy and receive corrective feedback from the teacher.
7. Students apply the strategy in different circumstances, for different purposes, and without teacher assistance.

To increase students' abilities to monitor their performance, they must be able to see the actions and hear the talk of skilled writers who are engaged in actual problem solving. This is why it is critical that, initially, you model the type of self-talk and vocabulary that writers use as they compose. You must demonstrate the task using a think-aloud procedure that leaves nothing to chance—in other words, explicit instruction is necessary. Students with writing difficulties require numerous opportunities to manipulate language in order to express their thoughts. You can easily incorporate guided discussions into the prewriting or planning components of writing.

Planning Strategies

Students write most easily when the topics are related and relevant to their background experience and knowledge. Sometimes students do not know much about a topic or have misinformation about the subject. Figure 7.2 illustrates two get well notes written by fourth-grade students, Taylor and Alexis, to their classmate, Aidan, who had just had his appendix removed.

Usually, when students do not write much it is not because they lack knowledge, but rather they do not know how to communicate their ideas through writing. Before creating text, all writers can benefit from various activities that help them develop, expand upon, and organize their ideas prior to writing. You can use prewriting activities for any type of text structure, either narrative or expository.

Observation

To help students develop ideas prior to writing, you might want to use observation activities. Following are suggested activities using pictures, objects, or events designed to help students record their observations (Tompkins & Friend, 1986):

1. Observation (Pictures)
   a. Provide students with an interesting picture with details.
   b. Ask students to name all the things that can be seen in the picture.
   c. List the responses on the chalkboard.
   d. Help students categorize the words.
   e. Have students use the words to write sentences to describe the picture.
2. Observation (Objects)
   a. Gather a collection of common objects such as combs, rocks, and toothbrushes.
   b. Distribute the objects among the students.

Dear Aidan,   Apri 21

How are you feeling? It reely stincks that you had to get your appendix removed. It's good you didn't live back in 1803. I hope you are feeling better.

Sincerely,
Taylor

Dear Aidan,

I'm sorry about your appendix. I hope your other ones ok. We all miss you so come back soon!!

From,
Alexis

PS: Hope you feel better.

Figure 7.2. Get Well Notes from Fourth-Grade Students.

   c. Have each student list five observations about his or her object.
   d. Have the students combine the five observations into five sentences, without naming the object.
   e. Collect all the objects and the written descriptions.
   f. Read the descriptions aloud and have the students guess which object is being described.

    g. As skill develops, make the task more difficult by distributing items that are similar.

3. Observation (Events)

    a. Have students observe an event such as a candle burning or a dog eating.

    b. Help students write down words to describe the event.

    c. Help students organize the list of words into a logical sequence.

    d. Ask students to write a description of the event with the help of the organizer.

Following are several additional strategies that you may use to help stimulate the writing of your students:

1. Ask students to record their observations in a sequence, noting the beginning, middle, and end of the activity or observation.

2. Provide your students with incomplete sentences that offer choices to complete the sentences. As students improve their skills, have them create their own responses.

3. Create different exercises for summarizing material. For example, have students rewrite sentences for different audiences. Or, have students write summaries of lower-grade books that are then attached on the inside cover of the book for younger readers.

4. Have students create the dialogue for cartoon or fictional characters. Several computer programs are available, or you can use newspaper cartoons and delete the dialogue.

5. Correspond with your students. Have students write in a personal notebook that you review. Write an entry in each student's notebook that emphasizes the communicative aspect of writing and encourages the student to reply.

Fifty Journal Topics

Sometimes students cannot think of anything to write about and need assistance selecting a topic for journal or story writing. The following list, compiled by Wendy Randall Wall (personal communication to author, August 15, 2008), provides possible starters for journal entries.

1. If I could visit any place I would . . .
2. I think life on another planet would be . . .
3. If I had three wishes I would . . .
4. My favorite sport is . . .
5. The last movie I saw was . . .
6. My favorite professional athlete (or movie star) is . . .
7. I love my pet because . . .
8. A person whom I admire is . . .
9. The best gift I have received is . . .
10. When I was younger I liked to . . .
11. I think an interesting experience would be . . .
12. Something I do well is . . .
13. The most incredible journey I have ever made is . . .
14. The season I like best is . . .
15. If I could be in charge of the world I would . . .
16. My favorite activity is . . .
17. A good book I have read is . . .
18. If I could be locked in a toy store I would . . .
19. I love my best friend because . . .
20. My family is . . .
21. Something I have always wanted to do is . . .
22. My ideal vacation would be . . .
23. My favorite subject in school is . . .
24. If I could be the teacher I would . . .
25. I felt proud when I . . .
26. When I am older I will . . .
27. If I won the lottery I would . . .
28. The funniest thing I ever did was . . .
29. What I like most about myself is . . .
30. If I could be the president of the United States, I would . . .
31. Something people don't know about me is . . .
32. After school I like to . . .
33. The best choice I ever made was . . .
34. If I could be any animal, I would choose to be . . .

35. My favorite place to be is . . .
36. Something I like to do for others is . . .
37. When I go to the mall, I like to . . .
38. One day I would like to learn to . . .
39. What really drives me crazy is . . .
40. Someone who has really helped me is . . .
41. A country I would like to visit is . . .
42. One of my goals is . . .
43. A fun game to play is . . .
44. A person I would like to meet is . . .
45. I am thankful for . . .
46. If I could fly I would . . .
47. I was mad (or scared or surprised) when . . .
48. Something I have always wanted to do is . . .
49. My favorite superhero is . . .
50. If I could change something about myself, it would be . . .

In considering the importance of topic selection, Wendy relayed this story regarding a friend of hers who teaches sixth grade in an inner-city school. For the state writing exam, her students were given a writing prompt asking them to imagine discovering a treasure chest. They were to write about what they would do with it. One-third of her class came from homes where they had limited experiences and had no idea whatsoever what a treasure chest was. A few of the students wrote about finding a chess set. They automatically received zeros on their writing tests because they were off the topic. Obviously, it didn't matter if they could write; their limited cultural experiences (lack of exposure to stories or movies involving treasure chests) ruined their opportunity to show what they knew about written language. Of course, these kids were invited to summer school to remediate their obvious written-language deficits.

Twenty-Five Story Starters

Often students like to be provided with the first sentence or two of a narrative. The following list provides twenty-five story starters. You might prefer to substitute a name for the word *I* in order to provide variety.

1. One dark, rainy night, as I lay in my bed, I heard . . .
2. I woke up with a start. The room was filled with a bright light, and there in front of me was . . .
3. It was an ordinary Saturday in August. Or so I thought. Everything changed, however, when I went to the store . . .
4. I was reading peacefully when, all of a sudden, my brother ran into the room, screaming . . .
5. I walked into the store and couldn't believe my eyes. There in front of me was the man I had seen on *America's Most Wanted* . . .
6. At last, I was going to get the chance to play on my school's baseball (or soccer) team . . .
7. At last, I was going to get the chance to dance (or sing) in my school concert . . .
8. I was walking to school, minding my own business, when all of a sudden . . .
9. I didn't believe in ghosts. That's why I was happy to stay in the haunted house. Little did I know . . .
10. Once upon a time, a princess was walking in her garden when . . .
11. I thought our trip to the beach would be quite boring, but I was wrong . . .
12. I couldn't believe my ears when my teddy bear winked at me and said . . .
13. The day was a disaster. Everything went wrong from start to finish . . .
14. I thought I was a good driver until last Saturday in the rain. As I was driving down the highway, the car skidded out of control and . . .
15. I am so excited. I have been waiting for this day to come for what seems like eternity. Tonight is the night that I . . .
16. "Stop," the man shouted, "You cannot go in there." We looked at each other and . . .
17. It could only have happened at Halloween when witches and goblins roamed the streets . . .

18. The doctor spoke with a soft voice, but I saw the evil glint in his eye . . .
19. "That's an odd request," exclaimed my fairy godmother, "but I shall see what I can do . . ."
20. I smiled, thanked my principal for the reward money, and thought back to the events of the day . . .
21. Imagine my surprise when I saw that Santa had left me some magic stardust. What fun I would have that day . . .
22. It was a beautiful, warm day. I was sipping juice in my backyard and listening to the birds when . . .
23. I smiled at my brother (or sister) and whispered, "Today is going to be the best day of our lives because . . ."
24. I felt myself falling down the deep, smelly hole. I hit the bottom with a thud. With dazed eyes, I looked up and saw . . .
25. I noticed that my teacher looked strange. Suddenly, she leaned forward and . . .

Twenty-Five Story Endings

As a variation, you can provide students with story endings instead of starters. Many students comment that writing a story with a given ending is more difficult than writing one that has a given beginning. Before using story endings, ensure that students' skill levels are sufficient for them to experience success.

1. I opened my eyes and, to my delight, saw that the creature had disappeared.
2. The kangaroo grew to like the zoo and lived there happily for many years.
3. I turned back and glanced at the house, and I knew that I would never return.
4. The magic potion had worked. I had saved the world.
5. Cold sweat was running down my face. I could not believe that it had all been a dream.
6. After cheering me, the villagers returned safely to their homes.
7. I was so happy. My little sister (or brother) was safe in my mother's arms.

8. The king changed his ways and soon became one of the kindest people in the world.
9. I shall cherish my prize for the rest of my life.
10. The animals took a last look at the cage and ran quickly into the forest.
11. I had had my day with the magic lamp. I wondered who would be the next to discover it.
12. I was in the hospital for two weeks and have never forgotten how lucky I was to escape.
13. After the spacecraft left, I wondered if it all had been a dream.
14. Never again did I look at dinosaur fossils in the same way.
15. The wind blew gently in my hair and the sun warmed my skin. I was free at last.
16. I knew that I would never see anything as beautiful as this again.
17. The giant became friends with the villagers, and they all lived happily ever after.
18. I knew that no one would forget April 17th, the day of the flood (or fire or earthquake or volcano).
19. They ran into each other's arms and promised that they would never again be parted.
20. Twenty years have passed since then. I wonder if they still remember me.
21. We laughed and danced in the rain.
22. Now I understand why the door must always be kept locked.
23. The noise quieted down slowly, and the people left gradually. It was finally over.
24. It was so long ago. Today, the island is only a memory.
25. It was the happiest day of my life.

Even when provided with topics, students still need to spend time thinking about the details they will include, as well as receiving feedback about their ideas. Mikalah, a third-grade student, was planning to write a descriptive paragraph about her cat. Figure 7.3 presents her first draft. She talks about how much she loves her cat and then starts writing a letter to a friend. Her teacher then helped Mikalah create categories for a web so that she could think of additional ways to describe her cat. Figure 7.4 presents Mikalah's web. Because of more time spent planning, her next draft included much more detail and maintained the topic.

Older students also experience the same types of problems. Figure 7.5 presents an assignment by Don, an eighth-grade student. He was asked to write advice to the president about how he should handle some current concern regarding the economy. Although Don spent an entire class period on this assignment, you can see that he had not developed his ideas. Don needed to spend more time planning before writing.

Similarly, Jack, a tenth-grader, was asked to write specific questions regarding chapters of *Huckleberry Finn*. Figure 7.6 illustrates his questions with a note from the general education teacher to the special education teacher.

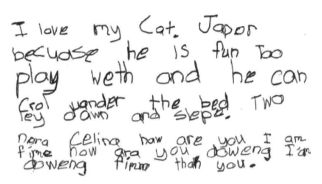

Figure 7.3. Mikalah's Description of Her Cat.

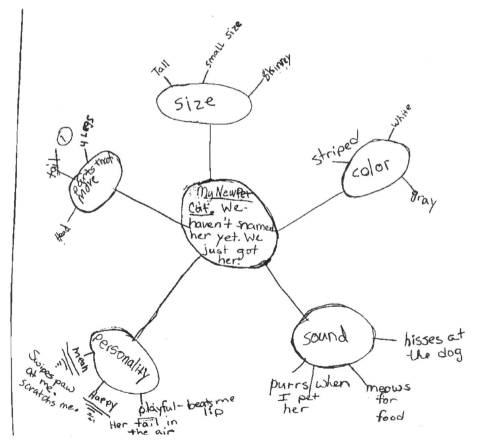

Figure 7.4. Mikalah's Web.

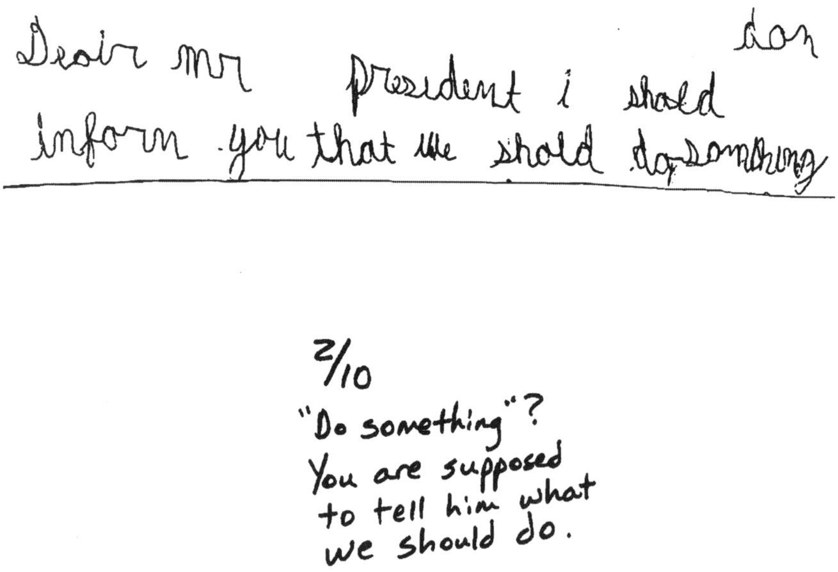

Dear mr President i shold don inform you that we shold do something

²⁄₁₀
"Do something"?
You are supposed
to tell him what
we should do.

Figure 7.5. Don's Advice to the President.

who was Huck
Who was TOM
who was Jim
who was Marr
who was Dad

This was a paper to write 5 questions on a couple of chapters of *Huckleberry Finn*. There was no effort that went into this that could show that Jack read these chapters, although I believe he did.

Figure 7.6. Jack's Questions on *Huckleberry Finn*.

Jack had read the chapters, but the process of generating questions was much more difficult for him.

Mapping and Graphic Organizers

Use of a variety of maps and graphic organizers can help students such as Don and Jack develop and organize their thoughts prior to writing. Graphic organizers can help students depict the important ideas and then show their relationships to each other. Students may list their ideas and then expand and organize them. In addition, graphic organizers can help students learn to recognize and use common organizational patterns or text structures (for example, compare-contrast, cause and effect, or sequential).

Procedure

The process of developing graphic organizers does not change, no matter which style of map, web, or frame students use. Develop the organizer, model the steps, and provide cues or guided practice until the student learns to use the strategy independently. Essentially, you use explicit instruction to introduce any new organizer or strategy. The first step in mapping is the brainstorming of ideas. The purpose of brainstorming is to increase background knowledge and help students retrieve prior knowledge. During brainstorming, place the emphasis on divergent thinking and the rapid production of ideas. View all ideas as both pertinent and worthy. You can use the following steps to introduce graphic organizers:

1. During brainstorming, write one- or two-word cues to represent concepts or ideas as they occur.

2. When no more ideas are being generated, return to each cue, elaborating upon the idea within.

3. Color-code ideas that can be grouped or categorized together.

4. Write the ideas on a graphic organizer developed for the text type (for example, compare-contrast).

5. Develop paragraphs for each category, expanding on the ideas already formulated.

As students become more familiar and confident with the use of mapping and graphic organizers, help them to categorize the ideas as they are generated. At this point, color-coding becomes unnecessary. Once students can construct their own organizers, they can explain their organization to others.

Types

Many different types of graphic organizers exist. Figure 7.7 illustrates and describes several types of commonly used graphic organizers. You can also include a small version of the graphic in the bottom right-hand corner of the page. Students can fill in the appropriate part of the small visual as they complete the steps on the full-size model. As students' familiarity with graphic organizers increases, they can develop their own models. Figure 7.8 illustrates a graphic organizer developed by Cecilia, a fifth-grade student, who was studying the ocean.

The use of graphic organizers can also help students increase their vocabulary. For example, students can place a word in the center of the map, often referred to as a semantic map or web, and then generate synonyms or antonyms for the word in the outside circles.

VOCABULARY

The difference between the right word and the almost right word is the difference between lightning and a lightning bug.
—Mark Twain

Sequential Paragraph Organizer

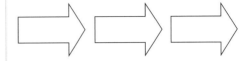

Compare-Contrast Organizer (Venn Diagram)

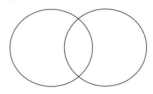

Descriptive Organizer

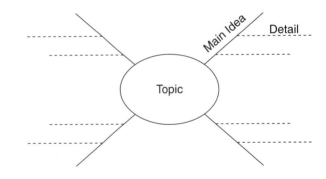

Cause and Effect Organizer

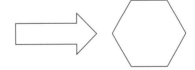

Figure 7.7. Sample Graphic Organizers for Different Text Structures.

You can use a variety of instructional strategies to help students expand their word knowledge. For some students, a limited vocabulary is the primary reason for their written expression difficulties. A good language base is necessary for written language, even though other factors can inhibit performance also. Although many teachers have students look up and write the definitions of new words, this is not an effective procedure for several reasons: the activity is not engaging, usually only one meaning is written, numerous exposures are not provided, and

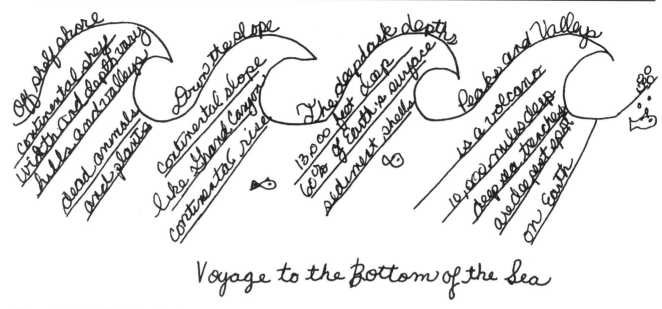

Figure 7.8. Cecilia's Graphic Organizer of the Ocean.

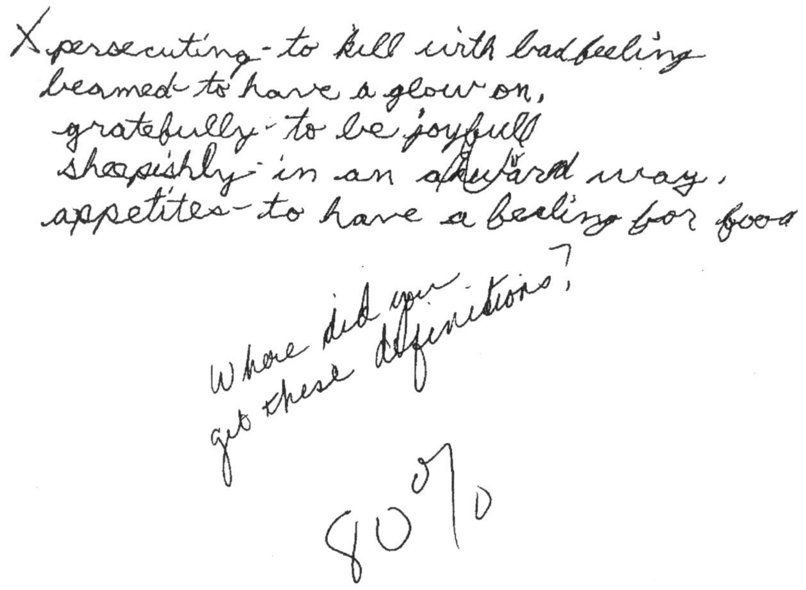

X persecuting - to kill with bad feeling
beamed to have a glow on,
gratefully - to be joyfull
shapishly - in an akward way,
appetites - to have a feeling for food

Where did you get these definitions?

80%

Figure 7.9. Zack's Word Definitions.

the word is viewed in only one context. Also, many students with language difficulties do not understand the meanings of the dictionary definitions. Figure 7.9 presents words and definitions written by Zack, a ninth-grade student. His teacher asks where he got the definitions. It seems that Zack is relying on his own or a friend's knowledge to define the words.

Principles of Effective Vocabulary Instruction

Effective vocabulary instruction is based on the following principles:

1. Provides numerous exposures to words in a variety of contexts.

2. Provides illustrations of usage in differing contexts.
3. Makes connections among words with similar meanings.
4. Teaches strategies to help students remember word meanings.
5. Integrates knowledge of new words with known words.
6. Provides review of word meanings.
7. Provides opportunities for meaningful use.

Fortunately, the visual nature of writing provides an excellent opportunity for helping students expand their vocabularies.

Word Retrieval

Some students benefit from specific training in word-retrieval strategies. This instruction is designed to help students replace common words with more descriptive words. You can encourage vocabulary development by having students brainstorm about a variety of words prior to writing. For example, prior to writing, ask students to think of different words that could replace *said* (for example, *shouted*, *whispered*, and *yelled*). When students learn to classify words, they can select more precise vocabulary prior to or during writing.

Classification

You can use several different prewriting activities to enhance skill in the ability to classify, rehearse, and recall vocabulary (Israel, 1984).

1. Association between the category names and the names of members of the category:
   a. An ostrich is a _____
   b. Is an ostrich a bird or a fish?
   c. Ostrich, eagle, and osprey are _____
2. Identification of an item that does not belong in a particular semantic category:
   a. Which does not belong—boy, girl, dog, man?
   b. Why doesn't *cheese* belong in this list—milk, cheese, water, juice?

3. Selection of an item from a heterogeneous list that represents a named category:
   a. Tomato, girl, leg, elephant, rose: Which one is a food? Which one is a flower?
   b. Which one of these is a fruit—potato, apple, or yogurt?
4. Identification of object features to help differentiate between objects:
   a. How are a book and a newspaper alike?
   b. How are a book and a newspaper different?
5. Identification of subcategories within a general classification: zebra, dog, cat, elephant, giraffe, rabbit
   a. What is the general classification of the list above?
   b. In the list above, what are the two subcategories within the general classification of "animals"?
6. Association of items with some specific shared feature(s):
   a. List (or Find) all objects that need air to breathe.
7. Visual-imagery of items to help classify and subcategorize:
   a. Close your eyes and imagine you are in a spaceship. Name all of the things you see.

Cuing Strategies

When learning words or connected information, instruction in various cuing strategies can help students with word retrieval. Cuing strategies can be most beneficial when learning information for a test or examination. Examples of the most widely used cuing strategies are

1. Linking the word with its classification (for example, zebra—animal).
2. Pairing highly associative words with each other (bread and butter).
3. Using sentence completion or fill-in-the-blank strategies (Italians eat *pasta*).
4. Using chunking or the recoding of individual items into a superordinate system. As an example, the superordinate system of

animals would include "cows," "horses," and "zebras." Or, students can practice chunking words into semantic categories, regardless of their position in the list (for example, apple, *tea*, orange, lemon, *coffee, juice*, banana, *water*).

5. Using phonemic cuing with the production of the initial sound or syllable ("ant," "peg," "herc" for Antigone, Pegasus, Hercules).

6. Forming sentences from the phonemic cues ("*Richard of York gave battle in vain*" to remember the sequential order of the colors of the rainbow (red, orange, yellow, green, blue, indigo, violet).

7. Using visual imagery for remembering lists, for first-word cuing, or for remembering important, connected facts (for example, imagining an *elephant* wearing a *crown* and holding a *noose* to remember the fate of an individual who tried to capture the ruler of Burma).

Morphology

You can teach students morphological rules through systematic exposure to the rules. For example, encourage students to check the endings of words and to note tense markers (such as *-ed*) or plural markers (such as *-s* or *-es*). You can also use any of the activities described in the following to help students increase their knowledge of the relationships and meanings of various word forms.

Structural Analysis Maps

You can use graphic organizers to demonstrate the relationships among prefixes, suffixes, and root words. Write the root word in the middle of the map and then place prefixes and suffixes extended from the side. After completing the map as a class activity, students can attempt to write all of the words that can be formed through the addition of various affixes.

Figure 7.10 illustrates several adaptations of this type of procedure. In the first map with the root word *cover*, the student can read across from prefix to root word to suffix, creating various derivations of the word. Students can make separate maps for adding prefixes or suffixes. Or, as an alternative, you can place a prefix or suffix in the center of the map.

Prefixes, Suffixes, and Roots

You can use additional activities to increase students' understanding of prefixes, suffixes, and roots. For the first activity, you can use the following steps:

1. Explain that many words consist of prefixes, suffixes, or roots.

2. Give examples of some common ones and explain their meanings.

3. List common prefixes, suffixes, or roots horizontally along a line.
   For example, UN DIS FRIEND TION LY

4. Under each of the headings, have students list appropriate words.
   For example, *unhappy, disappear, friendship, action, gladly*

5. Discuss both appropriate and inappropriate words with the students (for example, explain why the word *uniform* does not fit under *un*).

6. Encourage the students to "mix and match." For example, *unfriendly, disagreeing*.

7. Have the students brainstorm about additional prefixes, suffixes, and roots and discuss the meaning of those.

8. Repeat the activity with new morphemes.

You can also use the following activity to help students increase their knowledge of the meanings of affixes:

1. Introduce the concept of prefixes, suffixes, and roots to students.

2. Brainstorm about examples of prefixes and suffixes.

3. Have students think about and attempt to identify the meaning of each affix.

4. Write the affixes and the meanings on the chalkboard.

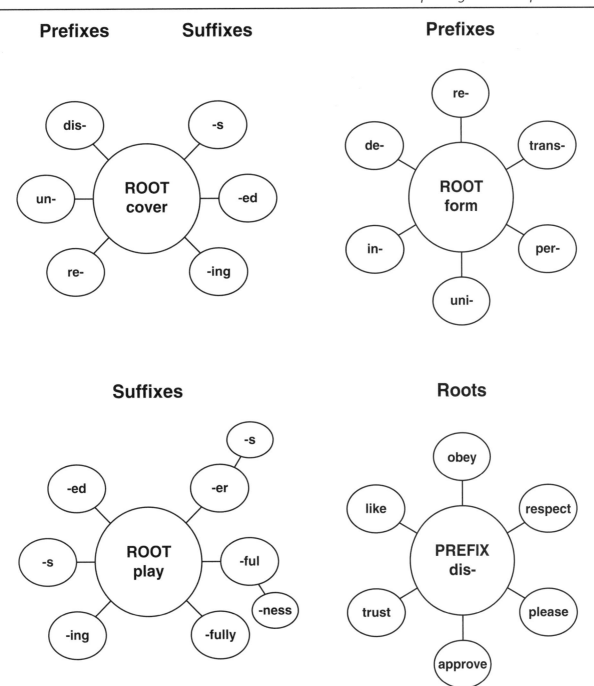

Figure 7.10. Examples of Graphic Organizers for Affixes.

5. Asking leading questions to help students infer the meanings (for example, "Who has ever heard of a manicure?" "What does it involve?" "So what do you think the prefix 'mani' means?").

6. Have students copy the affixes and meanings onto their papers.

7. Have students combine the prefixes, suffixes, and roots to make multisyllabic real or nonsense words. For example, the phrase

"micropolycephalus monster" (small, many-headed monster) would be an example of a nonsense word.

Morphological Cloze

You can also use the cloze procedure to help draw attention to morphological rules. Prepare a cloze passage in which the endings have been deleted from several nouns and verbs within the passage. Ask the student to read the passage and then write in the correct endings.

As an alternative procedure, prepare a cloze passage from the student's own writing. Place a blank where the correct endings were not included or use Wite-Out to delete endings. Ask the student to reconstruct the passage. Practice with this type of procedure is particularly effective for students who tend to omit word endings in their writing. As Penny, a sixth-grade student, commented, "When I am writing, I just don't notice the endings of words. *Walk* and *walked* look just about the same to me."

Word Knowledge

Perhaps the most difficult vocabulary problem to address is a student's understandings of word meanings. A student who has difficulty with word associations has developed qualitatively different understanding of word meanings. These difficulties influence writing performance, as well as communication skill. Recently, in a high school English class, two students, Chad and Hal, were paired together to provide revision suggestions on their papers. Chad offered feedback to Hal, and Hal made appropriate revisions to his paper. When Hal initiated feedback to Chad, he began with the comment, "You have probably done a lower level of analysis on this paper than anyone else." Chad became defensive at the implied insult of "lower level." Later, Hal explained that his intention was to tell Chad that he had done a "deeper" level of analysis and put more work into the paper than others. Hal did not understand the differences in meaning between lower and deeper.

Semantics includes the various shades of meaning a word may have, as well as knowledge of word use. Semantic knowledge helps one to differentiate between the meanings of words, such as *disagreement* and *squabble, house* and *residence*, and *sympathy* and *empathy*. Students like Hal tend to select the wrong word at the wrong time. Inappropriate word choices in speaking and writing are symptomatic of a need for in-depth vocabulary instruction.

You can use a variety of strategies to help students increase their breadth and depth of vocabulary. Fortunately, the visual nature of writing provides an excellent way for working with vocabulary difficulties by allowing us to (a) teach differences in meaning as they correspond to differences in spelling (homophones), (b) highlight by underlining or color-coding the repetition of words in text so that students become sensitive to the need for rephrasing, (c) highlight simplistic words and phrase choices and guide the student toward more sophisticated choices, and (d) construct semantic maps that depict the relationships between and among words. For increasing word knowledge, students appear to benefit from methods that illustrate conceptual relationships. In addition to the use of graphic organizers, you can find other activities for enhancing word knowledge, such as semantic feature analysis.

Semantic Feature Analysis

The purpose of semantic feature analysis is to help students analyze the meanings of specific words and integrate new words into their vocabularies (Johnson & Pearson, 1984). When introducing this activity, use categories that are concrete and familiar to students. Later, you can progress to less familiar or more abstract categories. Figure 7.11 provides an example of a semantic feature analysis related to modes of transportation. You can use the following steps:

1. Select a category and the key words that relate to the topic to be studied.
2. Make a chart with a topic heading at the top, key words down the side, and columns

Transportation	Wheels	Engine	Speed	Cost
Horses	−	−	−	−
Bicycle	+	−	−	−
Car	+	+	+	+
Train	+	+	+	+
Airplane	+	+	+	+

Figure 7.11. Example of Semantic Feature Analysis.

across the page. Label columns with terms that represent features that are shared by some of the words.

3. Have students record a plus or minus sign in each column depending on whether the word has the feature or not. Have students place a question mark if the relationship is unknown.

4. Have students discuss the meanings of each word, the reason for selecting a plus or minus, and how the word is similar to or different from the other words.

5. Present information that clarifies remaining relationships and have students change or complete the signs in the matrix.

6. Guide a discussion about the relationships between the words.

IT FITS Strategy

IT FITS is a strategy to help students recall difficult terminology, such as new words to be learned for a science or history lecture (King-Sears, Mercer, & Sindelar, 1992). The first-letter acronym has the following steps:

I   *Identify* the term.
T   *Tell* the definition of the term.
F   *Find* a key word.
I   *Imagine* the definition doing something with the key word.
T   *Think* about the definition doing something with the key word.
S   *Study* what you imagined until you know the definition.

The key word may be a rhyming word or a word that evokes specific visual imagery. You can expand this strategy by having the student write several sentences that contain the target word.

Self-Regulated Strategy Development

Self-Regulated Strategy Development (SRSD), a model for teaching strategies, has been developed over the past two decades by Steven Graham and Karen Harris. Over thirty research studies have demonstrated that SRSD can be effective for a wide range of students with varying levels of abilities. Numerous applications of SRSD have been created to promote written language development. Students can work on vocabulary development and expansion using a five-step strategy (Harris, Graham, Mason, & Friedlander, 2008). You can target a certain type of word, such as nouns, adjectives, or verbs (action words). To begin, select a picture and then present the following five steps on a chart:

1. Ask the student to look at the picture and write down a list of the type of targeted words, such as adjectives or action words.
2. Have the student think of a story idea that will use the selected words.
3. Ask the student to write a story that makes sense and uses as many of the words as possible.
4. Have the student read the story and ask these questions: Did I write a good story? Did I use the selected words?
5. Have the student edit the story and try to use more of the type of words selected.

Prior to writing, you may also have students set a goal for the number of describing words to be used in the story. After completion of the story, students can count the number of targeted words used and chart this number on a graph. Students can also do this type of activity in pairs or small cooperative groups. The additional dialogue with classmates can help students expand their own word knowledge.

Synonyms and Antonyms

Many students tend to over-rely on certain words. This is particularly true for individuals with learning disabilities who overuse words that they have written successfully in the past. Use the following procedure to teach synonyms and antonyms:

1. Discuss with students the meaning of a word.

2. Have students write the word in the middle of a circle with lines going out.
3. Ask students to try to write synonyms for the word on each of the lines.
4. Encourage students to use the synonyms in writing assignments.

You can use the same procedure for antonyms. If the central word is *happy*, help students think of words such as *unhappy*, *sad*, *miserable*, *glum*, and *depressed* to write on the lines. As skill improves, students can use a thesaurus to help in selecting synonyms or antonyms.

For increasing challenge, have students list the words by degree and place them on a graphic organizer that is shaped like a pyramid. For example, *glum*, *unhappy*, *sad*, *miserable*, and *depressed* could be recorded by gradients of severity. Accept any logical order that the student can explain.

Synonym Cloze

You might also use a modified cloze procedure to help students select more precise words. Once students have written a story, identify several words that are overused or imprecise. Delete each word from the line, replace it with a blank, and then write the word below the line. For example, Omar, a fifth-grade student, began his story with the sentence, *It was a nice day*. His teacher deleted the word *nice* and placed it below the line.

It was a _____ day.
                    nice

Omar was then asked to think of and write a more precise adjective. He wrote, *It was a glorious day*.

Effective vocabulary instruction involves providing students with multiple exposures to words, with attention focused on morphology, using activities to increase understanding of word structure, and using words in a variety of sentence contexts. Making connections between known words and new words and incorporating their use in all types of language activities—reading, writing, listening, and speaking—will help students expand their knowledge of word meanings. For effective word learning, students need to be active participants in their pursuit and mastery of new vocabulary.

TEXT STRUCTURE

Instruction in various text structures can help students organize their ideas. As with other areas of written language, such as vocabulary, students who struggle with writing require direct instruction to increase their knowledge and use of text structure. Fortunately, many strategies exist to help students improve their knowledge of text structures and increase their ability to organize and sequence ideas logically. You might use story grammar cue cards or a check-off system in which students mark off the story parts as they are completed. Or, you might have students complete a paragraph planning guide prior to writing a paragraph. Whatever strategies you select, you will want to ensure that students understand the various organizational structures.

Principles for Teaching Text Structure

Several guidelines exist for teaching text structure organization. Some basic principles are

1. Provide direct, explicit instruction by modeling and teaching different text structures.
2. Show students how to use text structure to plan, generate, and monitor their writing.
3. Help students plan, implement, and monitor their use of strategies.

Explicit instruction in the use of cohesive ties will also help students learn to organize and integrate concepts in writing, whereas explicit instruction in text structure strategies will help students improve both narrative and expository writing.

Coherence and Cohesion

Successful communication in writing requires adherence to three main factors. First, the writer must establish communicative intent and clarify the goal. Next, the writer must select descriptive words and phrases. Finally, the writer must organize his or her thoughts in a logical, readable way. A fundamental principle of writing is that all ideas in a single piece of writing relate in some way to one another. This creates a coherent text, one that makes sense to the reader. *Coherence* then refers to how a text is organized, how the ideas are developed, and how the content hangs together. Creating a coherent text relies on *cohesion*, or making the relationships between and among the words and phrases clear. Cohesion is the "glue" that holds the text together and helps create a coherent text but does not ensure it. Ultimately, the reader of the text decides if the text is coherent by considering whether or not the expressed ideas make sense.

A skilled writer needs to attend to: text coherence, sentence-level cohesion, and word-level cohesion. Text coherence involves the overall plan for a composition that dictates sentence order. Sentence- and word-level cohesion involve the specific ways that sentences are linked together, as well as the transitions within and between sentences. In addition, specific types of words, such as prepositions and conjunctions, play a major role in cohesive writing.

Text Coherence

Text coherence includes both maintaining the topic and sequencing and organizing ideas within the text. The text structure, or underlying organizational schema, allows the writer and reader to communicate more easily because what has been written reflects an anticipated organization. For instance, the schema for a descriptive paragraph differs from the schema for a chapter in a book. Examining text coherence can help you determine a student's problem-solving strategies and gain insights into instructional planning. You can evaluate essays to see if students can state and expand upon opinions and group-related ideas, formulate an argument, and use the appropriate expository text structure.

Sentence-Level Cohesion

Analyzing sentence-level cohesion involves thinking of audience considerations, attending to the given-new paradigm within and across sentences, and using appropriate reference. Writers must make a conscious effort to evaluate their writing from the reader's perspective. They make a conscious effort to reduce the assumptions between the writer and the reader and to ensure that the reader can share the perspective. You will want to remind students frequently that the purpose of writing is communication with the reader or readers. Often, oral reading of text can help students hear the clarity of expression.

One way that writers consider how they sequence information is to pay attention to both the given and the new information within and across sentences. Information that has been established previously (explicitly or implicitly) is termed "given." Communication that adds to or expands previous knowledge is considered "new." Both in speaking and writing, the "given first" order is evident, where given information is followed by new information. Given and new ideas may be presented in a variety of ways. Whenever one word makes reference to another, a semantic tie occurs. Strategies for using pronouns and other references are provided later in this chapter in the section on cohesive ties. Some students misuse reference because of inadequate understanding of the difference between spoken and written language. When speaking, information is derived from both verbal and nonverbal cues, whereas in writing, such assumptions can produce misunderstandings between the writer and the reader. Strategies for helping students think about the given and new information are provided later in this chapter.

Word-Level Cohesion

Word-level cohesion involves the correct use of function words, such as prepositions and prepositional phrases. Prepositional words and phrases help a writer to integrate material and vary sentence structure. Although some students understand how to use prepositions, others do not. Prepositions that have multiple meanings are particularly difficult. For example, "He stood *by* her" differs from "He finished *by* noon," "Multiply 6 *by* 7," "or "The concert was over *by* midnight." Students who do not understand the concepts underlying simple words such as *by* will have difficulty generating written text.

At a deeper level, embedding meaning within and between sentences is also accomplished through the use of cohesive devices. Children with language impairments typically have problems with words indicating temporal and spatial concepts. A student may not understand that *beyond* means going past a certain distance. The same student may have trouble with the cause-effect relationship inferred by the word *because*. Many students can benefit from direct instruction in how to use words that signify a variety of semantic relations. The use of both prepositions and conjunctions can be difficult for some students.

Prepositions

Prepositions link nouns, verbs, and phrases within sentences. The preposition is used to introduce a prepositional phrase. For example, in the sentence, "The child plays with her cat," the word *with* is the preposition that introduces the prepositional phrase "with the cat." These phrases may modify nouns (for example, the scenery *in Paris*) or verbs (for example, jump *over the fence*). The most commonly used prepositions are *for*, *in*, *of*, *on*, and *to*. Explicit instruction in the use of prepositions can help students integrate these words and phrases into their writing. Exhibit 7.2 provides a list of common prepositions presented in alphabetical order.

Conjunctions

The purpose of instruction in cohesion is to help students connect the sentences and paragraphs within their compositions. Students who only use *and* and *and then* as conjunctions can only write

Exhibit 7.2. Examples of Common Prepositions and Compound Prepositions.

about	in addition to
above	in spite of
according to	inside
across	instead of
after	into
against	like
along	near
among	of
around	off
at	on
because	out
because of	into
before	over
behind	past
below	prior to
beneath	since
beside	through
besides	throughout
between	to
beyond	toward
by	under
down	underneath
during	until
except	upon
for	with
from	within
in	without

first-letter mnemonic FAN BOYS to help them recall the seven coordinating conjunctions that are used to write compound and compound-complex sentence patterns (Schumaker & Sheldon, 1985). These conjunctions and their meanings are explained as follows:

For: Means the same as because when used as a conjunction. It differs from the preposition because it is always followed by a subject and a verb.

And: Shows that two ideas are equally important and connected.

Nor: Is used to introduce the second clause of a negative statement and shows that the second clause is also negative. The verb comes before the subject in the second independent clause.

But: Shows contrast.

Or: Joins two ideas when there is a choice between them.

Yet: Shows contrast.

So: Shows that the second clause is the result of the first.

sequential concepts. They will need to be taught how to use more complex conjunctions, such as *because*, *however*, and *furthermore*.

Students with writing difficulties often do not use a variety of conjunctions in their writing, so specific instruction will be necessary. Conjunctions link together words, phrases, and clauses. Writers may use three basic types of conjunctions: coordinating, correlative, and subordinating. Coordinating conjunctions join single words, groups of words, and complete ideas of equal syntactic importance, such as boys *and* girls (nouns) or He waited *but* his ride did not come (two complete ideas). They may combine a noun plus a noun, a verb plus a verb, or a sentence and a sentence (which results in a compound sentence).

As part of the comprehensive Sentence Writing Strategy, you can teach students the

Correlative conjunctions always occur in pairs, and they work together to coordinate two or more ideas (for example, Neither Barb nor Nancy wanted to write another book). When joining singular and plural subjects, the noun closest to the verb determines whether the verb is singular or plural (for example, *Neither* my sisters *nor* my <u>mother was</u>; *Neither* my mother *nor* my <u>sisters were</u>). Subordinating conjunctions are used to introduce dependent adverbial clauses. They subordinate a clause to make it dependent on the main clause. These clauses are usually followed by commas (for example, As the game was about to end, the players became more excited), and may come at the beginning or ending of the main (independent) clause. Some of the coordinating conjunctions can also serve as prepositions (such as *after*, *before*, *since*, *until*, *as*).

Conjunctive adverbs are words that establish the relationship between two or more independent clauses and are often used to join sentences. When the job of an adverb is to

Exhibit 7.3. Examples of Common Conjunctions and Conjunctive Adverbs.

FANBOYS

Coordinating	Correlative	Subordinating	Conjunctive Adverb
for	both . . . and	after	for example
and	not only . . . but also	although, though	furthermore
nor	either . . . or	before	in addition
but	neither . . . nor	if	therefore
or	whether . . . or	unless	meanwhile
yet		until	indeed
so		as	nevertheless
		when, whenever	finally
		where, wherever	however
		since	consequently
		while	likewise
		than	instead

put together two ideas, it is called a conjunctive adverb. Exhibit 7.3 presents examples of the three types of conjunctions and examples of conjunctive adverbs. When you are teaching students about conjunctions, begin with coordinating, then correlative, and finally subordinating conjunctions, and conjunctive adverbs.

You can use the following additional types of strategies to help students increase skill in sequencing, organizing, and connecting their thoughts.

Categories of Cohesive Ties

Prepositions, conjunctions, and adverbs can be grouped into various categories that share similar meanings. These cohesive ties provide signals as to how a previous clause or statement is related to another. Examples of several types of cohesive ties follow:

Adding: and, also, in addition, additionally, furthermore, again
Explaining: furthermore, moreover, in the same way, for example, as an illustration

Contrasting: but, however, in contrast, nevertheless, on the other hand, yet, although
Causing: if-then, because, due to, as a result, for
Ending: therefore, accordingly, consequently, in conclusion, so, for this reason, thus
Timing: after, meanwhile, whenever, previously
Sequencing: first, second, then, next, lastly, finally, earlier, later
Spacing: next to, between, in front of, adjacent to, in back of
Continuing: after all, again, finally, another
Comparing: likewise, similarly, or
Restating: in other words, that is, in summary
Excluding: except, barring, beside, excluding

Transition Device Strategy

Simply possessing the knowledge that good writers use transitions among sentences and between paragraphs does not ensure that students can accomplish this in their writings. Criselda, a fifth-grade student, was asked to use a transition for the following two sentences: *I was told that all kindergarten students loved music. I soon found out that Vic did not.* After much thought, Criselda wrote, *I was told that all kindergarten students loved music. On the other hand, I soon found out that Vic did not.* Criselda, like many other students, needs to be taught how to use cohesive ties. One simple procedure for writing a sequential paragraph is to have students fold the paper into four squares and write a word in the upper left-hand corner of each box, such as First, Then, Next, and Finally. Although Adam, a fifth-grade student, did not copy the cohesive ties correctly, his paper in Figure 7.12 about how to brush your teeth illustrates this procedure.

Cloze for Cohesive Ties

You can use the following adapted cloze procedure to help students increase their use of cohesive ties:

1. Delete any of the following cohesive ties that signal the organizational pattern of a passage:
    a. Words signaling organizational patterns, such as *first*, *next*, or *finally*.
    b. Words signaling time, such as *before*, *after*, or *when*.

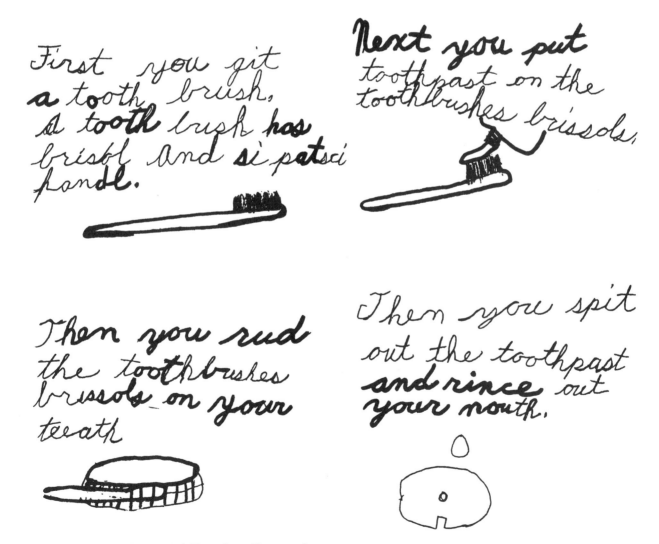

Figure 7.12. Adam's Sequential, Expository Paragraph.

    c. Words signaling a comparison or contrast organizational pattern, such as *however, but, as well as,* or *yet.*

    d. Words signaling a cause-and-effect organizational pattern, such as *because, therefore,* or *consequently.*

2. If necessary, provide students with a list of words that they may use to fill in the blanks.

3. Discuss with students alternative choices that could be used in each blank.

Example:

When you start to write a paper, _____ research your topic and _____ make an outline or organizational plan. _____, you are ready to begin writing.

Pronoun Referents

Many writers seem to learn to use pronoun referents without explicit instruction. Some individuals, however, continue to use pronouns incorrectly. Use of the following procedure can help students learn to use pronoun referents:

1. Provide students with a passage in which names and words are repeated rather than being replaced by pronouns or demonstrative articles (for example, *Mary went on a trip to China. Mary had never been to China before.*).

2. Show students how to rewrite the sentence (*Mary went on a trip to China. She had never been there before.*).

3. Teach the meanings of specific pronouns.

4. Provide students with sentence pairs in which pronouns in the second sentence refer to nouns in the first sentence. Underline the pronouns and draw arrows to their referents.

5. Ask students to replace pronouns with the words they represent.

6. Expand the exercise to include longer passages and have students answer questions regarding pronoun referents.

7. Have students find and circle pronouns with an arrow to their referents on copies of passages from their textbooks.

Kerrigan's Method for Connectives

Kerrigan's method for connectives (Kerrigan, 1979) is an easy way to teach students to use cohesive ties in essay writing. The goal of the strategy is to ensure that every sentence is connected with, and makes a clear reference to, the previous sentence, which can be accomplished in one of these seven explicit ways:

1. In the second sentence, repeat a word that has been used in the first sentence.

2. In the second sentence, use a synonym of a word used in the first sentence.

3. In the second sentence, use an antonym of a word used in the first sentence.

4. Use a pronoun in the second sentence to refer to an antecedent in the first sentence.

5. Use a word in the second sentence that is commonly paired with a word in the first sentence (for example, *bacon, eggs*).

6. Repeat the sentence structure.

7. Use a cohesive tie in the second sentence to refer to an idea in the first (such as *for, therefore, as a result, for example, however, and, but*).

The four basic connective types are:

1. *Identity connectives.* These indicate that one idea is the same as another. A colon is usually used to punctuate this relationship.

2. *Opposite connectives.* These indicate something contrary or contradictory to what has previously been stated. Words used to indicate this opposite relationship are *but, though, yet, still, however,* and *nevertheless.*

3. *Equivalent connectives.* These words denote parallel ideas with no new ideas being introduced. Words used to indicate this relationship are *and, too, also, besides, in addition, moreover, similarly, in the same way,* *again, furthermore, another, a similar*, and *the same*.

4. *Cause-and-effect connectives.* These denote a cause-and-effect relationship between the two ideas. Words used to indicate this are *therefore, so, as a result, as a consequence, thus we see*, and *it follows that*.

Once students have mastered more concrete connections, teach them the more indefinite connections such as *in fact, indeed*, and *now* that do not explicitly point out the relationship between ideas previously discussed. Let students know that a guiding rule when writing is to determine the relationship between two consecutive sentences and then, if possible, use a connective to indicate the relationship.

Given-New Strategy

Some students need help in understanding how to relate the given information, or information the writer assumes the reader knows, and the new information, or information that requires explanation. In most situations, the given information is usually in the subject position of the sentences, whereas the new information is usually in the predicate. You can use the following procedure, adapted from Cooper (1988), to help students understand the relationship between given-new principles. To begin, teach students how the concepts presented in sentences often overlap, and then follow these steps:

1. Write two sets of sample sentences, one in which the concepts are all new and another in which the concepts are related.
2. Provide further examples in regard to cohesion using graphic depictions that incorporate overlapping or non-overlapping boxes. Use non-overlapping boxes under sentences that contain only new concepts (NEW). Use overlapping boxes under successive sentences to depict how given information is transformed to relate to new or extended information. Figure 7.13 presents an example of unrelated and related sentences.

3. Have students organize cut-up sentence strips to create a chain of overlapping concepts. Ensure that all the sentence strips pertain to one topic.
4. Have students practice writing the first sentence of a paragraph. Help them to create a chain of overlapping concepts in the sentences that follow. Draw boxes underneath the sentences and label the information as being "old" or "new."
5. Demonstrate to students the relationships between paragraphs based on the graphic information given by the boxes. Sentences with overlapping boxes would remain in one paragraph with a constant topic and linear progression. A sentence with non-overlapping boxes would be the starting point for a new paragraph.
6. Repeat step 3 using two or three different topics. Explain to students how they can link the different paragraphs together.
7. Continue providing assistance in linking information within and between paragraphs until students can incorporate cohesive ties into their writing.
8. Provide further practice with transitions, linking expressions, and repeated terms, such as the use of pronoun referents, as needed.

Students may also use synonyms to carry meaning from one sentence to the next. For this process of reiteration, the writer purposefully uses synonyms or derivatives to remind the reader of the "given" information. For example, when describing a concert in the park, the writer would refer to the concert as an event in the next sentence. Reiteration helps the reader focus on the topic.

Narrative or Story Grammar

I keep six honest serving men. (They taught me all I know); Their names are What and Why and When and How and Where and Who.

—Rudyard Kipling

Unrelated Sentences

Sam loves to ride horses.

NEW

The show will be exciting.

NEW

Ralph hopes to win a blue ribbon.

NEW

Related Sentences

Sam loves to ride horses.

NEW

He . . . plans to compete in a horse show.

OLD	NEW

The event . . . is this Saturday.

OLD	NEW

Figure 7.13. Examples of Given-New Sentences.

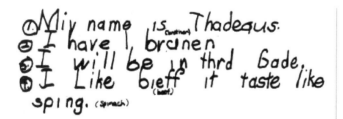

Figure 7.14. Thadeaus's Attempt to Write a Story.

Story grammar is the underlying framework that writers have in their memory that allows them to organize the text as they write. Understanding story structure allows a student to (a) understand new stories, (b) organize and predict new information, and (c) critique what has been presented. You can use a variety of techniques to help students develop and improve their narrative writing skill. Some strategies provide specific instruction in story grammar, whereas others involve special applications of the writing process approach. Students often do not know how to write stories without specific instruction and practice. Figure 7.14 shows the responses of Thadeaus, a student at the end of second grade, when he was asked to write a story.

Beginning Story Grammars

You may introduce the concept of story grammar to students as early as kindergarten or first grade. In the early grades, you might tell students that every story has three parts: a beginning, middle, and an end. Draw three circles and connect them with arrows to illustrate the progression. Or, you can draw a simple mnemonic with a face representing first (F), then (T), and finally (F), as illustrated in Figure 7.15.

You also might give students a series of prompts or questions for guiding their writing.

Figure 7.15. Beginning Story Grammar: First-Then-Finally Face.

A first-grade teacher provided her students with the following prompts for writing: Who? Did what? And then . . .

Another example of a simplified story grammar is based on the following four questions (Carnine, Silbert, Kame'enui, & Tarver, 2010): "Who is the story about? What is the main character trying to do? What happens when the main character tries to do it? What happens in the end?" (p. 236). You write the story on the board, then introduce the questions, have students read the story and respond orally to the questions, and then model how to summarize the story using the four questions. For further practice, you can read examples of stories that either adhere or do not adhere to these questions. You may also read stories that are missing parts and ask students how to resolve the missing information. When writing stories, students can use the four questions as a guide and write one or more paragraphs to address each question.

Story Maps

You can also have students develop story maps for writing. One example would be:

1. Develop or choose an appropriate story map for a writing assignment.

2. Put a copy of the map on the board or overhead and provide each student with a copy.
3. Discuss the purpose and benefits of using story maps to plan narrative writing.
4. Brainstorm about ideas with students and show them how to place the ideas within the different sections of the map.
5. Write the information on the board and have students copy it onto their maps.
6. Have students write stories using the maps, either individually or in pairs or small groups.
7. As their skill improves, have students develop their own maps individually.

Adaptations of the Language Experience Approach

You can also combine the language experience approach (LEA) with strategies, such as semantic mapping. The basic procedure of the LEA involves these steps:

1. Have the student share an experience.
2. Write or type the ideas as the student dictates a story about the experience.
3. Have the student read the story back.

You can adapt the LEA using the following steps:

1. Help students construct a graphic organizer to describe an experience.
2. In the middle of the map, write an idea or word that is central to the experience.
3. Have students brainstorm about different words or ideas that can be arranged in categories around the topic.
4. After the map has been developed, have students orally dictate the story into a tape recorder.
5. Have students listen to the recording and evaluate and critique the taped text for clarity, organization, and specificity of each part of the story. In addition, you can have students decide what type of story frame or text structure is best suited to their narrative.

6. Have students discuss the organization of their narrative and then dictate their story a second time.
7. Have the students write the dictated story and then read it aloud to other students.

Story Grammar Elements

You can teach students how to include the following elements in their stories. Have them:

1. Introduce the main characters and the time and place of the action.
2. Describe the actions and how the main characters respond in terms of their actions and their feelings, hopes, and goals.
3. Describe what the main characters do to try to achieve the goal.
4. Discuss whether the characters' attempts succeeded or failed, and the changes that resulted from the attempt.
5. Describe how the main characters feel and think about the outcomes.
6. Write an ending that resolves the story.

Organization Strategy

Initially, some students will require increased structure to incorporate elements of story grammar into their writing. Prior to writing, you might provide students with specific questions or guidelines pertaining to the setting, problem, and conclusion. The following is an example adapted from Stein and Glenn (1979):

1. Discuss the setting:
   Characters
      Who is the main character?
      Who are the other characters?
   Time
      When does the story take place?
   Place
      Where does it take place?
2. Discuss the problem:
   What is the problem confronting the main character(s)?
   How did they respond and what did they do?
3. Discuss the ending:
   What happened to resolve the story?

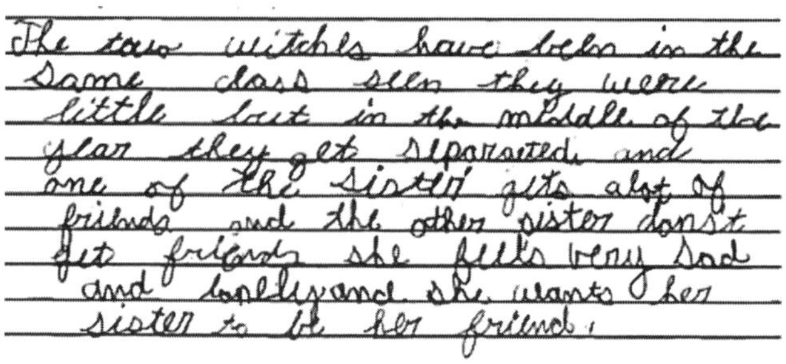
The two witches have been in the same class seen they were little but in the middle of the year they get separated and one of the sister gets alot of friends and the other sister don't get friends she feels very sad and lonleyand she wants her sister to be her friend.

Figure 7.16. Lynne's Problem for Her Story.

You may also read stories to students and then ask them to write about aspects of the story, such as the problem or conclusion. Figure 7.16 illustrates the response of Lynne, a third-grade student, who was asked to describe the problem that occurred in a story about witch twins.

SPOT

Some students benefit from having a mnemonic strategy to help them remember the important elements of story grammar. The mnemonic SPOT may be used as a prewriting strategy. Prior to writing, ask the students to think about their audience and the kind of story they want to write. Next, have the students take notes on the story, using the mnemonic:

S—What is the *setting* and who are the characters?
P—What is the *problem*?
O—What is the *order* of events?
T—What is the end of the *tale*?

You could incorporate this strategy with a picture of a dog, as presented in Figure 7.17.

STORE the Story

STORE the Story is a strategy that incorporates elements of the writing process through

Setting (S)

_____

_____

_____

_____

_____

Problem (P)

_____

_____

_____

_____

_____

SPOT

Order of Events (O)

_____

_____

_____

_____

_____

_____

Ending of the Tale (T)

_____

_____

_____

_____

Figure 7.17. SPOT Story Strategy.

the use of a story frame (Schlegel & Bos, 1986). You can use the following adaptation (Mather & Jaffe, 2002):

STORE is an acronym for:

S = *Setting* (Who? What? Where? When?)
T = *Trouble* (What is the trouble or problem?)
O = *Order* of events (What happens?)
R = *Resolution* (What is done to solve the problem?)
E = *Ending* (How does the story end?)

A. Introduction of the Cue STORE

  1. Discuss the meaning of the verb *to store* (save, hold, keep for a while, put away).

  2. Discuss the purpose: to help understand and remember (store) any story the students read by recognizing and recalling each part.

  3. Explain the parts of a story. Every story has a beginning, middle, and end. Every story also has a Setting,

Trouble, Order of events, Resolution, and Ending.

B. Demonstration or Modeling

1. Model the prewriting stage of the writing process approach by thinking aloud the steps of topic selection and brainstorming of ideas. Brainstorm about ideas for the story and fill in the STORE cue sheet, crossing out ideas and adding others until satisfied.

2. Read over the cue sheet to make sure that all parts of the story make sense and fit in relation to other parts.

3. Model how to write a first draft, and, subsequently, revise, edit, and rewrite. Explain how the use of STORE ensures continuity of the story line.

C. Guided Practice

1. Guide the students to create a group story using the STORE format. This requires close monitoring and immediate, corrective feedback to ensure a successful experience.

D. Independent Practice

1. Have the students create their own stories.

E. Adaptations or Extra Support

1. Provide picture cards to aid in generating story ideas.

2. If necessary, provide the Setting, Trouble, and some Events. Have the student add some Events and finish the story, or provide the Setting or the Trouble and have the student generate the other parts of the story.

Figure 7.18 presents a sample worksheet for this strategy.

W-W-W, What = 2, How = 2 Strategy

You can use a similar mnemonic strategy, W-W-W, What = 2, How = 2 as a prewriting strategy (Graham & Harris, 1989a). Show students a picture or have students create their own stories. Prior to writing, have the student answer the following questions:

1. *Who* is the main character? Who else is in the story?
2. *When* does the story take place?
3. *Where* does the story take place?
4. *What* does the main character do?
5. *What* happens when he or she tries to do it?
6. *How* does the story end?
7. *How* does the main character feel?

Character Description

In addition to strategies to assist with organization, some students benefit from instruction in character description. Figure 7.19 presents a story by Shannon, a fourth-grade student. Although she mentions the princess, all we know about Tammy is that she has "pretty shoes." Nothing is mentioned about the prince except his marriage proposal. Clearly, Shannon can benefit from explicit instruction in story grammar, as well as character development. She did, however, recognize that she needed to move her margins over!

You might present students with a series of questions that will help them expand their descriptions of the physical appearance, the mannerisms, the actions, and the thoughts and feelings of the main characters:

1. What does the person look like? What color is their hair? What color are their eyes?
2. How does the person act?
3. What does the person say and do?
4. What does the character think about?
5. How does the character feel about what is happening throughout the story?

When discussing character development, you can read sample paragraphs to students in which the main character has been developed fully and ones in which only minimal information is given. Encourage the students to discuss the differences between the descriptions and note how detailed descriptions can help readers increase their understanding of the characters.

Store the Story

Name: _____   Date: _____

Working Title: _____

Setting

     Who _____

     What _____

     Where _____

     When _____

Trouble _____

_____

Order of Action

     1. _____

     2. _____

     3. _____

     4. _____

     5. _____

Resolution

     1. _____

     2. _____

     3. _____

     4. _____

     5. _____

Ending _____

_____

Figure 7.18.   Worksheet for STORE the Story Strategy.

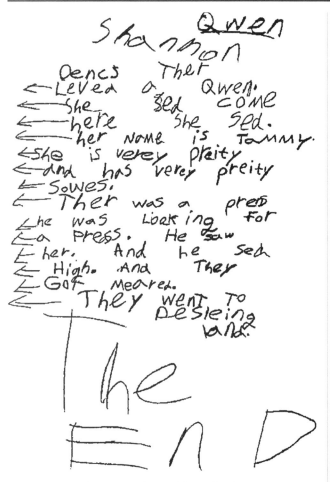

Figure 7.19. Shannon's Story About the Queen.

Branching Narratives

You also can have students write stories modeling the "Choose Your Own Adventure" genre (Mather & Jaffe, 2002). The student begins by writing the opening of the adventure and then stopping at appropriate places in the adventure to write several options that will have different outcomes. For example, after describing the characters entering a haunted house, Donavan, a fourth-grade student, writes,

   1a. If you decide to go up the stairs, turn to page _____.
   1b. If you decide to enter the dining room, turn to page _____.

Ms. Randall, Donavan's teacher, helped him to develop a branching narrative using the following steps:

Figure 7.20. Austin's Story About Little Dude.

1. After writing the beginning of the story, Donavan decided to write the outcome to 1a. He wrote 1a at the top of a separate page, followed by the opening sentence: *You decide to go up the stairs.* He then proceeded to complete this outcome.
2. After writing the outcome for 1a (which may result in new choices, 2a and 2b, or an ending), Ms. Randall had Donavan put a slash through 1a on the first page to show that it had been completed.
3. Donavan next wrote the outcome for 1b. He began with the sentence: *You decide to enter the dining room.* He decided to end this branch and wrote: *Bad choice. The chandelier fell on your head and you've never been heard from since. The End.*

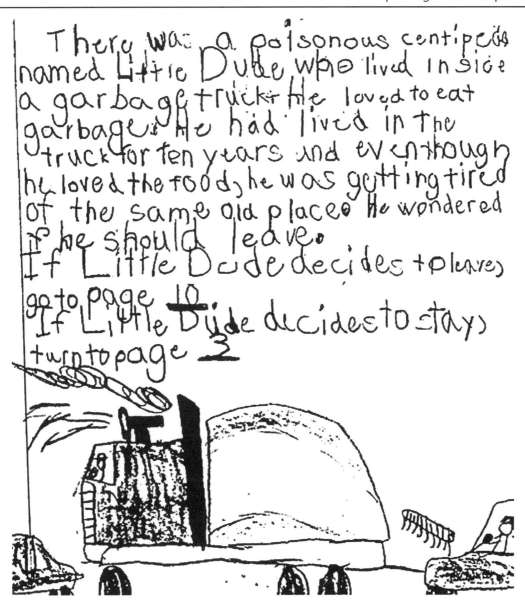

There was a poisonous centipede named Little Dude who lived inside a garbage truck. He loved to eat garbage. He had lived in the truck for ten years and even though he loved the food, he was getting tired of the same old place. He wondered if he should leave.
If Little Dude decides to leave, go to page 10.
If Little Dude decides to stay, turn to page 3

Figure 7.20. *(Continued)*

After writing this outcome, he put a slash through 1b on the first page to show that it had been written.

Students then add the page numbers after the story is completed and all the various paths have been resolved.

Figure 7.20 illustrates the cover and the first page of the final draft of a branching narrative written by Austin, a third-grade student. His final story about Little Dude, the centipede, was twenty pages long.

Shared Writing

Students may also collaborate on a writing assignment. You can use these steps to motivate reluctant writers:

1. Explain to students that they will be writing a story with another person and the goal is to produce a story that sounds like it was written by one person.
2. Provide a topic or have the pairs discuss and choose a topic.

3. Have one student write the first sentence of the story and pass the paper to his or her peer.
4. The other student reads the sentence and then adds another sentence.
5. The pairs take turns contributing sentences and discussing their additions, until they agree that the story is complete. Occasionally, encourage the students to stop and read the entire story before adding a sentence.
6. When the story is completed, have the pair read it together.

Students can share writing by alternating sentences, single words, or paragraphs. When writing sentence-by-sentence, perhaps the least difficult compositional unit is when coauthors are encouraged to maintain the topic and determine the direction of the story as they take turns adding sentences. Word-by-word composition is a more difficult procedure, as it requires greater facility with syntax; partners must adapt word choice with each turn. Creating stories at the paragraph-by-paragraph level requires skill in organization and story cohesion. You may use this type of shared writing with cooperative learning groups as well. You might also add alternative rules such as "no talking" while the story is being written, or after reading the story, peers can give feedback on how the story can be improved and then the pair can revise the story.

You may also have a quiet dialogue with students where you ask them a relevant question and they must write the response. For very reluctant writers, you might start out with simple questions that require a "yes" or "no" response. Figure 7.21 indicates a dialogue with Matthew, a fifth-grade student with a learning disability.

Writing with others can help reduce anxiety and encourage students to participate more fully. Make sure, however, that all students participate, including those who are shy, quiet, or have difficulty writing. Robin, a fifth-grade student with limited writing skill, became even more discouraged about her writing because in her cooperative learning group, she was always told to just draw the illustrations. As a group member, Robin also needs to be spending time writing.

Writing Process: Scaffolding Activities

Even when you focus on writing as a process and provide plenty of opportunities to write and revise, some students will need more assistance in different facets of writing skill. You can incorporate the following adapted principles and procedures (Moulton & Bader, 1986):

Prior to Writing

1. Provide ample time for prewriting activities.
2. Help students choose a topic for writing based on their knowledge, interest, and motivation, and then gather information about the topic from numerous sources.
3. Encourage students to write down lots of ideas.
4. When no more ideas are forthcoming, have students try to put the ideas into some order. To help them organize their ideas, you can:
   a. Provide a simple graphic organizer or chart
   b. Provide a simple outline or frame

First Draft

1. Encourage students to write on every other line or use double-spacing if keyboarding.
2. Encourage students to focus on ideation, not mechanics.
3. Give immediate responses to ideas as they are written and discuss the positive aspects of the student's writing. You might read a sentence or phrase from a student's writing that is well written, has good content, or reinforces an important concept.

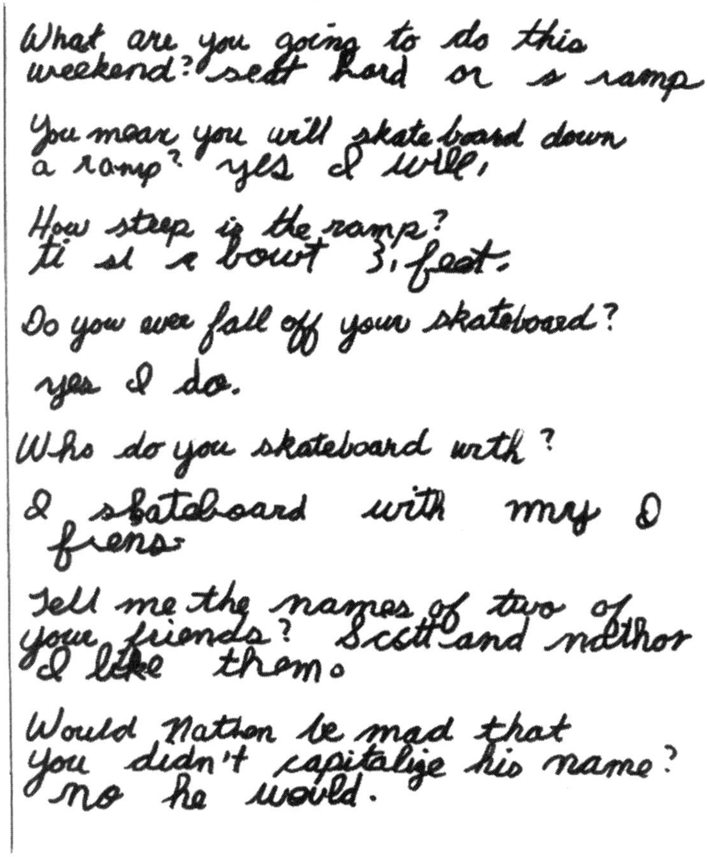

What are you going to do this
weekend? seat hard or a ramp,
You mean you will skateboard down
a ramp? yes I will,
How steep is the ramp?
ti si a bowt 3, feet.
Do you ever fall off your skateboard?
yes I do.
Who do you skateboard with?
I skateboard with my
fiens.
Tell me the names of two of
your friends? Scott and nathor
I like them.
Would Nathon be mad that
you didn't capitalize his name?
no he would.

Figure 7.21. Matthew's Responses to His Teacher's Questions.

Revising

1. Have students read stories to peers and discuss any suggested changes and incorporate them into another draft.
2. Prepare a list of questions about the draft, such as:
   a. How well does the draft maintain the topic?
   b. How well does the draft stick to the plan?
   c. Is the information well organized?
   d. Is the word choice appropriate?
3. Discuss the questions and how the student can improve the writing in individual teacher-student conferences. Tell the students why a specific comment or suggestion was made and how it will improve their composition.

Editing

1. Depending on student skill, editing may be performed by the writer, by peers, or with a teacher or aid.
2. Provide the level of assistance necessary for the individual. Some students will need line-by-line guidance, whereas others will need only a checklist of general reminders.
3. Do not expect students to correct errors that are beyond their current skill level, such as using quotation marks when they have not yet learned about dialogue.
4. Remember that improvement, not perfection, is the expectation during editing.
5. Have students share their writings with other students, parents, and so on.

Expository

Although instruction in writing stories and story grammar, or narrative writing, is often an appropriate place to begin with young writers, you will also want to ensure that students of all grade levels improve their proficiency with expository writing. After being taught a narrative strategy, some students are able to adapt it to expository writing without specific instruction, whereas others require direct and assisted practice with the new type of text structure.

Figure 7.22 illustrates first drafts of opinion essays written by six high school students from an English class. Their assignment was to write an essay about a person whom they admired. Although several of the students have a few ideas on the topic, their failure to develop organizational frameworks for their writing is apparent.

Students who struggle with writing often have trouble developing and organizing their ideas. They often do not understand how related information is assembled into one paragraph or how to break information into different paragraphs. Wendy Wall, a special educational consultant, told us about an interesting "strategy" of Aaron, one of her new fourth-grade students. When they were discussing organizing paragraphs, she asked him if he felt he had trouble figuring out when to begin new paragraphs. He said, "Yes, I do. What I do, though, is look at the three holes on the left of my paper. When I get to one of those, I indent and make a new paragraph." He felt that, at about the place where one comes to a new hole, it was time to change paragraphs and that seemed to work for him.

Clearly, students such as Aaron will have difficulty writing specific and well-focused assignments and will fail to describe and develop a topic clearly and completely. As part of every writing assignment, students need to identify the audience, organize their ideas, consider the perspectives of the readers, select the type of format, and maintain discussion of the topic or topics. Your choice of a strategy will depend upon student need and preference.

Fortunately, you can use many strategies to help students improve their skills in collecting and organizing the factual information that they wish to include in their paragraphs, essays, or reports. Most of the strategies can be applied to any type of text structure. Figure 7.23 presents the most common types of expository text structures. This figure provides a brief description of each text structure, a sample sentence as a model for informal evaluation of a student's writing, and examples of the cohesive ties that are most common to each type. These basic expository text structures can form the basis for instruction in paragraph or essay writing. Most students benefit from formal instruction that presents models of different text structures followed by practice writing these structures.

Expanding, Interviewing, and Oral Histories

Three activities for helping students write paragraphs begin with prewriting and progress to paragraph or essay writing. Following is a description of each activity: expanding, interviewing, and oral histories (Tompkins & Friend, 1986).

Expanding

1. Select a broad topic (for example, Things I Have Lost).
2. Have students name several events or objects that the topic brings to mind (such as baby teeth, dog, or homework assignments).
3. Have students brainstorm about words that make the experience more vivid in their memories.
4. Have the students write a paragraph in a small group.

Interviewing

1. Have a group of students work together in choosing a topic (for example, a favorite movie star).

I Admire all the people in the world that resisted the temtation of Evils and wrong doings from the start of there lives But I also Admire the people like me that relized the stoopidity and changed.

I don't Have no FRiends
They get you in trouble

I don't like alot of people for different reasons but thats already Settled that I don't like them and I Never will

Pat, pretty cool dude has a temper. He can get on your nerves some times, but he's still cool so I dont care because I get on his nerves to.

a person I admire
The person I admire is my friend Juan because I've known him forever, we've been friends and enimes in the past but we alyae see it troph so thats who I admire

Description about a Parent
My mom is cool, but I really don't talk to her to much. And my dad lives in P.A. so oh well, I try to look out for my self.

Figure 7.22. First Drafts of Opinion Essays by High School Students.

SEQUENTIAL: A series of events presented in temporal order, that tells how to do or make something.

Cohesive Ties and Key Words

first	finally	at night
second	in the past	in the fall
third	eventually	during the spring
last	now	at breakfast
then	soon	toward the afternoon
to begin	before	in the morning
next	after	

Sample: "To bake a cake, you must complete several steps. First, you buy your ingredients . . . "

ENUMERATION: A series of facts or details related to a specific topic, listed as points.

Cohesive Ties and Key Words

in addition	finally
furthermore	for example
besides	for instance
likewise	in other words
of course	such as
to illustrate	next
moreover	

Sample: "Garlic can be used in many ways. For instance, in folklore garlic was used to ward off vampires. It was also used . . . "

DESCRIPTION: A series of attributes and characteristics that tells about the subject. The description may include spatial characteristics, physical attributes, behavioral characteristics, or affective characteristics.

Cohesive Ties and Key Words

refers to

can be explained as

can be defined as

can be described as

is a method for

is a way to

Sample: "The London Bridge is located in Arizona. The bridge spans . . . "

Figure 7.23. Types of Text Structures for Expository Writing.

CAUSE AND EFFECT: An explanation of the situation and the reasons for why something happened.

Cohesive Ties and Key Words

to begin with	because
most important of all	consequently
for one thing	therefore
furthermore	for this reason
as a result	thus

Sample: "During the past year, physical fitness at our school has improved. These programs have been beneficial in a number of ways . . . "

PROBLEM AND SOLUTION: The statement of a problem and possible alternative solutions.

Cohesive Ties and Key Words

last and most important	as a result
in addition	currently

Sample: "If you're unlucky enough to have a flat tire on the highway, you will need to find ways to cope with the problem. You might start by . . . "

COMPARE-CONTRAST: Two or more topics compared according to their likenesses and differences along one or more dimensions.

Cohesive Ties and Key Words

in contrast	even so	although
conversely	otherwise	instead of
on the contrary	still	similarly
however	yet	while
but	whereas	on the other hand

Sample: "Uganda has a different topography than Kuwait. Uganda is lush and green, whereas Kuwait is arid. The two countries, however, . . . "

ARGUMENT OR PERSUASION: Statement of a position on an issue with justification.

Cohesive Ties and Key Words

the first

therefore

consequently

the major reason

subsequently

Sample: "The government should spend more money on the prevention of AIDS. The first reason . . . "

Figure 7.23. (*Continued*)

2. Separate students into pairs.
3. Ask each pair to interview approximately eight of their peers, with one of the pair asking the questions and the other recording the answers.
4. After the interviews are completed, help students synthesize the responses.
5. Have the group write three paragraphs, one on what was done, one on the results, and one on the conclusions.
6. As skill develops, have each pair choose a topic of interest to them. Help the two collaborate, and provide support as they write the paragraphs at the conclusion of the study.

Oral Histories

1. With a group of students, develop a set of questions that will explore an individual's history.
2. Have the students collect data from a family member by asking the questions and recording the answers.
3. Model how to organize the data.
4. Help students organize their data.
5. Model how to integrate the data into a written report.
6. Provide individual support as students write their reports.

Questioning Strategy

Having students complete a series of questions prior to writing will increase their awareness of the purpose for writing. For example, before they draft an assignment, have students answer the following questions:

1. What do I know about this topic?
2. What experiences have I had with it?
3. What do I think about it?
4. What do I want to try to explain or discuss?

If preferred, you can present the questions in written form and ask students to jot down a short answer to each. Alternatively, you might have students answer the questions orally either to you or to a peer. Sharing the answers with others will help students increase their own understanding.

K-W-L Procedure

To help students increase their factual knowledge and participate more actively in the writing process, you can employ the K-W-L procedure (Ogle, 1986). Provide students with a strategy worksheet with the following three columns across the top of the paper:

K   What I *know*
W   What do I *want* to learn
L   What I *learned*

Follow these steps in completing the worksheet:

1. In the first column (K), have students brainstorm and list any information that they already know about the topic. This is activating prior knowledge, an effective teaching technique.
2. In the second column (W), have students develop questions about what they want to learn about the topic. This step actively engages the student in setting personal goals for the lesson.
3. In the third column (L), have students record what they have learned from reading and library research. This step actively engages the students and reinforces learning.

Upon completion of the worksheet, ask students to write an expository paragraph that summarizes what they have learned about the topic.

K-W-L Plus

An adaptation of the K-W-L strategy, K-W-L Plus, adds mapping and summarization, which increases writing (Carr & Ogle, 1987). To add the mapping component, students categorize the information listed under *L*. The topic forms the center of the map. For example, if students were learning about the planet Saturn, they would write *Saturn* in the center of the map. Lines are then added to show the relationship between the main topic and the facts that have been learned.

For the summarization component, students can use the map that depicts the organization of the information. The center of the map becomes the title of the essay, and each category is used as the topic for a new paragraph. Supporting details are then added to expand the paragraph or explain the topic further. After practice with this procedure, some students are able to omit the mapping step and write their summaries directly from the K-W-L worksheet. Summarization is a powerful strategy and will help your students become more effective learners.

Paragraph Frames

Paragraph frames can be used to help students improve their expository writing (Nichols, 1980). For each genre, the frames contain the key words or phrases that are often used to structure and organize ideas. Different frames can be developed for all types of expository writing, such as sequential, chronological order, cause and effect, and compare-contrast. In general, when constructing these frames, leave spaces for the student's writing and provide surrounding words that will help the student decide what should be written in the spaces. Although the technique does not produce creative expository writing, the frames serve as scaffolds for students who have more limited writing skill. Figure 7.24 presents examples of several frames.

Question-Answer-Detail (QAD) Method

The purpose of the QAD method is to help students organize paragraphs and reports (Weiss & Weiss, 1993). Three columns are made with the following headings at the top: Question, Answer, and Detail. In the first column, help the students generate several questions that will be answered in the report. In the second column, have the students answer the questions. In the third column, have the students write additional details about the topic.

To write a three-sentence paragraph, the student cuts across the paper including one question, an answer, and a related detail. The question is then rephrased as an expository statement. As students become more proficient in paragraph writing, more details can be added with additional columns.

SLOW CaPS

You might also use the SLOW CaPS strategy with the following four different types of paragraphs: (a) enumerative or descriptive, (b) sequential, (c) compare-contrast, and (d) cause and effect (Schumaker & Sheldon, 1985). The small *a* in the mnemonic denotes that it is not used in the reminder.

S   *Show* the type of paragraph being used. This is done in the first sentence.
L   *List* the details that will be discussed.
O   *Order* the details.
W   *Write* the details in complete sentences.
In conclusion, CAP the paragraph with one of the following:
C   A *concluding* sentence
P   A *passing* sentence (transition sentence)
S   A *summary* sentence

PLEASE Strategy

The PLEASE strategy was designed to promote metacognitive problem solving for prewriting, planning, composing, and revising for students in upper grades (Welch, 1992; Welch & Jensen, 1991). The acronym represents the following steps:

P   *Pick* a topic, the audience, and the appropriate textual format.
L   *List* your ideas about the topic. Using various techniques, such as brainstorming or mapping, list information about

Sequential

In order to _____ a _____, you must follow several steps.

First _____

_____

Then _____

_____

Next _____

_____

Finally_____

_____

_____

Chronological

At the beginning _____

_____

After that _____

_____

Next _____

_____

The_____ ended when _____

_____

_____

_____

Enumerative

Several reasons explain _____

_____

First, _____

_____

Second, _____

_____

Finally, _____

_____

_____

Figure 7.24. Samples of Expository Paragraph Frames.

Descriptive

The following provides a description of _____

_____

The _____

looks like _____

If you look around you will see _____

_____

You will also see _____

_____

You will also see _____

_____

In general, _____

is very _____

_____

Compare-Contrast

_____ and _____

are alike and are different in several ways. First, they are alike because

_____

_____

but they are different because of _____

_____

Secondly, one is _____

while the other is _____

Finally, they are alike because _____

_____

but different because _____

_____

Problem-Solution

The problem began when _____

_____

The _____ tried to_____

_____

After that _____

_____

Figure 7.24. *(Continued)*

Then _____

_____

The problem was finally solved when _____

_____

Cause and Effect

The _____

was caused by _____

As a result, _____

_____

Another consequence was _____

_____

Furthermore, _____

_____

The effects of the _____

_____

are clearly apparent.

Figure 7.24. Samples of Expository Paragraph Frames. (*Continued*)

the topic. This information will be used in generating, organizing, and evaluating sentences.

E *E*valuate whether the list is complete and organize the ideas into a logical order in preparation for sentence generation.

A *A*ctivate the paragraph idea by writing a short, simple, declarative, topic sentence.

S *S*upply supporting sentences. The sentences are generated from the list of ideas recorded earlier.

E *E*nd with a concluding sentence, and *e*valuate the work using an error monitoring strategy such as COPS.

Audience

Audience considerations are an important part of the writing process. As noted by Blatt (1985), "When he's writing, the writer must take distance. But when he's reading, he must get involved" (p. 366). Some students have difficulty considering the needs of the reader. For example, they may assume erroneously that their readers have prior knowledge about the topic. Ask a student the following questions:

1. What does your audience already know about the topic?
2. What new information do you want your audience to know?
3. Does your audience need more information to understand the topic?

You can also use the AUDIENCE strategy to remind the writer to consider and identify the needs of the reader prior to and during writing. This type of strategy may help writers attend to the relationship between the information presented in the text and the readers' comprehension of the purpose and meaning.

The first-letter mnemonic represents the following steps:

*A*sk who the readers are. For example, ask, Who are my readers? What do they already know about the topic?

*U*nderstand the readers' needs. For example, ask, What information will be new to my readers?

*D*elve into the topic.

*I*ntegrate background information with new information.

*E*nsure that all material makes sense.

*N*ote the most important information.

*C*onstruct a passage.

*E*valuate the passage for clarity by asking questions such as: Is all the information presented clearly? Will any of the sentences confuse the readers? Is there more that I need to explain?

PLANS Strategy

When asked to write a paper, many students have only a vague idea about how to locate the necessary information or how to evaluate their work. One way of dealing successfully with a writing assignment is to complete a means-end analysis. This involves deciding how the final draft of the assignment will look, selecting the means to attain the end goal, and using the PLANS strategy (Harris & Graham, 1992).

The goals can include (a) general purpose of the paper (for example, "Write a paper that is fun to read"); (b) completeness of the paper (for example, "Write a story that has all the basic parts"); (c) length (for example, "Write a paper that has five paragraphs"); (d) specific attributes (for example, "Share with the reader four things about the main character"); (e) vocabulary (for example, "Write a paper containing fifteen describing words"); and (f) sentence variety (for example, "Write a paper in which you use six complex sentences").

Use of these steps involves a means-end analysis:

1. Use PLANS
   P *Pick* goals (from among a number suggested by the teacher).
   L *List* ways to meet the goals.
   A *And* make
   N *Notes.*
   S *Sequence* notes.
2. Write and say more.
3. Test the goals. If the goals have not been met, help the student revise the paper in order to meet them.

Paragraph-Organization Strategy

You can teach students how to write effective formula paragraphs by modeling the writing of different types of paragraphs using the following steps:

1. Discuss with students how to develop a topic sentence.
2. Discuss how to create details and supporting statements and a concluding statement. Elicit a topic and supporting details from the group to develop a model paragraph. Write the topic and details on a board so all can see.
3. Have students write their own practice paragraphs and then compare their paragraphs to the model paragraph.
4. Discuss with students how to revise their paragraphs so they are like the model.
5. Provide practice with different paragraph types, such as enumerative, sequential, and compare-contrast.

Graphic Organizers

Some students will benefit from the use of graphic organizers. Students may write a central theme or main idea in the middle circle, and then delineate on branches the major subtopics to be discussed. As students research the topic, they may add more details to the map. You may also have students write several topic headings on papers or poster boards and then write their notes on index cards or sticky notes and place them under the appropriate headings.

Students can then move the notes easily from category to category as they organize and reorganize their reports.

Writing Wheels

Writing wheels may help your students organize their essays, paragraphs, compositions, or term papers (Rooney, 1990). The wheels are used to separate the main ideas and the details. The first page is a five-circle overview and is developed using the following strategy:

1. Write the title at the top of the paper.
2. Draw five wheels on the first sheet. In the first wheel write the word *START* and in the last wheel write the word *END* or *THEREFORE*. Write a word or phrase or sentence in the first wheel that identifies the ideas that will be used in the Introduction.
3. Write one main idea inside each of the three middle wheels that will be developed.
4. In the last wheel, marked *END*, write a word, phrase, or sentence that will be used as the conclusion.

After the five-circle overview page is completed, the information from each of the five circles is placed on a separate page for further development. The writer then adds details, ideas, and thoughts in a spoke-like fashion around each wheel. When all the ideas have been recorded, the writer then numbers the ideas in each wheel in the sequence in which they will be presented. The pages of wheels are then used to write an outline or a rough draft. Figure 7.25 illustrates the first five-circle overview sheet. Figure 7.26 shows an example of the single wheel that may be used when developing details or ideas for one of the main ideas.

Statement-Pie

Statement-Pie is another strategy that might help your students develop expository paragraphs (Hanau, 1974). In this strategy, *statement*

refers to a topic statement, and *pie* refers to the details:

P   Proofs
I   Information
E   Examples

You can also use the following adaptation (Wallace & Bott, 1989):

1. Give students a completed paragraph guide as a model of the strategy.
2. Explain the meaning of *statement* and *pie*.
3. Model the detection and generation of pies.
4. Give students a statement.
5. Have students verbally generate appropriate pies. Use the planning guide as follows:
   Statement: topic statement
   Pie: a detail related to the topic statement
   Pie: another detail related to the topic statement
   Pie: another detail related to the topic statement
6. Give immediate feedback in regard to the appropriateness of each pie.
7. Give students another statement in an area that is age appropriate and in which students have background knowledge.
8. Have students generate and write appropriate pies to be used as paragraph planning guides on the given topic.
9. Give immediate feedback in regard to the appropriateness of each pie.

Use the following steps for outlining statements and pies in expository paragraphs:

1. Model the outlining of statements and pies in chosen expository paragraphs.
2. Give students paragraphs for guided practice.
3. Circle the statements and underline the pies.
4. Write the statements and pies in a planning guide such as that noted above.

Title: _____

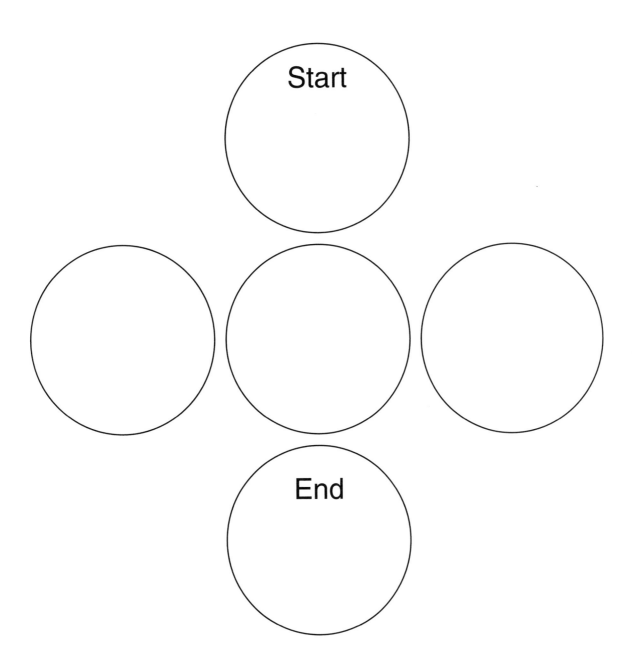

Figure 7.25. The First Page of Writing Wheels.

Main Idea: _____

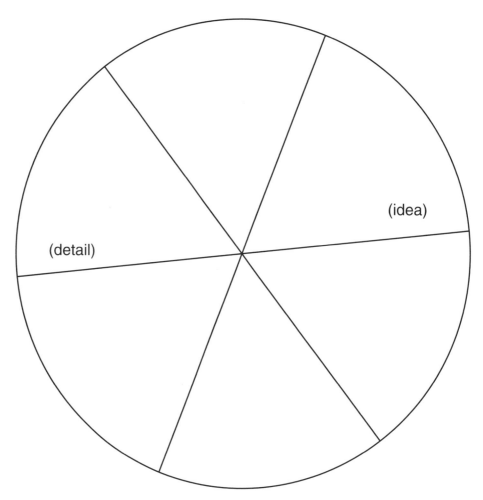

Figure 7.26. Single Wheel for Developing Main Idea.

Writing Paragraphs

1. Model paragraph writing by:
   a. Selecting a topic
   b. Writing a paragraph planning guide
   c. Using the guide to construct sentences
   d. Forming the sentences into a paragraph
   e. Emphasizing key words and cohesive ties (such as *first, next, afterwards, finally*)
2. Have students choose a topic from a list generated by you.
3. Have students generate statement-pie paragraph planning guides.
4. Have students write a paragraph.
5. Provide immediate feedback with regard to the appropriateness of the pies.

Essays

Essentially, essays are composed of several well-written paragraphs that contain transition sentences to make the ideas among and between the paragraphs clear. You will want to teach students how to organize information by writing an introductory paragraph, supporting paragraphs, and a concluding paragraph. You will want to provide both direct instruction and guided practice. You can use the following procedure to teach students how to write a paper containing several paragraphs:

1. Have students select a familiar topic.
2. Explain to students that the topic sentence is the controlling idea of the essay. Help students write a clear topic statement.
3. Have students brainstorm about ideas related to the topic.
4. From the ideas, select three to four central ideas that can be developed into separate paragraphs to support the topic and write headings for those ideas.
5. Have students brainstorm about ideas for each paragraph and list the most relevant details under each paragraph heading.
6. Write examples of transition words that may be used to connect the paragraphs.
7. Keep a copy of all notes on the board so that all students can see the information.
8. Have students write an essay using the information, as well as any new information they would like to add.
9. Have students read their essays to other students and discuss with other students.

TOWER Strategy

Several mnemonic strategies have been designed to help students remember and follow steps for essay writing. One such strategy, developed by researchers at the University of Kansas, uses the mnemonic TOWER to represent the following steps (Schumaker & Sheldon, 1985):

T *Think* of the content. Write down:
   a. A title
   b. Major areas for discussion
   c. Details within each area
O *Order* the major topic areas and the details under each topic area.
W *Write* a rough draft.

E *Error* monitor the work using an error monitoring strategy such as COPS:
   C Capitalization
   O Overall appearance
   P Punctuation
   S Spelling
R *Revise* the rough draft.

WRITER Strategy

The acronym WRITER refers to another process-oriented strategy (Schumaker & Sheldon, 1985). It represents

W *Write* the first draft on every other line of the paper choosing a sentence formula, such as subject + verb, for each sentence.
R *Read* for meaning. Inappropriate sentences must be revised.
I *Interrogate* yourself using the COPS strategy:
   C Capitalization
   O Overall appearance
   P Punctuation
   S Spelling
T *Take* the written work to someone else to check if unsure about a potential error.
E *Execute* a final draft of the work, incorporating the corrections made on the first draft and writing as neatly as possible on every line.
R *Reread* the work and make any necessary final edits.

Comparison-Contrast Organization Strategy

You may also use a strategy for helping students write compare-contrast essays (Englert & Raphael, 1989). The use of this type of essay format is signaled by key words such as *alike, different from, in contrast to*, and *similar to*. Have the student ask the following questions:

1. What is being compared or contrasted?
2. On what aspect are they being compared or contrasted?

3. How are they alike (mention all similarities)?

4. How are they different (mention all differences)?

Explanatory Essay Organization Strategy

A similar procedure helps students write an explanatory or sequential essay (Englert, Raphael, & Anderson, 1989). Have your students ask:

1. What is being explained (for example, steps involved in making a cup of tea)?

2. What materials are needed to accomplish the task?

3. In what setting is the task to be accomplished?

4. What are the steps involved? Normally, the steps are sequenced (first, next, third, then, last).

Opinion Essay: TREE Strategy

Some individuals require extra instruction to develop the necessary skills for writing opinion essays. The mnemonic TREE is used as a planning strategy with the following steps (Graham & Harris, 1989b):

T Generate a *Topic* sentence
R List the *Reasons* supporting the argument
E *Examine* the reasons
E Provide an *Ending*

Subordination

An important aspect of writing competence is an understanding of how to subordinate ideas. Most expository writing involves at least three levels of ideas:

Main idea statements—these often introduce the paragraph or essay
Major details (paragraph) or subtopics (essay)
Minor details

Students can learn how to subordinate by writing simple paragraphs, consisting of one main idea sentence followed by two major details. For example, Andrea, a second-grade student, was given the following prompt: *I have two favorite activities when we go to the beach.* Andrea then wrote two detail sentences: *I love to make sandcastles. I like to jump into the waves.* Next, she can develop each major detail into a paragraph by adding minor details about each activity.

Kerrigan's Method

A comprehensive procedure for teaching students how to write essays uses the following steps to help students write clearly organized papers (Kerrigan, 1979):

1. Have the student write a sentence in which a person or an object is or was something, or does or did something. The sentence must follow seven rules:

   a. Create a sentence about which you can say more.

   b. Concentrate on what the person or object *does*.

   c. Be specific—what *exactly* did the person or object do?

   d. Until you become proficient, keep the sentence short.

   e. Write the sentence as a *statement*, not as a question or command.

   f. Ensure you have only *one* statement.

   g. Do not use a descriptive or narrative sentence.

2. Have the student write three sentences about the original sentence. Encourage the student to use simple, declarative sentences that give information clearly and directly about the original sentence. The information must pertain to the whole of the original sentence, and not to a piece of it. It should not repeat the same idea in different words, but instead provide more specific information.

3. Ask the student to write four or five sentences about each of the three sentences in step 2.

4. The sentences in step 3 must be specific and concrete. Encourage the student to go into detail, and use examples. Specify that the goal is to give *more* information about what has already been introduced; thus there must be no new ideas. Sharing short anecdotal stories with the student can be effective during the fourth stage.

At this point, help the student review the content to ensure that the subject has not changed, and that the central idea or theme is obvious from the first paragraph. Have the student focus on being understood by the prospective audience, not on being entertaining. Encourage the student to use vocabulary that is pertinent to the audience and to concentrate on making the theme clear, real, and convincing.

5. Have the student insert a clear, explicit reference to the theme of the preceding paragraph in the first sentence of the following paragraphs.

6. Have the student work to ensure that every sentence is connected with, and makes a clear reference to, the previous sentence. (See Kerrigan's method for connectives.)

Use of these six steps will ensure that your students' writing is to the point and that the whole theme is thoroughly connected. Figure 7.27 illustrates these six steps in the first draft written by Jenn, an eighth-grade student. The assignment was to describe your favorite holiday.

Kerrigan described additional steps for writing specific types of themes such as contrast, comparison, argument, and expression.

The following rules apply to themes of contrast:

1. Have the student select important, noticeable differences for discussion.

2. Have the student contrast specifics that can be compared (in other words, shapes with shapes, not shapes with colors).

3. Remind the student to contrast opposite qualities as well as contrasting differences.

4. Remind the student not to include material that does not imply contrast.

5. Have the student sequence the contrasts as they are initially presented (for example, if contrasting an apple and an orange, in each sentence attributes of the apple must precede those of the orange).

6. Suggest that the student not use the word *contrast* in the theme as a synonym for *difference*, as *contrast* is the name of an operation performed. Instead, have the student use words such as *difference*, *dissimilarity*, *likeness*, *similarity*, and *resemblance*.

7. Encourage the student to use the expressions *whereas* and *in contrast*.

For themes of comparison, all rules relevant to themes of contrast can also be applied, but with likenesses, not contrasts, being discussed. Remember that items described as similar are not identical, but the point of comparing them is to show how they are alike. The following precautions apply to teaching students to write themes of contrast and comparison:

1. Teach the student not to note individual points about A in one paragraph and about B in another. Rather, contrast and compare point by point within each paragraph.

2. Remind the student that the essay must consist of more than a two-paragraph theme. Suggest to the student that if only two major qualities can be used to compare or contrast, a third paragraph should be added at the beginning that briefly establishes the similarity or contrasting points, as well as one at the end that states some point about the contrasts or similarities.

When writing themes of argument, the writer seeks to persuade or convince the reader. It is important to teach students that the point of these types of essays is not to argue to win,

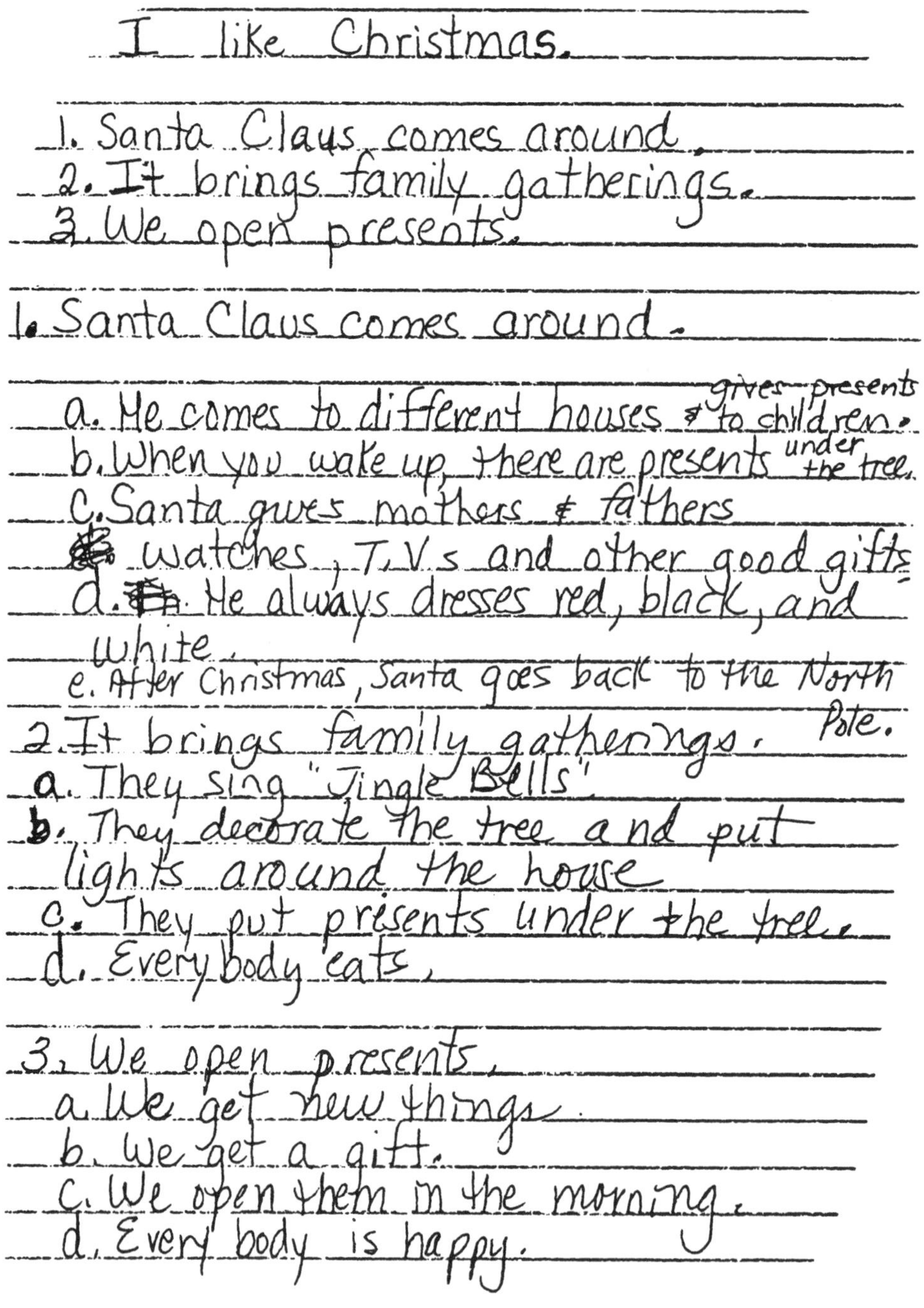

I like Christmas.

1. Santa Claus comes around.
2. It brings family gatherings.
3. We open presents.

1. Santa Claus comes around.

a. He comes to different houses & gives presents to children.
b. When you wake up, there are presents under the tree.
c. Santa gives mothers & fathers watches, T.V.s and other good gifts.
d. He always dresses red, black, and white.
e. After Christmas, Santa goes back to the North Pole.
2. It brings family gatherings.
a. They sing "Jingle Bells".
b. They decorate the tree and put lights around the house
c. They put presents under the tree.
d. Everybody eats.

3. We open presents.
a. We get new things.
b. We get a gift.
c. We open them in the morning.
d. Everybody is happy.

Figure 7.27. Jenn's First Draft Using Kerrigan's Method.

but rather to find the truth. The following rules apply:

1. The student must support ideas with reasons, examples, and facts that have been researched.
2. The student must choose topics that have two sides, ones that can be supported adequately, regardless of which side is chosen. Remind the student to mention the contrasting views and refute them as expertly as possible.
3. Have the student use connectives so that the reader knows which side of the argument is being discussed (such as *true, admittedly, of course, naturally, even now*).

Tell the student that *but* may also be used to show when the other side of the argument is about to be presented.

Themes of expression may be the most difficult to write, as style and eloquence are required. In this style of writing, the writer seeks to make his or her intention and attitude clearer. Eloquence may be developed by:

1. Reading every day, sometimes reading aloud.
2. Frequent writing (letters or journals) in order to practice what has been learned.
3. Observing rules of grammar and taking the time to learn common errors made (both oral and written errors).
4. Increasing one's vocabulary.
5. Being succinct in speech and writing, and eliminating words not contributing to the point.
6. Varying sentence length and form.

REVISION

Once students have written their first drafts of stories, paragraphs, or essays, they should be encouraged to revise and improve their products. Do not have students revise everything that they write, but rather only the pieces that will be published or shared with others. Ms. Gorski, a fourth-grade teacher, has her students select one of their writings every two weeks to revise for their writing portfolios. Students choose the piece that they wish to include and then revise and edit their work. Figure 7.28 presents the final version of Donavan's essay on space. He used the six-step Kerrigan method to develop the first draft. He began with his main idea that he knew a lot about space, and then developed paragraphs with specific facts and supporting details.

When revising their work, encourage students to focus on the meaning of the text, not on detecting the errors in basic writing skills.

Although some of the revision strategies provide an editing step, the focus of revision activities is on organization, clarification, and elaboration of ideas. As with other areas of writing, several strategies have been developed for revision.

TAPS Strategy

Students can provide feedback to each other during the revising stage by using the simple strategy of TAPS to help them focus on the ideas and provide constructive feedback to each other. The mnemonic TAPS represents:

T   *Tell* the person what you liked about the paper.

A   *Ask* questions about parts that are unclear.

P   *Provide* suggestions for making the paper better.

S   *Share* the revised paper.

Student Editor Strategy

The student editor strategy is designed to help students in the writing and revision stages of the writing process (MacArthur, 1994; MacArthur, Schwartz, & Graham, 1991). The strategy helps students increase awareness of their audience and the clarity of their writing. Students may write papers on a computer in order to ease the physical process of revision.

Strategy Instruction

Specific teaching guidelines are provided for teaching the student editor strategy. Ideally, strategy instruction is provided to groups of four to six students, although it can also be taught to pairs. First, teach those students who are most likely to learn the strategy easily as, with mastery, they will be able to help teach the strategy to peers. In general, use the following seven stages when teaching the strategy:

1. *Developing necessary preskills.* Ensure that students have experience with the process

I know a lot about space. I know a lot about space because of what I've seen on television, read in books or learned from my parents.

I know that there are planets with moons in space. Moons orbit around planets. Jupiter has sixteen moons. Mars has two. Saturn has three moons. Mercury has no moons. Our Earth has one moon orbiting around it.

I know spaceships have the power to go up in space. A spaceship divides into five parts on its journey through space. It takes a spaceship around twenty-eight years to go out of the "Ork Cloud." I know this because I saw it on television. If the spaceship goes at the speed of light to the closest neighbor in space; if it takes the spaceship thirty-eight years to get there, then on Earth 8,000 years will have passed.

I know astronauts go up in space to explore. A long time ago, scientists sent animals to see if it was safe

for humans to go up in space. Scientists discovered that humans could survive in space and on the moon. They sent up the first astronaut to explore the moon. That astronaut put the American flag on the Earth's moon to show that it was the property of the United States. Astronauts are sent in spaceships to explore in space. That way we may live a little better here on Earth because of what we learn from exploring on the moon and in space.

Figure 7.28. Donavan's Essay About Space.

approach to writing and feel comfortable with activities involving planning, writing, revising, and sharing their work.

2. *Providing an initial group conference.* Review students' performance levels in revision and discuss what revision techniques are currently known. Discuss the importance of revision when writing.

3. *Introducing and discussing the strategy.* Following the introduction of the strategy, discuss its importance and point out that all professional writers have editors who help them. Help students understand when to use the strategy. Provide direct explanation of the "how," "why," and "when" of the strategy.

4. *Modeling the strategy.* Use an assignment to model the strategy, verbalizing each of the steps and the mental processes involved. Statements that may be beneficial include problem definition ("What do I have to do next?"); self-regulation ("That's the first two steps completed, now for the third"); self-evaluation ("I was supposed to add details to the main character. Did I do that?"); and self-reinforcement ("I think I succeeded in making that description better.").

5. *Mastering the strategy.* Provide a few minutes each session for students to memorize the steps. Continue with this until each student can recite the steps from memory.

6. *Providing collaborative practice.* Have students take turns in being editors for their peers. Provide whatever support is necessary to ensure appropriate strategy use. Fade the support as each pair of students becomes more proficient at using the strategy independently.

7. *Practicing independently.* After students have attained mastery, provide periodic feedback and review as necessary. Make specific plans for generalization to other tasks and situations.

Steps

Have students work in pairs and take turns being the "author" and "editor." The editor follows these steps:

1. Listen to the author read the paper, and follow along on a second printed copy of the assignment.

2. Review the content of the paper and tell what part you liked best.

3. At this stage, the students switch roles and the first two steps are repeated. For the third step, each student works independently on a written copy or a computer printout of their partner's paper.

4. Read your partner's draft and make notes directly on the paper. Look for
    a. Clarity—is anything difficult to understand?
    b. Details—are there places where more details could be added?

5. Meet with your partner and discuss your queries and suggestions. The discussion should be interactive, with the author responding to the editor's comments. The editor focuses on content and communication, not on mechanics such as spelling or capitalization errors.

6. On the same day as the conference, the authors work separately making revisions to their papers.

Step-by-Step Revision and Editing Strategy

A strategy that begins with revision activities and progresses to editing strategies uses the following steps (Cohen, 1985):

1. Have the student complete a free writing assignment and share it with you.

2. Without correcting errors, react to the content of the draft.

3. Upon return, have the student read the assignment aloud to other students in

order to detect errors in structure and word usage.

4. Have the student revise and reorganize the assignment, integrating the feedback from peers.
5. Have the student turn in the assignment.
6. Place a check by each line that contains an error. When more than one error exists on a line, write the number of errors by the line in parentheses.
7. Have the student correct the teacher-indicated errors and turn in a third draft.
8. Mark any remaining errors.
9. Have the student incorporate the teacher's corrections into a final draft.
10. Use the approach with numerous writing assignments.
11. Have the student select an assignment for a final paper.

Revision Conferences

The easiest way to provide students with feedback on their writing is to conduct a revision conference. Your specific feedback during brief conferences will help students revise their drafts. Attempt to conduct frequent, but brief (two to three minutes) conferences. Effective student-centered conferences are based on the following steps:

1. Begin by providing feedback about what you like about the paper.
2. Help the student develop and clarify the selected topic.
3. Ask questions about the writing that will teach and provide direction.
4. Have the student answer the questions orally and then add in clarifications to the revision.

You might want to write down a few comments and questions for discussion prior to the conference. Through an interactive discussion, you can critique writing for clarity using the following procedure:

1. Identify the student's difficulties in the paper.

2. Discuss the identified problems with the student and explain why they are problematic.
3. Discuss ways to improve and clarify the writing.
4. Have the student make revisions and then review and discuss the student's revisions.

You can use the following procedure to conduct a revision conference (Moulton & Bader, 1986):

1. Write a list of comments and questions about the draft and share it with the student. The major questions might include:
   a. To what extent has the topic been covered in the draft?
   b. To what extent does the draft adhere to the prewriting plan?
   c. To what extent has the information been organized for clarity?
   d. To what extent has the choice of words been appropriate?
2. Hold a conference and have the student read the draft aloud and respond to the comments and questions.
3. Ask the student to suggest changes to the draft.
4. At the conference, have the student revise the draft using a colored pen.
5. Repeat the process until the student can identify and solve problems independently.

You might also have a small group of students meet together to read and revise their compositions. They should take turns reading their compositions aloud and then listening to the strengths of the paper, as well as suggestions for improvement from peers.

Ms. Rodriguez, a ninth-grade English teacher, conducts daily, individualized revision conferences with her students. Samples of first drafts of descriptive paragraphs from five of her students, Bart, Pearl, Craig, Jeremy, and Ethan, are presented in Figure 7.29.

Their assignment was to write paragraphs describing their perfect homes. Ms. Rodriguez reviewed the samples and then presented both

Bart

My house is very large and
my carpet is ~~no~~ really pulse I have a really
pig pool and its heat too & my house is
IN THE coUNTRY AWDI have cows and pig so I cold eat
them

Pearl

My Perfect home

If I had a choice, where my house
would be it would be in calf. with a
veiw on the beach. Ever seice I went
there I've had a dream of liveing there
but I've heard its not so bump I dont
realy know and I dont think I'll ever
find out but thats ok because its a
nice place to visit but I'm never gone
na live there.
Most of my friends say that place
is complished to whats going on around
every one. but I dont know.
And never will

Figure 7.29. First Drafts of Five Students' Descriptive Paragraphs.

Craig

Craig

My perfect home would be a nice big beach house in California. It would have alot of windows in the back so it would be easy to see the ocean from almost anywhere in the house. It would have a 3car garage. A basement made made into a game room with a pool table and a stereo. And a pool on the side of the house. It would have a exercise room. It would have atleast 3 bed rooms one for me and my future wife, and the others for my future kids. But untill then I would have big parties all the time.

Jeremy

My perfect home would call for me to win the lottery it would cost so mucha I would first take the second to bigest room and totally sound proof it for my band. Second I would tear out the floor thru one one the front room and put on indoor pool in. With a bridge leading down the hall. That is pretty much all I would do. Except for a 22 year old blond model for a maid.

Figure 7.29. First Drafts of Five Students' Descriptive Paragraphs. *(Continued)*

Ethan

<u>"My perfect Home"</u>

My perfect home would be most defenitly more suitable to be called a lazy richmans home because it would be furnished with black laqure furniture and Leather furniture evrywere I thought nessisary and a big screen tv w/ remote 4 head vcr in sterro and not to mention a very loud sterro system w/ cd pkyer and spekers all over the place and a big ... bed w/ silk sheets in my room w/ more spekers and evry thing I have can be controll by voice comand in any room even out side and the kitchen would also be voice comand evry thing to be cooked would just have to be told what to do and it would get it done and also a large wieght room and a pool table and a spa, pool to relax in this would be the some what mosterly explaned lazy Home.

Figure 7.29. *(Continued)*

positive comments and suggestions to her students in a revision conference. She provided suggestions for their topics, and helped them to expand upon their own ideas.

Bart

Bart wrote three sentences. In this short sample, his vocabulary is imprecise and he does not appear to have much to say. After looking at Bart's paragraph, Ms. Rodriguez notes that he would have benefited from increased planning time. These prewriting activities would have helped him develop a sequence for his description prior to writing. He does not introduce the topic, and the details describing his perfect house are not presented sequentially. In the opening sentence, he notes that his house is very large and the carpet is plush. He then writes that the house is in the country. The closing thought appears only tangentially related to the topic ("I have cows and pigs so I could eat them"). In their meeting, Bart and his teacher brainstorm about other observations he could include and develop a framework for sequencing his ideas. They also discuss possibilities for a concluding statement.

Pearl

Pearl begins by writing the title for her paragraph: "My Perfect home." She then informs the reader of the location of the house. She wants her house to be in California with a view of the beach. She then loses the focus of the assignment and fails to maintain the topic. She shifts to a discussion about the merits of living in California. The focus shifts as she reports the opinion of her friends and her own personal thoughts. She states that she's never going to live there and concludes that she will never know what it is like.

Pearl's vocabulary is simple and lacks clarity. Although she appears to have some knowledge of the meaning of the word *camouflaged*, the usage is incorrect as she writes: "Most of my friends say that place is camoflashed to what going on around every one."

As with Bart, Ms. Rodriguez notes that Pearl would have benefited from increased planning prior to writing. Her failure to maintain the topic suggests that she really did not have a plan in regard to the information she needed to describe her perfect home. In the conference, her teacher reviews with her the structure of a paragraph and helps her to identify her topic, develop her ideas, and consider a concluding sentence.

Craig

Craig begins his paragraph by introducing his reader to the topic and writes, "My perfect home would be a nice, big beach house in California." He uses humor by concluding that until he is settled with a family, he would have big parties all the time. Although descriptions are included, Craig's sentence patterns lack variety. The majority begin with "It would have . . . " In addition, one sentence is incomplete. In their revision conference, the feedback for improvement centers on ways several sentences could be rewritten and elaborated upon to increase interest. In addition, Craig and Ms. Rodriguez discuss ways that he could correct the incomplete sentence.

Jeremy

Jeremy begins with an interesting topic sentence, noting that he'll have to win the lottery to afford his perfect house. The organization of his paragraph is logical. He uses two cohesive ties (*first, second*) to connect his thoughts. He describes two improvements and then uses humor in his ending by describing his ideal roommate.

The first sentence consists of two sentences joined without a conjunction. Near the end of the paragraph, Jeremy has written two incomplete sentences. Jeremy's handwriting is small and difficult to read. He writes in the middle of the paper, rather than observing the margins.

As with Craig, Jeremy has a good start on his paragraph. In the revision conference, Ms. Rodriguez and Jeremy discuss the presentation of his ideas. Although he maintains the topic, the paragraph does not describe his perfect home, but rather the improvements he would make to an existing home. Ms. Rodriguez encourages Jeremy to clarify this in his topic sentence and to strengthen the paragraph by including one more home improvement.

Ethan

The overall appearance of Ethan's writing is neat and easy to read. He indents the first paragraph and uses margins. Although Ethan's paragraph is written as one long sentence, his introductory statements about his lazy rich man's home capture the reader's attention. His vocabulary is precise and his vivid descriptions enable the reader to create a visual image of the surroundings. For example, he notes that his house will contain black lacquer and black leather furniture and that his big water bed will have silk sheets.

In the revision conference, Ms. Rodriguez and Ethan determine what parts of the paragraph may confuse the reader and how these sections could be clarified. First, they identify where his sentences begin and end. Next they discuss a few of the thoughts that seem unclear. For example, when describing the voice command in the kitchen, he writes, " . . . everything to be cooked would just have to be told what to do," and in the concluding thought he writes, " . . . to relax in this would be the somewhat modernly explained lazy home."

The five descriptive paragraphs on "My Perfect Home" illustrate the variability that exists among students on any writing assignment. Although each of the students has written the first draft of a paragraph, the writings differ both in ideation and organization. In addition, a teacher would have different, specific comments for each student during a revision conference.

As a final reminder, make sure to tell students what you like about their paper. For students with minimal writing skill, you can make comments, such as "Great idea" or "You've written several complete sentences." Figure 7.30 presents the first draft of J. P., a tenth-grade student who was asked to write an opinion paper. The topic was whether or not students in high school should be allowed to select their own classes. At the beginning of the revision conference, his English teacher told him that he had done a good job of structuring his essay—the first paragraph telling about what some people think, the second paragraph about what other people think, and the final paragraph about your own personal opinion. She also told him that she liked his ending. They then discussed how he could add more details to his essay, such as describing examples of what he thought were the easiest classes.

Should Students be able to Pick Thar Clases

    Some parents thinck that kids shod not pick thar clases. Thay say it is to much responsabelty for the student or the student will pick the esest clases.

    Other peple say the students have a right to thare one life and the thing pick are part of thar life. If they ruine it it is not the schools falt.

    Ass the atter of this newspaper, I think it should be haf and haf you should have the clases that be importen be pikt. But if you whant other clases you shud get them. This wod satis fie most peple but remember you can't satis fie evaryone. J.P.

Figure 7.30. First Draft of J.P.'s Opinion Essay.

Technology

Students with writing difficulties can also benefit from the use of computers for writing and revising stories and essays. The quality of their writing often improves when students use a computer. Many computer software programs are also available to help students develop their skills in both narrative and expository writing. Many of the writing programs available integrate text and graphics. For writing narratives, students often begin the program by developing pictures to illustrate their compositions. These types of programs are often effective in motivating both beginning and reluctant writers. In addition, students can use the word processor to complete story starters, keep diaries or journals, text message, or send e-mail.

Students can also use word-processing programs to create their own reports, newsletters, and newspapers. They can arrange the layout in one or two columns, insert headings and captions, and add graphics to illustrate the text. In addition, students can use electronic encyclopedias and Internet searches to gather information for their essays and reports. Several software programs combine word processing with speech synthesis. This feature allows students to enter text as the synthesizer reads it back to them by repeating a word or an entire line. When they hear the text they have written, they are often able to catch and correct errors. Computer-supported writing is one characteristic of a positive teaching and learning environment.

EXAMPLES OF COMMERCIAL PROGRAMS

A variety of methods for teaching written expression have been presented in this chapter. These methods can often provide the key to effective writing instruction. Successful writing instruction requires a framework and common language for teachers and students to use. Several programs can help you implement an effective writing program. One widely used framework is Write Traits®, which incorporates the following six writing traits: ideas, details, organization, sentence fluency, voice, and conventions. These six traits also provide a common language that is used across all levels from kindergarten through college. Many resources exist for teaching the six writing traits. Great Source (www.greatsource.com) is one resource for obtaining materials and workshops related to *Write Traits*, as well as the popular *Write Source* series.

Another helpful resource is *Powerful Writing Strategies for All Students*, published by Paul Brookes (www.brookespublishing.com). This book describes many effective instructional practices in an easy-to-use format and

provides step-by-step guidance and scaffolding for students. The lessons also illustrate how to fade the supports to ensure transfer of the skills. Lessons range from twenty to sixty minutes and cover every phase of the writing process. Writing strategies and skills are reinforced through individual and group practice. Reproducible cue cards, graphic organizers, sheets for graphing writing performance, and mnemonic charts are included. This resource is based on the strategies used in the field-tested Self-Regulated Strategy Development approach discussed earlier in this chapter.

As described in Chapter Six, multisensory, structured language programs also include instruction that increases in complexity from the basic elements of writing to written expression. For example, *Language Circle/Project*

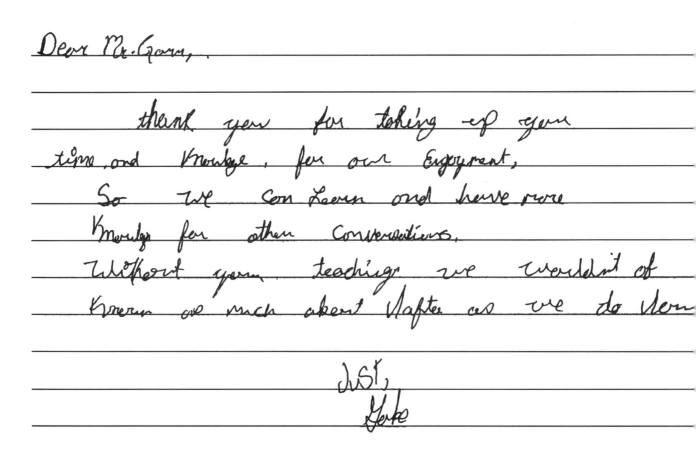

Figure 7.31. Gabe's Letter to His Teacher.

Translation: Thank you for taking up your time and knowledge for our enjoyment. So we can learn and have more knowledge for other conversations. Without your teaching we wouldn't have known as much about it after as we do now.

Read Written Expression Curriculum (www .projectread.com) provides a multisensory, systematic approach to teaching writing skills. A variety of software programs are also available. For example, *Kidspiration* for grades K–5 and *Inspiration* for grades 6–12 use proven graphic organizers, outlining, and visual learning principles to help students develop written expression skills by planning, organizing, and expanding their topics. Both programs are available from Inspiration Software (www.inspiration.com).

As another resource, Read & Write software from BrightEye Technology (www.brighteye.com) works within any application to help students read and write with greater ease. The software includes features such as translating text to speech, word prediction, and voice recognition. The National Writing Project (www.nwp .org) also offers many resources to assist with writing instruction. This professional development network is dedicated to improving student achievement by improving the teaching of writing. Its website includes publications and research related to writing, as well as professional development opportunities. One pertinent resource available for download is *30 Ideas for Teaching Writing*.

CONCLUSION

Many students who struggle with writing seem to make little improvement in skill across the grades. In the past, teachers may not have spent enough time on integrating writing into the curriculum. Today, more time is spent on writing, but the focus may be more on preparing students to pass writing exams than on helping them acquire the writing skills they will need as adults.

Presently, many students with language and learning difficulties are spending the majority, if not all, of their day in general education classrooms and, like their peers, are being asked to produce clear, coherent writing. These demands necessitate that both general and special education teachers work together to develop effective writing programs. The most important component of any writing program is the teacher. Gabe, an eighth-grade student, wrote the note presented in Figure 7.31 to thank his teacher for sharing his knowledge with the students. Our goal as teachers is to help students such as Gabe improve their skills in both oral and written language.

chapter
8

Informal Assessment and Curriculum-Based Measurement

While instruction and evaluation may prove helpful, the more valuable opportunity is the actual writing practice, the expression of ideas.

—Joan Lickteig (1981)

Frequent assessment and progress monitoring are important elements of good instruction and are essential when trying to meet accountability standards or when implementing a response to instruction or response to intervention (RTI) model. Many teachers use informal assessments or curriculum-based measures to determine if their students have acquired the skills being taught. As a teacher, your job is to ensure that students are learning. Without assessment and careful attention to progress, you will not know which students have mastered a skill and are ready to move on, or which students have not and need additional instruction. Good teachers "recognize the importance of ongoing assessments and continual adjustments on the part of both teacher and student as the means to achieve maximum performance" (McTighe & O'Connor, 2005, p. 11).

The goal of informal assessment and curriculum-based measurement (CBM) is to promote student learning. The focus is not on a score or a rank order, but rather on what the student is learning and what still needs to be learned to reach an instructional goal. You can incorporate these techniques into classroom routines easily and use them at any time without interfering with instruction. They can help you determine how your instruction is working and how your students are learning. You will be able to answer questions such as: Which students need additional instruction? Which students are at about the same level so they can be grouped for instruction? Do I need to change my teaching approach? Are my students making appropriate progress?

This chapter presents various informal assessment techniques and tips on using CBM for spelling and written expression. Throughout the chapter writing samples illustrate how to evaluate different types of writing for the purpose of determining instructional needs.

INFORMAL ASSESSMENT

Teachers are constantly gathering information about their students. Good teachers use this information to guide instruction. For informal assessment to be most effective, you have to know what it is you want your students to be able to do. Clear instructional goals are important. Regular use of informal assessments helps you see if you are meeting your instructional goals. Many types of informal assessments are available or you can make your own. Both structured and unstructured activities provide opportunities to evaluate student performance. Spelling tests or checklists are examples of structured activities. Journal entries or student portfolios are examples of unstructured activities. To make good sense of the information you gather, it is important that you know what to expect regarding developmental variations in performance.

Developmental Differences

Tremendous variation exists in the writing skill of students. As a teacher, you must be aware of this diversity of development so that you can plan instruction accordingly. This variation is evident as early as the kindergarten level and increases with each year. Figure 8.1 provides samples of several beginning kindergarten students having written their names. Although all of the students understood that some type of writing was required, the skill level was extremely varied.

Some students spelled their names correctly. Dominic started his name with an uppercase letter and wrote the remaining letters in lowercase. Others had correct spelling, but awkward letter formation. Jenni spelled her name correctly, but the letters increased progressively in size, and Kyle made an uppercase E with four horizontal lines, rather than three. Jana reversed the letter J and added a stick to a circle to form an a. Others have learned a few letters in their names. For example, Heather wrote her name as *Het*, Sam wrote his name as *AS*, and Brian spelled his name as *OBD*. Some students understand that their names are composed of a series of letters, but are uncertain as to which ones. For example, Tina wrote her name as *Tliibbothu*, and Jonathan wrote his name as *Em*. Ryan and Sarah produced scribbles or circles, although Ryan understood that some form of discrete symbols was needed.

Similarly, Figure 8.2 provides samples from several beginning first-grade students who drew self-portraits and wrote a sentence about a favorite activity to include in a class directory. Diversity in development of visual-motor skill as well as writing skill is apparent. Several of the students used "temporary" spellings that have some of the sounds, whereas a few used spellings that have all of the sounds. Many times the differences in writing skill persist throughout the grades, and may intensify. Figure 8.3 illustrates the handwriting and spelling skills of two seventh-grade students. Notice the variation in letter formation as well as the differences in spelling. There is nothing fair or equitable about requiring the same writing tasks for these two students; nor would it be appropriate to provide the exact same instruction to both.

Qualitative Analysis

Informal evaluation of what your student can and cannot do is at the heart of instructional planning. Simply observing the work of your students is the first step in qualitative analysis. Notice the errors they make when writing. Is a student struggling with letter formation? If you observe this as a problem area, you may need to make adjustments to instruction or provide an accommodation. For example, if a student is struggling with the motor demands of writing, you might want to introduce keyboarding skills as soon as possible, or shorten writing assignments. Is a student struggling with spelling? If you observe spelling difficulties, provide direct instruction in the elements that are most troublesome for that student. Are students struggling with organizing their writing? Teach them about text structure. Use the observable, qualitative information to guide instruction. Different chapters in this text provide in-depth information about each aspect of writing. Once you have identified the problem area or areas, consult the appropriate chapter: Chapter Five for handwriting, Chapter Six for spelling and usage, and Chapter Seven for written expression.

Observation

Sharpen your powers of observation, and you will gain key data about your students. One method used by many teachers is called "clipboard

Figure 8.1. Written Names of Kindergarten Students.

Figure 8.2. Sentences Written by First-Grade Students.

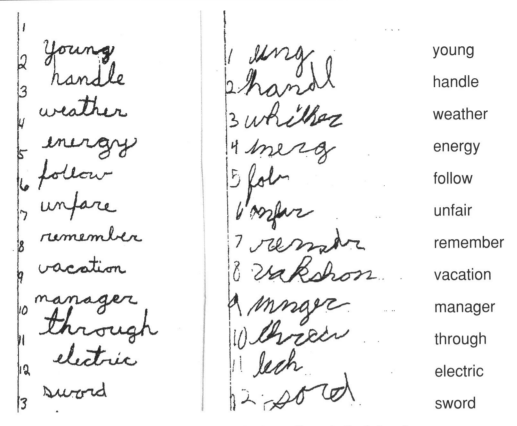

Figure 8.3. Two Examples of Variation in Spelling and Writing at Seventh-Grade Level.

cruising." This method requires only a clipboard, a set of self-adhesive address labels, and a notebook or folder with a page for each child. Move, or cruise, around the room observing your students at work. Record the student's name, date, and your observational comments on one of the labels. After completing an observation, place the sticker on the child's page in your notebook or folder. Once you have completed several observations, review the data you've collected looking for patterns of behavior that affect performance.

Error Analysis

Errors are opportunities. They reveal where learning is breaking down. Because writing provides a permanent record of performance, it is easy to analyze errors. Chapter Nine of this text provides numerous examples of how to analyze errors. It also provides guided and independent practice in analyzing writing samples to inform instruction.

Handwriting

Quick and automatic letter formation is an important prerequisite skill for written expression. A simple way to evaluate your students' handwriting automaticity is to first ask them to copy a sentence using their best handwriting. After it has been copied, ask them to write that sentence as many times as they can in three minutes. Use a sentence that contains all the letters of the alphabet, such as "The quick brown fox jumps over the lazy dog." This allows you to look at the quality of letter formation for the entire alphabet. You can identify which letter or letters require more instruction and practice. In addition, you can calculate the letters per minute (lpm), an indicator of writing speed. After the three minutes is completed, you count the total number of letters and divide by three. That gives you the average lpm. Then compare your student's performance to a graded scale, such as the following one from Zaner-Bloser (Barbe, Wasylyk, Hackney, & Braun, 1984).

Grade 1: 25 lpm
Grade 2: 30 lpm
Grade 3: 38 lpm
Grade 4: 45 lpm
Grade 5: 60 lpm
Grade 6: 67 lpm
Grade 7: 74 lpm

Figure 8.4 illustrates the sentences written in three minutes by Jon, a fifth-grade student. The first sentence is the one he copied using his best handwriting. The ones that follow were completed in the three minutes allowed for this handwriting sample. Notice that the quality of his writing diminishes under pressure of time. He did produce a total of 153 letters. Divide his total by three to get his letters per minute (lpm). The fifth-grade standard

is 60 lpm, so Jon's writing at 51 lpm is slower than expected. Jon has difficulty with quick and automatic writing, and his letter formation is not of good quality. As a fifth-grader, Jon needs to be using word processing whenever possible. When handwriting is required, he needs shorter assignments or extended time.

Spelling

Informal assessment of spelling may be facilitated when using something like the Phonics Check-Off Chart (Figure 8.5). This chart presents common phonic elements that are important to spelling mastery. You can use the chart to direct assessment of spelling needs by dictating a group of key words that include a particular phonic element. For example, you know that Sonia often omits the second letter in words with consonant blends when she is writing. You begin with the *L* family, asking Sonia to write the words *block, clock, flock,*

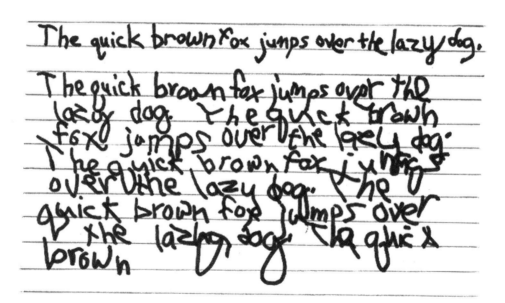

Figure 8.4. Jon's Three-Minute Handwriting Sample.

Figure 8.5. Phonics Check-Off Chart.

Consonants
- b
- c — cat
- c (+ e, i, y) — city
- d
- f
- g — gum
- g (+ e, i, y) — gem
- h
- j
- k
- l
- m
- n
- p
- qu
- r
- s — sock
- s — bugs, visit
- t
- v
- w
- x — fox
- x — xylophone
- y
- z

Initial Digraphs
- ch — chip
- ch — chorus
- ch — chef
- gh — ghost
- gn — gnat
- kn — know
- ph — phone
- sh — ship
- th — that (voiced)
- th — thin (unvoiced)
- wr — write

Initial Consonant Blends
- *L*-family
- bl
- cl
- fl
- gl
- pl
- sl
- spl
- *R*-family
- br
- cr
- dr
- fr
- gr
- pr
- tr
- *S*-family
- sc
- sk
- sm
- sn
- sp
- st
- sw
- 3-letter *S*-family
- scr
- spl
- spr
- squ
- str
- *W*-family
- dw
- tw

Initial Digraph Blends
- chr — chronic
- sch — school
- shr — shrill
- thr — thrill

Final Consonant Blends
- -ct — fact
- -ft — lift
- -ld — cold
- -lf — elf
- -lk — milk
- -lp — help
- -lt — melt
- -mp — jump
- -nd — end
- -nk — sink
- -nt — mint
- -pt — kept
- -rd — bird
- -rm — farm
- -rt — hurt
- -sk — ask
- -sp — lisp
- -st — list
- -xt — next
- -mpt — tempt

Final Digraphs and Trigraphs
- -ck — duck
- -gh — tough
- -lf — half
- -lk — walk
- -mb — thumb
- -ng — sing
- -dge — fudge
- -tch — match

Final Digraph Blends
- -fth — fifth
- -lfth — twelfth
- -lch — mulch
- -lth — filth
- -nch — inch
- -nth — seventh

Short Vowels Closed Syllable		Long Vowels Open Syllable		Long Vowels CVe Syllable		R-Controlled Vowel/Syllable		Vowel Digraphs		Vowel Diphthongs		Common Prefixes	Common Suffixes
a	cat	a	baby	a-e	cake	ar	car	ai	rain	oi	oil	un-	-s, -es
e	met	e	me	e-e	Pete	er	her	ay	day	oy	boy	re-	-ed
i	fit	i	hi	i-e	pine	ir	sir	au	sauce	ou	out	in-, im-, ir-, il-(not)	-ing
o	mop	o	no	o-e	bone	or	for	aw	claw	ow	cow	dis-	-ly
u	nut	u	flu	u-e	rule	ur	fur	ea	meat			en-, em-	-er, -or
y	gym	y	fly	u-e	mule			ea	head			non-	-ion, tion, ation, ition
		y	happy	y-e	style			ea	great			in-, im-(in, into)	-ible, -able
								ee	feet			over-	-al, -ial
								ei	seize			mis-	-y
								ei	vein			sub-	-ness
								eigh	eight			pre-	-ty, -ity
								ey	key			inter-	-ment
								ey	grey			fore-	-ic
								eu	sleuth			de-	-ous, -eous, -ious
								eu	feud			trans-	-en
								ew	blew			super-	-er, -est
								ew	pew			semi-	-ive, -ative, -itive
								ie	piece			anti-	-ful
								ie	pie			mid-	-less
								igh	high			under-	-est
								oa	boat				
								oe	toe				
								oo	moon				
								oo	book				
								ou	soup				
								ow	snow				
								ue	clue				
								ue	cue				
								ui	fruit				
								ui	build				

Figure 8.5. Phonics Check-off Chart. (*Continued*)
Source: Developed by L. E. Jaffe and N. Mather.

glow, play, slow, and *splash*. When you look at the list, you note that Sonia left out the letter *l* on three of the words: *block, glow*, and *splash*. Your next spelling lesson for Sonia would then focus on groups of words that begin with those specific blends, *bl-, gl-*, and *spl-*. Once those blends are mastered, you can progress to other common elements in the chart. You can also use the chart to develop spelling lists to reinforce a specific pattern or provide certain students with more practice spelling certain patterns, such as common consonant digraphs of suffixes. Using this information to guide instruction for spelling may provide the additional benefit of improving the student's decoding skills. The Phonics Check-Off Chart is also a helpful progress-monitoring tool. Once a certain element has been mastered, you or the student may place a check in the box.

Written Expression

Many teachers have students write in a journal each day, or maintain a portfolio of writing samples. Both of these sources can be used for qualitative analysis of writing skill. In addition, there are a number of checklists available that can be used to help evaluate the quality of the writing sample. One example of a checklist that provides a holistic evaluation is shown in Figure 8.6. The Writing Evaluation Scale includes the components of written language we have presented through this text. You can use this scale for both holistic (overall impression) and analytic (evaluation of parts) scoring. Each category can be rated from a low of 1 (least advanced on the skill being rated) to a high of 5 (most advanced on the skill being rated). For holistic scoring, you can assign an overall rating for the writing, based on your impression of the entire piece. When evaluating the overall quality of writing, consider the student's writing in relation to his or her peers. Focus on all components of writing except handwriting. Try not to let poor handwriting affect your judgment of the content. If necessary, students can keyboard their papers so that handwriting is not a factor.

For the major components in bold, such as "Handwriting," assign a general rating for overall legibility. If you want to analyze the samples in more detail, you can rate the various categories included with the component. This will involve more attention to error analysis. For example, under spelling, you will see Phonology, Orthography, Morphology, and Semantics. When considering these elements, you may ask, Does the student spell words the way they sound and sequence sounds correctly? (Phonology) Does the student spell the irregular elements of words correctly? (Orthography) Does the student include meaning units in spelling, such as endings, prefixes, past tense, and so on? (Morphology) Does the student spell homophones correctly, such as *pear* and *pair*? (Semantics) You might want to evaluate samples from students on a weekly basis and keep their papers in a writing portfolio, where you can work together for setting goals to improve writing.

Other checklists help document the types of errors that were made, or you can simply track the types of errors. For example, how many errors did the student make in spelling, or capitalization, or punctuation, or grammar? In addition, you can record the actual errors so that you can target instruction to address the specific errors that the student made.

Syntax

Some students have difficulty with the structure of language, which limits their written expression. You can use informal assessment techniques to check your student's knowledge of syntax. Use a student's writing sample to see if he or she can identify different parts of speech. For example, ask the student to find the action word in a sentence. Start with a sentence that has an obvious verb. Then move to more complex sentences, such as ones with helping verbs (for example, *is running*). Use a cloze procedure to see if the student can fill in the correct form of a word that is missing. This can be used to

Writing Evaluation Scale

Name: _____   Date: _____

Directions: Rate the student's writing performance in relationship to classmates.

Component	Least Advanced		Typical		Most Advanced
OVERALL	1	2	3	4	5
Handwriting	1	2	3	4	5
Letter formation	1	2	3	4	5
Rate	1	2	3	4	5
Spelling	1	2	3	4	5
Phonology	1	2	3	4	5
Orthography	1	2	3	4	5
Morphology	1	2	3	4	5
Semantics	1	2	3	4	5
Usage	1	2	3	4	5
Capitalization	1	2	3	4	5
Punctuation	1	2	3	4	5
Syntax/Grammar	1	2	3	4	5
Vocabulary	1	2	3	4	5
Word retrieval	1	2	3	4	5
Morphology	1	2	3	4	5
Breadth and depth	1	2	3	4	5
Text structure	1	2	3	4	5
Cohesion	1	2	3	4	5
Narrative	1	2	3	4	5
Expository	1	2	3	4	5

Notes for instruction:

Figure 8.6. Writing Checklist for Holistic and Analytic Evaluation.

evaluate verb tenses, as well as "to be" constructions. For example:

He walk _____ the entire length of the school yesterday.
She swim _____ every day.
We _____ been shopping for school clothes.
They _____ waiting for you.

Another simple idea for checking a student's understanding of syntax is to use scrambled sentences. Prepare some sentences in advance and write each word on a separate card. Place the cards for a sentence in random order in front of the student. Ask the student to construct a sentence using all the cards. All of these sources of informal assessment are invaluable in guiding instruction.

CURRICULUM-BASED MEASUREMENT

The federal mandates of No Child Left Behind (NCLB, 2001) and the Individuals with Disabilities Education Improvement Act of 2004 (IDEA, 2004) have resulted in a national agenda to develop comprehensive writing standards, to teach writing in all subjects at all grade levels, and to align writing standards and instruction with best practices in writing assessment. Student progress must be tracked, and those at risk of failing to meet important academic standards must be quickly and accurately identified. Curriculum-based measurement (CBM) provides such a framework for monitoring progress (Deno, 1985).

CBM is a simple and time-efficient way for you to gather important instructional information. Typically, CBM involves brief, timed tests called probes, and covers material from the curriculum. CBMs are standardized in that the teacher reads the same instructions to all students each time the probe is administered, but they are not usually norm-referenced unless a district has gathered norms for each grade.

Several positive features of CBMs are worth noting. First, they are quick and easy to administer. You can even make your own. Second, they can be given multiple times without invalidating the test. Third, they are more sensitive to small changes than most norm-referenced tests. Because CBMs evaluate content from the curriculum they help the teacher determine which students are learning the required content and which students are lagging behind.

CBM for Spelling

Curriculum-based measurement allows frequent monitoring of your students' progress in spelling and only requires a small investment of time. In a typical CBM for spelling, you read aloud a list of words for the students to try to spell. You would dictate the words at a prescribed pace, such as one every seven to ten seconds, for a total of two minutes. For example, for first-through third-grade students, you would administer twelve grade-level words at the rate of one word every ten seconds. For older students in grades four through eight, you would administer seventeen words at the rate of one word every seven seconds. You can create your own spelling lists by consulting a variety of grade-level spelling resources, or by using words that will be encountered throughout the year. Some districts have created their own graded spelling lists for this purpose, or you can use a commercial program. Aimsweb Spelling Curriculum-Based Measurement is a commercially available program that provides graded spelling lists for grades 1–8. See aimsweb.com for more information. In any event, the goal is to create a master list of words appropriate for the targeted grade. From this master list, you would select either twelve or seventeen words, depending on the grade level, for each spelling probe.

Administering spelling probes is simple and usually done with groups of students. First you give the directions and tell the students how much time they will have to write each word (that is, seven or ten seconds) and that they will get credit for each correct letter they write.

Also tell them to go on to the next word once it is given, even if they haven't finished the previous word. Once the assessment begins, you pronounce each word twice. No sentences are used unless the word is a homophone, such as *wood* or *would*. In these cases, you would provide a sentence to clarify which word to spell.

When using CBM spelling probes, you can base the score on two elements: (a) the number of words spelled correctly (WSC); and (b) the number of correct letter sequences (CLS).

Words Spelled Correctly (WSC)

It is easy to count the number of words spelled correctly. Some teachers circle words that are spelled correctly so they are easy to spot. Figure 8.7 shows spelling probes for two third-grade students scored for words spelled correctly (WSC). As you can see by the circled words, Juris spelled ten out of the twelve words correctly, whereas Ricardo only spelled one word correctly. Dramatic differences between these two classmates are easily apparent when comparing their responses. Juris has over 80 percent accuracy whereas Ricardo has only 8 percent accuracy. Their instructional needs are different, and the teacher must adjust instruction accordingly. Remember that spelling probes for grades 1 through 3 typically include twelve words, and the words are dictated at the rate of one

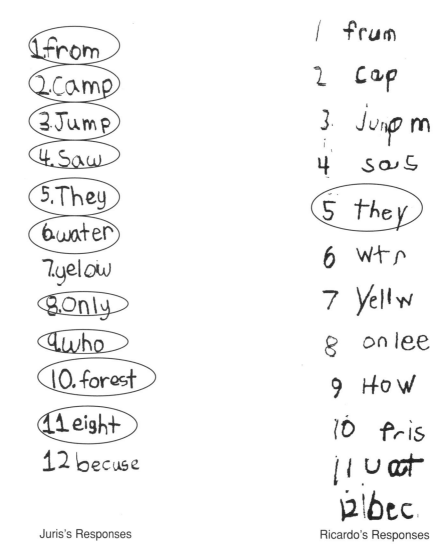

Juris's Responses   Ricardo's Responses

Figure 8.7. Third-Grade Spelling Probes Scored for Words Spelled Correctly (WSC).

word every ten seconds. Students are told to move on to the new word when it is dictated, even if they have not finished the prior word. You can see an example of this in Ricardo's spelling list. He did not have time to complete his spelling of the last word dictated. Remember that even the last word in a spelling probe is given only the prescribed amount of time, ten seconds in Ricardo's case.

Correct Letter Sequences (CLS)

Correct letter sequences are pairs of letters in a word that are written in the correct sequence. Scoring correct letter sequences gives partial credit for words that are misspelled and helps pinpoint growth and monitor progress. Calculating the number of correct letter sequences takes a bit more concentration. Include both correctly spelled words and misspelled words. Words that are spelled correctly will receive maximum points for correct letter sequences (CLS). Maximum credit for correct letter sequences is always one point more than the number of letters in the word: a four-letter word has five correct letter sequences; a six-letter word has seven correct letter sequences, and so on. For example, the word *boat* has four letters, but it has five correct letter sequences possible. A blank or empty space that occurs both before and after the word creates five possible letter sequences (for example, _b_o_a_t_). One method you can use when marking correct letter sequences is to place a caret (^) above each correct letter pair, or space and letter. If the student spelled the word *boat* as *bot*, it would be scored as ^b ^o t ^ for a score of 3 CLS.

Let's look at Juris's and Ricardo's spelling probes again, but this time scored for correct letter sequences (Figures 8.8 and 8.9). Juris had ten of the twelve words spelled correctly, so he will receive maximum credit for those ten words. Remember, maximum credit is the number of letters in a word plus one. So for example, the first word, *from*, has four letters. Because Juris spelled it correctly, his number of correct letter sequences for this word is 5. Although he misspelled number seven, the word *yellow*, he will

still earn points for correct letter sequences. Yellow has six letters, so maximum credit for CLS would be 7. Because Juris spelled *yellow* as "yelow," he has spoiled two letter sequences (ll) and (lo). Therefore, he earns 5 CLS points on this word. His total CLS for this spelling probe is 63. The maximum possible on this probe is 67, which results in 94 percent accuracy for Juris.

Now let's look at Ricardo's probe (Figure 8.9). Although Ricardo only spelled one word correctly, he will earn more points for correct letter sequences. Using CLS helps identify progress that might not be apparent when looking only at the number of words spelled correctly. Notice that Ricardo seemed to change his mind about word number 3, *jump*. He had written "jum" and then decided to put "jupm," spoiling three letter sequences: (um), (mp), and (p_). So instead of earning 5 points, he earns 2 points for the correct sequences of (_j) and (ju). As with Juris's spelling probe, the maximum number of correct letter sequences on this spelling probe is 67. Ricardo had 31 correct letter sequences, resulting in 46 percent accuracy. While Ricardo only had 1 word spelled correctly, he had nearly half of the letter sequences correct. Considering both WSC and CLS allows you to monitor progress more carefully, especially for students who are not meeting grade-level expectations for spelling.

Practice Scoring Spelling Probes

Maria's responses to the same spelling probe for grade 3 are shown in Figure 8.10. The list of spelling words dictated is also shown to assist you in determining correct spelling and correct letter sequences. Try scoring Maria's responses. First, count the words spelled correctly (WSC). Second, determine the number of correct letter sequences (CLS).

How many words did Maria spell correctly? If you answered none, then you are correct. Her WSC is 0. How many correct letter sequences did Maria have out of the 67 possible? If you found 29 CLS for Maria, then you are correct. Let's review the scoring of correct letter sequences: ^f^rum^ = 3, kap^ = 1,

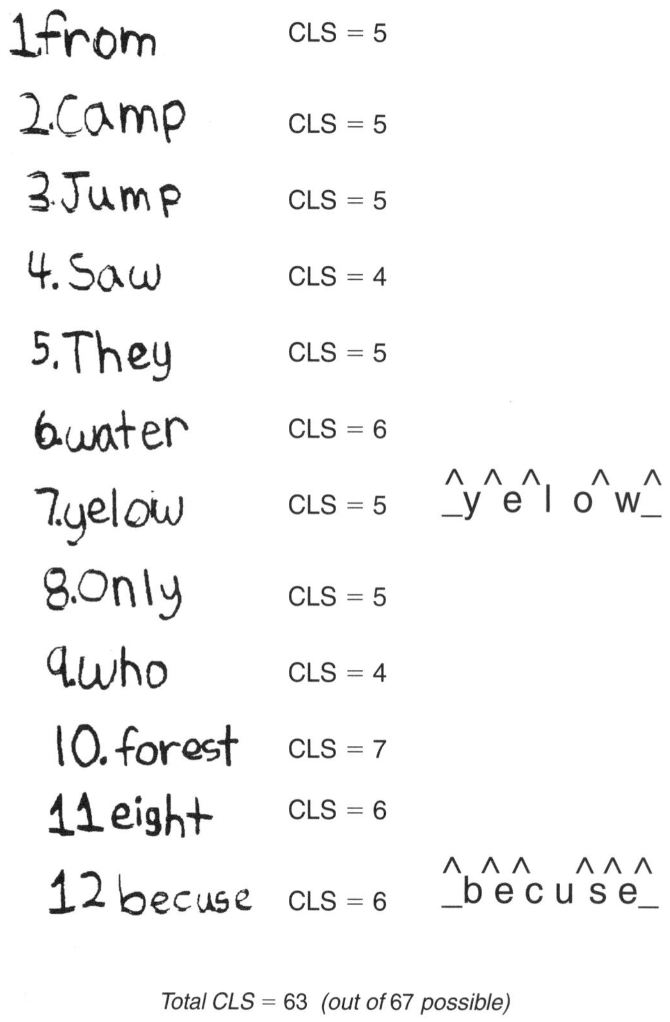

1. from   CLS = 5

2. Camp   CLS = 5

3. Jump   CLS = 5

4. Saw   CLS = 4

5. They   CLS = 5

6. water   CLS = 6

7. yelow   CLS = 5   ^ ^ ^   ^ ^
_y^e^l o^w_

8. Only   CLS = 5

9. who   CLS = 4

10. forest   CLS = 7

11. eight   CLS = 6

12. becuse   CLS = 6   ^ ^ ^   ^ ^ ^
_b e c u s e_

Total CLS = 63 *(out of 67 possible)*

Figure 8.8. Juris's Spelling Probe Scored for Correct Letter Sequences (CLS).

Note: Juris received maximum credit for all words except numbers 7 and 12.

^jep^ = 2, ^soll = 1, ^t^hay^ = 3, ^wodr^ = 2, ^y^e^lo^w^ = 5, ^oley^ = 2, ^woh = 1, ^f^o^ris^t^ = 5, ^eate = 1, and ^b^e^cks = 3. Some of these may have tricked you. For example, her spelling of *camp* as "kap" has only one correct letter sequence, and it is the final *p* with a space after. Her spelling of *eight* as "eate" also has just one correct letter sequence, and it is the initial space followed by the first *e*. On *water*, spelled "wodr," Maria has two correct letter sequences, the beginning and the ending. So Maria has 0 percent accuracy when looking at words spelled correctly,

but 43 percent accuracy when considering correct letter sequences.

Figure 8.11 shows the responses of two seventh-grade students who were administered the same spelling probe. The responses are scored for words spelled correctly (WSC). One of the students, Hayden, had four of the seventeen words spelled correctly whereas the other student, Jamie, had fourteen of the words spelled correctly. Hayden's accuracy is about 23 percent, while Jamie's accuracy is 82 percent. Using the criterion of WSC is quick and easy to do, plus it helps us quickly determine instructional needs.

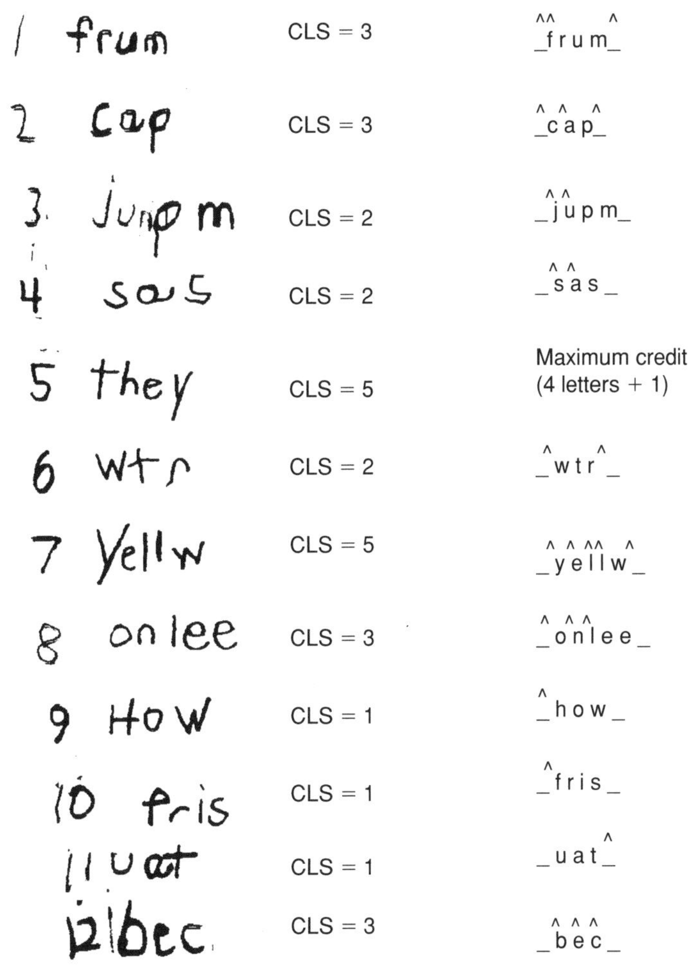

1 frum   CLS = 3   ^^_frum_^

2 cap   CLS = 3   _^c^a^p^_

3. Junpm   CLS = 2   _^j^upm_

4 sas   CLS = 2   _s^a^s_

5 they   CLS = 5   Maximum credit
(4 letters + 1)

6 wtr   CLS = 2   _^wtr^_

7 Yellw   CLS = 5   _y^e^l^^l^w^_

8 onlee   CLS = 3   _^o^n^l^ee_

9 HoW   CLS = 1   _^how_

10 fris   CLS = 1   _^fris_

11 uat   CLS = 1   _uat^_

12 bec   CLS = 3   _^b^e^c_

Total CLS = 31 *(out of 67 possible)*

Figure 8.9. Ricardo's Spelling Probe Scored for Correct Letter Sequences (CLS).

Clearly, Hayden needs more intensive instruction in spelling and close progress monitoring. For someone with so few words spelled correctly, it is important to consider correct letter sequences (CLS), especially when trying to document progress. Practice scoring Hayden's responses for CLS. After you complete your scoring, consult the Answer Key (Figure 8.18) at the end of this chapter.

Using grade-appropriate spelling probes is a quick and easy way to monitor your student's progress in spelling. It takes just two minutes to administer, and scoring takes little time as well. You could administer the probe to the entire class, or just to the students who are not responding adequately to spelling instruction and therefore require frequent progress monitoring. The students can maintain their own progress charts. Engaging students in recording their own progress not only frees up your time, but actually motivates the students.

CBM for Written Expression

CBM is also an attractive option for monitoring progress in written expression. As with spelling, you can administer the writing probes to groups or individual students. A common

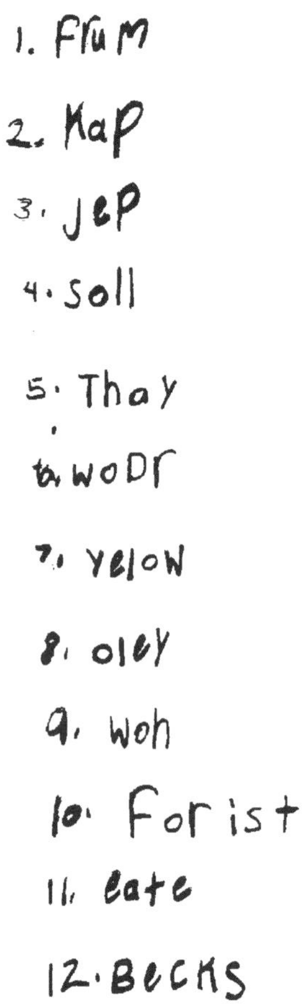

Words dictated:

1. Frum — 1. from

2. KaP — 2. camp

3. JcP — 3. jump

4. soll — 4. saw

5. Thay — 5. they

6. woDr — 6. water

7. YeloN — 7. yellow

8. oily — 8. only

9. woh — 9. who

10. Forist — 10. forest

11. eate — 11. eight

12. BeCHS — 12. because

Figure 8.10. Maria's Spelling Probe.

method is to provide a grade-appropriate story starter sentence printed at the top of a lined composition sheet of paper. If each student has a spiral notebook for writing, they can respond to all of the probes in the notebook, making it easy to see progress across time. Even if you are just monitoring the progress of a few students in your class, you can have the entire class write a response to the story starter.

To conduct ongoing CBMs of writing, you must have a collection of equivalent story starters that are grade appropriate and are essentially of equal interest. You can purchase story starters organized by grade levels from Aimsweb (aimsweb.com) if you are using the Aimsweb system. As another example, you can purchase the *Story Starters: Card Decks* from Teaching & Learning Company (teachinglearning.com).

An Internet search for story starters reveals numerous websites that provide story starters at no charge. Or, you can just use one of the samples provided in Chapter Seven or make up your own.

Ideally, the first time you administer a CBM writing task, you would do three equivalent story starters to obtain three samples during the same session. If necessary, you can collect the three samples on consecutive days. The purpose of getting three samples is to determine the median score for the student. The median, or middle score, becomes the first data point in your progress monitoring of that student's writing performance. You are establishing the student's baseline, or the beginning average performance level.

When administering the story starter probe, allow the students one minute to think

Hayden's responses   Jamie's responses

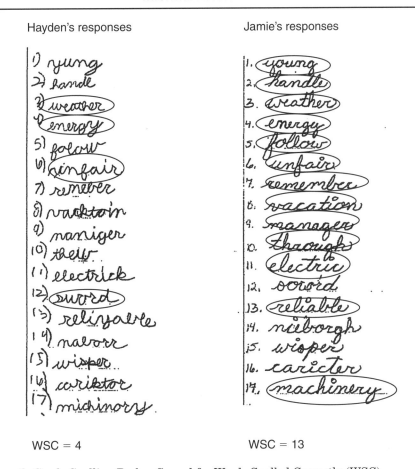

WSC = 4   WSC = 13

Figure 8.11. Two Seventh-Grade Spelling Probes Scored for Words Spelled Correctly (WSC).

about the story suggested by the sentence. Then give the students three minutes to write the story. The emphasis should be on the quality of what they write instead of on speed. These types of probes may be scored on the basis of several different criteria: (a) the total number of words written (TWW); (b) the words spelled correctly (WSC); (c) the total number of letters written (TLW); or (d) the number of writing units in correct sequence (CWS).

At the secondary level, correct word sequences minus incorrect word sequences (CIWS) is a better indicator of writing proficiency than either TWW or WCS. Also, longer samples are needed at the secondary level. At this level, the writing task should require seven to ten minutes rather than the three to five minutes needed at the elementary level.

Total Words Written (TWW)

When using this criterion, count up all the words written, including misspelled words. Include a letter or group of letters separated by a space, even if they are misspelled words or nonsense words. Also, if the student wrote a title, include those words. Do not include numerals that may appear, such as 3 or 10. This criterion is easy to score, but only gives a limited view of writing fluency. You are tracking the number of words written in three minutes without regard to accuracy or content. In Figure 8.12, you can see how to score a sample based on total words written. Carla, a second-grade student, wrote a total of twelve words. Remember that you count every word written, even those that are misspelled. Some teachers underline each word and then

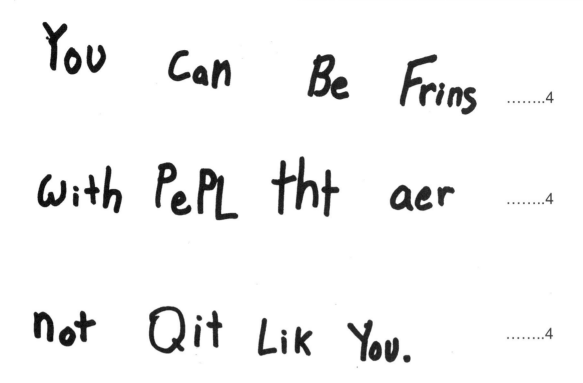

Figure 8.12. Carla's Writing Sample Scored for Total Words Written (TWW).

count the number of underlines to obtain the total words written.

Words Spelled Correctly (WSC)

To determine the WSC, you identify each correctly spelled word in the writing sample. Consider each word in isolation rather than in the context of the sentence. If the word in isolation is a real word spelled correctly, give it credit. If a word is a proper noun or the pronoun *I*, it must be capitalized to receive credit. This criterion allows you to look at the student's spelling accuracy. Figure 8.13 illustrates the scoring of Carla's passage based on words spelled correctly. Of the twelve words that Carla wrote, only six of them were spelled correctly.

Total Letters Written (TLW)

This criterion is also easy to score. Simply count up all the letters written, including the

misspelled words. Once again, you do not include numerals that may be written. This criterion may help you identify students who use more advanced writing vocabularies, such as using longer words. Figure 8.13 also illustrates the scoring of total letters written by Carla. She wrote a total of thirty-nine letters. Because she wrote a total of twelve words, her average word length is approximately three letters.

Correct Writing Sequences (CWS)

When using this criterion, you will be considering accuracy of spelling, grammar, capitalization, and punctuation. Although this criterion requires more effort and time to score, it is worthwhile due to the additional information it provides about the quality of the student's writing. The other criteria discussed previously evaluate primarily fluency

13 ...... You Can Be Frins 3

14...... With PePL tht aer 1

12...... not Qit Lik You. 2

TLW: 39　　　　　　　　　　　　　　　　　　　　WSC: 6

Figure 8.13. Carla's Writing Sample Scored for Words Spelled Correctly (WSC) and Total Letters Written (TLW).

and spelling, providing a more limited view of the student's writing.

To evaluate CWS, you begin at the start of the writing sample and consider each successive pair of writing units. A writing unit is defined as a word or an essential punctuation mark, such as a period or question mark. Commas are not essential and are not scored. To receive credit, the writing unit must be spelled correctly, be grammatically correct, and make sense within the overall context of the sentence. In addition, capital letters must be used appropriately. For example, the first word in each sentence must be capitalized, as well as proper nouns. If a capital letter is used inappropriately, that word will be scored as incorrect. Reversed letters are acceptable as long as they do not create a misspelled word. Essentially this means if the reversed letter makes a new real letter, this will be counted as a spelling error

(for example, *b* becomes a *d*). However, if the reversed letter does not become a different letter, it can be overlooked (for example, *c* does not become a new letter if it is reversed). If the student has included a title on the writing sample, include that in your scoring. Once again, do not count numerals that may appear unless they represent a date. In that case, you can count the dates as part of a sequence. As with scoring correct letter sequences in spelling, you may use a caret (^) to mark between each of the correct writing sequences.

To begin, first identify all of the misspelled words by drawing a circle or box around them, for example. This will make it easy to see which words cannot be counted in evaluating correct writing sequences. Figure 8.14 illustrates the scoring of Carla's sample using the criterion of correct writing sequences. Carla has a total of two correct writing sequences.

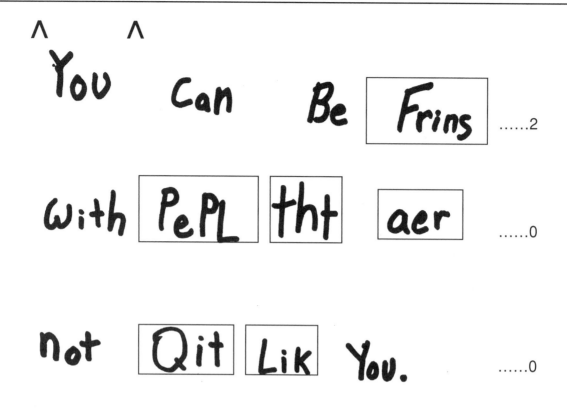

Figure 8.14. Carla's Sample Scored for Correct Writing Sequences (CWS).

She receives credit for her first word, *You*, because it is capitalized. An appropriate first word that is spelled correctly and capitalized is scored as a correct writing sequence. The next correct sequence is the words (*You can*). These are both spelled correctly and semantically and syntactically correct. The next sequence (*can Be*) is not correct because she capitalized the *B*. Due to her misspelled words and inappropriate use of capitals, Carla has no more correct writing sequences. She did end her sentence with a period, which is considered essential punctuation and therefore would have been counted as part of a correct writing sequence. However, the last word (*You*) spoils the final sequence because it is capitalized.

A fifth-grade class was given the story prompt, "I was walking to school minding my own business, when all of a sudden...." The students were given one minute to think about the prompt and then three minutes to write. Figure 8.15 illustrates the written responses of two of the students, Reshad and Sheila. Reshad's story contains many misspelled words and almost no punctuation. In fact, the entire paragraph is written as one sentence. However, Reshad shows a good imagination and sense of humor. Sheila's story also contains many misspelled words and very little punctuation, but she demonstrates more difficulty with vocabulary. When scoring these types of passages, do not include the story starter prompt when counting any of the criteria.

Review Reshad's writing sample. First, you count the total words written (TWW). Spelling does not matter for this criterion. Reshad wrote a total of twenty-eight words. Next, look at how many words Reshad spelled correctly (WSC).

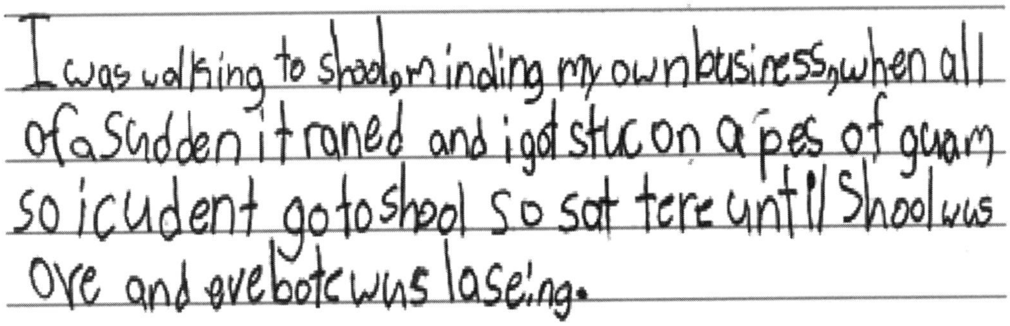

I was walking to shool, minding my own business, when all of a Sudden it raned and i god stuc on a pes of guam so icudent go to shool so sat tere until Shool was ove and evebotc wus laseing.

Reshad's writing sample

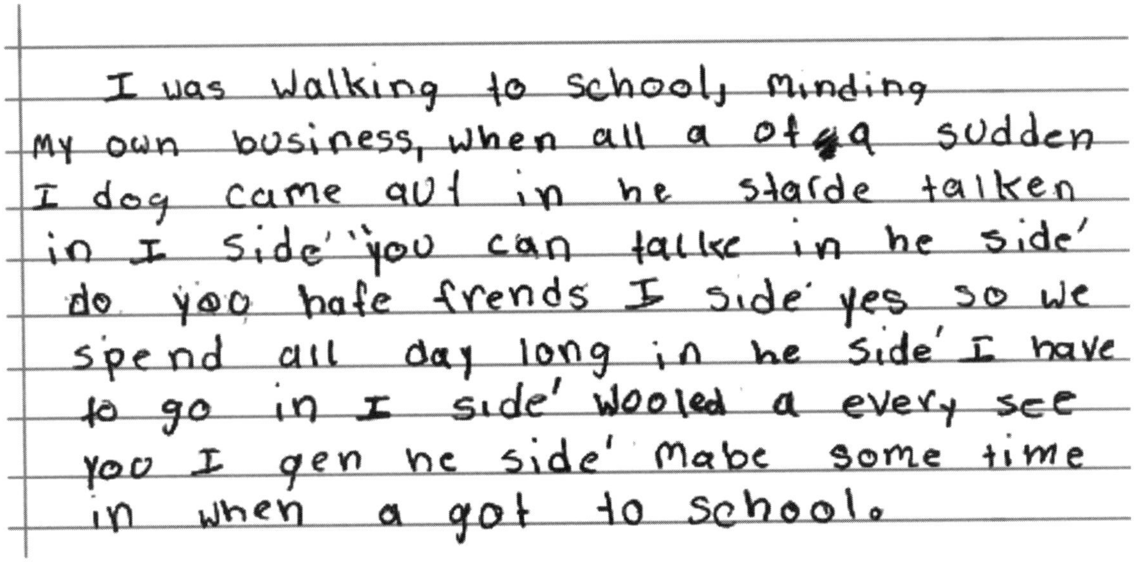

I was walking to school, minding
My own business, when all a of a sudden
I dog came aut in he starde talken
in I side' "you can talke in he side'
do yoo hafe frends I side' yes so we
spend all day long in he side' I have
to go in I side' wooled a every see
you I gen he side' Mabe some time
in when a got to school.

Sheila's writing sample

Figure 8.15. Reshad's and Sheila's Responses to a Story Starter Prompt.

Context does not matter because you look at the words in isolation. However, if a word is a proper noun or the pronoun *I*, capitals must be used to receive credit. This is why Reshad does not receive spelling credit for the correct spelling of the word *guam*. Even though we know that was not his intended word (that is, *gum*), he would have received credit for *Guam*. Reshad had fifteen words spelled correctly. To help document word length, count the total letters written (TLW). Reshad had a total of ninety-two letters. Now evaluate for correct writing sequences (CWS). Everything matters when counting CWS—essential punctuation, capitals, spelling, and usage. Remember that commas are not essential, but ending punctuation is essential. Following is Reshad's written response scored for CWS. His correct writing sequences are shown below marked with a caret (^). Due to his many misspelled words he ends up with only three correct writing sequences out of a possible thirty. Because he did not capitalize the word *I* he cannot receive credit for the sequences around that word.

> ... ^ it raned and i got stuc on ^ a pes of guam so i cudent go ^ to shool so sat tere until shool was ove and evebote was laseing.

Translation: . . . it rained and I got stuck on a piece of gum so I couldn't go to school so sat there until school was over and everybody was leaving.

Summarizing the information we gathered from Reshad's story, he wrote twenty-eight words with fifteen of them spelled correctly, or about 54 percent accuracy. He wrote ninety-two letters in twenty-eight words, so his average letters per word is between three and four. He had three correct writing sequences out of a possible thirty, or 10 percent correct. We can see that his problems are related primarily to spelling, capitalization, and punctuation. Reshad's teacher must focus on instruction in these areas.

Let's look at Sheila's story and score it for the same four criteria. Remember, do not include the story prompt. How many words has she written (TWW)? She has fifty-eight words written. We do not worry about spelling or capitalization when counting words written. How many words did Sheila spell correctly? She has forty-nine words spelled correctly (WSC). Remember that we look at each word in isolation. It just has to be a real word spelled correctly, and the proper nouns or the pronoun *I* have to be capitalized. In Sheila's writing, she spelled *side* correctly, even though she really meant *said*. She has many usage errors, but they do not count for TWW or WSC. Next we count total letters written (TLW). She has 177 letters written. We count every letter, whether or not the word was spelled or used correctly. Finally, we look at correct writing sequences (CWS). Following is Sheila's written response scored for CWS. Her correct writing sequences are shown below marked with a caret (^).

> . . . I dog ^ came aut in he starde talken in I side you ^ can talke in he side do ^ you hafe frends I side yes ^ so ^ we spend all ^ day ^ long in he side I ^ have ^ to ^ go in I side wooled a every see ^ you I gen he side mabe some time in when a got to ^ school ^.
> *Translation*: . . . a dog came out and he started talking and I said you can talk

and he said do you have friends I said yes so we spend all day long and he said I have to go and I said would I ever see you again he said maybe sometime in when I got to school.

Sheila has thirteen correct writing sequences out of a possible sixty sequences. If punctuation had been used correctly, there would have been additional sequences available. She had forty-nine out of fifty-eight words spelled correctly, even though many of the correctly spelled words do not make sense in her story. As you can see, looking only at the percentage of correctly spelled words (84 percent) can be misleading. Sheila had 177 total letters written and fifty-eight words, so her average word length was three letters. The words Sheila used were very basic, limiting the quality of her writing. It appears that she tried to incorporate quotation marks in a couple of spots, but they were not used correctly. Like Reshad, Sheila needs instruction to focus on spelling and punctuation. However, it also appears she needs to engage in activities to promote vocabulary development.

Practice Scoring Written Expression

Armando, a seventh-grade student, was asked to write about how he feels about math. Review his writing sample shown in Figure 8.16 and score his writing for the following: total words written (TWW), words spelled correctly (WSC), total letters written (TLW), and correct writing sequences (CWS).

Let's review your scoring of Armando's writing sample. First, how many words did he write? Did you remember to include all words, spelled correctly or incorrectly, as well as any group of letters, or even nonsense words? Be sure to include the title in your calculations, but do not include any words or letters that have been crossed out. Armando's total words written (TWW) is thirty-nine. Next, how many words did he spell correctly (WSC)? Remember to consider each word in isolation rather than in the context of the sentence. If it is spelled

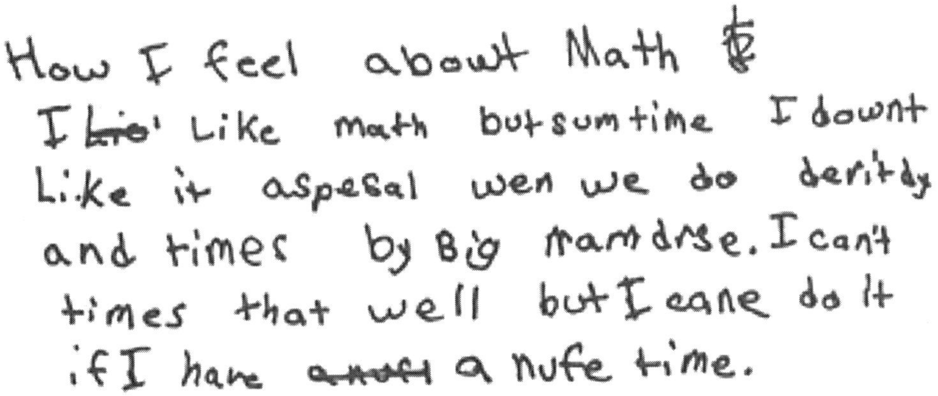

How I feel abowt Math
I [Lric'] Like math butsumtime I downt
Like it aspesal wen we do deritdy
and times by Big namdrse. I can't
times that well but I eane do It
if I have [anoth] a nufe time.

Figure 8.16. Armando's Writing Sample About Math.

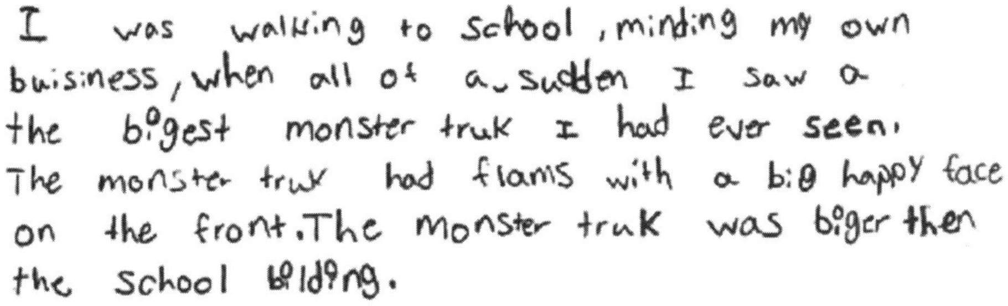

I was walking to school, minding my own
buisiness, when all of a sudden I saw a
the bigest monster truk I had ever seen.
The monster truk had flams with a big happy face
on the front. The monster truk was biger then
the school blding.

Figure 8.17. Jason's Writing Sample in Response to a Story Starter Prompt.

correctly it receives credit even if it is grammatically incorrect. Armando has thirty-one words that are spelled correctly. Were you tricked by "cane" for *can*? Because we look at each word in isolation, we give *cane* credit because it is a real word spelled correctly. Misspelled words include *abowt, sumtime, downt, aspesal, wen, devidty, namdrse,* and *anufe.* Counting the number of letters written results in a TLW of 135. Remember to include all letters written whether the words were spelled correctly or incorrectly. Do not include crossed-out letters. Armando had thirty-nine words written and 135 letters. His average number of letters per word is three to four. He is using many short words, focusing more on ones he can spell. As you can see, the longer words he attempted are misspelled.

The final criterion is correct writing sequences (CWS). Now spelling and grammar will matter, as will capitalization and essential punctuation. Armando has a total of twenty correct writing sequences. In the title, Armando has three CWS: ^How^ I feel abowt Math^.

He does not receive credit for the other sequences in the title because he did not capitalize *Feel* or *About*, plus he misspelled *about*. In his paragraph he has an additional seventeen CWS. Remember that misspelled words spoil correct writing sequences, as do words that are inappropriately capitalized. The period after the final word is essential and creates a correct writing sequence with the correctly spelled word *time*.

^I Like math ^ but sumtime I downt Like it aspesal wen we ^ do devidty and ^ times ^ by Big namdrse. ^ I ^ can't ^ times ^ that ^well ^but ^I cane do ^ it ^ if ^ I ^ have anufe time. ^

Translation: I like math but sometimes I don't like it especially when we do division and times by big numbers. I can't times that well but I can do it if I have enough time.

Figure 8.17 illustrates the writing of a fifth-grade student, Jason. Practice scoring his writing sample for all four criteria: total words written (TWW), total letters written (TLW), words spelled correctly (WSC), and correct writing sequences (CWS). After you complete your scoring, consult the Answer Key (Figure 8.19) at the end of this chapter.

Resources for Learning About CBM

Several excellent resources are available for learning more about CBM. The CBM Warehouse is a free, online resource that is located at www.interventioncentral.org. Of particular interest at the Intervention Central website is a complete CBM manual for teachers written by Jim Wright that may be downloaded at no cost. There are also links to Aimsweb (www.aimsweb.com). Aimsweb, now part of Pearson Education, Inc., has CBM products available for sale. However, you can look at manuals and samples that are helpful when learning about CBM. The National Center on Student Progress Monitoring (www.studentprogress.org) offers a variety of resources as well. In addition, *The ABCs of CBM: A Practical Guide to Curriculum-Based Measurement* is a book that is written by experts in the area of CBM and provides practical guidance (Hosp, Hosp, & Howell, 2007).

CONCLUSION

Informal assessment is essential for monitoring student progress. It provides invaluable, immediate feedback about the performance of students on curriculum-based standards. A skilled teacher takes this information and uses it to identify specific instructional needs and then to customize instruction for students. Frequent assessment and progress monitoring make it possible for you to know if your instruction is working and students are learning. Informal assessment is the key for documenting the results of your efforts and the impact on student learning.

Not only does informal assessment help guide instruction, it also helps the students develop an awareness of their own performance. For students to be active participants, responsible for their own learning, they must have a clear picture of what is expected of them and how they are progressing toward that goal. Both teachers and students benefit when informal assessment is integrated into the classroom. Wiggins (2006) suggested, "Here's a radical idea: We need more assessment, not less. Seem crazy? Substitute feedback for assessment and you'll better understand what I mean" (p. 49).

Answer Key

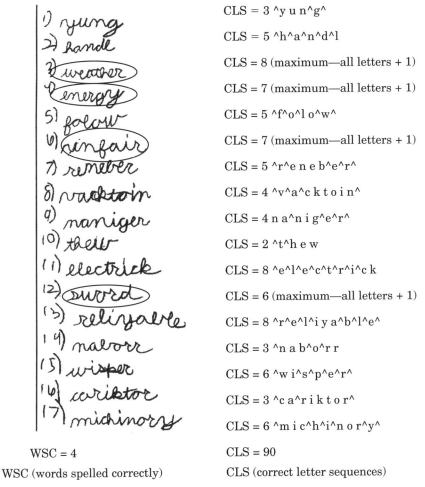

CLS = 3 ^y u n^g^

CLS = 5 ^h^a^n^d^l

CLS = 8 (maximum—all letters + 1)

CLS = 7 (maximum—all letters + 1)

CLS = 5 ^f^o^l o^w^

CLS = 7 (maximum—all letters + 1)

CLS = 5 ^r^e n e b^e^r^

CLS = 4 ^v^a^c k t o i n^

CLS = 4 n a^n i g^e^r^

CLS = 2 ^t^h e w

CLS = 8 ^e^l^e^c^t^r^i^c k

CLS = 6 (maximum—all letters + 1)

CLS = 8 ^r^e^l^i y a^b^l^e^

CLS = 3 ^n a b^o^r r

CLS = 6 ^w i^s^p^e^r^

CLS = 3 ^c a^r i k t o r^

CLS = 6 ^m i c^h^i^n o r^y^

WSC = 4   CLS = 90

WSC (words spelled correctly)   CLS (correct letter sequences)

Words dictated:

young, handle, weather, energy, follow, unfair, remember, vacation, manager, through, electric, sword, reliable, neighbor, whisper, character, machinery

Figure 8.18. Hayden's Sample Scored for Correct Letter Sequences (CLS).

Answer Key

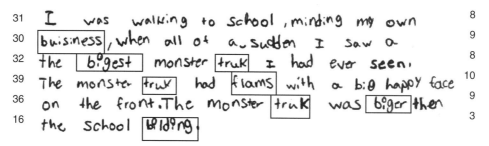

TLW: 184   TWW: 47

Misspelled words are boxed. Eight words are misspelled out of 47. WSC=39

Scored for Correct Writing Sequences:

^I^was^walking^to^school^minding^my^own buisiness

when^all^of^a^sudden^I^saw a the bigest monster truk I^had^ever^seen^.

^The^monster truk had flams with^a^big^happy^face^on^the^front^.

^The^monster truk was biger then the^school bilding.

Summary:

Total Words Written (TWW): 47 (count all words, even misspelled words)

Total Letters Written (TLW): 184 (count all letters written, even in misspelled words)

Words Spelled Correctly (WSC): 39 (consider all words in isolation)

Correct Writing Sequences (CWS): 31 (out of 49 possible)

Spelling accuracy is almost 83% (39/47=82.9%)

Average letters per word is almost 4 letters per word (184/47 = 3.9)

His overall accuracy considering spelling, punctuation, and usage is about 63% (31/49 = 63.2%)

Figure 8.19. Jason's Sample Scored for Four Criteria: TWW, TLW, WCS, and CWS.

Analysis of Writing Samples

Hence the well-known fact that young children cannot express their thoughts fluently by writing. The mechanics of the writing process stand in the forefront of attention and interrupt the flow of thought. As practice proceeds, these steps follow one another more rapidly and more closely so that they interrupt the thought process less. The writing process becomes more nearly automatic—that is, it becomes capable of being carried on without the direction of attention. The attention can then be occupied more fully with the meaning which is to be expressed.

—F. N. Freeman (1914)

Early identification of potential writing difficulties is important to the goal of providing each student with successful learning opportunities. Analyzing your students' writing samples is a means to identifying problems early and adjusting instruction accordingly. To further develop your writing analysis skills, this chapter provides examples of completed analyses, followed by examples for guided practice. It concludes with some samples for you to analyze independently. The samples provided in this chapter may be used for self-study or in classes designed to increase diagnostic skill.

As we discussed in Chapter Eight, informal assessment and curriculum-based measurement (CBM) may be useful in identifying the learning needs of your students and evaluating the effectiveness of instruction. Those practices, combined with writing sample analysis, can help you identify a student's strengths and weaknesses. Analysis and interpretation of error patterns in writing can often help detect and diagnose the specific factors that are inhibiting writing performance. One caution: you would not determine that a student has a learning disability or language impairment solely on the basis of written language samples. In most instances, this type of diagnosis would be made by a team that would base that decision on a multiplicity of factors, including classroom performance and teacher observations. In-depth analysis of writing samples can, however, provide invaluable information for programmatic decisions and instructional design.

ANALYZED WRITING SAMPLES

Different types of samples are included to illustrate a variety of writing difficulties. Some of the students have their greatest difficulty with spelling, whereas others have problems with the development of ideas. For some students, only one sample is provided. For other students, two or more samples are included to allow for a more in-depth evaluation of writing skill. The majority of samples are students' first drafts of assignments. For a few students, samples are presented from different time periods to illustrate development in writing skill. For each sample, the writing is evaluated in regard to the student's strengths, as well as his or her instructional needs. Recommendations are then made for instructional programming.

To get the greatest benefit from these examples, prior to reading an analysis, study the writing sample shown in the figure. Attempt to identify both the strengths and weaknesses in that student's writing skill. Next, think about the instructional needs of the student and what educational recommendations you might make. As a final step, read the analysis and note the similarities and differences between your observations and those stated in the text.

Following is an index of the completed analyses that includes the students' names, grades, and their major difficulties in writing.

Index

Student	Grade	Areas of Greatest Difficulty
Jose	1st	Handwriting and Spelling
Hannah	3rd	Spelling and Ideation
Frankie	3rd	Spelling and Usage
Brian	4th	Spelling and Usage
Emily	5th	Spelling and Ideation
Malika	6th	Usage, and Organization and Ideation
Helen	7th	Appearance, Usage, and Organization and Ideation
Chantelle	9th	Language, and Organization and Ideation
Tim	10th	Spelling

Student: Jose
Grade: 1st
Assignments: Journal entries

Several samples from mid-year were taken from Jose's journal. Earlier in the year, Jose had been evaluated and accepted in the school's gifted and talented program. Although

his teacher was pleased with Jose's ability to express his ideas, she was concerned about the development of handwriting skill (Figure 9.1).

Analysis

Handwriting

Presently, Jose writes using uppercase letters. He attempts to make his letters fill the space between the lines in his writing journal. The spacing between words is inconsistent. In general, the writing is not pleasing to the eye, but the majority of his letters and words are recognizable. His human figure drawings are somewhat immature.

Spelling

Jose is using "temporary" spelling successfully. Although he omits a few sounds, he sequences the sounds that he writes accurately (for example, "grad ma," for *grandma*, and "monene" for *morning*). Jose appears to be progressing from including most sounds toward including all sounds. As is to be expected, he writes the major consonant sounds and omits the vowels in several words (for example, "frst" for *first*, "hs" for *his*, "wr" for *were*, "strts" for *starts*, and "wrk" for *work*). He also omits the nasal sound in *grand*, another characteristic of early spelling. Other spellings are good phonetic equivalents (for example, "kising" for *kissing*, "bak" for *back*, and "kusins" for *cousins*). With the exception of two instances ("re left" for *relieved* and "grad ma" for *grandma*), Jose appears to recognize word boundaries, and he realizes that separations should occur in the phrase "10 O CLOK."

Usage

Jose attempts to write in complete sentences. Although several of his periods are too large, he appears to understand the function of a period. Because all of the letters written are capitals, it is unclear as to whether or not Jose knows that sentences begin with uppercase letters. Jose is

Figure 9.1. Jose's Journal Entries.

Translations: Today Mom and Dad came back and I was relieved.

Attention. First day of school. Sam starts kissing me.

Grandma came and Mom and Dad were going to San Diego this morning

I got up too late.

Scott make me do his work.

My cousins came last night at 10 o'clock.

consistent in verb tense. He uses both present and past tense appropriately in his writing.

Vocabulary

Although unsure of the spelling, Jose attempts to use descriptive words. He notes that when his mom and dad came back, he was *relieved* ("re left") and that his *cousins* ("kusins") came.

Organization and Ideation

Jose has ideas that he wants to share through writing. Although letter formation appears to be difficult, he likes to write and has clear ideas that he wants to express.

Recommendations

Handwriting

1. Have Jose work on handwriting daily for short lessons. Provide review and practice of formation of lowercase letters. Show him how to be consistent in the spacing between words. Have him apply the skills that he is learning in context.

2. Teach Jose to write on primary paper that has a clear dotted middle line. Encourage

him to form letters properly within the boundaries of these lines.

3. Recognize Jose's effort in trying to write neatly. Give plenty of encouragement as he develops his handwriting skill.

4. As motor skill improves, encourage Jose to reduce the size of his periods.

5. Date all handwriting samples and keep them in a portfolio so that Jose can see evidence of his progress.

6. Encourage Jose to engage in a variety of activities to promote fine-motor skill development, such as completing dot-to-dot drawings, solving mazes, or drawing illustrations for his writing. Because Jose is highly motivated to write, explain to him how spending time on fine-motor activities will help make handwriting easier for him.

7. Select a structured handwriting program to use with Jose, such as D'Nealian or Handwriting without Tears.

8. Conduct an informal handwriting assessment, such as a three-minute timed writing of a practiced sentence, to identify Jose's letters per minute and specific letter formation difficulties. Compare his letter per minute to grade-level standards (25 lpm).

Spelling

1. Praise Jose for his logical attempts to spell.

2. Teach Jose that all words contain a vowel. Initially, take some of his misspellings from his writing, and rewrite the words with a blank placed for the missing vowel (such as f_rst). Help him determine what vowel belongs in the missing space. Gradually, help him determine where the vowels should be inserted.

3. Introduce and provide practice with common English spelling patterns (for example, *ck* and *ight*.)

4. Teach Jose basic spelling rules, such as how to spell consonant-vowel-consonant (CVC), and consonant-vowel-consonant-silent e (CVCe) words.

5. Use CBM to monitor Jose's progress in spelling. Track words spelled correctly and correct letter sequences.

Usage

1. Teach or review with Jose that sentences begin with uppercase letters.

2. Reinforce Jose for his skill in maintaining consistency with verb tense.

Organization and Ideation

1. Provide many opportunities for writing. Discuss with Jose the ideas that he is communicating.

2. Remind Jose that development of spelling and handwriting skills will improve his ability to communicate ideas to others through writing.

Student: Hannah
Grade: 3rd
Assignments: Letters with illustrations

As part of an in-depth Social Studies unit on the origins of ceremonial masks, Hannah was asked to write two letters to a fictional friend and draw an illustration. The samples were written within the same week (Figure 9.2).

Analysis

Handwriting

On these two samples, the size of Hannah's letters is inconsistent. Formation of a few letters also appears problematic. Her lowercase *a* is sometimes formed like an uppercase *Q*. On several occasions, Hannah substitutes an uppercase *R* for the lowercase letter, and her lowercase *g* does not extend below the line. In addition, the spacing between words is inconsistent and results in some words being difficult to decipher.

Spelling

Presently, Hannah is attempting to write words the way they sound (such as "solger" for *soldier*) but omits many sounds so her writing is difficult to read. Although she appears to have knowledge with regard to masks, it is difficult to decipher many of the words that she is writing.

Usage

Hannah begins both letters with correct capitalization and punctuation. Although Hannah produces several complete sentences, she does not start them with uppercase letters or end them with periods. She has used present-tense verbs consistently throughout both samples.

Vocabulary

Although the words are difficult to identify, Hannah's choice of words is representative of her good conceptual and topical knowledge. She uses precise vocabulary. Examples include the words *crucified, Roman soldier, Fariseo, sign language*, and *purity*.

Organization and Ideation

Hannah has good background knowledge in regard to ceremonial masks. She is motivated to share her ideas and organizes them in a logical way. As noted, however, her ideas are difficult to decipher because of poor spelling.

Figure 9.2. Hannah's Two Letters.

Translation:

Dear Alicia,

It is a Roman soldier that crucified God on the cross. The red is blood. The black is for when some one dies. The white is purity.

Dear Alica,
tes is a frisae Mask and hes
secs the secs are hes soz
ehy Can Notitol eo toe
thy hav sin laue gweh sec

Figure 9.2. Hannah's Two Letters. (*Continued*)

Translation:

Dear Alicia,

This is a Fariseo mask and his sticks. The sticks are his so as they can not talk together. They have sign language when speaking.

Recommendations

Handwriting

1. Provide Hannah with primary paper with a dotted middle line to use on all writing assignments.
2. Review and provide practice with formation of the following lowercase letters: *a, g,* and *r.*
3. Conduct an informal handwriting assessment, such as a three-minute timed writing of a practiced sentence, to identify Hannah's letters per minute and specific letter formation difficulties. Compare her letter per minute to grade-level standards (30 lpm).

Spelling

1. Remind Hannah that the purpose for learning to spell correctly is to enhance her ability to communicate thoughts in writing. Praise her efforts and provide encouragement about skill development.
2. Use an activity such as the Elkonin procedure or Making Words to help Hannah increase her knowledge of the sequence of sounds within words.
3. As skill develops, encourage Hannah to listen to sounds more carefully as she attempts spellings. Ask Hannah to say the word slowly while pronouncing and then writing the sounds. Re-teach sound-symbol correspondences as needed.

4. Use a spelling flow list to help Hannah master the spelling of words she uses frequently in her writing. Teach only a few spelling words at a time. Provide daily review and practice until the words are mastered. Review the words weekly to help with retention.

5. Determine an appropriate spelling study strategy for Hannah. One effective approach may be to have Hannah (a) look carefully at the word, (b) cover the word, (c) write the word while pronouncing it slowly, and (d) then check the word against the original. If Hannah has difficulty writing the word from memory, add in a tracing component.

6. Until her spelling skill improves, have Hannah read her stories to a scribe immediately after writing. Without this accommodation, the next day Hannah cannot read her writing.

7. Use CBM to monitor Hannah's progress in spelling. Track both words spelled correctly and correct letter sequences.

Usage

1. Teach Hannah how to recognize sentence boundaries and include the appropriate ending punctuation marks.
2. When editing, remind Hannah to start sentences with uppercase letters.
3. Teach Hannah a specific editing strategy, such as COPS.

Organization and Ideation

1. Continue to provide Hannah with frequent, purposeful writing activities.
2. Provide Hannah with activities based on her interest and talent that include the opportunity for both artistic and written expression. For example, have Hannah illustrate a story that she is writing or write a brief description of a picture she has drawn.

3. For some written assignments, use a modified language experience approach with Hannah. Have her dictate a story to a scribe and then recopy it as a final draft.
4. When evaluating her papers, emphasize the clarity of the message over basic writing skills so that Hannah's interest and willingness to write do not diminish.

Student: Frankie
Grade: 3rd
Assignments: Two creative writing assignments, two journal entries, picture with title

---

For the first assignment, Frankie was asked to write a story titled "What Bad Luck." The second and fourth assignments were journal entries, and the third assignment was written in response to the title "What I Want to Be When I Grow Up." The picture was drawn to illustrate a video that Frankie had just rented. All of these assignments are shown in Figure 9.3.

Analysis

Handwriting and Appearance

The handwriting on the printed sample is adequate, whereas that on the three cursive samples is good for a third-grade student. The slant is consistent and all the letters are formed correctly. Frankie observes the left and right margins in all samples. The paragraphs are not indented. In addition, only one of the assignments has a title ("What Bad Luck"), and it is not capitalized.

Spelling

Although Frankie's writing is legible, a number of different spelling errors can be seen in his assignments. Frankie has mastered the spelling of some high-frequency sight words such as *there, want, the, that*, and *was*, but still misspells others such as *when, went, him*, and *but*. Of the 184 words written, 64 or 35 percent are

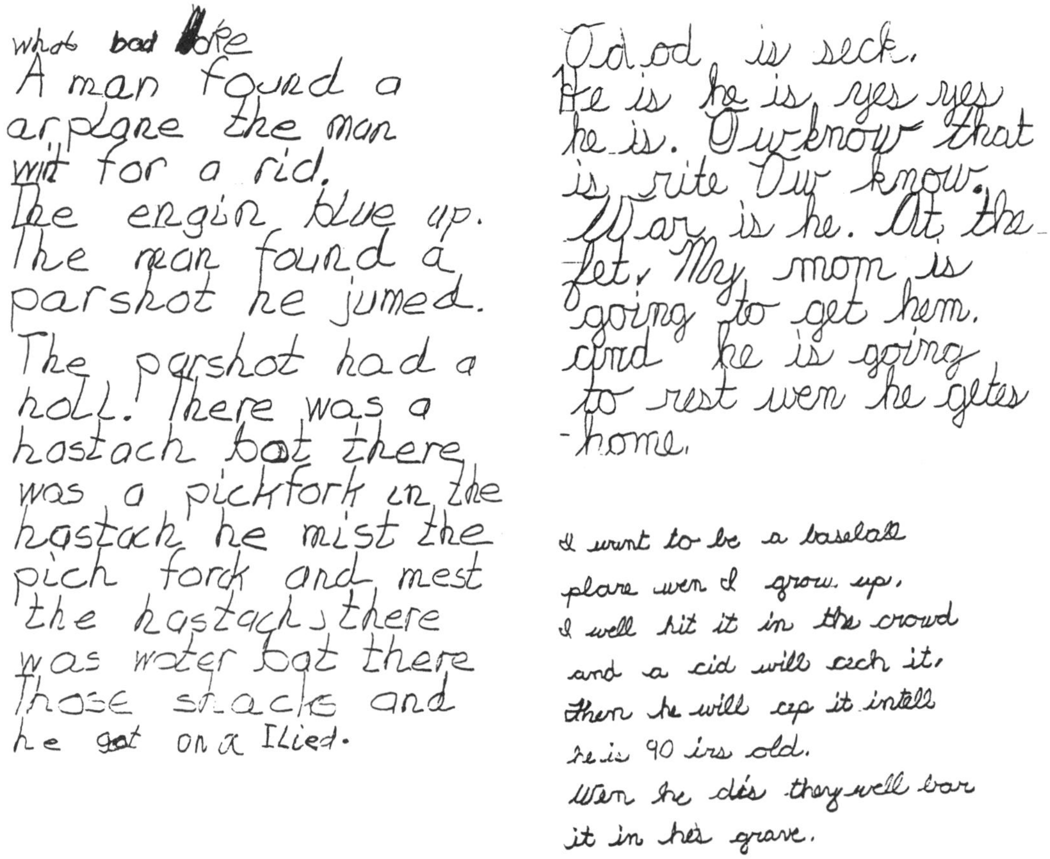

Figure 9.3. Frankie's Assignments and Journal Entries.

Translations: What bad luck. A man found a airplane. The man went for a ride. The engine blew up. The man found a parachute. He jumped. The parachute had a hole! There was a haystack but there was a pitchfork in the haystack. He missed the pitchfork and missed the haystack, there was water but there those sharks and he got on a island.

Hobo is sick. He is. He is. Yes, yes, he is. Oh no. That is right. Oh no. Where is he? At the vet. My mom is going to get him and he is going to rest when he gets home.

I want to be a baseball player when I grow up. I will hit it in the crowd and a kid will catch it. Then he will keep it until he is 90 years old. When he dies they will bury it in his grave.

either spelled incorrectly or are homophones to the correct word. Some of the homophones that Frankie confuses are *know* for *no, blue* for *blew, wood* for *would, there* for *their,* and *mist* for *missed.*

Frankie appears to have some confusion distinguishing certain vowel sounds in words, as illustrated by some of the misspellings such as "well" for *will,* "intell" for *until,* "wint" for *went,* "ceds" for *kids,* and "hem" for *him.* Clearly, Frankie has difficulty with the spelling of medial vowel sounds. The short *e* and *i* sounds seem to be particularly troublesome for

Frankie, and numerous examples are evident throughout the writing samples.

Some of Frankie's spellings look similar although they represent different words. For example, "ceds," "cech," and "cep" represent the words *kids, catch,* and *keep,* respectively. Frankie sometimes omits sounds from words. He writes "parshot" for *parachute,* "shacks" for *sharks,* "Ilied" for *island,* "bar" for *bury,* and "olowen" for *Halloween.* Perhaps the best example of Frankie's confusion with speech sounds is in his writing the well-known phrase from the movie *ET* "ET phone home" as "pt foam home."

kown want my
brouther did on olowen
wen the ceds woud
coom up to oc house
he wood jump out
and skar the ceds
they would run of
and drop there candy

pt foom home.

Figure 9.3. Frankie's Assignments and Journal Entries. *(Continued)*

Translations: Know what my brother did on Halloween. When the kids would come up to our house he would jump out and scare the kids. They would run off and drop their candy.

ET phone home.

Although Frankie tends to spell words the way they sound, he has not yet mastered some of the simpler patterns. For example, he sometimes misuses and sometimes omits the digraph *ch* in words, as in "hastach" for *haystack* and "pickfork" for *pitchfork*. Difficulties with the spelling of other patterns can be seen in Frankie's spelling of "coom" for *come*, "dis" for *dies*, and "skar" for *scare*.

In addition to problems distinguishing between speech sounds, Frankie appears to struggle with the visual retention of spelling patterns. This is evidenced by the different spellings of the same word, particularly when the different spellings are in close proximity. Examples of this can be seen in the first writing sample with "mist" and "mest" for *missed* on consecutive lines, and "bot" and "bat" for *but* only five lines apart. He also spells the high-frequency word *know* as "kown."

Usage

Frankie consistently capitalizes the word *I* but is erratic with his capitalization of the first letter in a sentence. He capitalizes the first letter in sentences about 50 percent of the time in the first sample, 100 percent of the time in the next two samples, and 0 percent of the time in the third. In addition, the name "ET" is not capitalized. Frankie's use of a period is also sporadic. In one instance on the first writing sample, he uses a comma instead of a period.

Other usage problems are evident. He uses the article *a*, even when the noun begins with a vowel. Most of the sentences are simple and without explanation or elaboration ("The man went for a ride. The man found a parachute. He jumped."). Also, some problems with pronoun reference can be seen in the second sample when Frankie refers to a ball that was never mentioned as "it" throughout.

Vocabulary

On the whole, the vocabulary Frankie uses is simplistic. The majority of words are one syllable. The words *haystack* and *pitchfork*, however, are more complex and demonstrate some background knowledge of farming. More advanced words are found in the printed sample. This may indicate that Frankie is able to focus more on vocabulary when not having to concentrate on the mechanics of cursive writing.

Organization and Ideation

Frankie writes information sequentially. Some of his assignments, however, are limited in the information they convey.

Recommendations

Handwriting and Appearance

1. Teach Frankie to indent the first word in each paragraph.
2. Teach Frankie to write titles for his stories that are centered and have each word capitalized.

Spelling

1. During editing, help Frankie listen carefully to words that he is attempting to spell. Have him check his spellings as he pronounces the words slowly. Encourage Frankie to pronounce words syllable by syllable as he checks the spelling.
2. Help Frankie improve his spelling of high-frequency words. Take words from the "300 Instant Words" list (Figure 6.22) and use a multisensory technique to practice the words.
3. Teach the spelling of word families around those words taught using a method that incorporates writing words from memory, such as look-cover-write.
4. Provide review of spelling words and practice of particular orthographic patterns (e.g., *ch*).
5. Teach the difference between the spellings of homophones (such as *wood* and *would*) in context using sentences to illustrate the difference in meaning.
6. Provide Frankie with a copy of *A Spelling Dictionary for Beginning Writers* to use at his desk. This reference contains approximately fourteen hundred of the words most frequently used in writing by children in kindergarten through second grade.
7. Help Frankie learn to differentiate the spellings of vowels and vowel patterns. Work with pairs of words (for example, *him-hem, pet-pit*) and have him write the spellings from dictation.
8. Use CBM to monitor Frankie's progress in spelling. Keep track of both words spelled correctly and correct letter sequences.

Usage

1. Review the use of capitalization rules with Frankie.
2. Review the use of periods at the end of sentences and help Frankie see the relationship between the use of periods and uppercase letters.
3. Teach Frankie to use a mnemonic editing strategy such as COPS (capitalization, overall appearance, punctuation, and spelling) for all of his assignments.
4. Review the difference between words beginning with vowels and those beginning with consonants. Teach Frankie the rules for when the article *an* is used instead of *a*.
5. Help Frankie write more complex sentences. Use sentence-combining activities, for example, to help Frankie combine his ideas into varied sentence structures.

Vocabulary

1. Reinforce Frankie for using more difficult words and do not penalize him for incorrect spellings. Arrange for a peer editor to work with Frankie on the final draft.
2. Help Frankie create a personalized thesaurus and encourage him to use it when writing an assignment.

Organization and Ideation

1. Work on prewriting strategies with Frankie that will help him organize and present more information.

2. Encourage Frankie to use graphic organizers to help expand his ideas and sequence them logically.

3. Teach a procedure such as the given-new strategy to help Frankie consider the reader in determining what is known information and what needs further explanation.

4. Use CBM to monitor Frankie's progress in written expression. Keep track of total words written, total letters written, words spelled correctly, and correct writing sequences.

Follow-Up

Frankie received assistance from a special education teacher for one year. The major goals were to improve reading and writing skills. A sample of a first draft from a story starter is presented in Figure 9.4. Frankie's story is creative and sequenced, and he attempts to offer the reader good advice.

Although his sentence patterns are more complex, he still needs some assistance with identifying sentence boundaries (such as where to put a period) and spelling. His spelling has improved greatly, but Frankie continues to misspell some common words, writing *will* as "well" and *chocolate* as "choclet." He does not double the middle consonants in *offer* and *better*. Fortunately, spellings of this nature may be corrected easily during the editing stage, and he could be taught spelling rules for when to double consonants.

Student: Brian
Grade: 4th
Assignments: Three journal entries and one follow-up entry

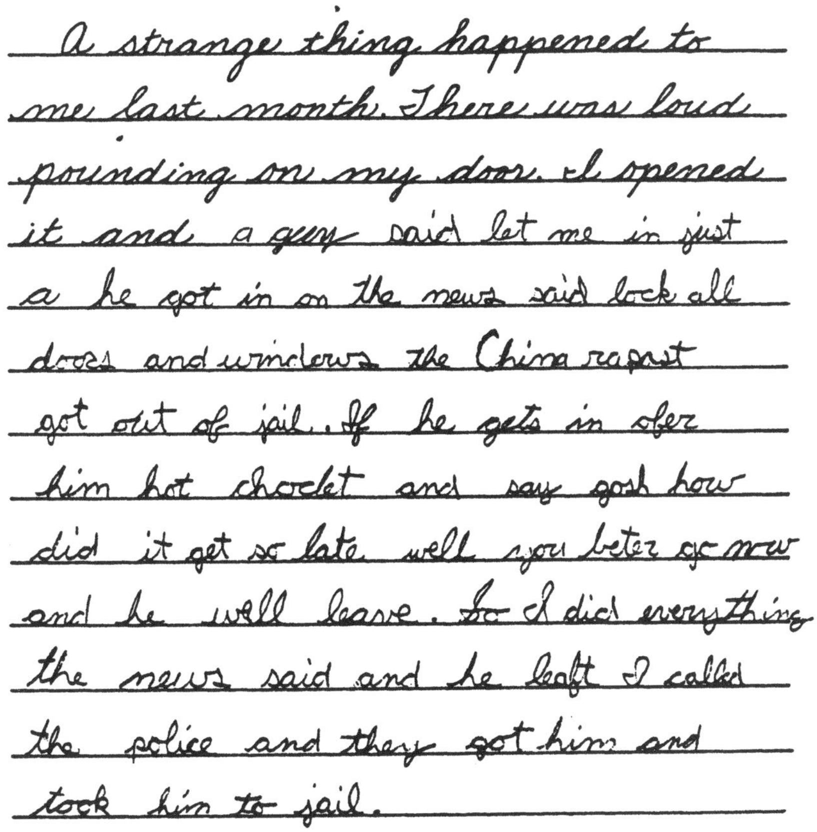

A strange thing happened to me last month. There was loud pounding on my door. I opened it and a guy said let me in just a he got in on the news said lock all doors and windows the China rapist got out of jail. If he gets in ofer him hot choclet and say gosh how did it get so late. well you beter go now and he well leave. So I did everything the news said and he left I called the police and they got him and took him to jail.

Figure 9.4. Frankie's Writing One Year Later.

Brian selected the topics for the writing samples and wrote them in his journal (Figure 9.5). No brainstorming or prewriting activities had occurred.

Analysis

Handwriting and Appearance

The handwriting in the printed sample is adequate, but that in the cursive samples is better. The spacing between words is inconsistent and, on the whole, too large. With one exception, Brian observes the margins in the samples. His paragraphs, however, are not indented.

Spelling

Spelling is difficult for Brian. He appears to have a significant problem representing the sequence of sounds in words correctly. Numerous examples of poor sound-symbol correspondence exist in the samples, including the spelling of *half-back* as "uafbk," *beach* as "betche," *shovel* as "shvle," *watch* as "sawsh," and *mighty* as "mindy." In addition, Brian appears to have difficulty remembering how words look and, consequently, misspells high-frequency sight words. For example, he spells *went* as "wint," *house* as "houns," and *made* as "mand." The letter *n* is added incorrectly to several words such as "rint" for *right*, "mand" for *made*, "houns" for *house*, and "inind-ing" for *exciting*.

Brian tries to spell phonetically. He does not seem to understand basic spelling patterns, such as CVCe patterns. He spells *pile* as "pill" and *hole* as "holl." He does not seem to understand common spelling rules, such as when to double consonants when adding suffixes (for example, "diging" and "biger"). He tends to confuse some common digraphs, such as *sh* and *ch* in his spellings of "shire" for *church*, and "sawsh" for *watch*. He also confuses certain similar-sounding vowel sounds, such as spelling *went* as "wint." When spelling, not all of the syllables in words are represented. At times, he records fewer syllables than exist, as in the writing of "rocus" for *firecrackers*, "chapyn" for *championships*, "foull"

for *Fort Lowell*, and "or" for *over*. At other times, Brian writes more sounds than are necessary, as demonstrated by his spellings of "firends" for *friend's*, and "cnandy" for *candy*. Although able to read his work immediately following writing, Brian is unable to remember what he has written after a short interval.

Usage

Brian uses commas correctly when in a list, as can be observed in "fowrd, uafbk, folbk." Apart from the list, commas were not used. Brian appears not to have mastered the correct usage of periods and uses them in the middle of sentences. He does not seem to understand the concept of writing in complete sentences. Examples of this are "The foull soute out." "Is fun and we came in frist plass." "At my firends houns." At times, periods do not occur where necessary, as in "I got to go to shire it fin and . . ." In addition, Brian has a tendency to overuse the conjunction *and* and to write only simple sentences. Even though his use of periods is incorrect, Brian consistently remembers to capitalize the first letter after the period. He also consistently capitalizes the word *I*.

Although exclamation points are not used in many places, too many have been used in one place in the first sample. Brian also appears to make assumptions with regard to the information that the reader already possesses. For example, he writes that the shootout is fun and "we" came in first place. The reader may infer that the pronoun refers to a team, but has no information with regard to which team. Although much of the selected vocabulary is simplistic, Brian demonstrates good knowledge and vocabulary pertaining to soccer. He uses words such as *shootout, forward, halfback, fullback, championships*, and *dog pile*. The majority of the other words are one syllable.

Organization and Ideation

Brian does include a title on his second sample. In all samples, he presents information that he wants to share. A few organizational problems

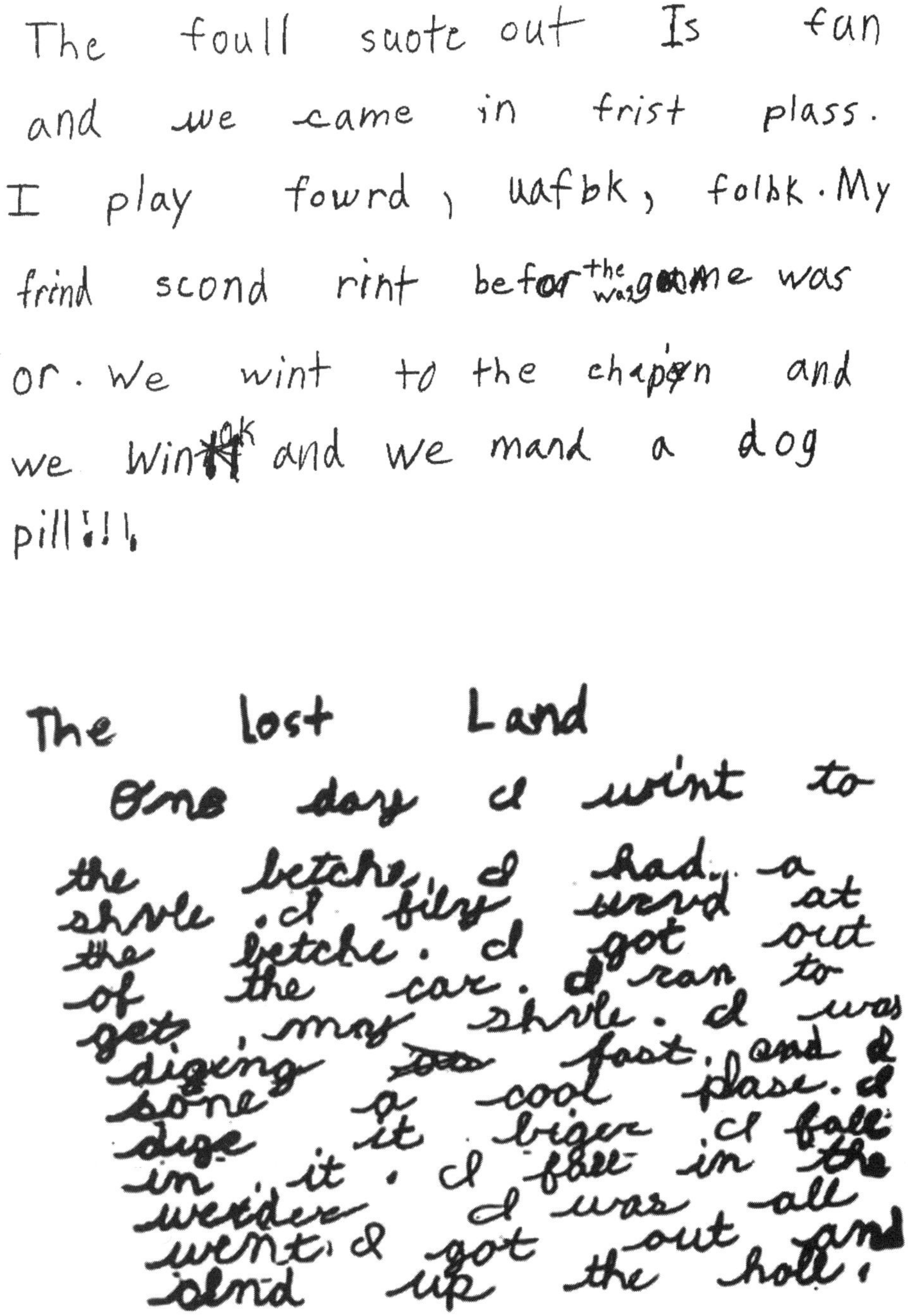

The foull suote out Is fun
and we came in frist plass.
I play fowrd, uafbk, folbk. My
frind scond rint befor the was game was
or. We wint to the chapen and
we wint ok and we mand a dog
pill.

The lost Land
One day I wint to
the betche. I had a
shvle. I fily wird at
the betche. I got out
of the car. I ran to
gets may shvle. I was
diging too fast. and I
sone a cool plase. I
dige it biger. I fall
in it. I fall in the
weider. I was all
went. I got out and
clind up the holl.

Figure 9.5. Brian's Three Journal Entries.

Translations: The Fort Lowell shoot out is fun and we came in first place. I play forward, halfback, fullback. My friend scored right before the game was over. We went to the championships and we won and we made a dog-pile.

The Lost Land

One day I went to the beach. I had a shovel. I finally arrived at the beach. I got out of the car. I ran to get my shovel. I was digging fast and I soon (got to) a cool place. I dig it bigger. I fall in it. I fall in the water. I was all wet. I got out and climbed up the hole.

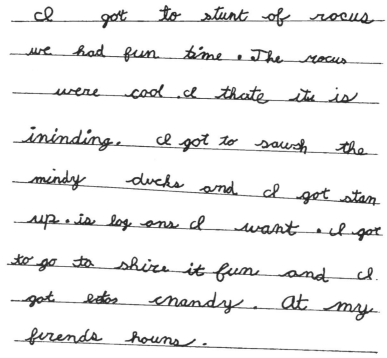

Figure 9.5. Brian's Three Journal Entries. *(Continued)*

Translations: I got to set off firecrackers. We had fun time. The firecrackers were cool. I thought it is exciting. I got to watch the Mighty Ducks and I got stay up as long as I want. I got to go to church. It fun and I got to eat candy at my friend's house.

exist, however. In the "shootout" sample, Brian introduces the topic and then lists the positions that he can play. Although the intent was not to infer that he played all three positions in the shootout, the placement of the information suggests otherwise. A different organizational problem is evidenced in the second and third samples. In the second sample, he has his shovel in the second sentence and then he runs to get his shovel in the fifth sentence. In the third sample, Brian writes about firecrackers, the Mighty Ducks, and church. No explicit connection exists among the activities other than they all pertain to Brian. The activities are not sequenced in any logical way.

Recommendations

Handwriting and Appearance

1. Because of its neater appearance, encourage Brian to use cursive writing for all assignments.

2. Review with Brian the amount of spacing that should occur between words. Show him how to hit one space on the keyboard, and that that is the right amount of space to put between words and sentences.

3. Reinforce the appearance of his written work regardless of content or spelling.

Spelling

1. Ensure that Brian is not penalized in any situation for his spelling attempts.

2. Encourage Brian to generalize the phonic spelling patterns that he has mastered. Initially, work with word families using the phonograms that he knows and then teach new ones. Ask Brian to suggest a word that he would like to spell, then teach him both the word and the word family pertaining to it (for example, if Brian chooses to learn the word *dictionary*, also teach *fiction* and *friction*).

3. As Brian has difficulty both sequencing sounds in words and picturing words in his mind, use a multisensory approach to teach spelling. Have Brian say and trace the word as many times as needed until he can write the word correctly three times from memory.

4. Provide Brian with a spelling box for storing the words he learns. Encourage him to alphabetize the words in the box and then provide weekly review.

5. As the number of words in the bank increases, ask Brian to build sentences using the cards and then copy them onto paper.

6. Help Brian understand the connection between the number of syllables in words and their length. Play games involving clapping or giving counters for each syllable in a word. Ask Brian to "read" his written work by tapping a pen on the table for every syllable.

7. Teach Brian common spelling rules, such as the doubling rule. Provide practice adding various vowel and consonant suffixes to words.

8. Use CBM to monitor Brian's progress in spelling. Keep track of words spelled correctly and correct letter sequences.

Usage

1. Teach Brian how to write complete sentences. Begin with simple sentence structures and then progress to compound sentences and then complex sentences. Teach him that a sentence consists of a complete thought and that a period is placed at the end.

2. Encourage Brian to limit use of the conjunction *and*. Help Brian edit his work by either replacing *and* with another word or beginning a new sentence.

3. Review the use of pronouns such as *we*. Explain to Brian how all pronouns must have clear referents. Provide practice by having Brian write pairs of sentences. The first sentence would include a noun or proper noun. The next sentence would add more information and contain a pronoun.

4. Through questioning, help Brian clarify pronoun referents.

5. Teach Brian the given-new strategy to help him learn to connect consecutive sentences. Encourage Brian to assume that the reader has no prior knowledge of the topic.

6. Discourage Brian from using too many exclamation points. When they are used, help him understand that one exclamation point is all that is necessary. Remind Brian that writers place only one period at the end of a sentence, not three.

Vocabulary

1. Help Brian to select more precise words to use in his assignments. As a prewriting activity, have Brian and a peer think of all the descriptive words they can. Encourage Brian to keep this list in front of him as he writes his first draft. Upon completion, have him count the number of targeted words that he has used.

2. Use a synonym cloze procedure to help Brian increase his writing. After a draft of a story is complete, underline words that could be more descriptive. Delete each word to be changed and then write it under the line. Have him work with a peer to determine other words that would make the writing more interesting.

Organization and Ideation

1. Prior to writing, have Brian engage in discussions about his ideas.

2. Work on prewriting strategies using graphic organizers. Stress the importance of keeping information in an organized order and not including information that does not belong.

3. Help Brian organize and sequence details. For example, have him list all the information that he thinks is important and then help him think of ways to sequence the points. Teach Brian to use mapping or webbing in order to provide structure to the organization.

Follow-Up

A special education teacher began working with Brian on these recommendations for one hour, twice weekly. During the fourth session, Brian was asked to write a journal entry (Figure 9.6).

Analysis of the assignment indicates a marked improvement in Brian's writing from two weeks prior. The problems discussed in his previous writing still exist but the effectiveness of the specific recommendations can be clearly seen. Brian is encouraged by his improvement and motivated to work at improving his writing further. In addition, to document progress, Brian and his teacher have compared journal entries on a weekly basis and charted CBM graphs for both spelling words and written stories. Brian's comment with regard to his latest attempt was "Boy, this is better. My handwriting isn't good so I should write in cursive, shouldn't I? But my spelling is so much better. You were right. I *can* write."

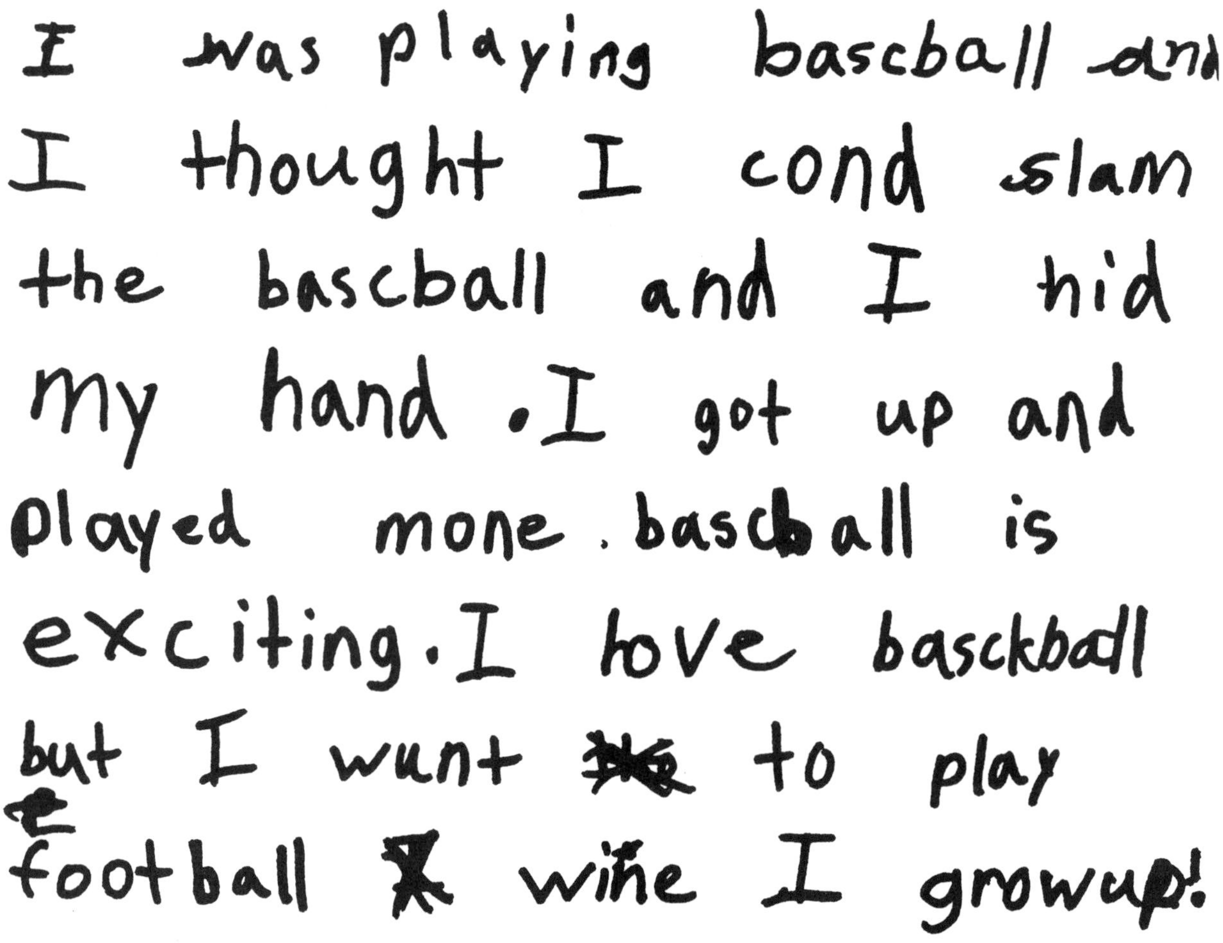

Figure 9.6. Brian's Journal Entry After Recommendations Were Implemented.

Translation: I was playing basketball and I thought I could slam the basketball and I hit my hand. I got up and played more. Basketball is exciting. I love basketball but I want to play football when I grow up.

Student: Emily
Grade: 5th
Assignment: Sequential paragraph

Emily was asked to write a sequential paragraph about what she does in the morning before coming to school (Figure 9.7).

Analysis

Handwriting

In general, Emily's cursive writing is legible. She appears, however, to have some difficulty with the formation of a lowercase *b* when it is joined with the letters *r* and *u*. In one instance,

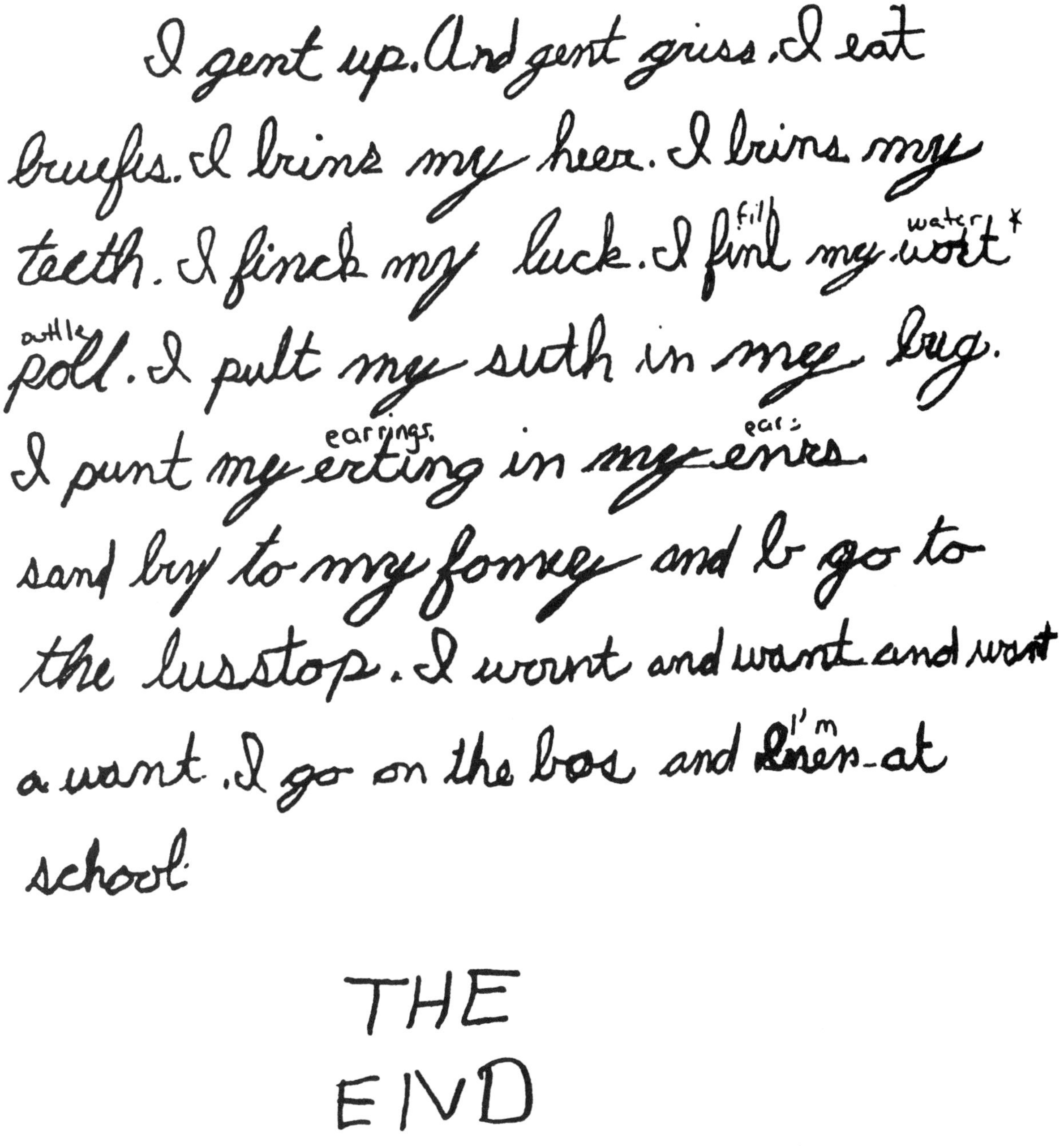

Figure 9.7. Emily's Sequential Paragraph.

Translation: I get up. And get dress. I eat breakfast. I brush my hair. I brush my teeth. I fix my lunch. I fill my water bottle. I put my stuff in my bag. I put my earrings in my ears said bye to my family and I go to the bus stop. I wait and wait and wait and wait. I go on the bus and I'm at school.

she reverses an uppercase *I*. The letters below the line extend too far to the left. The spacing between sentences is inconsistent.

Spelling

Emily's greatest difficulty appears to be spelling. Although one may suspect that some of Emily's misspellings are based on articulation errors (for example, "griss" for *dress*, "bruefis" for *breakfast*, and "poll" for *bottle*), these types of sound confusions are not present in her oral language. She also includes unnecessary sounds, particularly confusing the sounds of /n/ and /l/ (for example, "gent" for *get*, "pult" for *put*, and "finl" for *fill*). In general, her spellings indicate poor phonological awareness with difficulty placing the sounds in sequence.

Several of Emily's spellings have limited sound-symbol correspondence but begin with the correct consonant sound. For example, she spells *stuff* as "suth," *family* as "fomey," and *fix* as "finck." Emily does appear, however, to realize that the spelling of words does not vary. As long as the words are close together in the passage, she maintains her spelling. For example, she spells the word *get* twice as "gent," *brush* twice as "brins," and *wait* three times as "want."

Usage

Emily begins all sentences with an uppercase letter and ends with a period. Her sentence patterns are relatively simplistic. With the exception of one incomplete sentence beginning with the word *And*, she starts each sentence with the word *I*. Although verb tense is mostly consistent, Emily has made two errors, writing "dress" instead of *dressed* and "said" instead of *say*. It is unclear, however, whether these errors are due to problems with spelling or usage.

Organization and Ideation

The activities described contain little detail. In addition, Emily does not introduce her topic

or use linking words to order her actions. She does, however, relate her morning activities in an appropriate sequence.

Recommendations

Handwriting

1. Provide Emily with additional practice with letters that require a bridge or handle when joined to other letters (*b, o, v,* and *w*).
2. Review with Emily the correct formation of letters that extend below the line, such as *y* and *g*.
3. Remind Emily to leave a space after sentences.

Spelling

1. Provide Emily with an individualized spelling list. Select words that are frequently misspelled in her writing. Initially, select spelling words for Emily that have phonically regular spelling patterns and also teach the families of the chosen spelling words (for example, alongside *part*, teach *cart, dart, start*, and so on).
2. Help Emily learn to determine the number of syllables that she hears in a word and then the number of sounds. Have her pronounce the word slowly as she pushes out a counter for each sound. Then have her write the sounds that she hears.
3. Dictate simple spelling words to Emily and have her build the words with magnetic plastic letters or Scrabble tiles. Have her form the word with the letters, then scramble the letters and reconstruct the word from memory.
4. Teach Emily how to spell the sounds of words in sequence. Encourage her to pronounce a word slowly as she writes each sound. This will help Emily sequence letters in the correct order.

5. Use CBM to monitor Emily's progress in spelling. Keep track of words spelled correctly and correct letter sequences.

Usage

1. Teach Emily how to write a variety of sentence patterns.
2. Encourage Emily to start sentences in different ways. Suggest that only two sentences may begin with the same word. Reinforce Emily when she attains the goal.
3. Analyze additional writing samples and listen to Emily telling a story to determine whether she is consistent in use of verb tense. If not, provide instruction in how to maintain consistency in verb tense throughout a paragraph. Provide feedback when editing by underlining all of the verbs and helping Emily check them.

Ideation

1. Provide opportunities for daily writing.
2. Use a modified cloze procedure to help Emily expand her sentences. Take a paragraph that she has written and put in blanks where the sentence can be elaborated. Have her add adjectives, adverbs, phrases, and clauses.
3. Teach Emily how to write a topic sentence that introduces the main idea and then to write details to support that idea. Also teach her how to write a final sentence that summarizes the main idea or provides a transition to a related idea.
4. Teach Emily to use simple cohesive ties, such as *afterwards, then, next*, and *finally*, to help the reader follow the organization of her sequential paragraphs.
5. Use CBM to monitor Emily's progress in written expression. On a weekly basis, administer a three-minute writing task using a grade-appropriate story starter. Keep track of the total words written, total letters written, words spelled correctly, and correct writing sequences. Have Emily chart her own progress.

Student: Malika
Grade: 6th
Assignments: Two opinion essays

Before the production of the assignments, a prewriting class discussion had occurred. Malika and her peers were then asked to record their personal ideas of "A Perfect Classroom" and "A Perfect Teacher." Figure 9.8 illustrates Malika's essays.

Analysis

Handwriting and Appearance

Malika remembered to put a title to the first assignment, but proceeded to place an equal sign after the title, turning the assignment into

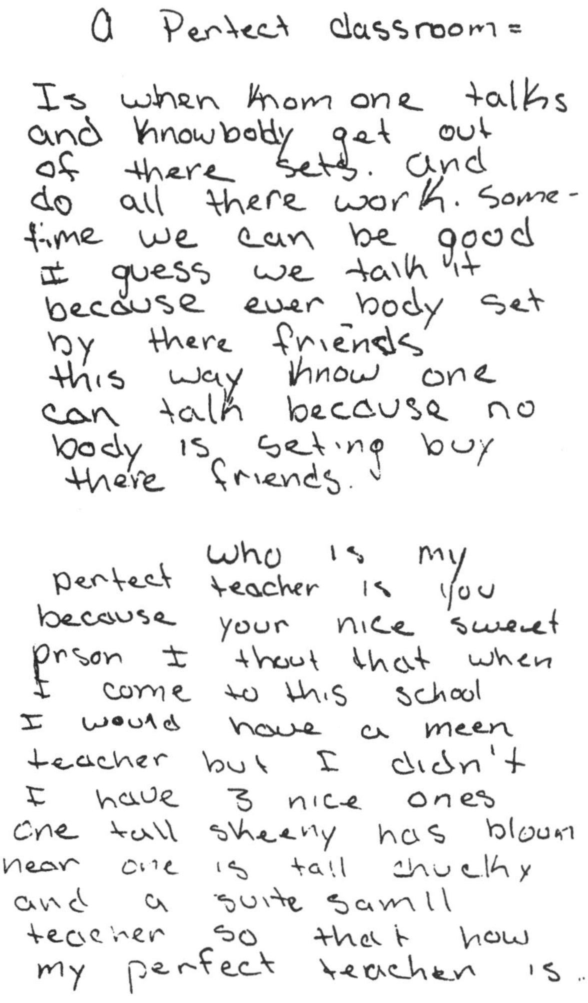

Figure 9.8. Malika's Opinion Essays.

a form of equation. No title was recorded for the second assignment. Malika printed both assignments. Although her handwriting is easy to read and all letters are recognizable, formation of the letter *k* detracts from the overall appearance. She does not indent the paragraphs and seems to have tried to create the appearance of a title from the first sentence in the second assignment. Malika has attempted to observe both left and right margins.

Spelling

A number of spelling errors appear in the "Perfect Teacher" sample. As examples, she writes "thout" for *thought*, "meen" for *mean*, "bloun" for *brown*, "samil" for *smile*, "hear" for *hair*, and "skeeny" for *skinny*. Only a few errors are made, however, in the "Perfect Classroom" sample (for example, "seting" for *sitting* and "sets" for *seats*). The words, although incorrectly spelled, are close approximations, and therefore easy to recognize.

Malika shows confusion in her spelling of common homophones. For example, she spells *no* in the compound words *nobody* and *no one* as "know." In addition, she spells *by* as "buy," *their* as "there," *you're* as "your," and *sweet* as "suite."

Usage

Malika's use of periods and uppercase letters is incorrect. Although she capitalizes the first letter in the first sentence of each paragraph, the sentences do not make sense as written ("Is when knom one talks and knowbody get out of there sets," and "Who is my perfect teacher is you because your nice sweet prson . . . "). Malika capitalizes the first letter after two of the three periods used. She does not, however, always place periods where needed and has several run-on sentences (for example, "One tall skeeny has bloun hear one is tall chucky and a suite samll teacher so that how my perfect teacher is.").

Malika has not yet mastered correct sentence formation. She often writes unfinished sentences and clauses that represent incomplete thoughts (for example, "and do all there work," and "Sometime we can be good I guess we talk it because ever body set by there friends . . . "). Analyses of the syntactic errors suggest that Malika may have expressive language difficulties (for example, "I thout that when I come to this school . . . ," and "Sometime we can be good I guess we talk it because ever body set . . . "). She tries, however, to write compound sentences connected by the conjunction *because*. Malika's use of subject-verb agreement is incorrect after the words *everybody* and *nobody* ("knowbody get out . . . ," and "ever body set . . . ").

Vocabulary

Although her vocabulary is simple, Malika attempts to use colorful and descriptive words, particularly in the "Perfect Teacher" sample. For example, she describes her teachers as being "skinny," "chunky," and "sweet small."

Organization and Ideation

The samples are rather limited in content and lose focus at times. For example, when describing a perfect classroom, Malika discusses when her class is quiet. In the description of the perfect teacher, she mentions three teachers briefly instead of fully describing one.

Recommendations

Handwriting and Appearance

1. Encourage Malika to write a title for every written assignment she attempts.
2. Remind Malika that every paragraph needs to be indented.
3. Teach Malika the correct formation of lower- and uppercase *k*. Reinforce her for using the correct formation in her written work.

Spelling

1. Help Malika increase the number of high-frequency words that she knows how to

spell. Take the words to be taught directly from her writing. Have Malika select additional words that she is interested in learning.

2. Develop an individualized spelling program for Malika using a flow list rather than a fixed spelling list. Test her on the words daily. When a word has been spelled correctly on three consecutive days, replace it with a new word from her writing.

3. Show Malika the difference in the spellings of common homophones, such as *your* and *you're, no* and *know, by* and *buy*, and *there, their*, and *they're*. Teach the homophones out of context, but reinforce the meaning of the homophones by providing the opportunity for Malika to use these words in context.

4. When editing her work, provide Malika with a peer who will help her identify and correct any misspelled words.

5. Use CBM to monitor Malika's progress in spelling. Keep track of words spelled correctly and correct letter sequences.

Usage

1. Review with Malika the correct use of periods. Encourage her to place a period at the end of every complete thought. Discourage her from beginning a new sentence with the word *and*.

2. Have Malika place an uppercase letter immediately after a period.

3. Tape Malika telling a story in order to assess whether the syntax and language problems are evident in both her oral and written language. If they are, Malika would benefit from receiving speech and language services. Alternatively, a speech and language consultant could collaborate with the classroom teacher to provide various language activities for Malika.

4. Teach Malika the correct subject-verb agreement with the words *nobody* and *everybody*. Extend the lesson to include the words *no one* and *everyone*.

5. Teach Malika a variety of sentence structures such as simple statements (declarative), questions (interrogative), and compound sentences. Provide ample opportunity for her to practice using the different sentence patterns.

6. Use a modified cloze technique and sentence-combining exercises to help Malika expand her sentences.

7. Review and provide opportunities to practice the correct use of conjunctions such as *because, however*, and *so*.

8. Encourage Malika to edit her work to check for the correct use of periods and uppercase letters. In addition, encourage Malika to edit for syntax errors by reading the assignment aloud either to herself or to a peer.

Vocabulary

1. Encourage Malika to use more complex vocabulary. Underline two or three words in each of her assignments and ask her to replace the words with more complex or descriptive ones.

2. Before assigning a descriptive paragraph, help Malika generate a number of words in different categories. For example, before writing about a teacher, help her generate five categories (such as physical attributes, emotional attributes, likes and dislikes, teaching style, and grading policies). Under each category, the teacher or a peer would help Malika list descriptive words (under "teaching style," she may list "clear voice," "steady pace," "appropriate use of visuals," and so on).

Organization and Ideation

1. Help Malika develop her sense of audience. Prior to writing, help her identify the reader and encourage her to write to that specific audience.

2. Provide opportunities for the sharing of assignments. Publishing work will help Malika become more sensitive to audience

needs. It will also give her a sense of purpose and encourage her to take pride in the work.

3. Although a prewriting discussion had occurred before Malika attempted either assignment, she would benefit from more structured prewriting strategies. Provide her with an appropriate graphic organizer and help her organize her thoughts into a logical order.

4. Provide Malika with the opportunity to read her essays to a peer in order to get feedback with regard to missing elements or those that need expansion. Encourage her to integrate the feedback into her work during the revision process.

5. Use a structured revision conference with Malika.

6. Use CBM to monitor Malika's progress in written expression. On a weekly basis, administer a three-minute writing task using a grade-appropriate story starter. Track total words written, total letters written, words spelled correctly, and correct writing sequences. Have Malika chart her own progress.

Student: Helen
Grade: 7th
Assignment: Descriptive essay

Instead of writing a descriptive essay titled "A Person I Shall Never Forget," Helen wrote a narrative essay (Figure 9.9). Her introduction was consistent with the assignment, but she quickly veered off track. Apart from being given the title, no prewriting activities were conducted.

Analysis

Handwriting and Appearance

Although Helen tends to have an inconsistent slant in her cursive writing, the words are legible and formed correctly. Some variability

exists, however, in her letter size. She leaves a space to create a boundary between each word, but the space tends to be too large. Helen has not indented her paragraph. Although margins have been observed, the appearance of the assignment is marred by overzealous scribbling and the numbering of lines.

Spelling

On this assignment, spelling does not appear to be a problem for Helen. One reason is that the majority of words that she writes are simple and repeated several times. Her spelling of the words *with* as "wiht" and *Chris* as "Chisr" suggests that she may have experienced spelling problems in earlier grades. Helen uses a few words incorrectly, writing "to" instead of *too* and "won't" for *want*.

Usage

Helen correctly capitalizes the first letter of her story. She does not use any periods in the twenty-seven carefully counted lines. She remembers to capitalize the first word in the name "Big Boy," and capitalizes the word *I* throughout the story. She does not use commas or quotation marks throughout the assignment even though the majority of the story is written as dialogue.

Inconsistencies may be noted in verb tense. Helen begins by writing in the past tense, changes to the present, reverts to the past tense, and then back to the present tense for the dialogue. In addition, subject-verb agreement is incorrect in at least one instance ("he like me"), and possibly in another ("he doesn't like me"), where the error could be due to incorrect usage or spelling.

Vocabulary

The vocabulary Helen uses is simple and uninteresting. She writes only a few words that are longer than one syllable (for example, *very, going, Honda, sometime,* and *puppy*).

1. There was a man ~~that~~ (that) was

2. be a nerd to my friend

3. his name is ~~chior b~~ he is very

4. ~~mean~~ ~~cool~~ to me he was sad d ~~saying~~ scind

5. dm going to hurt ~~you no~~ you are not

6. yes am going to hurt you ok

7. you won ok d get to hurt you

8. yes you can hurt me ok but d

9. don't wont to fine then d like you

10. you are cool ~~chior~~ do you like cars.

11. yes d do good d have a lot

12. of them they are cool hot honds

13. d have a big car to for you

14. to play ~~with~~ wiht d have 3 big dog

15. they are cool they are mean

16. to my friend d do ~~not~~ like

Figure 9.9. Helen's Descriptive Essay.

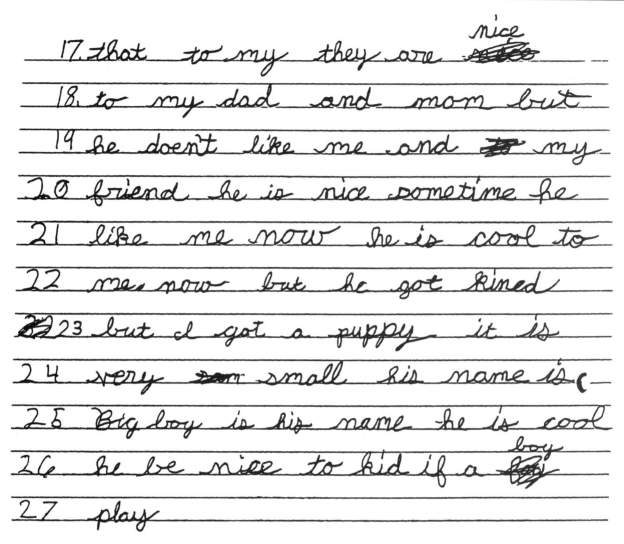

17. that to my they are ~~nice~~ *nice*
18. to my dad and mom but
19. he doesn't like me and ~~I~~ my
20. friend he is nice sometime he
21. like me now he is cool to
22. me now but he got kined
23. but I got a puppy it is
24. very ~~sm~~ small his name is (
25. Big boy is his name he is cool
26. he be nice to kid if a ~~boy~~ *boy*
27. play

Figure 9.9. Helen's Descriptive Essay. *(Continued)*

Organization and Ideation

The assignment is not the requested descriptive essay but rather a narrative one. Within the framework of a narrative, the dialogue is somewhat disorganized and uninteresting. The assignment begins with an introduction of Chris, then moves on to someone wanting to hurt him. Chris then appears to become a "cool" person. The discussion then moves to Chris's dog that does not appear to like many people and from there to the writer's dog. Adding confusion to the story is the lack of a clear reference. Apart from Chris, no other person is introduced, though "my friend" is referred to several times.

In addition, some problems with ideation occur. Helen seems to write a lot of words, but her story is not well developed. The content is dull, and some of the thoughts are difficult to understand (for example, "he be nice to kid if a boy play").

Recommendations

Handwriting and Appearance

1. Encourage Helen to indent each paragraph.
2. Remind Helen not to number the lines. Look over some passages in books with Helen and discuss why authors do not number each written line.

3. Encourage Helen to leave less space in between words.
4. To increase self-monitoring of her paper's appearance, teach Helen the HOW strategy (heading, organized, written neatly).

Spelling

1. Using a visual strategy, such as the look-cover-write method, review the spelling of high-frequency words, such as *with*.
2. For spelling instruction, select words that are misspelled in Helen's writing.

Usage

1. Encourage Helen to place a period after each complete thought. Provide help in checking for the correct use of periods during editing.
2. Review the use of uppercase letters. Begin with the use of uppercase letters to start each sentence and then in proper nouns.
3. Teach or review all punctuation marks in a logical sequence.
4. Review usage rules pertaining to subject-verb agreement and verb tense. Provide Helen with the opportunity to work with the teacher or a peer with more advanced writing skill when editing her work.
5. Teach Helen a variety of sentence structures and reinforce her attempt to use them. Use sentence-combining exercises to help her increase sentence complexity.
6. Show Helen how sentences can be combined using a variety of conjunctions. Provide her with ample opportunity for combining sentences. Reinforce her when she generalizes the skill into her written assignments.
7. Have Helen skip lines when writing her first drafts. Provide Helen with the time and help needed to edit her work. Have her write edits in the space above each line and then write the final draft using each line.
8. Teach Helen the mnemonic COPS (capitalization, overall appearance, punctuation,

spelling) or SCOPE (spelling, capitalization, order of words, punctuation, express a complete thought) as an error-monitoring strategy for use in editing.

Vocabulary

1. Help Helen develop a personalized thesaurus and encourage her to use the new words in her written assignments.
2. Use prewriting strategies to help enhance vocabulary.
3. When revising her papers, underline a few words and help Helen replace them with synonyms that are more complex and descriptive. Remind Helen to add these words to her thesaurus.
4. Use structural analysis maps to show Helen how the addition of morphemes alters word meaning. Provide practice using the various forms of words within sentences.

Organization and Ideation

1. Have Helen spend sufficient time on prewriting activities. Use different types of graphic organizers to help her sequence her thoughts. Encourage her to use the ideas from her graphic organizers as she writes her story. For example, use an organizer shaped as a star. Have Helen shade in each point of the star after she has included the information in her story or essay.
2. Review the major elements in a story.
3. Teach Helen a prewriting strategy, such as C-SPACE, to help her remember the steps to follow when writing a narrative.
4. Help Helen understand that writing has multiple steps and is recursive.
5. Teach Helen how to write different types of expository paragraphs. Begin with a sequential paragraph. When this form is mastered, teach her how to write a descriptive paragraph.
6. Use CBM to monitor Helen's progress in written expression. On a weekly basis,

administer a three-minute writing task using a grade-appropriate story starter. Keep track of the total words written, total letters written, words spelled correctly, and correct writing sequences. Have Helen chart her own progress.

Student: Chantelle
Grade: 9th
Assignments: Five descriptive paragraphs

The five assignments represent Chantelle's attempts to write descriptive paragraphs (Figure 9.10). She wrote these assignments over a period of five weeks.

Analysis

Handwriting and Appearance

Variation exists in Chantelle's handwriting from assignment to assignment. Although her printed samples are neat, the writing appears immature. The appearance of the three cursive samples varies across samples. The handwriting in the "Dorm" sample is similar in appearance to the printed stories. The appearance on "About Kangaroo" is the best. All paragraphs are indented. Chantelle uses titles in all of her assignments and leaves a space between the title and the body of the assignments.

All of Chantelle's letters are formed correctly, and her writing is easy to read even when the overall appearance is sloppy. She leaves adequate space between words, but not quite enough space after a period.

Spelling

Chantelle spells most words correctly. She separates a few compound words (such as *class room, baby sitter, Hand writing*, and *after noon*). She mistakenly writes "wishing" instead of *washing* and "dential" for *detail*. On two occasions, she sequences letters incorrectly and writes "Secince" for *Science* and "Sutdy"

for *study*. On a few occasions, Chantelle writes a word that sounds similar to the correct word (for example, she writes "he's" for *his*, "life" for *live*, "them" for *then*, and "below" for *blow*).

Usage

Chantelle uses uppercase letters correctly most of the time, both to start new sentences and in proper nouns. On one occasion, however, she capitalizes the word *Dorm* unnecessarily, and on another, she forgets to capitalize the letter beginning a new sentence. She consistently capitalizes the word *I*. She capitalizes her titles, with the exception of the title "Spring break."

Although periods are evident in the samples, they are sometimes omitted (for example, "Then we came back from jr. high school we go to . . . "). On one occasion, a comma is used instead of a period. Commas are used correctly in the list of school subjects, but are not used in other places. No comma appears in Chantelle's recording of her birth date.

Chantelle's main difficulties are in the area of language, primarily syntax and usage.

In general, her sentences are awkward in construction, and the words are often not written in the correct order. As examples, she writes, "In my birth is April 13 I also get my gift in there my mom do the cake and I blow the candle then we eat the cake." Chantelle has not fully mastered English syntax and sentence structure, and some of her sentences tend to confuse two or more patterns (for example, "I like to do my work is Language for meaning, Hand-Writing, Math, Secince, S. Sutdy and Creative Writing that I like it," and "They long about 7 feet long that about men"). Although correct in her choice of verb tense most of the time, Chantelle sometimes writes the incorrect tense. For example, she writes, "Sometime . . . we just sitting around, . . . then we came back . . . , and He was work at . . . " At times, the verb is omitted, as in "They (are) long," "They (live) in the cave," and " . . . that (is) all. . . ."

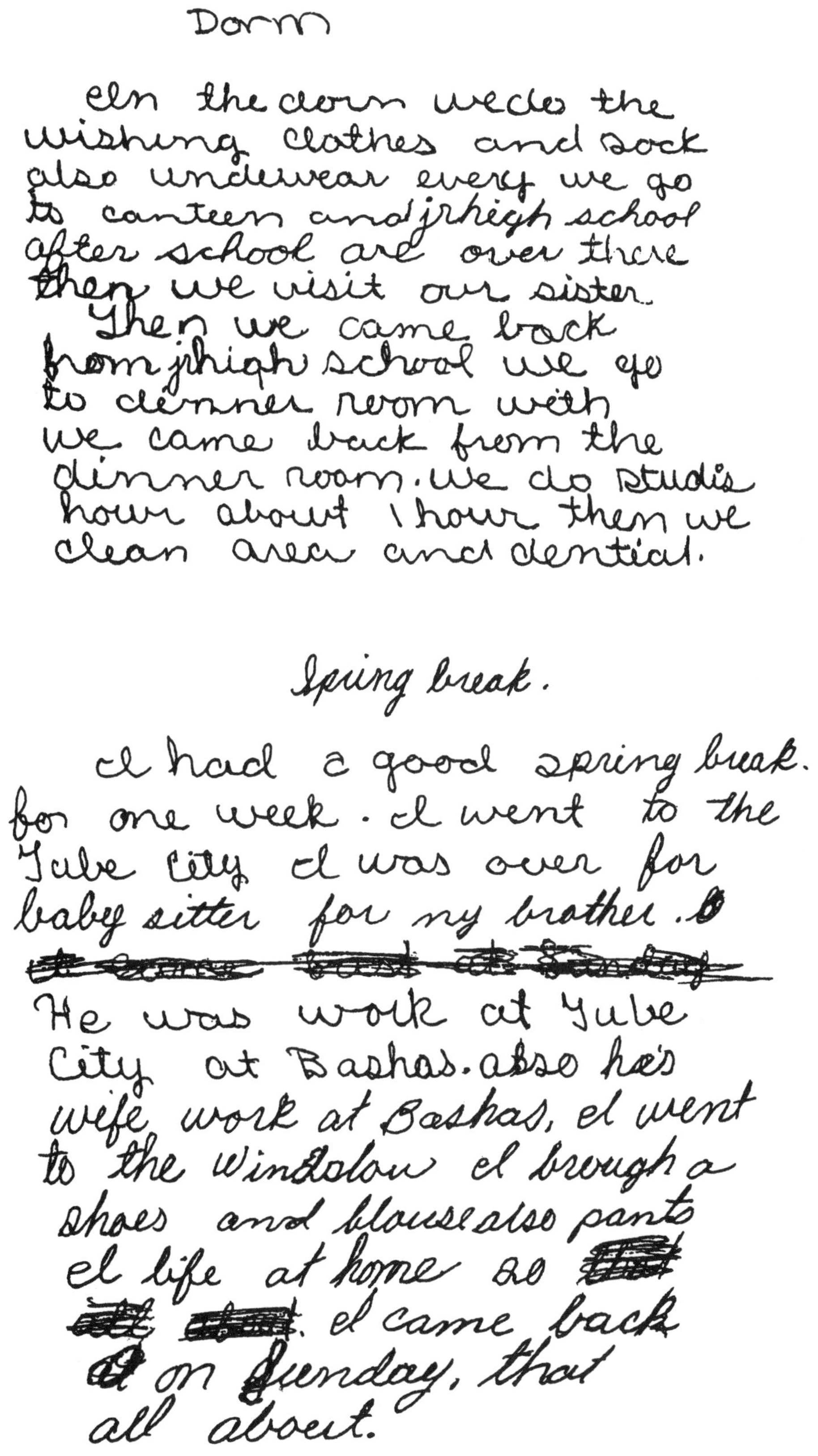

Dorm

In the dorm wecd the wishing clothes and sock also underwear every we go to canteen and jr high school after school are over there then we visit our sister.

Then we came back from jr high school we go to dinner room with we came back from the dinner room. We do studie hour about 1 hour then we clean area and dential.

Spring break.

I had a good spring break. for one week. I went to the Yube city I was over for baby sitter for my brother. ~~I came back I Sunday~~ He was work at Yube city at Bashas. also he's wife work at Bashas, I went to the windolow I brough a shoes and blouse also pants I life at home so ~~that~~ ~~my that~~. I came back ~~I~~ on Sunday, that all about.

Figure 9.10. Chantelle's Descriptive Paragraphs.

My classroom

In my classroom I do my work. I like to do my work is Language for meaning, Hand-Writing, math, Secince, S.Sutdy and Creative writing that I like it

In after noon we do lots of work. Sometime we don't do anything we just sitting around.

My Self

My Self I do my work and do my thinng that way all these year also I always help the aids at Dorm and class room and any people that I can help with them.

In my birth is April 13 I also get my gift in there my mom do the cake and I below the candle them we eat the cake

About Kangaroo

In the pouch the little Kangaroo is sitting in it. They live in Australia and zoo and they eat grass and nuts. They run about 35 miles per hours. They long about 7 feet long. that about men. The ladys are small. They in the cave.

Figure 9.10. Chantelle's Descriptive Paragraphs. *(Continued)*

On occasion, Chantelle uses incorrect plurals, writing "bodys" for *bodies* and "studis" for *studies*, "35 miles per hours," and "wishing clothes and sock." In one instance, she omits the *t* from *brought*. This omission may be a usage rather than a spelling error, as she appears to have a tendency to omit word endings (such as "work" for *working* and "sometime" for *sometimes*).

Chantelle uses prepositions and prepositional phrases incorrectly in several places. She writes, for example, "I help . . . any people I can help with them. I always help the aids at Dorm," and "I was over for baby sitter for my brother." In addition, she has not yet mastered the use of the articles *a* and *the*. On occasion, Chantelle omits the article ("at Dorm," "They live in Australia and zoo," and " . . . we go to canteen"), or incorrectly includes one ("the Windslow," and "a shoes").

Chantelle also writes both incomplete and run-on sentences. ("That all about" and "Sometime we don't do anything we just sitting around.")

Vocabulary

Chantelle's use of vocabulary is adequate at times, but not precise. For example, Chantelle writes about doing her work and her "thing," about her mom "doing" her birthday cake, and about herself "doing" the washing and her studies.

Organization and Ideation

Chantelle's assignments lack both organization and ideas. Although her ideas are difficult to follow because of poor sentence structure, she does attempt to maintain the topic in all five samples.

Recommendations

These samples document Chantelle's difficulties with written expression because of weaknesses in language. In this case, you would also want to consult with the speech and language therapist for additional recommendations. The speech and language therapist and the classroom teacher(s) would have ongoing communication in regard to procedures for reinforcing newly developing language skills in the classroom. In general, the selected procedures and techniques would be designed to enhance both oral and written language.

Handwriting and Appearance

1. Encourage Chantelle to observe both the left and right margins on all of her assignments.
2. Encourage the use of cursive writing on all of her assignments. Provide Chantelle the "About Kangaroo" sample, or one similar in appearance, as a model of the neatness expected for final drafts.
3. Using her reading book as a model, review with Chantelle the amount of spacing to place after a period.

Spelling

1. Review the spellings of common compound words.
2. Encourage Chantelle to listen to the sounds in a word and to try to sequence them correctly when she is uncertain of the spelling. Review the difference in meanings between similar sounding words such as *he's* and *his*; *life* and *live*; *below* and *blow*; and *then* and *them*.

Usage

1. Remind Chantelle to capitalize the first word in sentences.
2. Until Chantelle's mastery of syntax has improved, provide many opportunities for her to edit her work with a more knowledgeable other (such as a teacher, a parent, or a peer).
3. Encourage Chantelle to use a variety of sentence patterns. Begin by helping her

understand basic sentence structures (for example, subject-verb-object). Provide extensive practice with these structures. Once she has mastered simple sentence patterns, introduce more complex patterns and have her practice them.

4. Provide extensive oral practice with sentence-combining exercises. Present Chantelle with several clauses or short sentences and have her generate as many sentence patterns as she can using a variety of connecting words. As an alternative activity, provide her with a specific word or words to use in joining clauses or sentences.

5. Help Chantelle clarify and expand her written statements through questioning. For example, when she writes a sentence such as "We do lots of work," ask, "What kind of work do you do?"

6. Explain the importance of using consistent verb tense. Have Chantelle write a paragraph in present tense. When she has mastered the consistent use of present tense, have her write paragraphs in the past tense.

7. Help Chantelle note the errors in her work and encourage her to correct these errors when editing.

8. Provide Chantelle with practice using prepositions. Begin by providing examples out of context, and, as skill develops, provide her with practice in context. Help Chantelle correct any errors in preposition use when editing.

9. Explain the correct use of articles and help Chantelle correct any errors when editing.

10. Review the formation of the plurals of words ending in *y* (for example, *study* and *baby*).

11. Review the difference between *brought* and *bought*. Link the verbs to their present tense forms and point out the *r* in *bring* and *brought*.

12. Teach Chantelle an editing strategy such as COPS or SCOPE.

13. When grading Chantelle's papers, make allowances for language and usage difficulties. For example, overlook grammatical errors in a paper with good conceptual content.

Vocabulary

1. Encourage Chantelle to choose more precise vocabulary. Use graphic organizers to help illustrate the relationships among similar words. Reinforce Chantelle for using more complex or descriptive words in her writing.

2. Underline one or two words in each assignment that could be clarified or improved on. Work with Chantelle to replace these words with ones that are more complex or more precise.

3. Read stories with Chantelle that are slightly above her language level. Discuss any unknown words using pictures or known synonyms. Encourage Chantelle to practice and use the new words in her writing.

Organization and Ideation

1. Use prewriting strategies with Chantelle, such as graphic organizers, to help her develop her thoughts.

2. Teach Chantelle to consider what information the reader has and what information must be explained. Provide her with practice in identifying the sections in her writing that may confuse a reader.

3. Teach Chantelle to introduce and describe what she is discussing.

4. Teach Chantelle how to subordinate information. Have her practice writing a topic sentence, followed by three or four supporting details. Once she has mastered paragraph structure, teach her how to organize paragraphs into essays.

Student: Tim
Grade: 10th
Assignments: Two letters

Two of Tim's letters are presented in Figure 9.11. One is written to his friend, Annie, and the other is written to his mother and brother. Tim attends a private boarding school for students with severe learning disabilities.

Analysis

Handwriting

In his first letter, Tim combines lowercase and uppercase manuscript letters and cursive letters. In his second letter, he begins writing in cursive and then switches to print. Although neither his manuscript nor cursive writing is attractive in appearance, the major difficulty with legibility is poor spelling rather than letter formation.

Spelling

Although incorrect, several of Tim's spellings are good phonetic approximations (such as "mite" for *might*, "skrach" for *scratch*, "cume" for *come*, and "eze" for *easy*). In general, however, Tim's ability to communicate effectively in writing is severely hampered by his extreme spelling difficulties. He has mastered the spelling of very few words. It seems that every time he comes to a word, he has to start again to try and spell it as if for the first time. For example, within the first sample, he spells the word *probably* as "parll" and "prabble." He misspells many high-frequency words ("ass" for *as*; "ween," "win," and "wew" for *when*; "tray" for *try*; and "wall" for *while*). He confuses word boundaries (for example, "abager" for *a bagger*, "ajob" for *a job*, "Newyurk" for *New York*, and "Afabter" for *Alpha Beta*). With the exception of the correct spelling of *-ing* in several words, many of his spellings indicate lack of sensitivity to common English spelling patterns (for example, "woork" for *work*, "dowin" for *down*, "monee" for *money*, and "wew" for *when*). He also transposes sounds within a few words ("gart" for *great*, "rorg" for *Roger*, "pells" for *please*, and "sifn" for *sniff*).

Usage

Tim places a period at the end of most sentences. He expresses his thoughts in complete ideas. He makes three errors in subject-verb agreement (". . . my dad dont," "Tom call," and "he get"). It is unclear whether these are spelling or usage errors.

Both letters begin with a salutation and end with a closing. Tim does not place a comma after his salutation, however, and in the second letter the first sentence is merged with the greeting.

Organization and Ideation

Tim has a lot to say to his friend Annie. His letter is informative, and the sequence of his thoughts makes sense. He describes what he plans to do in the summer months. He adds a postscript that reiterates when he will call his friend. Perhaps indicative of other types of sequential difficulties, he writes the dates as "25-24 of Feb," proceeding backward in time. He also repeats information in one sentence ("I will probably go to New York this June to work tearing down a building in New York this June").

Recommendations

Tim has a severe spelling problem that is affecting his ability to communicate in writing. Because of the severity of the problem and his age, he will require specific accommodations and modifications to succeed in academic settings.

Accommodations

1. Limit or eliminate copying requirements from both the blackboard and textbooks.
2. Provide tape recordings of the class lectures rather than requiring Tim to take notes.
3. Provide specific instruction in how to use technology as a substitute for writing.

Figure 9.11. Tim's Letters.

DeAR ANNY I goT YouR LitteR I WiLL

Be going To NewYuRK This June. MABy IF IDowT go Home

iN MAY30ARS1. FOR good. I WILL give you a CALL

you oN The 24 OR 25 OF FcB. I MiTe geT u JoB

Ass Buger iN PSFOR iN SANTA CRUZ Wew I

Cume home iN MAY MApe. IF I geT A JoB

Ass A BAgeR iN The STORY iN SANTA CRUZ

ILL TRAY TO FLY BACK TO see you.

my DaD is Thing aBNTe TACKing MY home FOR

good iN MAY. IFF he gET The MaNee The

Nashll garD iN MAY Then I WILL PRLL go

home FOR good. IF My DAD DowT geT The

MONEY iN MAY Thew I WILL PRABLLc go

TO New YuRK This June To WOORK TARiNg

DONin a BiLLing iN NewYuRK This June iN

~~Be ToDDy S~~ Jll 30 I WILL FLY home

RND STAY with AY MOM FOR a WRLL iN

SANTA CRUZ.

Love Timmy

P.S. ILL CALL you 25-24 OF FEB

WEEN I go home ON MY home VisT

Figure 9.11. Tim's Letters. *(Continued)*

For example, teach Tim how to use voice recognition software. He may also use a tape recorder to complete different types of assignments. Provide practice in taking an oral examination and preparing and giving oral reports, essays, and short stories.

4. Accept tape-recorded assignments as an alternative to written assignments.

5. When necessary, administer content area exams orally. Give exams individually or have Tim dictate responses into a tape recorder for grading at a later time.

6. On some assignments, provide a scribe for Tim. Have him dictate his thoughts to another who will write them or type them on a word processor. Have Tim then read the printed copy and discuss revisions.

7. Help Tim advocate for himself by discussing the possible accommodations that he may require to be successful in both school and vocational settings.

Computer

1. Teach Tim keyboarding skills. Provide practice word-processing assignments. Give Tim as much time as is necessary to complete his assignments.

2. Teach Tim how to use a word-processing program. Teach the various functions, such as spell checking, moving and revising text, and saving and printing assignments.

3. Encourage Tim to write his letters and school assignments on a word processor.

Spelling

1. Presently, Tim's level of spelling skill is too low for him to be able to use a spell checker independently. Pair him with a peer who spells well enough to use a spell checker, and provide the time for the two to check and correct spellings on an assignment.

2. Develop a program to teach Tim the spelling of high-frequency words. Because retention has been so poor, Tim is likely to require some type of multisensory method that provides substantial practice and review.

3. Use a program such as Making Words or Phoneme-Grapheme Mapping to help Tim learn to record the sounds of words in the correct sequence.

Usage

1. Provide intensive assistance with correcting all usage errors during editing.

2. Review with Tim the format of informal letter writing.

Organization and Ideation

1. Continue to provide real purposes for writing, such as writing letters to communicate with friends and family members.

2. Provide structured strategies to help Tim develop his skill in expository writing. Begin by teaching him how to write paragraphs using a mnemonic strategy such as SLOW CaPS. Once Tim is able to write different types of expository paragraphs successfully, teach him how to write compare-contrast essays, followed by opinion essays using a technique such as the TREE strategy (topic, reasons, examine, ending).

GUIDED PRACTICE SAMPLES

Just as you would scaffold instruction for your students, this next section provides support while transferring more responsibility for analyzing the writing samples to you. When answering the guided questions, try to provide specific examples from the student's writing that illustrate and clarify the points. Following the analysis, suggest instructional strategies and methods for resolving each area of concern. In addition, consider what accommodations the student may need to participate fully in classroom writing activities. Although the process of analysis can be time consuming, the investment is worth the effort. A careful analysis, resulting in appropriate recommendations, can be the key to success for many students. In addition, you will be rewarded by your students' progress.

Index

Student	Grade	Assignment
Rachel	2nd	Reaction to a story and a short story
Angela	3rd	Book reports
Mayling	4th	Two journal entries
Darrell	4th	Social studies essay
Adam	5th	An imaginary story
Brad	6th	A story
Pascal	7th	A short story
Maria	8th	Several journal entries

Student: Rachel
Grade: 2nd
Assignments: Reaction to a story, story about helping people

Rachel wrote the two assignments on the same day, and they are linked to each other by content (Figure 9.12). The first is a reaction to a story that was read aloud whereby the hero, Jeff, helped someone. For the second, Rachel was asked to write a story about a time that she helped someone.

Guided Questions

Handwriting

- Does Rachel form all the letters correctly?
- Is letter size consistent?
- Is the spacing between the letters and words consistent and correct?
- Comment upon Rachel's use of uppercase and lowercase letters.

Spelling

- Are high-frequency sight words spelled correctly?

Figure 9.12. Rachel's Reaction to a Story and a Short Story.

Translations: I liked the story because it was nice and it was what Jeff did.

Because my dad's chest was hurting him really bad and he told me to call people but I phoned my mom to be with us. My mom and dad were surprised.

- Does Rachel attempt to spell words as they sound?
- How well does Rachel associate letters with their sounds?
- What letter sounds are represented incorrectly and correctly in words?

Usage

- Are capital letters used correctly throughout the samples?
- Are periods used correctly?
- Does Rachel use conjunctions appropriately?
- Does she write in complete sentences?

Vocabulary

- Comment upon Rachel's vocabulary and suggest a possible reason for her choice of words.

Organization and Ideation

- Is the information presented in the samples elaborate or limited?
- Is the information easy to follow and well organized?
- What factors may be affecting Rachel's written expression?

Supplementary Analyses

- Discuss any additional concerns you may have.
- Is there a need for further analysis?

Instructional Programming

- What accommodations or modifications may Rachel need to succeed on classroom writing tasks?
- What specific instructional strategies may help Rachel improve her writing skill?
- Would Rachel benefit from progress-monitoring (such as CBM) in any area of writing?

Student: Angela
Grade: 3rd
Assignments: Book reports

Angela wrote two book reports. One was on the book *Never Snap at a Bubble* and the other was on *Mrs. Spider's Beautiful Web* (Figure 9.13).

Guided Questions

Handwriting and Appearance

- Is Angela's handwriting legible?
- Does she use uppercase letters correctly?
- Is her letter size consistent?

- Is the spacing between letters and words consistent?
- Does she reverse any letters? If so, which ones?

Spelling

- Does she spell common sight words correctly?
- Do most of the misspellings include the sounds in the words?
- From the types of misspellings, what conclusions can you draw regarding Angela's knowledge of sound-symbol correspondences?
- Why does Angela add the letter *u* to the end of certain words, such as "aroundu"? Why does she spell the word *by* as "biy"?
- Are her spelling difficulties related more to phonological or orthographic awareness? What errors make you think this?

Usage

- Does Angela use and indent paragraphs?
- Does she include a title and observe the right and left margins?
- Does she use uppercase letters and periods correctly?
- Does Angela use a variety of sentence patterns?
- Does she follow basic syntactic rules (such as subject-verb agreement, consistent verb tense)?
- Are her errors more related to usage or spelling?

Vocabulary

- Are the words Angela writes appropriate for her reports?

Organization and Ideation

- Does Angela seem well prepared to write about the topic?
- Does she follow the elements of basic story grammar when writing her reports?

Never Snap at a Bubble

Ther was a Littl frog
and a Mother and a Fother
and Mothen ahl Fother wor
eating and Littl frog was
etena the Bubble
Then Littl frog was stil
eating bubbles
Then Littl frog was fat
and hiy eat 4 bubbles
Win Littl frog eat the
bubbles hi flow away

Figure 9.13. Angela's Book Reports.

mrs. spider's
beautiful web
mrs.spider was going to
mack a web to cach a fly
first she mad the web to
the leru. so it can hod
The web then she mad
The lins so she cah web
arawndu The web
She Mad The lins
She web a aroundu
and a aroundu a Gena
now She is dun weth hor web
and she hisu ih The lefu
Then a fly past biy and
it in stuck then zhes wed in
brocin ahd she isint

Figure 9.13. Angela's Book Reports. *(Continued)*

- Are her ideas sequenced in a logical manner?
- Does she use cohesive ties? If so, give examples.

Supplementary Analyses

- Discuss any additional concerns you may have.
- Is there a need for further analysis?

Instructional Programming

- What accommodations or modifications may be needed to help Angela succeed on classroom writing tasks?
- Identify specific instructional goals that will help Angela improve her spelling skill.
- What would be your main instructional goals for usage?
- How would you teach Angela about sentence structure?
- Would Angela benefit from progress-monitoring (such as CBM) in any area of writing?

Student: Mayling
Grade: 4th
Assignment: Two journal entries

Mayling was asked to record a journal entry on a daily basis. Figure 9.14 presents two samples that were written on two consecutive days. No assistance was provided.

Guided Questions

Handwriting and Appearance

- Is Mayling's handwriting legible and easy to read?
- Are her paragraphs indented and the margins observed?

Spelling

- What types of words are spelled correctly?
- Are words spelled correctly consistently?

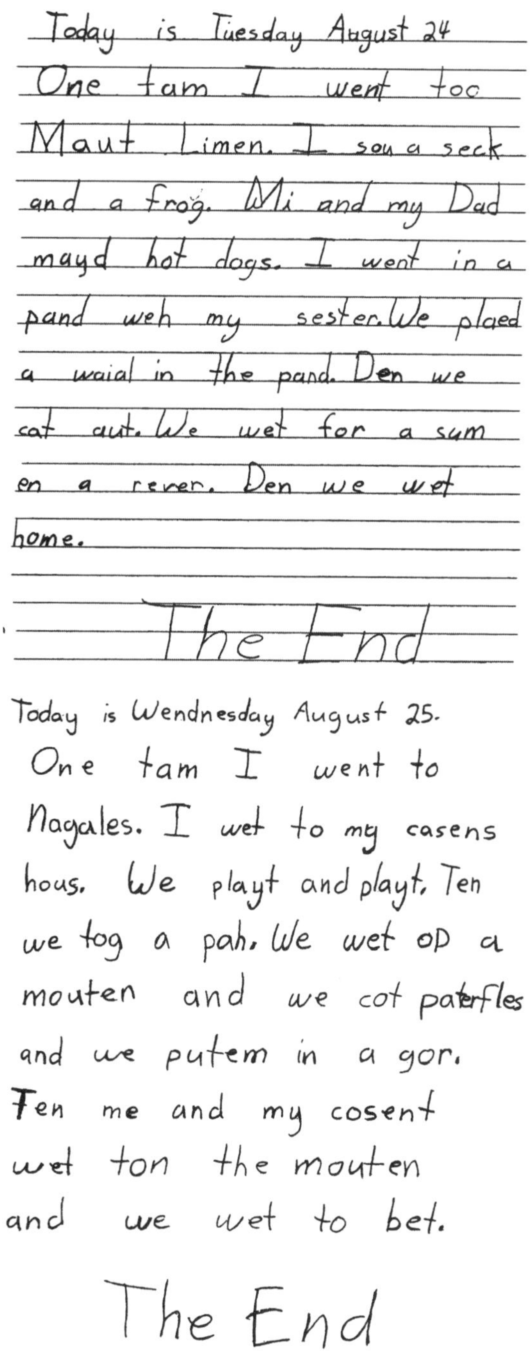
Today is Tuesday August 24
One tam I went too
Maut Limen. I sou a seck
and a frog. Mi and my Dad
mayd hot dogs. I went in a
pand weh my sester. We plaed
a waial in the pand. Den we
cat aut. We wet for a sum
en a rever. Den we wet
home.
The End

Today is Wendnesday August 25.
One tam I went to
Nogales. I wet to my casens
hous. We playt and playt. Ten
we tog a pah. We wet op a
mouten and we cot paterfles
and we putem in a gor.
Ten me and my cosent
wet ton the mouten
and we wet to bet.
The End

Figure 9.14. Mayling's Two Journal Entries.

Translations: One time I went to Mount Lemon. I saw a stick and a frog. Me and my dad made hot dogs. I went in a pond with my sister. We played a while in the pond. Then we got out. We went for a swim in a river. Then we went home.

One time I went to Nogales. I went to my cousin's house. We played and played. Then we took a path. We went up a mountain and we caught butterflies and we put them in a jar. Then me and my cousin went down the mountain and we went to bed.

- Consider Mayling's knowledge of sound-symbol correspondence. Which sounds does she seem to know well? Which sounds appear to cause confusion?

    List errors that she makes on vowel sounds.

    Find errors that she makes on voiced and unvoiced consonants.

    Find examples of where she omits nasal sounds before stop consonants.

    What consonant digraph does she confuse?

- Does she spell words the way they sound?
- Discuss Mayling's spellings of the past tense of verbs. Does she consistently add an -ed ending?

Usage

- Are uppercase letters and periods used correctly?
- What types of sentence constructions does Mayling use?
- Compare and contrast sentence structure between the two paragraphs.
- Discuss and compare the use of conjunctions in the two paragraphs.

Organization and Ideation

- Has Mayling developed her ideas fully?
- Do her journal entries follow a logical sequence?
- Does Mayling use cohesive ties?

Supplementary Analyses

- Discuss any additional concerns you may have.
- Is there a need for further analysis?

Instructional Programming

- What accommodations or modifications may be needed to help Mayling succeed on classroom writing tasks?

- How would you address Mayling's difficulties with certain speech sounds?
- How would you help Mayling write more descriptive sentences?
- What other specific instructional strategies may help Mayling improve her writing skill?
- Would Mayling benefit from progress-monitoring (such as CBM) in any area of writing?

Student: Darrell
Grade: 4th
Assignment: Social studies essay

After four weeks of learning about the solar system through books, videos, and experiments, Darrell was asked to write an essay about what he had learned from the unit (see Figure 9.15). When handing in his paper, Darrell commented to his teacher, "I know a lot more, but I just can't get it down on paper."

Guided Questions

Handwriting and Appearance

- Is Darrell's handwriting legible?
- Are all the letters formed correctly?
- Are any letter reversals apparent in the sample?
- Does he use uppercase letters correctly?
- Is letter size consistent?
- Is the spacing between letters and words consistent?
- Does Darrell observe word boundaries?

Spelling

- Are common sight words spelled correctly?
- Do most of the misspellings include the sounds in the words?
- From the types of misspellings, what conclusions can you draw regarding Darrell's knowledge of sound-symbol correspondences?

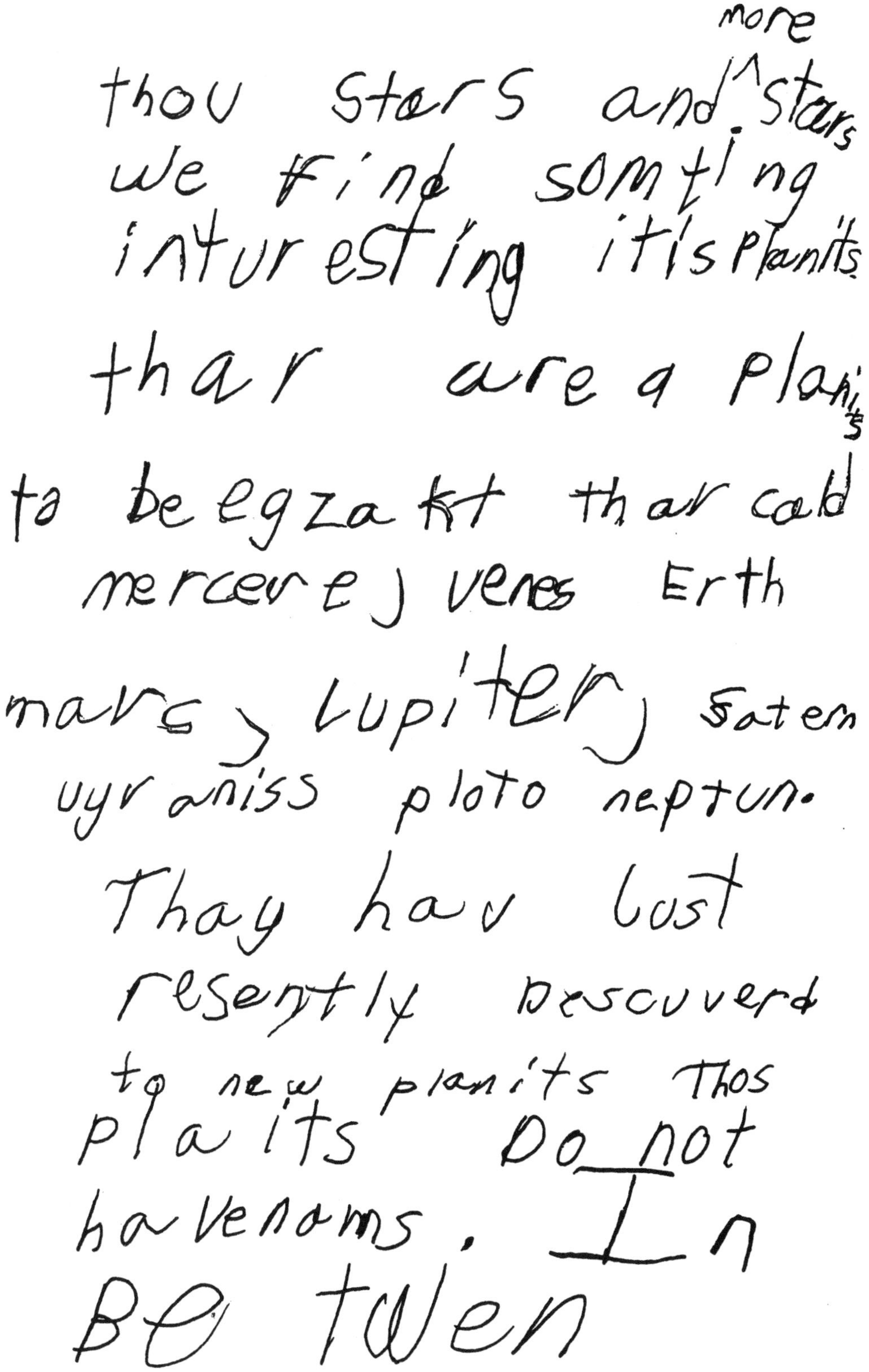

thou stars and ^more stars
we find somting
inturesting it is planits
thar are a planits
to be egzakt thar call
mercere) venes Erth
mars, Lupiter, Saten
uyraniss ploto neptun.
Thay hav last
resently Descuverd
to new planits Thos
plaits Do not
have noms. In
Be twen

Figure 9.15. Darrell's Social Studies Assignment.

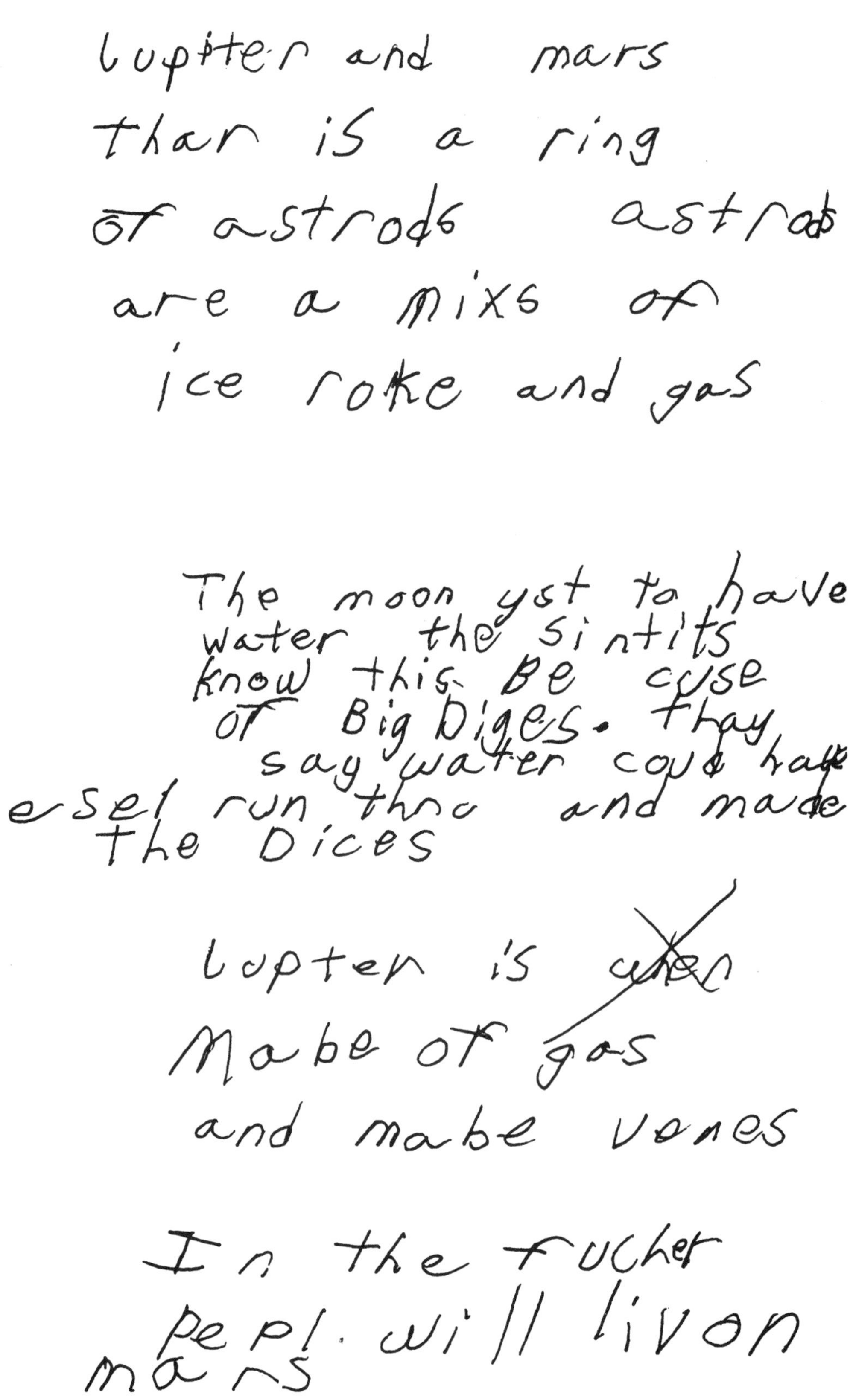

Jupiter and mars
than is a ring
of astrods astrods
are a mixs of
ice roke and gas

The moon yst to have
water the si ntits
know this. Be cuse
of Big Diges. thay
say water cou' hav
e sel run thro and made
the Dices

Jupter is ~~when~~
Mabe of gas
and mabe vanes

In the fucher
pepl. will liv on
mars

Figure 9.15. Darrell's Social Studies Assignment. *(Continued)*

- Are words spelled consistently, even if incorrectly?
- Does Darrell experience difficulties with the spelling of any homophones?
- Do you think his problems are more related to phonological or orthographic awareness? What were errors that made you think this?

Usage

- Are paragraphs used and indented?
- Does Darrell include a title and observe the right and left margins?
- Are uppercase letters and periods used correctly within sentences?
- Does Darrell use a variety of sentence patterns?
- Does he follow syntactic rules (such as subject-verb agreement, consistent verb tense)?
- Does he use commas correctly within sentences and lists?

Vocabulary

- Discuss Darrell's choice of words. Are words age- or grade-appropriate?

Organization and Ideation

- Does Darrell seem well prepared to write about the topic?
- What specific information has he learned from the unit?
- Are his ideas sequenced in a logical manner?
- Does Darrell expand upon and explain his ideas?

Supplementary Analyses

- Discuss any additional concerns you may have.
- Is there a need for further analysis?

Instructional Programming

- What accommodations or modifications may be needed to help Darrell succeed on classroom writing tasks?

- What kind of spelling program or materials would you use with Darrell?
- What specific instructional strategies may help Darrell improve his writing skill?
- Would Darrell benefit from progress-monitoring (such as CBM) in any area of writing?

Student: Adam
Grade: 5th
Assignment: An imaginary story

Adam was asked to write a story about wishes (Figure 9.16). Prior to writing, a class discussion had occurred with respect to the typical wishes of people. Members of the class were encouraged to think about their prospective story lines.

Guided Questions

Handwriting and Appearance

- Has a title been written?
- Does Adam use and indent paragraphs?
- Have the right and left margins been observed?
- Are all the letters formed correctly?
- Do Adam's letters have a consistent slant?

Spelling

- What types of spelling errors does Adam make?
- Are word boundaries observed correctly?
- Comment upon Adam's knowledge of sound-symbol correspondence.
- Does Adam have difficulty spelling any homonyms?

Usage

- Discuss Adam's use of periods and uppercase letters.
- Is the verb tense consistent and correct?

I found a little pebble it shined i brung it home every one kept telling me to through it away but i sill kept it later on i found out it was worth a lot of mony i was going to take it some where today but i wished it was worth millions of dollars. and the Pebble gave ne the mony i looked at it and i shold my mom and dad it, they said keep that rack wish on it a gain, this time wish for minllons of dollrrs. but i did not work it brung me to my room and it said to me and said i will not do it if you bring me aut there wish it in here ok. i wished it im my roon but we were wishing so much it said take me some where and sell me to day and i did, they said i'll give 1,000 dollers for that rock i thought about it and i said ok. but we were wish thow. The end

Figure 9.16. Adam's Imaginary Story.

- Analyze the different types of sentence structures that Adam used.
- Discuss Adam's use of dialogue.
- Does he use conjunctions correctly?

Vocabulary

- Has Adam chosen words that add to the story?
- Does Adam use many multisyllabic words in the assignment?

Organization and Ideation

- Does the story follow a logical order?
- Is the story easy to understand?
- Has Adam explained his ideas adequately?
- Are his ideas sufficient for telling the story?

Supplementary Analyses

- Discuss any additional concerns you may have.
- Is there a need for further analysis?

Instructional Programming

- What accommodations or modifications may Adam need to succeed on classroom writing tasks?
- How could you help Adam increase his written vocabulary?
- How could you help Adam write in complete sentences?
- How could you help Adam use varied sentence structures?
- What specific instructional strategies may help Adam improve his writing skill?
- Would Adam benefit from progress-monitoring (such as CBM) in any area of writing?

Student: Brad
Grade: 6th
Assignment: A story

Brad was asked to write a story on a topic of his choice. He did not engage in pre-writing activities. Although he was not asked to draw a picture, Brad spent more time drawing the picture than on writing the story (Figure 9.17).

Guided Questions

Handwriting and Appearance

- Are all the letters formed correctly?
- Has Brad mastered the use of uppercase and lowercase letters?
- Does Brad use consistent letter size?
- Is his slant consistent?

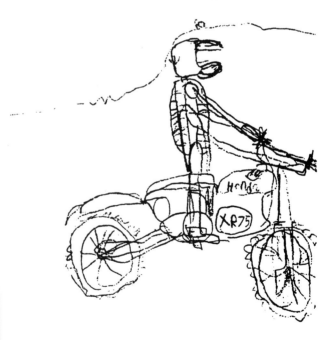

Figure 9.17. Brad's Motorcycle Story.

Translation: I like to ride my dirt bike. I have a Honda. It is the bestest. I like to do jumps. It is fun to jump. It feels good to jump and go fast.

- Is the spacing of letters within and between words appropriate?
- Does he observe left and right margins?

Spelling

- Does Brad spell high-frequency words correctly?
- Why do you think that he spelled the word *Honda* correctly?
- Does Brad omit sounds in his spellings? On what word does he omit a nasal sound?
- Does he spell words consistently, even if incorrectly?

Usage

- Does Brad use uppercase letters and periods correctly?
- What types of sentence structures does he use?
- What other errors do you see in usage?

Vocabulary

- Does Brad's choice of vocabulary promote reader interest?
- Why do you think he uses such simple words?

Organization and Ideation

- Does Brad fulfill the requirement of writing a story?
- Does he elaborate upon his ideas?
- Are his ideas sequenced logically?
- Does he use cohesive ties?
- Is there a difference between Brad's artistic ability and his writing skill?

Supplementary Analyses

- Discuss any additional concerns you may have.
- Is there a need for further analysis?

Instructional Programming

- What accommodations or modifications may Brad need to succeed on classroom writing tasks?
- What specific instructional strategies may help Brad improve his writing skill?
- What technology may help Brad?
- How would you monitor his progress?

Student: Pascal
Grade: 7th
Assignment: A short story

Pascal was asked to write a story for his English class and selected the topic of a murder investigation in a small town. Prior to writing, he discussed his ideas with his teacher and then a small group of peers. His final story was six pages long. The first several pages of the first draft are included for analysis (Figure 9.18).

Guided Questions

Handwriting and Appearance

- Does Pascal use and indent paragraphs?
- Are left and right margins observed?
- Discuss the formation and size of Pascal's letters.
- Is his slant consistent?
- Does Pascal use uppercase and lowercase letters correctly?
- Does he reverse any letters? If so, which ones?

Spelling

- Does Pascal spell most high-frequency words correctly?
- To what degree does Pascal rely on spelling words the way they sound?
- Do most of the words he spells have good sound-symbol correspondence?

- Does Pascal spell the same words consistently (for example, *people*)?
- What spellings suggest that Pascal has a weakness in orthography?
- What does Pascal know about spelling?
- Are there any transpositions, such as writing *was* for *saw*, evidenced in the sample?
- What phonological errors are apparent in the sample?
- What morphological errors are apparent in the sample?
- Does Pascal add or omit certain letters?
- Does he spell homophones correctly?

Usage

- Are uppercase letters used correctly?
- Are periods and question marks used consistently and correctly?
- Are articles used correctly?
- Does Pascal maintain consistency in verb tense?

Vocabulary

- Is Pascal's vocabulary appropriate for a narrative about a murder investigation?
- Do his spelling difficulties appear to inhibit his word choice?

Organization and Ideation

- Are the ideas well sequenced?
- Have all the ideas been clearly described and clarified?
- How has Pascal attempted to build suspense?

Supplementary Analyses

- Discuss any additional concerns you may have.
- Is there a need for further analysis?

Instructional Programming

- What accommodations or modifications may Pascal need to succeed on classroom writing tasks?
- What technologies may help Pascal improve his writing?
- What specific instructional strategies may help Pascal improve his writing skill?
- Would Pascal benefit from progress-monitoring (such as CBM) in any area of writing?

the baker kids

Ons Long ago ther were there
sHildrin thay casd Lotss
of trobool. thay Livd chose
to a old abanda hows
pepol shay thay se the

Figure 9.18. Pascal's Story for English Class.

Lits fliorig on and off.
pepol say it is the bakerkids
triy to skar the viligers
but wun mong thay wer misig
evry one loot foor them
Thay wer no were in site
ther was only one pase
thay did not look at toe
abadid hows on the hill
so the sheref went to the
hose wic he got ther he clamd
he soll the baker kids on the
floor ded so the hserif poot
owt a in westagashin that
moorng. the were no sadspees
pepol shay ther gostod by
an old man living thef
but he past away regentley
he was a stegy old man that
dint like to be botherd

   no wan liked him
but pepol shay thay se Him
in the fori. some times
with a shavol some pepol
think it was the sharif

Figure 9.18. Pascal's Story for English Class. (*Continued*)

win he wint up ther yesterday, evry one wos skard that ther was a killer on the loos that mornoning thay tok them to the morther tha morthichin clumd he fown boolit wons in ech of the kids. tha ~~next morning~~ the Acxds day the kids wer missing and the morthin was ded that niht a person sed he sell the old man with a shuvol and a gurdic bad walking in the forist pepole think ther are twins every onz gatherd tere wepens that moorning win thay got to the cadin the old man walkied owt boolits rang owt cry were

wen pepole retherd to there homs thay had a sledbashins for hoo thay that was the murder tow bays later a nother merder acherd. pepe were so skard

Figure 9.18. Pascal's Story for English Class. (*Continued*)

that thay Left oßown
pepol wer fcd opopcpol
we starting to think ther
was a gost in the town
nothing Like this has haping
cant so mouth ~~good~~ hapin
to an smoll comudity
werz efry one nose
evry one for one holl
whek every theig was
fineintell a nother merder
ocurd pcpoll started to
Loke there howssls up
wach thay have never
done befor

Figure 9.18. Pascal's Story for English Class. (*Continued*)

Translation: Once long ago there were three children. They caused lots of trouble. They lived close to a old abandoned house. People say they see the lights flickering on and off. People say it is the Baker kids trying to scare the villagers. But one morning they were missing. Everyone looked for them. They were nowhere in sight. There was only one place they did not look. At the abandoned house on the hill. So the sheriff went to the house. When he got there he claimed he saw the Baker kids on the floor dead. So the sheriff put out an investigation that morning. There were no suspects. People say there used to be an old man living there but he passed away recently. He was a stingy old man that didn't like to be bothered. No one liked him. But people say they see him in the forest sometimes with a shovel. Some people think it was the sheriff when he went up there yesterday. Everyone was scared that there was a killer on the loose. That morning they took them to the mortician. The mortician claimed he found bullets once in each of the kids. The next morning the next day the kids were missing and the mortician was dead. That night a person said he saw the old man with a shovel and a garbage bag walking in the forest. People think there are twins. Everyone gathered their weapons. That morning when they got to the cabin the old man walked out. Bullets rang out. Cries were. When people returned to their homes they had a celebration for who they that was the murderer. Two days later another murder occurred. People were so scared that they left town. People were fed up. People were starting to think there was a ghost in the town. Nothing like this has happened. Can't so much happen to a small community where everyone knows everyone? For one whole week everything was fine until another murder occurred. People started to lock their houses up which they have never done before.

Student: Maria
Grade: 8th
Assignments: Entries from her journal

Several excerpts were taken from Maria's journal from her Writing and Literature class (Figure 9.19), a few of which were presented in Chapter Three. You can sense how Maria is feeling about school and her school performance.

Guided Questions

Handwriting and Appearance

- Is Maria's handwriting adequate for journal entries?

Spelling

- What types of misspellings are evident in Maria's writing?
- Can you recognize the misspellings in context? Why or why not?
- Does Maria sequence sounds correctly in multisyllabic words?

Usage

- Does Maria use periods and uppercase letters correctly?
- Does she vary her sentence structures?
- Is Maria's writing style appropriate for the task?

Vocabulary

- Does her word choice seem adequate for journal entries?

Ideation

- Given that these journal entries were written over the semester from the earliest to latest entry, discuss changes in Maria's attitude toward writing, as well as her self-esteem.
- Do you think that Maria is motivated to write?
- Why do you think Maria chooses to write about her feelings?

Supplementary Analyses

- Discuss any additional concerns you may have.
- Is there a need for further analysis?

Instructional Programming

- What accommodations or modifications may be needed to help Maria succeed with classroom writing tasks?
- Do you think Maria could benefit from using a spell checker? Why or why not?
- What specific instructional strategies may help Maria improve her writing skill?
- Would Maria benefit from progress-monitoring (such as CBM) in any area of writing?

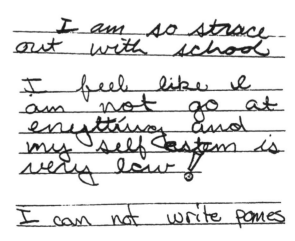

Figure 9.19. Maria's Journal Entries.

I mean it
it so hard for me. I wish
I could write pomes a lot
better. I gess I just have
to try more, but I just
have no time!

I learn best when I see
it and go over it all of
times not just one and then
have a quiz or test. And I
have to study!

My New Year's Resolution
is to start reading
abt and get better at
reading and spelling.

I am woried about W.+L.
becuse there is alot to do
and it sonds hard. I
want to do good.

I know more, but I
don't have time to wright
a whol essy.

I am really worded about
the reading contract
because I don't think I can
read all these pages and
boks. But I will do whet I
am do and I gess that is the best I can

I wrot poems is S.S.
today and I am
very happy with my
self want to hear them
Well I gess you really
dont have an anpam.

I am reamly proud I did it all on
my one.

Figure 9.19. Maria's Journal Entries. _(Continued)_

INDEPENDENT PRACTICE SAMPLES

Now that you have reviewed completed examples and have been guided through additional examples, you can practice several samples independently. You might first want to score the sample using CBM procedures for correct word sequences. When reviewing the five samples that follow, attempt to incorporate similar questions and recommendations as presented previously in the completed and guided examples. If you prefer, you can write and answer a series of your own questions.

Two sets of samples are provided for Charlie, several from fourth grade and a longer one from sixth grade. During the two years between samples, Charlie received intensive, individualized instruction from a learning disabilities specialist. Although significant progress can be seen, his difficulties with spelling are still apparent, as is the enduring nature of a learning disability.

Index

Student	Grade	Assignment
Omar	2nd	Description of a field trip
Charlie	4th	Two book reviews, a descriptive paragraph, a journal entry
	6th	An imaginary story
Shanika	5th	A descriptive paragraph
Karen	7th	A journal entry and a descriptive paragraph
Andrew	10th	An opinion paper and class notes

Student: Omar
Grade: 2nd
Assignment: Description of a field trip.

Following a field trip to a library and museum, the students in Omar's class were asked to write about their experiences. Prior to writing, an in-depth class discussion occurred. The title "My Field Trip" and the words *library* and *museum* were written on the chalkboard. Figure 9.20 presents Omar's description of the field trip.

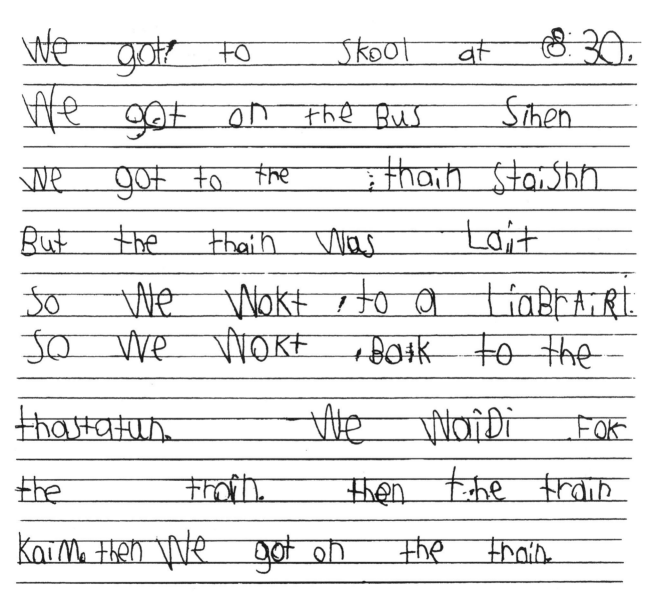

Figure 9.20. Omar's Description of a Field Trip.

Translation: We got to school at 8:30. We got on the bus. Then we got to the train station. But the train was late so we walked to a library. So we walked back to the train station. We waited for the train. Then the train came. Then we got on the train.

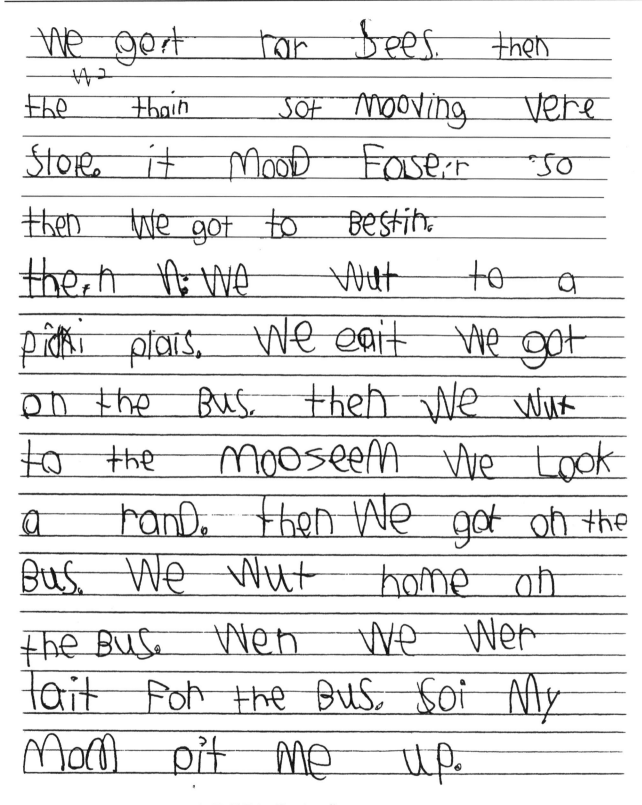

We got rar Sees. then
the thain sot Mooving vere
store. it MooD Foser so
then We got to Bestih.
then if We Wut to a
pidki plais. We eait We got
on the Bus. then We Wut
to the Mooseen We Look
a rand. then We got oh the
Bus. We Wut home oh
the Bus. Wen We Wer
lait Foh the Bus. Soi My
Mom pit Me Up.

Figure 9.20. Omar's Description of a Field Trip. *(Continued)*

Translation: We got our seats. Then the train start moving very slowly. It moved faster. So then we got to . . . Then we went to a picnic place. We ate. We got on the bus. Then we went to the museum. We look around. Then we got on the bus. We went home on the bus. When we were late for the bus so my mom picked me up.

Student: Charlie
Grade: 4th
Assignment: Two book reviews, a descriptive paragraph, and a journal entry

Charlie was encouraged to write as much as he could for all four assignments (Figure 9.21). The first and last were book reviews, the titles of which provide information with regard to Charlie's reading level. For the second assignment, the descriptive paragraph, the word *rattlesnake* was written for Charlie to copy. The third assignment, the journal entry, was the longest piece of writing produced by Charlie that year.

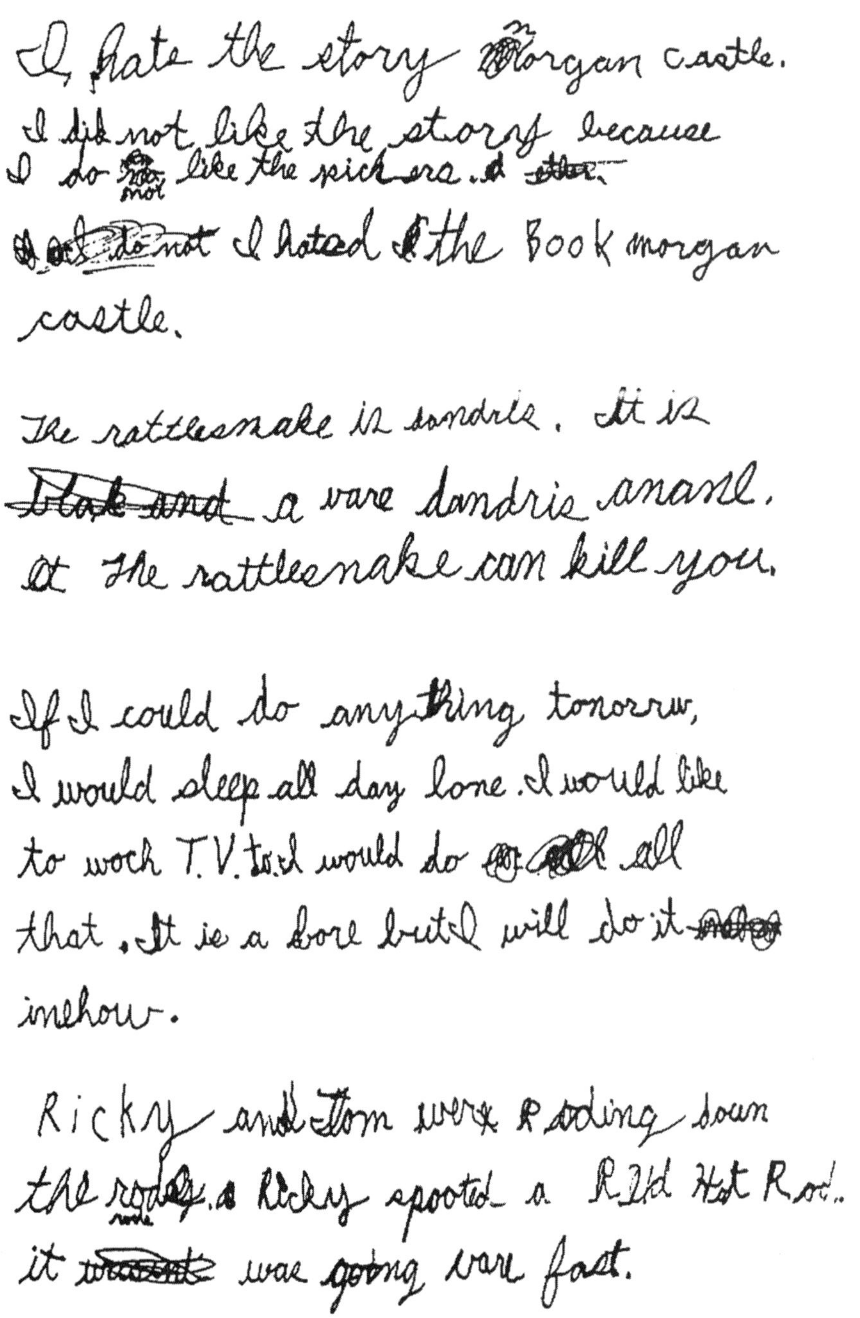

I hate the story Morgan castle.
I did not like the story because
I do not like the pichsra.
I hated the Book morgan
castle.

The rattlesnake is sondrie. It is
a vare dandrie anasl.
The rattlesnake can kill you.

If I could do anything tonorrw,
I would sleep all day lone. I would like
to woch T.V. to. I would do all
that. It is a bore but I will do it
inehow.

Ricky and Tom were riding down
the road. Ricky spotted a Red Hot Rod.
it was going vare fast.

Figure 9.21. Charlie's Four Assignments.

Student: Charlie
Grade: 6th
Assignment: An imaginery story

Charlie was asked to write a story on a topic of his choice. After choosing "The Invasion" as the title of his story, Charlie proceeded to write an unexpected story line (Figure 9.22). Prior to writing, he spent a number of minutes thinking about his content and jotted down some notes to help with organization.

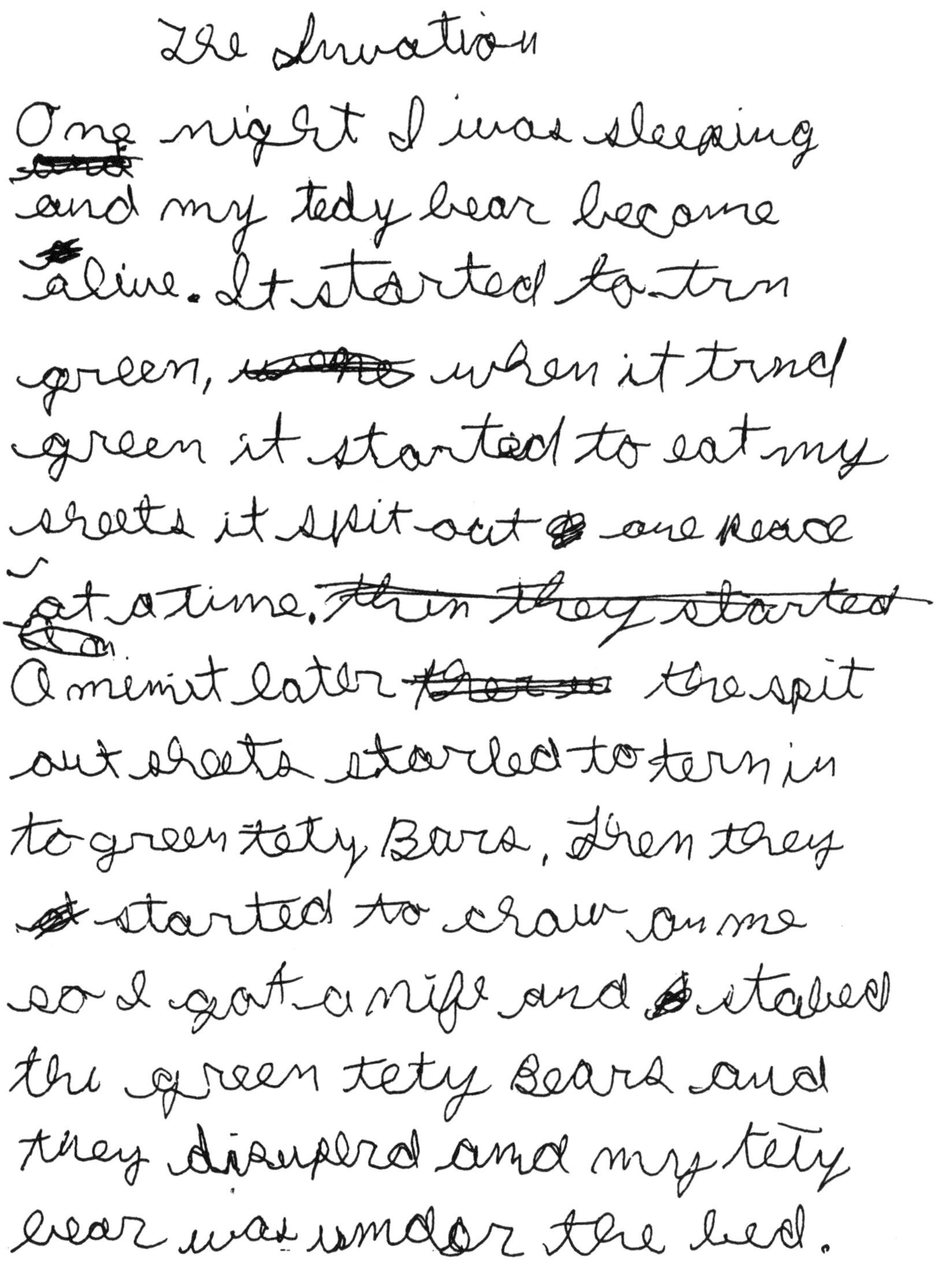

The Invation

One night I was sleeping and my tedy bear become alive. It started to trn green, when it trnd green it started to eat my sheets it spit out one peace at a time. ~~thin they started~~ A menit later the spit out sheets started to tern in to green tety Bars, Then they started to craw on me so I got a nife and stabed the green tety Bears and they disaperd and my tety bear was under the bed.

Figure 9.22. Charlie's Imaginary Story.

Student: Shanika
Grade: 5th
Assignments: A descriptive paragraph

Shanika was asked to write about her summer vacation. Prior to writing, she was encouraged to draw a semantic map or web to help with organization. After thinking for only a short time, Shanika wrote her assignment in less than ten minutes (Figure 9.23).

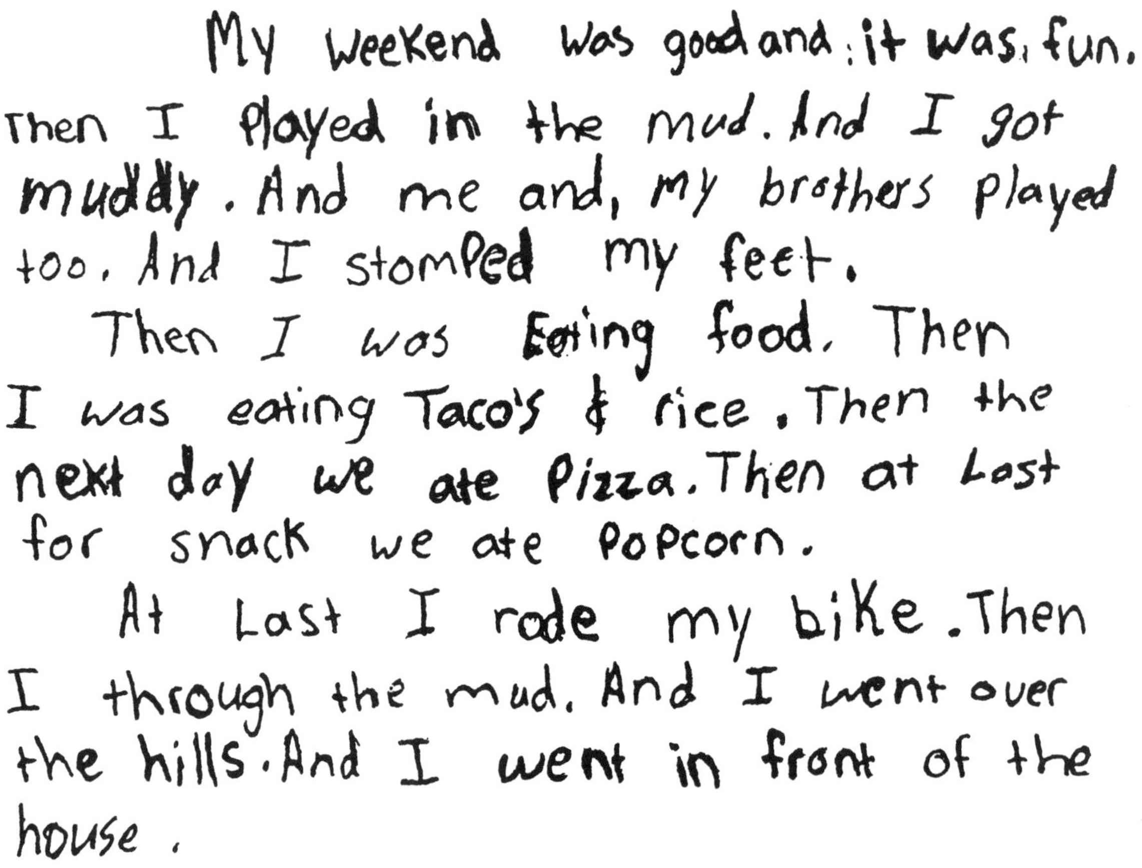

My weekend was good and it was fun. Then I played in the mud. And I got muddy. And me and, my brothers played too. And I stomped my feet.

Then I was Eating food. Then I was eating Taco's & rice. Then the next day we ate Pizza. Then at Last for snack we ate Popcorn.

At Last I rode my bike. Then I through the mud. And I went over the hills. And I went in front of the house.

Figure 9.23. Shanika's Paragraph.

Student: Karen
Grade: 7th
Assignments: A journal entry and a descriptive paragraph

The first sample, titled "Kites," was an entry from Karen's journal. The second sample, titled "Esther Island," was written on a topic chosen by Karen and is a final draft. On this assignment, Karen received help from a peer reviewer during the editing stage. Analyze both passages for content and form (Figure 9.24).

Kits

> One day me and my step father wemnt out to fly are Kits. My Kit is the same size as his but mine is a different color than his. For Christmas I got lights for my Kit.
> When I fly my Kit I half to look up and I get a stif neck. Some times I get pulled away from were I was starding.

Esther Island

> Esther Island has the second largest fish hatchery in the world. They raise salmons such as kings, silvers, dogs, and pinks. Esther does not raise red salmons. Esther gets it's power from the lake and Emergese generators. There are about twenty Eight people in the winter. and about one hundred people in the summer.
> At Esther Island I go to corespondence with my parents. I study by my self and my teacher corects and grads it all. But my parents are kind of my teachers.

Figure 9.24. Karen's Journal Entry and Descriptive Paragraph.

Student: Andrew
Grade: 10th
Assignments: An opinion paper and class notes

Andrew was asked to write an opinion paper for his Biology class about his reaction

to his lab experience of dissecting a pig. In addition, his class notes for the lecture that day are provided. What information can you learn about Andrew's writing skill by analyzing these brief assignments shown in Figure 9.25?

I think it was epecationl but very boring. I is hard to consentrat with that smell to, I did not like the lab and I had alredy lurned what was in it. Next year I siggjest you get some lisal.

Respiration

1) book lungs - stacked tissw
   Spiders

2) gills brething in whater
   crostation

3) trakel tubs

Circulation

1) dorsal heart - tube
2) Open air sistem few siters
   and vans

Excretion
1) solid whast - mouth → eofages - stomeh - intesten - anus
2) liquid whast; eses whater mineges nitrogen

Figure 9.25. Andrew's Opinion Response and His Class Notes.

CONCLUSION

An in-depth analysis of writing samples can provide invaluable information for programmatic decisions and instructional design. You can gather much information from one sample, providing that the sample is an accurate representation of the individual's ability. You must, however, examine a number of samples to ensure that the errors form a typical pattern.

One single, correct method or strategy for teaching writing does not exist. You must tailor the approach to meet the specific needs of the individual. The only criterion to be considered in choosing a particular approach is that the method is effective for the student. The strategies suggested in the analyses are considered methods that may work. Other techniques could be equally effective. Preference, familiarity, or convenience may lead you to choose a different approach from the ones we have presented. Over four decades ago, Otto and McMenemy (1966) stated, "The point here is that in remedial teaching there is no such thing as a universally good method. A method that works well with Clyde may have little value with Cynthia; its goodness or badness can be judged only in relation to its success or failure when used by a particular teacher with a particular pupil under particular conditions. Perhaps the only factor that should remain constant in remedial teaching is the positive, enthusiastic approach that characterizes successful teachers, whether they operate as remedial specialists or as regular classroom teachers" (p. 141). This is still true today.

Writing as Communication

*All authentic writing comes from an individ-
ual; but a final judgment of it will depend
not on how much individuality it contains,
but how much of common humanity.*
                              —John Peale Bishop

*"I quite agree with you," said the Duchess:
"and the moral is—'be what you would seem
to be' or if you'd like it put more simply—
'Never imagine yourself not to be otherwise
than what it might appear to others that
what you were or might have been was not
otherwise than what you had been would
have appeared to them to be otherwise.'" "I
think I should understand that better," Alice
said very politely, "if I had it written down;
but I can't quite follow it as you say it."*
                  —From *Alice's Adventures in Wonderland*

Writing is often our most precise and effective
method of self-expression and communication.
As noted by Alice, oral language can be difficult
to comprehend because it is fleeting, particularly
when the message, such as the one delivered
by the Duchess, is not expressed very clearly.
In contrast, written language is a permanent
record that may be studied, reread, interpreted,
shared, and discussed.

FACTORS AFFECTING WRITING

As we described in Chapter Three, writing is a
way to expand both our oral language and our
thinking abilities. For some students their oral
language and thinking abilities are much higher
than their written language abilities, whereas
for other students weaknesses exist in both
routes of communication.

The Impact of Oral Language

By high school, many students can write
nearly as well as they speak. As we have noted
throughout this book, students with learning
disabilities, however, often have better oral than
written language abilities. Melissa's sentence
in Figure 10.1 reminds us that she loves writing, but she hates spelling. Melissa has good
oral language abilities but has not yet mastered
phoneme-grapheme relationships. Hopefully, her
teachers will provide a supportive environment
that allows Melissa to continue to express her
ideas in writing or through other means and not
penalize her for spelling. In addition, she needs
explicit instruction in spelling.

Students who cannot write or whose
handwriting or spelling is so poor that their
writing is impossible to read are deprived of
a major means of communication and expression. Figure 10.2 depicts a part of a story about
Halloween by Elinor, a sixth-grade student.

Figure 10.1. Melissa's Sentence About Spelling.

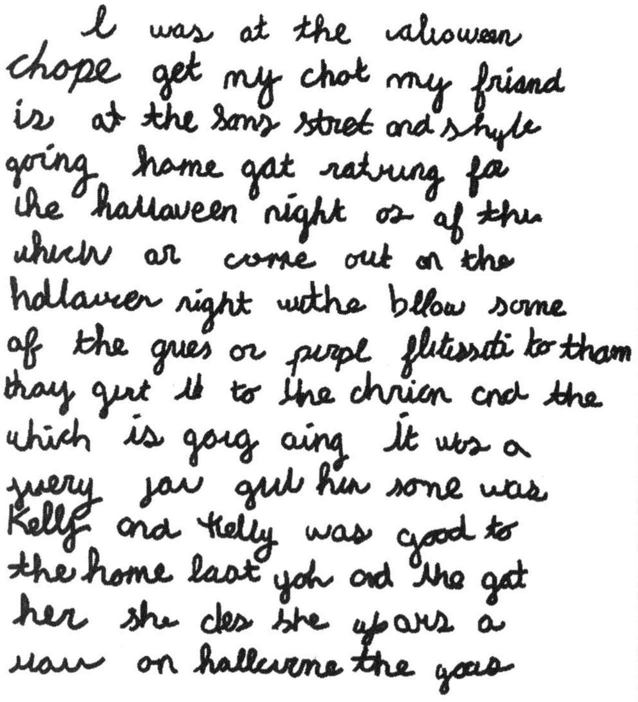
I was at the alhowean
chope get my chot my friand
is at the sons stret and shyle
going home gat ratrung fa
the halloveen night os af thu
which ar come out on the
hdllaveen night withe bllow some
of the gues or purpl flitssti to tham
thay gut it to the chrien and the
which is gorg aing it wos a
jvery jay gril her sone was
Kelly and kelly was good to
the home last yoh ord the gat
her she des she upars a
uaw on hallevrne the gaes

Figure 10.2. A Part of Elinor's Paper.

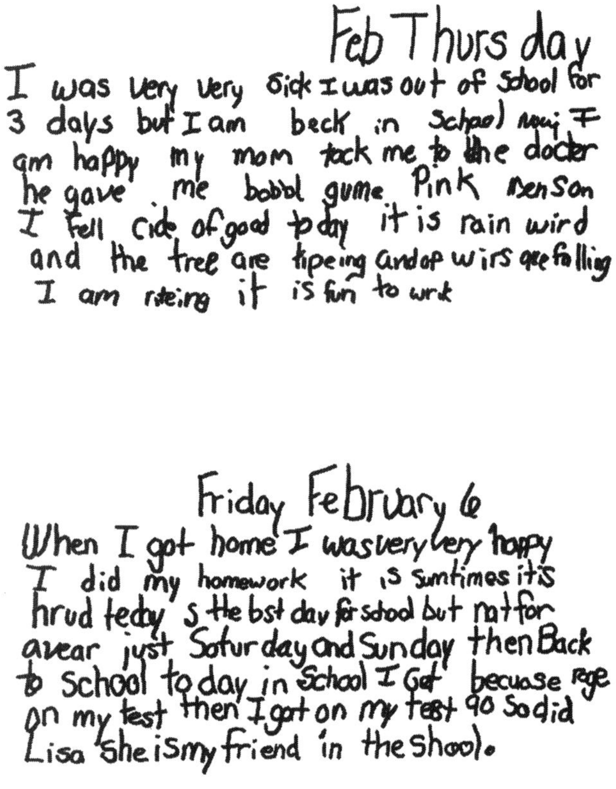
Feb Thursday
I was very very Sick I was out of School for
3 days but I am beck in School now I
am happy my mom tack me to the docter
he gave me bobbl gume Pink nenSon
I fell cide of good today it is rain wird
and the tree are tipeing and of wirs are folling
I am riteing it is fun to wrk

Friday February 6
When I got home I was very very happy
I did my homework it is Somtimes it's
hrud tedy s the bst dav for school but not for
avear just Soturday and Sunday then Back
to School today in School I Got because page
on my test then I got on my test 90 So did
Lisa She is my friend in the Shool.

Figure 10.3. Katy's Journal Entries.

Elinor writes a lot but her spelling is so poor that it is nearly impossible to decipher the content. Hopefully, in the following months, her teacher will help her learn how to sequence phonemes with the correct graphemes so people can read her writing.

In contrast to students with learning disabilities, students with language impairments and students who are just learning to speak English have weaknesses in both oral and written expression. Oftentimes their spoken and written language contain similar types of errors. Figure 10.3 illustrates two journal entries by Katy, a fifth-grade student. Katy has difficulty with syntax, as well as cohesion. These types of errors occur in both her spoken and written language. Katy's writing reflects both her thinking and language abilities. Instruction needs to focus on improving both oral and written language.

Some middle school students still have tremendous difficulty expressing their ideas in writing because of weaknesses in thinking with language. Figure 10.4 depicts a writing sample from Rosa, a seventh-grade student. Rosa was asked to write a story using her spelling words. She was then supposed to underline her spelling words in the story. You can see from this example that although Rosa attempted to complete the task, her thoughts are not cohesive. By the end of the story, it seems that she just got tired and decided to write in all of the remaining words, including some that were not in the list (such as "wersht").When we think of the concept of Vygotsky's zone of proximal development, it is clear that Rosa will require significant adjustments in classroom expectations and assignments in all of her middle school classes. Both lessons and assignments will need to be concrete.

We also must ensure that our writing assignments are meaningful to students. Arnold, a fifth-grade student, was asked to write a story using a list of compound words. His story is presented in Figure 10.5. Although Arnold has used all of the words in the list, we can see that he doesn't seem to understand the meanings of

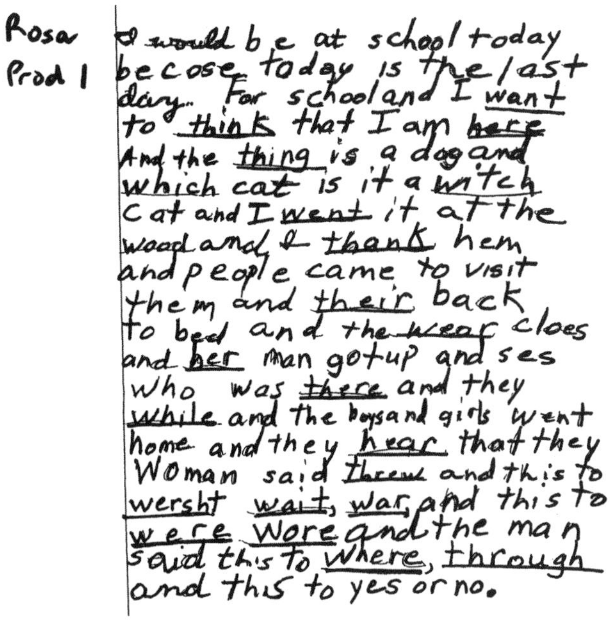

Rosa
Prod I

I would be at school today
becose today is the last
day. For school and I want
to think that I am here
And the thing is a dog and
which cat is it a witch
Cat and I went it at the
wood and I thank hem
and people came to visit
them and their back
to bed and the wear cloes
and her man got up and ses
who was there and they
while and the boys and girls went
home and they hear that they
WOman said threw and this to
wersht wait, war, and this to
were Wore and the man
said this to Where, through
and this to yes or no.

Figure 10.4. Rosa's Story with Her Spelling Words.

several of the words (for example, in comes a "toothbrush newcomer") or that he just wants to complete the task as quickly as possible. Although one wants students to be able to use compound words, having to write a story with a list of such words, or having to write a story with all of your spelling words, places too much restriction on content and results in papers with little meaning.

When teaching structured writing, such as how to include cohesive ties or how to write different types of expository structures, make sure that the students have developed and can express their ideas clearly before using scaffolded supports such as paragraph frames. The goal is to help students develop their oral language, so that they can express their thoughts more clearly in writing.

Figure 10.6 illustrates the writing of Delia, an eighth-grade student. Her assignment was to write an opinion essay about whether or not people should wear seat belts when driving their cars. Although Delia's first language is Spanish, she has been in English-speaking classrooms since the third grade. Clearly, Delia understands the appropriate use of cohesive ties for this type of text structure, but it is also clear that she has

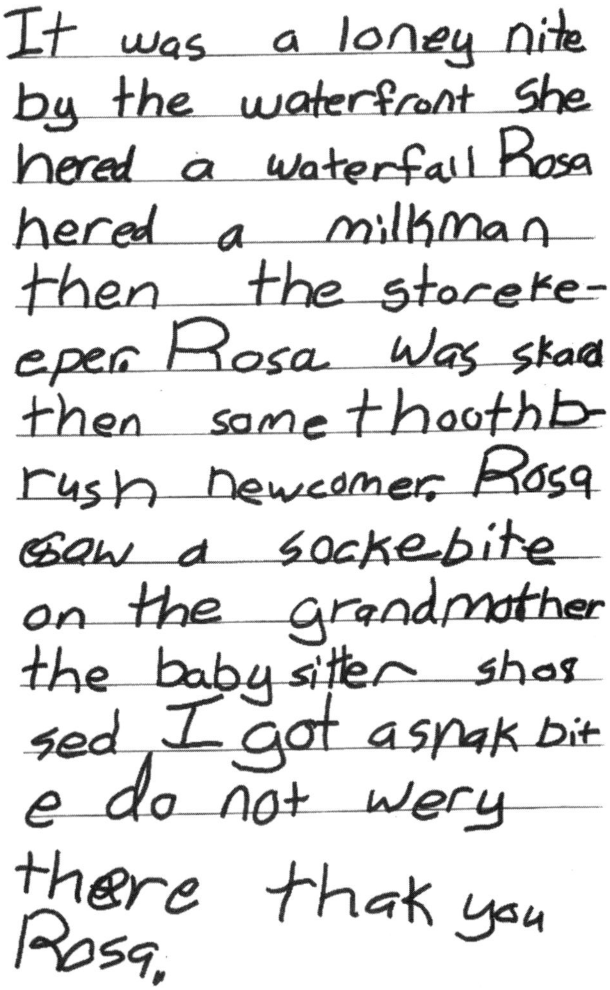

It was a loney nite
by the waterfront She
hered a waterfall Rosa
hered a milkman
then the storeke-
eper Rosa was skad
then some thoothb-
rush newcomer. Rosa
saw a sockebite
on the grandmother
the baby siter shos
sed I got a snak bit
e do not wery
there thak you
Rosa,

Figure 10.5. Arnold's Story Using Compound Words.

difficulty with English syntax. When we think about writing as the vehicle for communication, students such as Delia have extra challenges because English is not their first language. These students need our support and positive comments to keep improving their skills as writers.

The Impact of Thinking on the Quality of Writing

Because one can reflect when writing, writing is often far more elegant and precise than spoken language. Thus writing allows students to capture creative insights and transform them into print. Figure 10.7 presents a

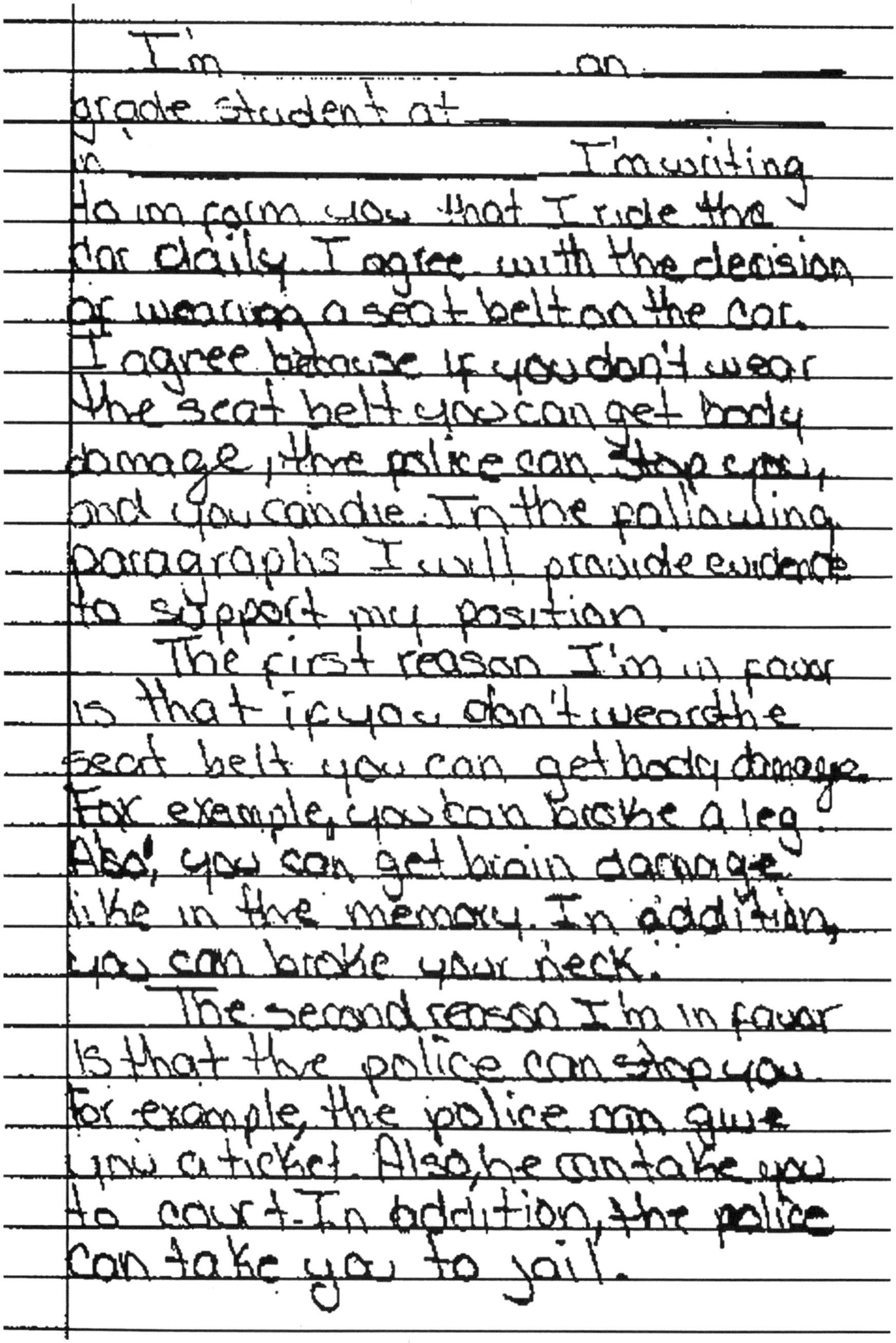

I'm an ___ grade student at ___ I'm writing to inform you that I ride the car daily. I agree with the decision of wearing a seat belt on the car. I agree because if you don't wear the seat belt you can get body damage, the police can stop car, and you can die. In the following paragraphs I will provide evidence to support my position.

The first reason I'm in favor is that if you don't wear the seat belt you can get body damage. For example, you can broke a leg. Also, you can get brain damage like in the memory. In addition, you can broke your neck.

The second reason I'm in favor is that the police can stop you. For example, the police can give you a ticket. Also, he can take you to court. In addition, the police can take you to jail.

Figure 10.6. Delia's Essay on Seatbelts.

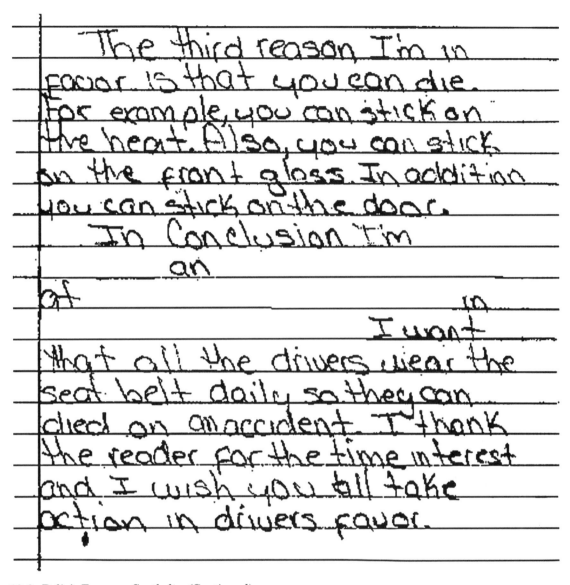

Figure 10.6. Delia's Essay on Seatbelts. *(Continued)*

Figure 10.7. Ramon's Haiku.

Translation: A cardinal flies its way around the wilderness It goes deep in it.

Source: Figure provided by Dr. Noel Gregg.

haiku written by Ramon, a gifted fifth-grade student with a severe writing disability. While it is virtually impossible to decipher Ramon's handwriting, we can see that his writing shows creativity. Clearly Ramon needs to use a computer for writing.

As another example, Figure 10.8 presents the first draft of a poem written by Jennifer, a fourth-grade student. Although Jennifer has difficulty with both spelling and handwriting, she has creative ideas to express.

Figure 10.9 presents the first draft of a story by Nathan, a high school student. The language

The moom the eternal Light in the Dark nice fore strols and walks in the park tenderly touchidg the clouds

Figure 10.8. Jennifer's Poem About the Moon.

Translation: The moon the eternal light in the dark Nice for strolls and walks in the park tenderly touching the clouds.

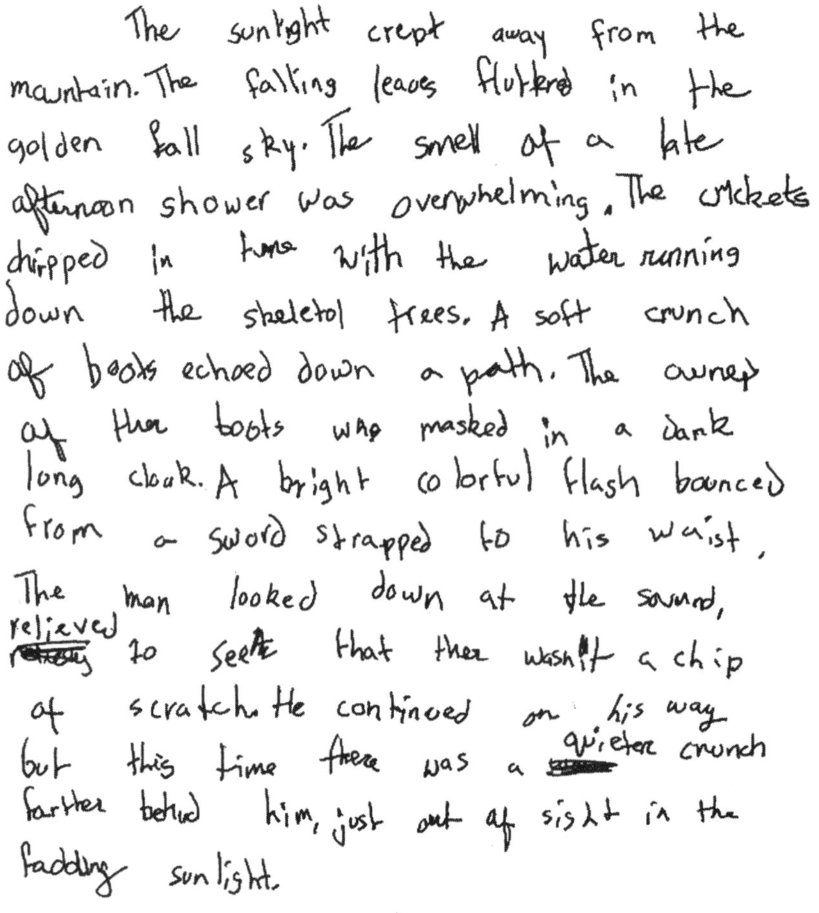

The sunlight crept away from the mountain. The falling leaves fluttered in the golden fall sky. The smell of a late afternoon shower was overwhelming. The crickets chirpped in tune with the water running down the skeletol trees. A soft crunch of boots echoed down a path. The owner of the boots who masked in a dark long cloak. A bright colorful flash bounced from a sword strapped to his waist. The man looked down at the sound, relieved to see that ther wasn't a chip of scratch. He continued on his way but this time there was a quieter crunch farther behind him, just out of sight in the fadding sunlight.

Figure 10.9. Nathan's Essay.

is alive and encourages the reader to develop visual images. These three students all have creative ideas. Through writing, they are able to capture and convey their experiences and thoughts in unique ways.

HEARING THE WRITER'S VOICE

Unlike other subject areas that require students to read the same assignment, or get the same answer, writing is individual. The result needs to be unique to the person. Just as we all have our own personalities, we each have our own "voice" when writing. When we write, the words we put on paper "sound" a certain way to the reader. How our words "sound" is called our voice. Our voice is communicated by the words we use, the tone we take, and the pattern of sentences. Our writing can be informal and friendly, or formal and distant. We can be chatty, flowery, or straight to the point. Not everything we write is written in the same voice. We adjust our voice and tone to match the purpose of the writing and the needs of the audience who will read our writing.

Students "hear" the teacher's voice in the feedback they receive on writing tasks. Students need to receive positive comments and feedback on their writing, not just identification of errors that were made. As we noted in Chapter One, remember to proceed gently with no red marks. Your voice, expressed through written feedback, communicates to students how you are responding to their ideas. Avoid writing rhetorical questions, such as, Did you try using a dictionary? or Did you even try on this assignment? Figure 10.10 presents two comments from different teachers. The first comment is from a sixth-grade teacher to a student who is having trouble following directions in class because of language and attentional difficulties. By telling the student that she might try listening, the teacher is placing the blame on the student. Instead, the teacher might have used this opportunity to set up a system that ensures

the student will understand the directions in the future. In the next comment, another teacher asks a student if he studied and then says he's capable of much more. Keep in mind that Dan, a third-grade student with labored handwriting, may not be capable of doing much better on this assignment. Again, this teacher is not showing awareness of the individual student. Writing provides observable information about a student's present skill level, as well as his or her strengths and weaknesses. Use that information to guide instructional planning.

If a student does not write much, try to figure out why this has occurred. Was the assignment too difficult? Did the student understand the topic? Did the student lack background knowledge? Was the student not interested in the topic? Was enough time provided? Were his or her ideas well developed before starting? Maybe the student was just not feeling well, or was distracted by other personal or environmental factors. In most instances, students are performing as well as they can given the interactions among their own unique personalities and temperaments, the characteristics of the classroom environment, and the amount of family support.

Nico, a fourth-grade student, had been diagnosed with Attention Deficit Hyperactivity Disorder (ADHD). Many times during the day his teacher would remind him to "Sit still," "Pay attention," or "Concentrate." One afternoon, Nico placed the note presented in Figure 10.11 on his teacher's desk. Nico wants to be able to concentrate, but it is just too difficult for him to do so.

We also must find the right balance for the number of corrections and the amount of feedback we include on papers. Figure 10.12 illustrates the first draft of a letter that Jimmy, a high school student in a special education residential school, was sending to a friend. Clearly, Jimmy has numerous spelling mistakes, but when one looks at the teacher's suggestions for edits, it seems that Jimmy's entire letter has been crossed out. In Jimmy's case, it would have been better if he had written his first draft

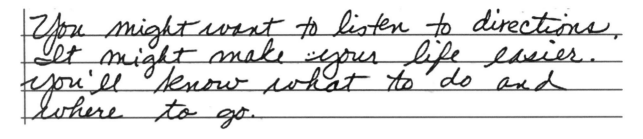

Figure 10.10. Teachers' Comments on Students' Papers.

on a computer so that it could be easily edited. One may surmise that after this type of feedback, Jimmy's letter will never be revised and sent.

Although Jimmy received too many markings on his paper, failure to make any comments regarding the content can also be inappropriate. We always want to remember to address ideas and feelings before spelling errors. When students express their thoughts and feelings, we must respond with understanding and insight. Figure 10.13 illustrates an example of completely inappropriate feedback. In this essay, Sabrina, a high school junior, revealed a traumatic event in her life. Unfortunately, her teacher's only comments were about her spelling and grammar errors. The teacher also assigned Sabrina a grade of 25/40. Although it is rare to come across examples like this, it is sad to think that such a lack of response can even occur. Clearly, a paper like this should not be assigned a low grade, and the only comments should be empathetic in nature.

Expressing Our Beliefs and Feelings

Writing is a basic, essential way to express our thoughts and feelings. Many times students express how happy they are through their writing. They write about how much they love their

I want to be able to concentrate.

Figure 10.11. Nico's Comment to His Teacher.

teachers, friends, parents, and pets. Students also write to express their unhappiness with aspects of school or their lives. Sometimes students are mad at a peer and want to write about a seeming injustice. Figure 10.14 presents a paragraph by Brooke, a fifth-grade student who is upset with Tony G. for the way he acted that day on the playground.

Other times students are unhappy with their teacher. Figure 10.15 illustrates a paragraph written by Jonathan, a fifth-grade student who did not get the teacher that he wanted. Notice how Jonathan identifies where he sits in the classroom in the upper-right corner. If the teacher takes this opportunity to "hear" Jonathan and then communicate with him empathetically, a dialogue can begin that may foster a more positive relationship.

Students may also express displeasure with a principal or authority figure. Jesse, a seventh-grade student, is often in trouble at school. Figure 10.16 depicts a paragraph in which he

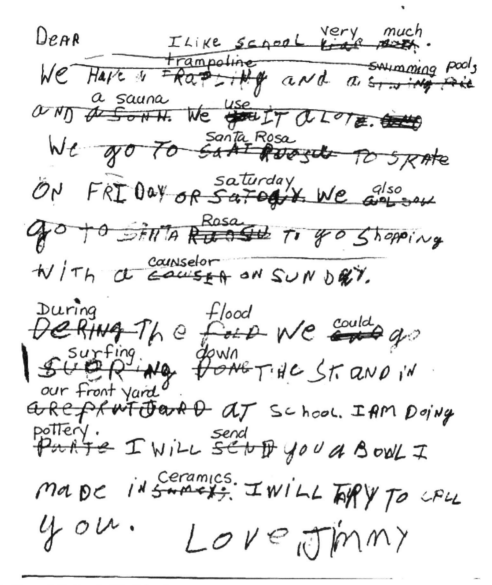

Figure 10.12. Jimmy's Letter to His Friend.

expressed his feelings about the principal because he is the person who often provides disciplinary actions. Although Jesse is thirteen years old, notice that he is still reversing the letters *b* and *d*.

Students also write papers that can raise concerns regarding how they are being treated by peers in the classroom or by their family at home. Figure 10.17 illustrates an essay written by Jared, a seventh-grade student. Jared lives alone with his father in a rundown trailer park on the outskirts of town. Jared wrote the essay during the first week of school. Ms. Morgan,

his teacher, shared the writing with the school counselor, who then started to meet with Jared on a weekly basis.

Writing is also a way that we express our condolences and gratitude to others. We write sympathy cards to let others know we are thinking of them. We write thank-you notes to let others know that we appreciate their efforts. Sometimes we write notes to apologize for misunderstandings or our own behavior. Figure 10.18 presents a note from Janet, a fourth-grade student, to her teacher. Janet had been reprimanded several times by her teacher at the family library night. Janet acknowledges that she is "not used to being good yet."

Similarly, Figure 10.19 presents an apology note from Boyce, a third-grade student, after he broke another child's toy. He assures his teacher that a problem like this will never happen again.

Students also write notes as excuses to explain why they don't have their assignments or are missing their homework. Figure 10.20

I woke up thinking today would be a wonderful day. It was sunny and unusually warm. After school a couple of us went to my Aunt's house. My cousin and I were going to hang out, since it was Friday. We decided we would go to the football game at our school. It was close to 7:00p.m., when my Uncle came home with my Aunt. I asked where my mom was, because I wanted to go home. My Uncle said she was at the hospital. I asked sadly, why? He said my dad committed suicide. I sat at the table in a confused state of mind. Things kept coming in and out of my mind, and I didn't know what to do. My Aunt came over and held me. She asked where is your brother? I told her he is out with his friend Dennis. We had to go find him. We got in the car and drove off. We went out searching everywhere for them. Finally, we found them walking along the street. We had to take Dennis home, before we could say anything to him. We got back at my Aunt's house and that is when we had to explain the situation to him. He stood trembling, tears came down his face, and he began to cry. My Aunt comforted him, as she did the same for me. My Aunt picked up the phone and was going to call the family. She would tell them the story and what had happened. The next day my mom sat down and called the funeral home to make the arrangements.

25/40

My family has their hard times, but we all worked together and help each other get through the hard times. We take one day at a time to make everyday work.

- Verb Tense Shifting
- Word Choice

Figure 10.13. Sabrina's Essay.

presents a creative explanation for missing homework by Kayla, a fifth-grade student. In Arizona, coyotes, not dogs, can be blamed for consuming homework. Through writing, students can express their unique circumstances.

All of these students are using writing as a tool for communication. This is perhaps the most important discovery our students can make about writing. It isn't just an assignment in school. It is a powerful means of expressing our beliefs, thoughts, and feelings. Helping your students discover writing as tool for communication should be an instructional priority.

Writing and Technology

When was the last time you received a handwritten letter? In this day and age, much of written communication is done through e-mail, text messaging, and instant messaging. A shorthand exists in instant messaging in which students abbreviate concepts and spell words

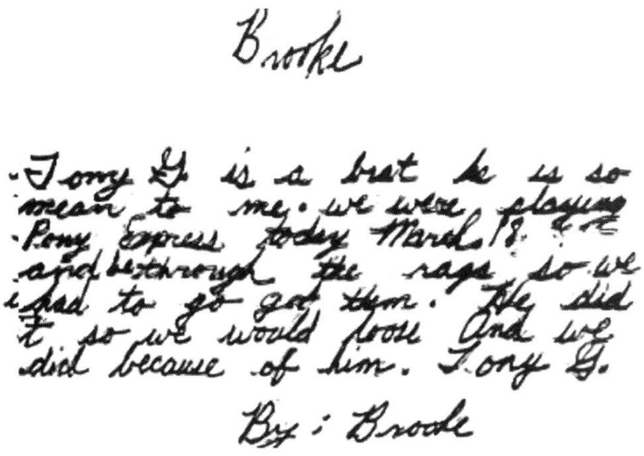
Brooke

Tony G. is a brat he is so mean to me. we were playing Pony Express today March 18. and he through the rags so we had to go get them. He did it so we would loose And we did because of him. Tony G.

By: Brooke

Figure 10.14. Brooke's Paragraph on Tony G.

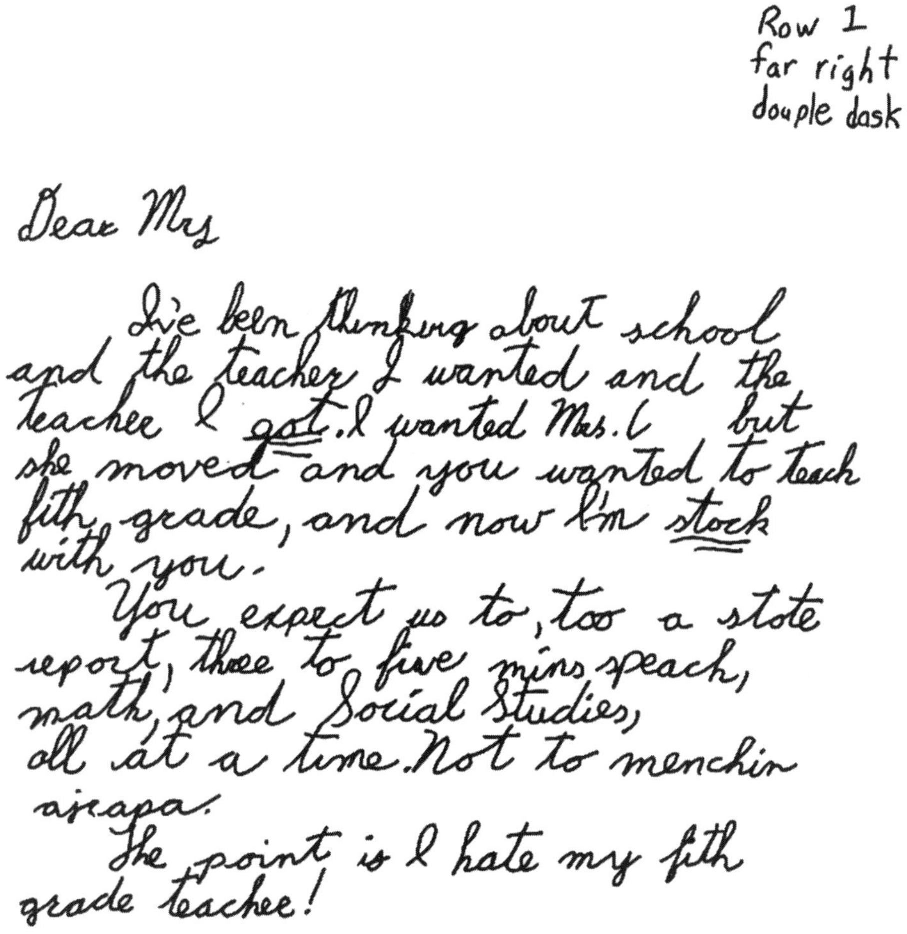
Row 1
far right
douple dask

Dear Mrs

I've been thinking about school and the teacher I wanted and the teacher I got. I wanted Mrs. C but she moved and you wanted to teach fith grade, and now I'm stock with you.

You expect us to, too a state report, three to five mins speach, math, and Social Studies, all at a time. Not to menchin aircapa.

The point is I hate my fith grade teacher!

Figure 10.15. Jonathan's Letter to His Teacher.

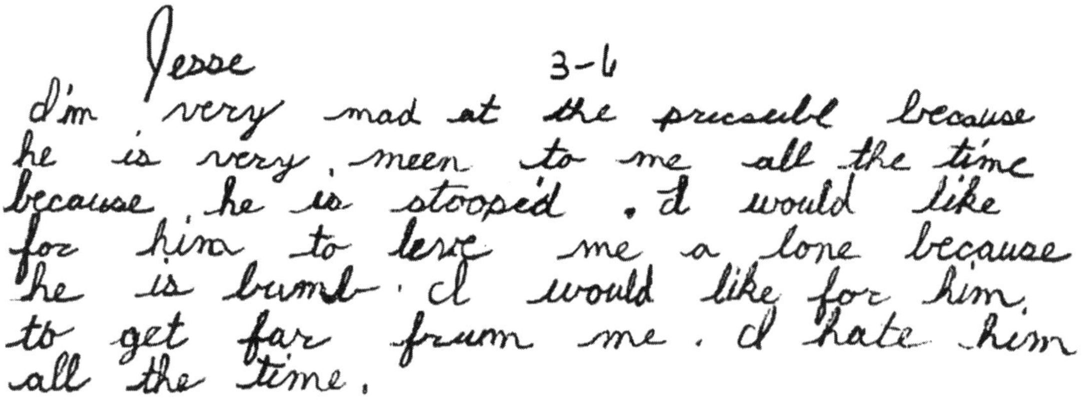

Jesse   3-6

I'm very mad at the precsubl because he is very meen to me all the time because he is stooped. I would like for him to leve me a lone because he is bumd. I would like for him to get far fruum me. I hate him all the time.

Figure 10.16. Jesse's Feelings About the Principal.

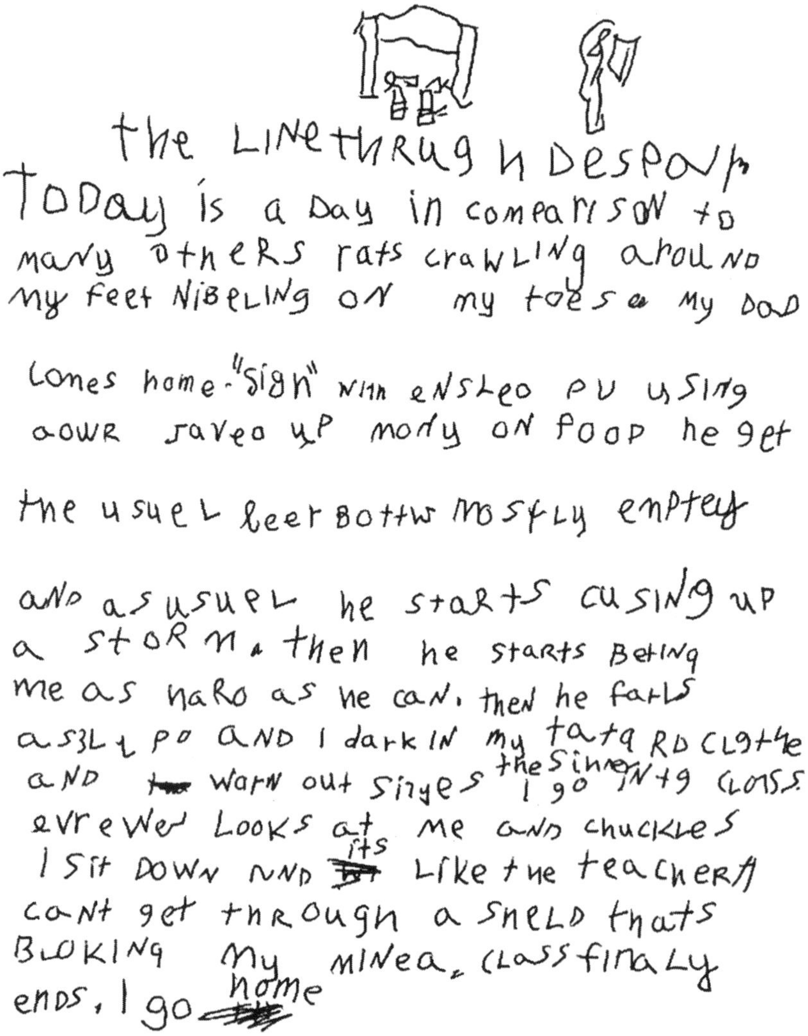

The LINE THRUGH DESPAIR

TODAY is a Day in comparison to many others rats crawling around my feet nibeling on my toes. My Dad

Comes home "sigh" with ensteo pu using aour saved up mony on food he get

the usuel beer bottw mostly emptey

and as usuel he starts cusing up a storm. then he starts beting me as hard as he can. then he falls asleep and I dark in my tatq red cloth and worn out shyes the sinnin I go into class evreweR Looks at me and chuckles I sit down nnd its like the teacher cant get through a sneld thats bloking my mind. class finaly ends, I go home

Figure 10.17. Jared's Essay About His Home Life.

Translation: The line through despair. Today is a day in comparison to many others. Rats crawling around my feet nibbling on my toes. My dad comes home "sigh" with instead of using our saved up money on food he gets the usual beer bottles mostly empty and as usual he starts cussing up a storm. Then he starts beating me as hard as he can. Then he falls asleep and I walk in my tattered clothes and worn out shoes to school. I go into class. Everyone looks at me and chuckles. I sit down and it's like the teacher can't get through a shield that is blocking my mind. Class finally ends. I go home.

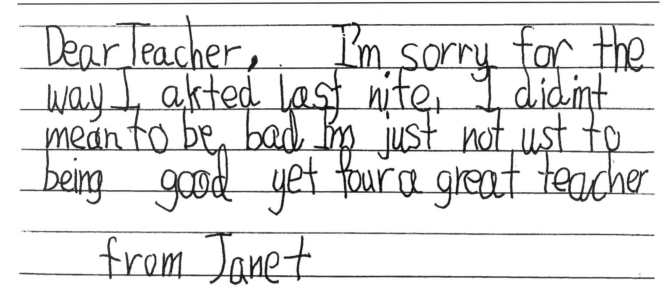

Figure 10.18. Janet's Apology for Misbehaving.

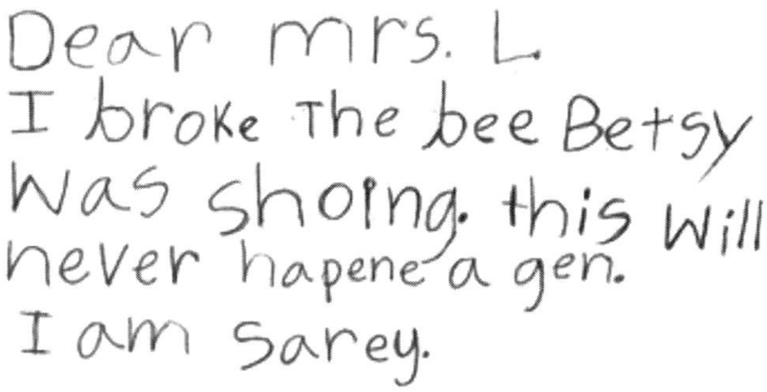

Dear mrs. L
I broke The bee Betsy
Was shoing. this will
never hapene a gen.
I am Sarey.

Figure 10.19. Boyce's Apology Note.

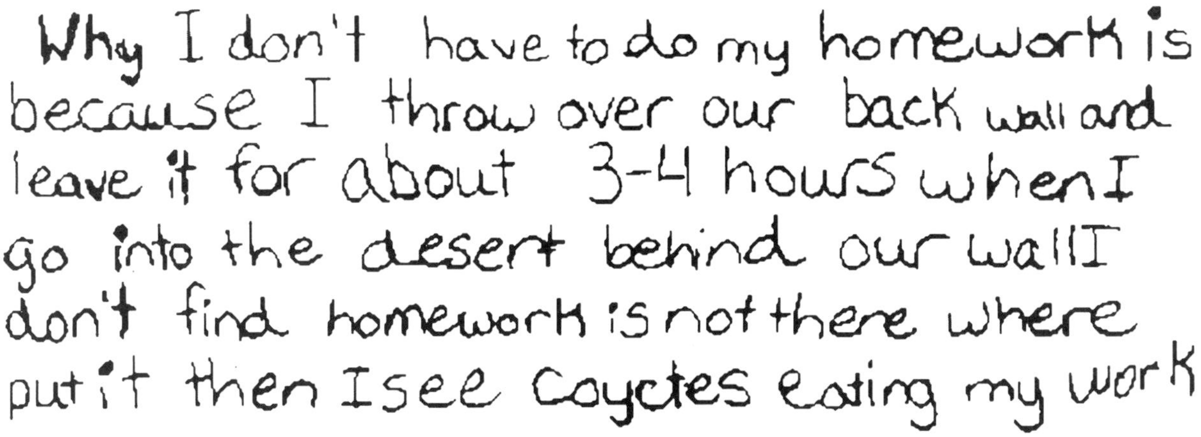

Why I don't have to do my homework is
because I throw over our back wall and
leave it for about 3-4 hours when I
go into the desert behind our wall I
don't find homework is not there where
put it then I see Coyctes eating my work

Figure 10.20. Kayla's Excuse for Missing Homework.

Figure 10.21. Sample of an E-Mail Message.

hey wuts up!! me not much jus livin in vages 4 now . . . sorry if it seemd like i was rude earlier on tha phone but i was tryin to tak to my gf thats y i was tryin to get off quickly . . . its good 2 kno ur still around tho . . . ive been doin really good tho workin full time n tryin to get into job corps or sumthing like that . . . i have plans to move back to ur area or somewhere around there since thats where my gf iz . . . but i wanna try to get involved wit sum sort of trade soo i kan make $ 4 tha time bein ya kno!! well get bakc at me n let me kno how ur doing n all dat good stuf!!! have a good one bro!

the way they sound rather than the way they look. Figure 10.21 depicts an e-mail from a high school senior to a friend living in another state.

Although this e-mail message communicates and is friendly in tone, one cannot help but wonder how this new form of communication will affect the development of writing skills of the students in this generation. The instant communication and the lack of attention to formal writing transform the intent of writing. Basic writing skills and conventions are of little concern, and many students do not take the time to check messages for spelling and punctuation errors. In addition, numerous abbreviations replace sentences with proper syntax. This type of instant writing is more spontaneous and interactive but less planned and reflective. As we have described in this book, written language helps shape and transform thought. Hopefully, the advantages of instant, informal written communications will not overshadow, diminish, or replace the need for writing competence.

CONCLUSION

Thought and language, which reflect reality in a way different from that of perception, are the key to the nature of human consciousness. Words play a central part not only in the development of thought, but in the historical growth of consciousness as a whole. A word is a microcosm of human consciousness.

—L. S. Vygotsky (1962)

Writing provides us with a venue for communication that is like no other. One's words and thoughts may be studied, critiqued, revised, quoted, and enjoyed. Writing provides us with the gift of reflection, a way to refine and expand our awareness. Its permanency allows one generation to share their visions and dreams with the next.

Figure 10.22 presents an entry from Tiffany's journal. This eighth-grade girl wants to become a writer so that she can share her imaginative thoughts with others. Writing allows us to transform our thoughts into words.

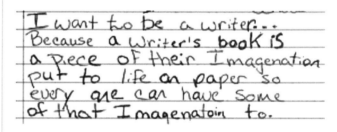

Figure 10.22. Tiffany's Journal Note.

Although tremendous variation will always exist among the writing skills of students, a caring teacher who possesses an understanding of language and writing development, as well as knowledge of a wide range of strategies, will be able to help students increase their

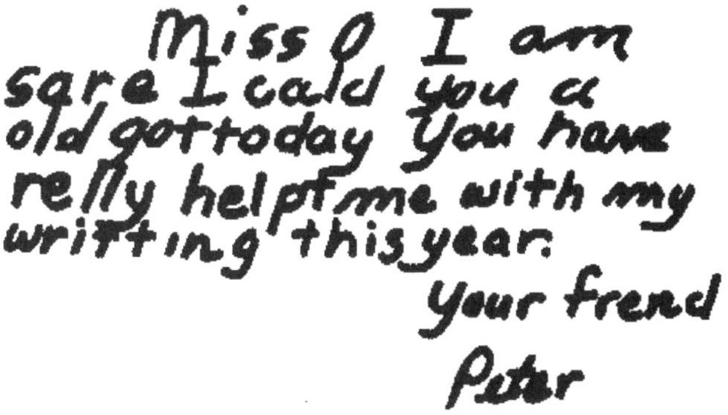

Miss Ø I am
sare I cald you a
old got today You have
relly helpf me with my
writting this year.
Your frend
Peter

Figure 10.23. Peter's Letter to His Teacher.

writing proficiency. Your students will be truly thankful for this help. Figure 10.23 presents a note written by Peter to his sixth-grade teacher. After apologizing for calling her an "old goat," he expresses his gratitude for her assistance with his writing.

Andrew, a third-grade student, was asked to write an idea about things or people who work together as a team to improve the world. He decided he would write about the "Garden Teams." His first draft is presented in Figure 10.24. Just as the rain at night makes the plants grow, your nurturing efforts and care help your students grow. You are the gardener. You plant the seeds of learning, teach and support your students, and watch them grow. Your efforts do make a difference, but as noted by Wong and Berninger (2005), ". . . learning to write is a long journey."

Figure 10.24. Andrew's Draft of the Garden Teams.

References

Alvarez, M. C. (1983). Sustained timed writing as an aid to fluency and creativity. *Teaching Exceptional Children, 15*, 160–162.

Americans with Disabilities Act of 1990, PL 101–336. H.R. 3195–110th Congress (2007): ADA Amendments Act of 2008.

Applebee, A. N. (1986). Problem in process approaches: Toward a reconceptualization of process instruction. In A. R. Petrosky & D. Bartholomae (Eds.), *The teaching of writing* (pp. 95–113). Chicago: National Society for the Study of Education.

Applebee, A. N., & Langer, J. A. (1983). Instructional scaffolding: Reading and writing as natural language activities. *Language Arts, 60*, 168–175.

Archer, A. L. (1988). Strategies for responding to information. *Teaching Exceptional Children, 20*(3), 55–57.

Barbe, W. B., Wasylyk, T. M., Hackney, C. S., & Braun, L. A. (1984). *Zaner-Bloser creative growth in handwriting* (Grades K–8). Columbus, OH: Zaner-Bloser.

Berninger, V. W., & Wolf, B. J. (2009). *Dyslexia and dysgraphia: Lessons from teaching and science.* Baltimore: Paul H. Brookes.

Blandford, B. J., & Lloyd, J. W. (1987). Effects of a self-instructional procedure on handwriting. *Journal of Learning Disabilities, 20*, 342–346.

Blatt, B. (1985). On writing, reading, and teaching. *Journal of Learning Disabilities, 18*, 366–367.

Carnine, D., Silbert, J., Kame'enui, E. J., & Tarver, S. G. (2010). *Direct instruction reading* (5th ed.). Boston: Pearson.

Carr, E., & Ogle, D. (1987). K-W-L plus: A strategy for comprehension and summarization. *Journal of Reading, 30*, 626–631.

Cohen, B. L. (1985). Writing: A new approach to the revision process. *Academic Therapy, 20*, 587–589.

Cohen, S. B., & Plaskon, S. P. (1980). *Language arts for the mildly handicapped.* Columbus, OH: Merrill.

Cooper, A. (1988). Given-New: Enhancing coherence through cohesiveness. *Written Communication, 5*, 352–367.

Cunningham, P. M., & Cunningham, J. W. (1992). Making words: Enhancing the invented spelling-decoding connection. *Reading Teacher, 46*, 106–115.

Deno, S. L. (1985). Curriculum-based measurement: The emerging alternative. *Exceptional Children, 52*, 219–232.

Elkonin, D. B. (1973). U.S.S.R. In J. Downing (Ed.), *Comparative reading: Cross-national studies of behavior and processes in reading and writing* (pp. 551–579). New York: Macmillan.

Englert, C. S., & Raphael, T. E. (1989). Developing successful writers through cognitive strategy instruction. In J. Brophy (Ed.), *Advances in research on teaching* (Vol. 1, pp. 105–151). Greenwich, CT: JAI Press.

Englert, C. S., Raphael, T. E., & Anderson, L. M. (1989). *Cognitive strategy instruction in writing project.* East Lansing, MI: Institute for Research on Teaching.

Fernald, G. (1943). *Remedial techniques in basic school subjects.* New York: McGraw-Hill.

Freeman, F. N. (1914). *The teaching of handwriting.* Boston: Houghton-Mifflin.

Fry, E. B. (1977). *Elementary reading instruction*. New York: McGraw-Hill.

Gage, G. T. (1986). Why write? In A. R. Petrosky & D. Bartholomae (Eds.), *The teaching of writing* (pp. 8–29). Chicago: National Society for the Study of Education.

Gearheart, B. R., & Gearheart, C. J. (1989). *Learning disabilities: Educational strategies* (5th ed.). St. Louis, MO: Times Mirror/Mosby College.

Gerber, A. (1993). *Language-related learning disabilities: Their nature and treatment*. Baltimore: Paul H. Brookes.

Gillingham, A., & Stillman, B. W. (1973). *Remedial training for children with specific disability in reading, spelling, and penmanship*. Cambridge, MA: Educators Publishing Service.

Giordano, G. (1982). CATS exercises: Teaching disabled writers to communicate. *Academic Therapy, 18*, 233–237.

Gould, B. W. (1991). Curricular strategies for written expression. In A. M. Bain, L. L. Bailet, & L. C. Moats (Eds.), *Written language disorders: Theory into practice* (pp. 129–164). Austin, TX: PRO-ED.

Graham, S. (1983). The effect of self-instructional procedures on LD students' handwriting performance. *Learning Disability Quarterly, 6*, 231–234.

Graham, S., & Freeman, S. (1985). Strategy training and teacher vs. student-controlled study conditions: Effects of LD students' spelling performance. *Learning Disability Quarterly, 8*, 267–274.

Graham, S., & Harris, K. R. (1989a). Components analysis of cognitive strategy instruction: Effects on learning disabled students' compositions and self-efficacy. *Journal of Educational Psychology, 81*, 353–361.

Graham, S., & Harris, K. R. (1989b). Improving learning disabled students' skills at composing essays: Self-instructional strategy training. *Exceptional Children, 56*, 201–214.

Graham, S., Harris, K. R., & Loynachan, C. (1994). The spelling for writing list. *Journal of Learning Disabilities, 27*, 210–214.

Graham, S., & Harris, K. R. (2005). *Writing better: Effective strategies for teaching students with learning difficulties*. Baltimore: Paul H. Brookes.

Graham, S., & Madan, A. J. (1981). Teaching letter formation. *Academic Therapy, 16*, 389–396.

Graham, S., & Miller, L. (1980). Handwriting research and practice: A unified approach. *Focus on Exceptional Children, 13*(2), 1–16.

Graves, D. H. (1985). All children can write. *Learning Disabilities Focus, 1*, 36–43.

Hanau, L. (1974). *The study game: How to play and win with statement-pie*. New York: Barnes & Noble.

Hanover, S. (1983). Handwriting comes naturally? *Academic Therapy, 18*, 407–412.

Harris, K. R., & Graham, S. (1992). *Helping young writers master the craft: Strategy instruction and self-regulation in the writing process*. Cambridge, MA: Brookline Books.

Harris, K. R., Graham, S., Mason, L. H., & Friedlander, B. (2008). *Powerful writing strategies for all students*. Baltimore: Paul H. Brookes.

Hosp, M. K., Hosp, J. L., & Howell, K. W. (2007). *The ABCs of CBM: A practical guide to curriculum-based measurement*. New York: Guilford Press.

Individuals with Disabilities Education Improvement Act (IDEA) of 2004, PL 108-446, 20 U.S.C. §§ 1400 *et seq.*

Isaacson, S. L. (1989). Role of secretary vs. author: Resolving the conflict in writing instruction. *Learning Disability Quarterly, 12*, 209–217.

Isaacson, S. L. (1994). Integrating process, product, and purpose: The role of instruction. *Reading & Writing Quarterly: Overcoming Learning Difficulties, 10*, 39–62.

Israel, L. (1984). Word knowledge and word retrieval: Phonological and semantic strategies. In G. P. Wallach & K. G. Butler (Eds.), *Language learning disabilities in school-age children* (pp. 230–250). Baltimore: Williams & Wilkins.

James, S. (1989). Assessing children with language disorders. In D. K. Bernstein & E. Tiegerman (Eds.), *Language and communication disorders* (2nd ed., pp. 157–207). Columbus: Merrill.

Johnson, D. D., & Pearson, P. D. (1984). *Teaching reading vocabulary* (2nd ed.). New York: Holt, Rinehart, and Winston.

Johnson, D. J. (1991). Foreword. In A. M. Bain, L. L. Bailet, & L. C. Moats (Eds.), *Written language disorders: Theory into practice* (p. ix). Austin, TX: PRO-ED.

Kerchner, L. B., & Kistinger, B. J. (1984). Language processing/word processing: Written expression, computers, and learning disabled students. *Learning Disability Quarterly, 7,* 329–335.

Kerrigan, W. J. (1979). *Writing to the point: Six basic steps* (2nd ed.). New York: Harcourt Brace Jovanovich.

King-Sears, M. E., Mercer, C. D., & Sindelar, P. T. (1992). Toward independence with keyword mnemonics: A strategy for science and vocabulary instruction. *Remedial and Special Education, 13*(5), 22–33.

Lavoie, R. (1990). *How difficult can this be?* (Videotape). Alexandria, VA: PBS Video.

Lickteig, J. (1981). Research-based recommendations for teachers of writing. *Language Arts, 58,* 44–50.

MacArthur, C. (1994). Peers + word processing + strategies = a powerful combination for revising student writing. *Teaching Exceptional Children, 27,* 24–29.

MacArthur, C. A., Schwartz, S. S., & Graham, S. (1991). A model for writing instruction: Integrating word processing and strategy instruction into a process approach to writing. *Learning Disabilities Practice, 6,* 230–236.

Maniet, P. (1986). *Mainstreaming children with learning disabilities.* Bayville, NY: Upward Bound Press.

Mather, N., & Goldstein, S. (2008). *Learning disabilities and challenging behaviors: A guide to intervention and classroom management* (2nd ed.). Baltimore: Paul H. Brookes.

Mather, N., & Jaffe, L. E. (2002). *Woodcock-Johnson® III: Reports, recommendations, and strategies.* New York: John Wiley & Sons.

McCoy, K. M., & Prehm, H. J. (1987). *Teaching mainstreamed students: Methods and techniques.* Denver: Love.

McTighe, J., & O'Connor, K. (2005). Seven practices for effective learning. *Educational Leadership, 63,* 10–17.

Moats, L. C. (2000). *Speech to print: Language essentials for teachers.* Baltimore: Paul H. Brookes.

Moulton, J. R., & Bader, M. S. (1986). The writing process: A powerful approach for the language-disabled student. *Annals of Dyslexia, 35,* 161–173.

Nichols, J. N. (1980). Using paragraph frames to help remedial high school students with written assignments. *Journal of Reading, 24,* 228–231.

No Child Left Behind Act (NCLB). Reauthorization of the Elementary and Secondary Education Act. PL 107–110, §§ 2102(4) (2001).

Ogle, D. M. (1986). K-W-L: A teaching model that develops active reading of expository text. *Reading Teacher, 39,* 564–570.

Otto, W., & McMenemy, R. A. (1966). *Corrective and remedial teaching: Principles and practices.* Boston: Houghton Mifflin.

Polloway, E. A., & Patton, J. R. (1993). *Strategies for teaching learners with special needs.* New York: Merrill.

Read, C. (1971). Pre-school children's knowledge of English phonology. *Harvard Educational Review, 41*(1), 1–34.

Rooney, K. J. (1990). *Independent strategies for efficient study.* Richmond, VA: J. R. Enterprises.

Schlegel, M., & Bos, C. S. (1986). *STORE the story: Fiction/fantasy reading comprehension and writing strategy.* Unpublished manuscript, University of Arizona, Department of Special Education and Rehabilitation, Tucson.

Schumaker, J. B., Deshler, D. D., Nolan, S., Clark, F. L., Alley, G. R., & Warner, M. M. (1981). *Error monitoring: A learning strategy for improving academic performance of LD adolescents* (Research Report No. 32). Lawrence: University of Kansas Institute for Research in Learning Disabilities.

Schumaker, J., & Sheldon, J. (1985). *The sentence writing strategy.* Lawrence: University of Kansas Institute for Research in Learning Disabilities.

Section 504 of the Rehabilitation Act of 1973, 29 U.S.C. 794, PL 93-112.

Stein, N., & Glenn, C. G. (1979). An analysis of story comprehension in elementary school children. In R. O. Freedle (Ed.), *New directions in discourse processes* (Vol. 2, pp. 53–120). Norwood, NJ: Ablex.

Strickland, R. G. (1972). Evaluating children's composition. In H. Newman (Ed.), *Effective language arts practices in the elementary school: Selected readings* (pp. 496–509). New York: John Wiley & Sons.

Tangel, D. M., & Blachman, B. A. (1992). Effect of phoneme awareness instruction on kindergaren children's invented spelling. *Journal of Reading Behavior, 24,* 233–258.

Tompkins, G. E., & Friend, M. (1986). On your mark, get set, write! *Teaching Exceptional Children, 18*(2), 82–89.

Thurber, D. N. (1983). Write on! With continuous stroke point. *Academic Therapy, 18,* 389–395.

Vaughn, S., & Bos, C. S. (2009). *Strategies for teaching students with learning and behavior problems* (7th ed.). Upper Saddle River, NJ: Pearson.

Vygotsky, L. S. (1962). *Thought and language*. Cambridge, MA: M.I.T. Press.

Vygotsky, L. S. (1978). *Mind in society*. Cambridge, MA: M.I.T. Press.

Wallace, G. W., & Bott, D. A. (1989). Statement-pie: A strategy to improve the paragraph writing skills of adolescents with learning disabilities. *Journal of Learning Disabilities, 22,* 541–543, 553.

Weiss, M. S., & Weiss, H. G. (1993). *Formulas to read and write*. Avon, CO: Treehouse Associates.

Welch, M. (1992). The *PLEASE* strategy: A metacognitive learning strategy for improving the paragraph writing of students with mild learning disabilities. *Learning Disability Quarterly, 15,* 119–128.

Welch, M., & Jensen, J. (1991). Write, P.L.E.A.S.E.: A video-assisted strategic intervention to improve written expression. *Remedial and Special Education, 12,* 37–47.

Wiggins, G. (2006, April). Healthier testing made easy. *Edutopia*, 49–52.

Wilde, S. (1997). *What's a schwa sound anyway?* Westport, CT: William Heinemann.

Wong, B. Y. L. (1986). A cognitive approach to spelling. *Exceptional Children, 53,* 169–173.

Wong, B., & Berninger, V. (2005). Cognitive processes of teachers in implementing composition research in elementary, middle, and high school classrooms. In B. Shulman, K. Apel, B. Ehren, E. Silliman, & A. Stone (Eds.), *Handbook of language and literacy development and disorders* (pp. 600–624). NewYork: Guilford.

Woodcock, R. W., McGrew, K., & Mather, N. (2001). *Woodcock-Johnson Tests of Cognitive Abilities and Tests of Achievement* (3rd ed.). Rolling Meadows, IL: Riverside.

Index

Page references followed by *fig* indicate an illustrated figure.

T